MW00646888

"Writing in the Trump moment when sweeping generalizations (and indictments) of evangelical populist thinking (and politics) easily prevail, Daniel Hummel takes the tougher route. With notable patience, careful attention to the granular as well as the big picture, and a sensitive touch with the pen, he guides readers through the centuries-long developments that saw a dissenting dispensationalist theology rise to the fore of mainstream evangelicalism and American apocalyptic culture. The result of his considerable efforts is a remarkably learned and readable book that surprises and entertains as well as enlightens."

—DARREN DOCHUK
Andrew V. Tackes College Professor of History,
University of Notre Dame

"As I write these words, I am looking at my bookshelf where I see a copy of the *Scofield Reference Bible* sitting next to my multivolume set of Lewis Sperry Chafer's theology and a few of the *Left Behind* novels. As someone whose teenage conversion to evangelical faith led him to study at a dispensationalist Bible college, I was reminded of my young-adult obsession with a brand of conservative Protestantism that shaped much of twentieth-century American evangelicalism. If you want to learn more about the evangelical fascination with the rapture, Israel, the antichrist, and the prophetic books of the Bible, *The Rise and Fall of Dispensationalism* is the place to start."

—JOHN FEA
distinguished professor of history, Messiah University
and author of *Believe Me: The Evangelical Road to Donald Trump*

"*The Rise and Fall of Dispensationalism* is the essential guide to a perplexing subject. Combining painstaking scholarship with an accessible style, Hummel shows how Christian theology influenced American culture—but also how American culture transformed Christian theology. Both experts and students will learn from this important book."

—SAMUEL GOLDMAN
associate professor of political science, George Washington University

"What do you say about a historical study that reads like a whodunit? Dan Hummel's book is a page turner, shedding light on details that I already knew from dispensationalist pop culture, filling in the gaps through patient analysis and good storytelling. Historians will love his patient analysis; it's the storytelling that hooked me. At the end of each chapter, I had to know what came next. Not only is *The Rise and Fall of Dispensationalism* a superb academic study; Hummel's analysis of the gap left by the decline of dispensationalism helps us understand the ideological crisis of the so-called evangelical church today."

—J. RICHARD MIDDLETON
professor of biblical worldview and exegesis, Northeastern Seminary

"Daniel Hummel has done us all a service by digging up the bones of a theological beast that left massive footprints across the land and then (all but) disappeared. Dispensationalism needs to be reckoned with. Its history of theological innovations, inclinations, obsessions, and curiosities is with us still, even if they're just skeletons buried in the backyard. Hummel's careful accounting and thoughtful interpretations are a gift to anyone trying to understand the contemporary landscape of evangelicalism."

—DANIEL SILLIMAN
author of *Reading Evangelicals:*
How Christian Fiction Shaped a Culture and a Faith

"In this brilliant and original book, Daniel G. Hummel traces the extraordinary history of one of the most influential religious groups in modern American life. His research is impressive, his writing is sharp, and his arguments will transform what we think we know about American religious history. An impressive achievement!"

—MATTHEW AVERY SUTTON
author of *Double Crossed:*
The Missionaries Who Spied for the United States during the Second World War

"*The Rise and Fall of Dispensationalism* is a lively, accessible, and erudite work. Hummel guides readers deftly through nearly two centuries of religious history as he illuminates the theological, political, and cultural evolution of dispensationalist thought—and influence—in the United States. Exploring key leaders, texts, and trends from John Nelson Darby to QAnon, this book is a must for anyone seeking to better understand the significance of eschatology and apocalypticism in American life."

—LAUREN TUREK
associate professor of history, Trinity University

"Daniel Hummel has written the best and most comprehensive history of dispensationalist theology currently in existence. Combining impressive historical research with an exceptionally nuanced attention to theological developments, Hummel's work offers a detailed, engagingly written historical survey of a movement that is often mentioned in studies of evangelical politics but rarely understood on its own terms. This is the book for people who want to go beyond the headlines to understand the long historical trajectory of the most influential end-times theology in American evangelicalism."

—DANIEL K. WILLIAMS
author of *God's Own Party: The Making of the Christian Right*

"A tremendous achievement, based on meticulous research and bold synthesis. Thanks to Dan Hummel, we can finally understand how these influential ideas moved through North American culture and politics."

—MOLLY WORTHEN
associate professor of history, University of North Carolina

THE RISE AND FALL OF DISPENSATIONALISM

*How the Evangelical Battle
over the End Times
Shaped a Nation*

DANIEL G. HUMMEL

WILLIAM B. EERDMANS PUBLISHING COMPANY
GRAND RAPIDS, MICHIGAN

Wm. B. Eerdmans Publishing Co.
4035 Park East Court SE, Grand Rapids, Michigan 49546
www.eerdmans.com

29 28 27 26 25 24   2 3 4 5 6 7

ISBN 978-0-8028-7922-6

Library of Congress Cataloging-in-Publication Data

A catalog record for this book is available from the Library of Congress.

Contents

Foreword

Daniel Hummel's great contribution in this book is to take a story that "everyone knows" and show that what "everyone knows" has barely scratched the surface. As a prime example, it is "well known" that John Nelson Darby was the key early promoter of "dispensational premillennialism," yet not until nearly fifty years after his death in 1882 did the word *dispensationalism* come into existence to describe some—but only some—of the theological principles Darby championed. Again, Darby belonged to the accurately named "Exclusive" branch of the Plymouth Brethren that emerged from Ireland in the nineteenth century, but bits and pieces of what he taught eventually came to exist in the most unregulated and aggressively *populist* varieties of twentieth-century American fundamentalism, evangelicalism, and Pentecostalism. Yet again, dispensationalists of whatever stripe are known to have never supported anything remotely progressive in politics, but A. T. Pierson not only drew on dispensational theology to drive his nonpareil advocacy of missionary service but also stood out by vigorously criticizing Jim Crow America.

Chronology is Daniel Hummel's great friend as, generation by generation, he explains how different individuals, movements, publications, and conferences first made "the new premillennialism" popular in the United States and then, with the addition of electronic media, sustained a great diversity of "dispensationalisms." While never leaving questions of theology or biblical interpretation behind, the book is a model of well-rounded history by showing how these questions were always answered in terms of specific cultural, social, media, and political developments.

Besides J. N. Darby, the book's burgeoning cast of characters includes many figures well known to historians as well as the general reading public: evangelist D. L. Moody, Bible-editor C. I. Scofield, Bible-school president

R. A. Torrey (Moody, BIOLA), financier of *The Fundamentals* Lyman Stewart, creationist George McCready Price, systematic theologians Lewis Sperry Chafer and Charles Ryrie, sensationalist Hal Lindsey, culture warrior and novelist Tim LaHaye. This book is even more illuminating for individuals who are not as well known, but who may have contributed even more to the popularity of dispensational themes: early systematizers Ethelbert Bullinger and Frederick Grant, Oxford University Press publisher Henry Frowde, the rare Lutheran dispensationalist J. A. Seiss, converted Jew Charles Feinberg, and many more. The book is just as informative on leading critics like the conservative Presbyterian Oswald Allis, theonomist Gary North, John MacArthur who abandoned the dispensationalism that he preached early in his career, and Philip Mauro who became as fierce a critic as he had once been a passionate advocate.

In a clever spin on the book title that made C. I. Scofield famous for explaining the dispensations he later spelled out in his study Bible, *Rightly Dividing the Word of Truth* (2 Timothy 2:15), Hummel employs the phrase "rightly dividing dispensationalism" to chart differences among new millennial, traditional, scholastic, progressive, national, and normative variations—differences contested every bit as seriously (though thankfully with less violence) as those among Shia, Sunni, and Sufi. Not the least of the book's many merits is to show why dispensationalists are largely responsible for pervasive confusion over the notion of "literalism" that bedevils Bible-reading America. (One of the very few cultural or social angles the book does not explore is the almost exclusively male leadership of whatever kind of dispensationalism, despite the fact that so many readers of the Scofield Bible, so many students at Bible schools organized by dispensationalists, and so many of those who bought volumes in the *Left Behind* series were women.)

The book's concluding section is particularly helpful in explaining why the academic dispensationalism long associated with Dallas Theological Seminary essentially collapsed in the very years when the *Left Behind* series of Tim LaHaye and Jerry Jenkins sold into the tens of millions, the Contemporary Christian Music industry churned out hit after hit laced with dispensational references, and a diverse range of singers, writers, film-makers, and journalists far removed from anything Christian exploited dispensational memes for their own purposes.

Serious readers will want to move carefully through the book's bibliography, which details the wealth of scholarship underlying the book's accessible, jargon-free, and frequently limpid prose. Alongside the debts acknowledged to landmark studies by the likes of Ernest Sandeen, George Marsden, Donald Akenson, Brendan Pietsch, and Timothy Gloege, Hummel also references an extraordinary range of other secondary literature that buttresses his en-cyclopedic harvesting from primary sources. Readers of whatever degree of seriousness will benefit from the well-chosen hymns or songs that begin each chapter and equally well-chosen images sprinkled throughout these pages.

This is a very good book on a very important subject.

Mark A. Noll

Preface

When I was growing up in the 1990s, my family's bookshelf held a line of theology texts that signaled something just by their presence. Along the spines of these books, the author names shone in capital and bold letters: WAL-VOORD, RYRIE, PENTECOST, CHAFER.[1] These titles were the products of thousands of hours of labor, collectively read by millions of Christians. The theologian authors were best known for their teachings on eschatology, or the study of the "end times," but they also ranged widely into every corner of Christian thought. These books were the crowning scholarly achievements of the theological tradition known as dispensationalism.

This bookshelf began a lifetime engagement with dispensationalism. In the early 2010s, as a graduate student at the University of Wisconsin–Madison, I would often peruse the vast stacks of Memorial Library, especially the shelves marked by the Library of Congress subject BT (Doctrinal Theology). Almost every book I opened had an insert tucked into its pages. On a three-by-five-inch sheet, in all caps, was printed "THERE IS NO RAPTURE!! . . . There were only 2 covenants, and Christ as our lasting one we must endure tribulation on earth." The anonymous writer identified the "many errors of Scofield and other dispensationalists" as the error to be combated, in this case by the guerilla tactic of book inserts.

A third encounter: in 2018 the largest-grossing film was the newest Marvel entry, *Avengers: Infinity War*. The plot centered on a villain named Thanos, whose scheme involved assembling a magical glove that could instantly disap-

---

1. After reading a draft of this paragraph, my father wanted me to include that there were also nondispensational authors on the shelves. For example, Louis Berkhof's *Systematic Theology* was his first choice for a quick reference.

pear half of humanity with the snap of a finger. When Thanos finally succeeds at the cliffhanger end of the movie, iconic superheroes are among the victims of what was dubbed by fans and critics as the "Snapture," a gloss on the dispensational teaching of the rapture.[2] When I saw the "Snapture" for the first time, a familiar wave of "rapture anxiety" from childhood briefly washed over me. The creators of *Avengers: Infinity War* had no interest in the doctrine of the rapture, but its distilled imagery, originally indebted to dispensationalism, still found its way to the commercial apex of American popular culture.

A fourth encounter: in the spring of 2022, in the wake of Russia's invasion of Ukraine, the ninety-two-year-old Bible prophecy forecaster Pat Robertson came out of retirement to warn that Russian president Vladimir Putin was being "compelled by God" toward war and that Ukraine was a "staging area" for a larger strike against the State of Israel that would scale, eventually, into the prophesied battle of Armageddon.[3] A day later a reporter called to ask me for an explication of Robertson's comments. "Is this what dispensationalists believe?" she asked me. I gave too complex an answer. Pieces of Robertson's remarks resembled the traditional dispensational end-times scenario: the importance of Russia as a geopolitical actor, the centrality of Israel, the site of Armageddon. There is a long history, dating at least to the Franco-Prussian War of 1870, in this vein. At the same time, no self-respecting dispensational scholar would so brashly lay out a detailed scenario of the ongoing war as did Robertson. The reporter thanked me, but I felt inadequate to the task: on paper Robertson couldn't be categorized, but in practice he was a prominent spokesman for the dispensational view.

Taken together, these moments illustrate some of the lives of dispensationalism in modern America. Many Christians have grown up with dispensationalism as part of their theological inheritance. Many of those Christians, and many other Americans, have probably come across evidence of an intense debate about dispensationalism that appears in slips of paper or online message boards. Almost all Americans know about the rapture because of its cultural adaptations, to the point that non-Christians might assume that the teaching is accepted theology for anyone who identifies as an evangelical Christian.

The following pages make sense of these different trajectories and manifestations of dispensationalism through the study of its history. I do so by telling

---

2. For the coining of "Snapture," see Glen Weldon, "OK, Let's Talk about the Ending of 'Avengers: Infinity War,'" NPR, April 30, 2018, https://www.npr.org/2018/04/30/607093337/ok-lets-talk-about-the-ending-of-avengers-infinity-war.

3. Patricia McKnight, "Retired Evangelist Pat Robertson Says Putin Is Fulfilling Biblical Prophecy," *Newsweek*, February 28, 2022, https://www.newsweek.com/retired-evangelist-pat-robertson-says-putin-fulfilling-biblical-prophecy-1683497.

the story of the ideas, institutions, and individuals that built dispensationalism in the nineteenth and early twentieth centuries, and the later generations who presided over its entrance into the mainstream of American popular culture in the twentieth and twenty-first centuries.

Even if you did not grow up with dispensational teachings, it is likely that you have encountered fragments of dispensationalism like the "Snapture." If you've watched films, read books, or listened to sermons that speculate on a coming one-world government led by the antichrist, then you have encountered a little more of apocalyptic dispensationalism. If you've consumed dystopian fiction or prestige television, you've probably come across popular vestiges of dispensational themes, from the HBO drama *The Leftovers* (2014–2017), which centers on survivors of a rapture-like event, to the comedian Marc Maron, whose Netflix special *End Times Fun* refers to the rapture as if it is common knowledge—"people just shoot up into the air like bottle rockets."[4] Dispensationalism in this popular form has managed to permeate vast sections of American culture.

Yet the end times are just one dimension of the theology of dispensationalism and its wider legacy. If you've contemplated the "plain meaning" of the Bible as the most authoritative interpretation of Scripture, you've encountered debates deeply shaped by dispensationalism. If you've met Christians who express strong support for the State of Israel based on interpretations of biblical prophecy, you've stumbled upon one of the geopolitical issues shaped by dispensational theology. If you've watched speakers teaching that the earth is headed for annihilation, that churches are outposts in a world careening toward decline, or that a conspiracy of satanic power is bringing about a one-world government—then you've seen patterns of thinking that have been deeply shaped by dispensationalism.

And so, the following pages are an entryway into reconsidering a wider swath of American religion and culture; they are an effort to capture the compelling power of a theological system and make sense of its ultimate fate while also tracing its influence writ large. This book is itself another entry into the long discourse on dispensationalism and its unique role in shaping American history.

4. Marc Maron, "End Times Fun (2020)—Full Transcript," *Scraps from the Loft*, March 12, 2020, https://scrapsfromtheloft.com/comedy/marc-maron-end-times-fun-transcript/.

Introduction

The term "dispensationalism" is unfamiliar, even to most Christians. It dates to 1927 and is attributable to Philip Mauro, a fundamentalist Christian who loathed the teachings of the rapture and other theological concepts that he would classify as dispensationalism. Mauro's dismissive coining of the term reveals a dynamic present since the creation of dispensationalism: it is a theology that has been indelibly shaped by the tensions between and among evangelicals and fundamentalists. These struggles have played an outsize role in modern-day evangelicalism.

In 1903, when the forty-four-year-old social critic and lawyer underwent a dramatic conversion experience at a Christian and Missionary Alliance church in New York City, Mauro joined a relatively new sect of Christianity. In his early years as a Christian, he embraced that community's view, later a part of dispensationalism, that the kingdom of God—the social order heralded by Jesus in the Gospels as "breaking in"—lay entirely in the future, awaiting its arrival on earth until the second coming. This teaching, which is called "new premillennialism" in the following pages, called on Christians to watch and pray for the kingdom of God but to harbor no illusions that it was currently established or expectations that its arrival could be hastened by humans.

Mauro initially agreed with the "future kingdom" view and its deeper philosophy of history that sketched a series of discrete ages, or dispensations, demarcated by God's divine testing and humanity's repeated failures. For Mauro and fellow new premillennialists, the dispensation of the kingdom, prophesied by the Hebrew prophets and New Testament writers, lay entirely in the future. Far from fragmenting his view of the world, the "dispensational truth" of God's purposes nurtured Mauro's budding faith. As he described the Bible in 1910, "The Holy Scriptures have a structure, exhibiting, when seen and comprehended even imperfectly, the same perfection of wisdom in design and of skill in execution that characterizes all His glorious and wonderful works."[1]

Yet, for all the beauty Mauro saw, his enchantment with dispensational truth was limited. By 1918 he was becoming obsessed with its failures, a process that happened alongside Mauro's increasing identification with the emergent Christian fundamentalist movement, which included both those who professed "dispensational truth" and those who did not. Identifying deep flaws in new premillennial teachings, Mauro unleashed a torrent of publications on the topic, effectively reversing his previous fifteen years of public theology and social commentary. "The leading feature of God's great work for this age," Mauro concluded in one of his books from 1918, "is the introduction into the world of 'the Kingdom of heaven.'"[2] The language he used was nuanced: Mauro was linking the kingdom to "this age" rather than the next one. "The Kingdom of heaven belongs wholly to this present age," he explained elsewhere.[3] Though camped out on a seemingly distant corner of Christian theology, the meaning of the kingdom and its implications loomed large in Mauro's mind and soon took center stage in the fundamentalist movement.

In the heat of World War I, in the throes of a mental breakdown in 1917, and in the wake of his wife's death in 1918, Mauro had come to a new understanding of the kingdom, and with it a wholesale rejection of "dispensational truth." No fewer than eight books, denouncing his old views, appeared in the next decade. After his reversal he explained, "The inconsistencies and self-contradictions of the system itself, and above all, the impossibility of reconciling its main positions with the plain statements of the Word of God, became so glaringly evident that I could not do otherwise than renounce it."[4] He wrote of specific "false assumptions" and "erroneous teachings," but he also recognized interlocking dispensational concepts with far-reaching implications.[5] The system was more than the sum of its parts.

Perhaps it was inevitable that Mauro would come to see dispensationalism—the name he gave for the bundle of his discarded views—as a coherent

1. Philip Mauro, *Man's Day*, 2nd ed. (New York: Gospel Publishing House, 1910), 7.

2. Philip Mauro, *After This, or the Church, the Kingdom, and the Glory* (Chicago: Revell, 1918), 9.

3. Philip Mauro, *The Kingdom of Heaven* (1918; reprint, n.p.: Philip Mauro Library, 2008), 3.

4. Philip Mauro, *The Gospel of the Kingdom* (1928; reprint, n.p.: Philip Mauro Library, 2008), 3–4.

5. Philip Mauro, *The Seventy Weeks and the Great Tribulation* (1921; reprint, n.p.: Philip Mauro Library, 2008; rev. ed. 1944), 18; Philip Mauro, *God's Present Kingdom* (1919; reprint, n.p.: Philip Mauro Library, 2008), 118.

intellectual project that he could package and then denounce. In any case, it took him until 1927—in what is likely the first use of "dispensationalism" in print—to name this "system of interpretation" that he once "had accepted wholeheartedly and without the least misgivings." The realization was painful. "I had eventually to learn with sorrow, and to acknowledge with deep mortification, that the modern system of 'dispensationalism,' or 'futurism' (or so-called 'rightly dividing the word of truth') to which I had thoroughly committed myself, not only was without scriptural foundation, but involved doctrinal errors of a serious character."[6]

Mauro intended for "dispensationalism" to bring into focus a theological tradition and social network encompassing ideas, institutions, and individuals that would dominate the fundamentalist scene. In fact, he insisted, World War I and the following years had exposed dispensationalists as peddlers of "a subtle form of modernism," by which he meant a dangerous theological innovation at odds with the chief aims of fundamentalism.[7] Dispensationalism was "a humanly contrived system that has been imposed upon the Bible, and not a scheme of doctrine derived from it."[8] Its teachings were "grotesquely absurd," "utterly fallacious," and "pernicious."[9] Its most important texts were "corrupt," "vile," and "clever."[10]

In some ways, Mauro's classing of dispensationalism merely acknowledged reality. A new subculture *had* appeared over his lifetime—one that by the 1920s played a critical role in the fundamentalist movement. In other ways, however, the coining of "dispensationalism" was itself a historical act, imposing order on a far-flung set of beliefs and practices, a sprawling network of people and institutions, that drew its inspirations from and exerted its influences upon many disparate groups. Its coherence as a "system" was not its creators' original intention, though it often became its detractors' primary concern. And yet, the classing of dispensationalism helped to shape a large swath of American Christianity for the next century and to amplify the influence of the "modern system of dispensationalism" beyond any scale Mauro could have imagined.

To his readers, Philip Mauro was, for good or ill, a turncoat. He generated significant controversy within theological circles, and in 1929 he suffered another mental breakdown that ended his status as dispensationalism's foremost critic. In the words of a friendly biographer, Mauro suffered "an onslaught . . .

---

6. Mauro, *How Long the End?* (1927), 1.

7. Mauro, *Gospel of the Kingdom*, 4, 9.

8. Mauro, *Gospel of the Kingdom*, 8.

9. Mauro, *Gospel of the Kingdom*, 4, 74; Philip Mauro, *The Hope of Israel* (Chicago: Revell, 1929), 15.

10. Mauro, *Gospel of the Kingdom*, 3.

which, to all appearances, seemed leveled by Satan himself against Mr. Mauro because of his valiant fight as champion of the Kingdom of God."[11] Mauro's protest burned hot and fast, yielding the name for one of America's most resilient and popular religious traditions, one that taught Christians to wait with anticipation for a coming kingdom of God that would wipe away the warring kingdoms of men, but just not yet.

Rightly Dividing Dispensationalism

The rise and fall of dispensationalism over the past two hundred years is a window into a fascinating tapestry of religion, theology, culture, politics, and social change in America. The story is expansive in scope as well as time, stretching from nineteenth-century dissenters in the Church of Ireland to the twenty-first-century New York Times Best Seller list. Mauro's creation of the term sits conveniently near the midpoint of this story. The twists and turns of the tradition, and the ebbs and flows of its relationships to competitors and American culture, are what propel dispensationalism, in this story, on its rise and fall trajectory.

Properly situated, the rise and fall of dispensationalism contributes in unique ways to explaining the state of modern American evangelicalism. A notoriously difficult group to define, evangelicals in America have been categorized as much by the tensions they manage between "head" and "heart" religion, and between populist and establishment aspirations, as by the theological commitments they profess or the sociological profile they share. And yet a history of dispensationalism, which has played a decisive role as a system of theology and a subculture, recasts our understanding of evangelicalism in at least two important ways.

First, dispensationalism brings to the fore the interdependent relationship between theology and culture that has shaped American evangelicalism. The quest to define evangelicalism in recent years has produced a variety of answers, many offering definitions that theoretically encompass everyone from seventeenth-century Pietists to twenty-first-century Christian nationalists. Such chronological and cultural breadth is difficult to capture in any case, and particularly so when undertaken in a political moment in which evangelicals are cast as key contestants.

This study approaches the problem of defining evangelicalism from a different angle, namely, by highlighting a more identifiable (if still difficult)

---

11. Gordon P. Gardiner, "Champion of the Kingdom: The Story of Philip Mauro" (1961; reprint, n.d.: Philip Mauro Library, 2008), 45.

term—"dispensationalism"—to make sense of how theology and culture became embedded in institutions that formed individuals and communities into a certain way of thinking and being Christian that we identify today as evangelical. In fact, dispensationalism has overlapped with a cluster of related movements that modern definitions of evangelicalism tend to subsume, including fundamentalism, Pentecostalism, Christian nationalism, and New Calvinism, among many others. By tracking these religious ideas and movements from the vantage point of dispensationalism, we can observe with fresh perspective the reception and contestation of theological ideas, the influences of cultural production and consumption, and the drives toward popularization and institutionalization that have shaped evangelicalism.

Second, a focus on dispensationalism illuminates contemporary trends toward polarization that have plagued evangelicalism in recent decades. These trends, I contend, are deeply intertwined with the "rise and fall" narrative of dispensationalism. While it was never the only theological tradition among fundamentalists or evangelicals, dispensationalism supplied at least four generations of white conservative Protestants, stretching from the late nineteenth century to the late twentieth century, with a theological framework to read the Bible and understand the world. Insiders and outsiders differed over how accurate or helpful dispensationalism was, but its teachings supplied a reference point to millions of Christians all the same.

With the fall of dispensationalism as a formal theological system in the 1990s, the white conservative Protestant community has deepened an ongoing crisis in theological identity, with many outside observers now questioning whether theology has much to do with evangelicalism at all. Rather than treat the current state of affairs as normative, a study of dispensationalism reveals the historical development of a theologically thin, while politically robust, popular evangelical culture. Conservative white Protestantism has always had other theological contenders, but the inherited theological tradition of dispensationalism, which now has fewer living theological proponents, played a significant role in shaping the "evangelical mind" until very recently. Diagnosing this situation through a historical approach reveals both the extent of the vacuum left by dispensationalism's fall and potential remedies for the future, one of which I end with in the book's epilogue.

Dispensationalists have often claimed that, to rightly understand the Bible, readers need to "rightly divide" Scripture using their theological schema. The dispensational perspective on the kingdom of God, which so rankled Mauro, was one teaching derived from a dispensational division of Scripture. We'll bracket the religious validity of that particular claim in favor of the more pressing historical task to "rightly divide" dispensationalism. Three distinctions are especially important to highlight at the outset: the historical boundaries of dispensationalism; the extent of dispensational theology beyond end-times beliefs; and the sociological scope of the dispensational tradition.

Historical Boundaries

In the 1830s, a group of Irish and English Protestant dissenters introduced a novel meaning for a dispensation, a term that is an English translation from the Greek *oikonomia*, a combination of *oikos* (household) and *nemein* (management). Because the word appears four times in the New Testament of the King James Bible, English-language Christians have used it to describe periods of time, especially sacred time, since the earliest days of the Reformation. The original dissenters were unique for teaching that all of history was divided into a series of dispensations that inevitably ended with the failure of humans to fulfill their obligations to God. They taught that the current dispensation was nearly complete, revealing the failure of organized Christianity, and that soon the state churches and the societies they enabled in Europe and North America, which they called Christendom, would be destroyed.

These dissenters originally congregated in cities like Dublin and London, with one of their largest assemblies in the southwestern English port city of Plymouth. As a group they refused to be called anything but "Christian," so they became known as "the brethren from Plymouth." The name stuck, and they became known as the Plymouth Brethren. A later schism created Open and Exclusive Brethren sects, the latter being a critical transmitter of theological teachings that would inform dispensationalism in the twentieth century.

One of the Exclusive Brethren's founders was a well-educated Englishman who grew up in Ireland by the name of John Nelson Darby (1800–1882). Darby taught that the Church of Ireland, and by extension the entire Anglican Communion, had failed the current dispensational testing by God and fallen into deep apostasy. The state church perpetuated false doctrine, gave cover to millions of nominal Christians, and subsumed its authority to worldly British imperial interests. For the early Brethren writers, and especially Darby, the teaching of dispensations and the hypocrisy of the churches combined with a "literal" or nonsymbolical interpretation of biblical prophecy to produce a new sect. The Brethren offered a new way to read Scripture, a new set of expectations for Christians, and a new vision of how God would ultimately redeem the world.

The story of dispensationalism invariably begins with Darby and his teachings, but it would be a mistake to think that dispensationalism was a simple transmission of Darby's teachings. True, key parts of what would become dispensationalism originated in Brethren thinking, but other aspects of Brethren teachings (such as radical separation from all denominations) found almost no resonance with dispensationalists. Americans used Brethren ideas to meet their own needs. To mention some examples, Americans held their own interests in religion and revivalism, in certain conceptions of geography, economics, race, class, gender, and American power, that supplied their interpretations of "dispensational time" with unique significance.

The Americans who adopted Brethren teachings in the nineteenth century were uniformly "premillennialists," meaning that they believed that Jesus would return before establishing the thousand-year kingdom of Revelation 20. But they did not all agree on what premillennialism ultimately meant. While premillennialism persisted in an old (sometimes called "historic") form dating to the Reformation, the understanding introduced by the Brethren carried different implications for Christians and churches. The first part of this history of dispensationalism, titled "The New Premillennialists, 1830–1900," is about this complex story of the transmission and reception of Brethren ideas in North America, from Darby's public ministry starting around 1830 through the end of the century.

Premillennialism was only one aspect of what Mauro called in 1927 the "modern system of biblical interpretation" known as dispensationalism. Dispensationalism was also deeply formed by other religious movements that appear in the following pages: revivalism, post–Civil War white sectional (North-South) reconciliation, commonsense realism, Higher Life and holiness movements, global missions, and fundamentalism, among others. As new premillennialists organized in the early twentieth century, they created an entire social and institutional complex infused with teachings adapted from the Brethren and these other strands of religion and culture. The resulting religious complex overlapped with the vast Moody movement, the sprawling network of people and institutions inspired by revivalist Dwight Moody that more or less governed early twentieth-century evangelicalism, and what became the early fundamentalist movement. In that later movement, which organized itself in the early 1920s, dispensationalists made up some (though not nearly all) of the leadership and lay support.

Even within fundamentalism, dispensationalism has always been controversial. The tensions of infighting are important for understanding the history of dispensationalism and can easily go unnoticed. The history of fundamentalism (and evangelicalism) would benefit from some of the insights scholars have gleaned about much more studied modern "isms" such as communism or fascism. The Cold War paradigm of communism confronting capitalism is, of course, vital to understanding the longer story of Karl Marx's ideas, but the Cold War does not exhaust the scope of Marxism. The struggles between Stalinists and Trotskyites, or the competing social visions of Vladimir Lenin and Mao Zedong, mattered greatly to the development of communism in the world. The same principle holds for fundamentalism. It is not an exaggeration to say that the shape of dispensationalism in the twentieth century is as much a product of its embrace and alienation within fundamentalism as any other factor.

By the mid-twentieth century, dispensationalism had become the basis for an entire fundamentalist subculture. Its adherents created seminaries, journals, and mission agencies; its theological concepts—the dispensations, the premillennial position and the future kingdom, the rapture—shaped the religious lives of millions of Americans. The success was stunning. One recent historian has remarked that dispensationalism is "perhaps the most resilient popular theological movement in American history."[12] Part 2 of this book, titled "The Dispensationalists, 1900–1960," explores the formation of this movement through the 1950s, which was the height of scholarly dispensational output, or, as I term it, the scholastic project of dispensational theology.

Alongside its career as a theological movement, dispensationalism began to influence large segments of American consumer culture and media. By the end of the twentieth century, its purported influence on political groups and politicians drove national headlines and its most successful cultural productions sold in the tens of millions. In many of these cases, the "system" of dispensational theology was reduced to its teachings on the end times—"pop dispensationalism"—which was especially focused on the sudden rapture. But like the Brethren and scholastic theologies that inspired it, pop dispensationalism assumed much more than end-times beliefs and helped drive evangelical engagement in politics and culture in the second half of the twentieth century.

By the 1970s, dispensationalism was at a crossroads. As a theological system, scholastic dispensationalism began a dramatic decline in authority, even while pop dispensationalism's success skyrocketed. By the early twenty-first century, the scholastic fate of dispensationalism looked bleak, even as its life as a folk religion and pop cultural influence was at an all-time high. The third and final part of this work, titled "The Pop Dispensationalists, 1960–2020," traces these two divergent but intertwined fates over the last sixty years as evangelicalism itself witnessed deep fissures in its theological, cultural, and political identity.

---

12. Christopher Hodge Evans, *Histories of American Christianity: An Introduction* (Waco, TX: Baylor University Press, 2013), 246.

As the story of Philip Mauro suggests, the term "dispensationalism," denoting an interlocking system of biblical interpretation and doctrines, is only about one hundred years old. To avoid anachronism, I do not normally use the term until reaching the year 1927. Not all premillennialists became dispensationalists—if they had, the history of dispensationalism would look very different. And not all evangelicals embraced dispensationalism—far from it. If they had, this, too, would have deeply imprinted on the history of dispensationalism. Projecting any term backward in time obscures a key insight that historical narratives can provide, namely, that the packaging of beliefs into an "ism" is often a contested process, and remains so even after an "ism's" seeming permanence is established.

The End Times and Everything Else

Dispensationalism is more than just a scenario of how the world will end. While many of its spokesmen have earned their reputation as purveyors of the apocalypse, the theology of dispensationalism encompasses much more.

And yet, eschatology deserves top mention. The eschatological content of dispensationalism finds its roots in Brethren teachings and has remained relatively stable in outline even as the details have changed every generation (or even more often). In summary, the close of this dispensation will be heralded by the imminent rapture, a sudden taking up into heaven of all true Christians to meet Jesus in the air. With the church removed from the earth, God will unleash judgments for seven years as part of the plan for world redemption. God will allow evil to reign and will permit the rise to power of the antichrist, a perversion of Christ's incarnation that sees Satan fuse with the human dictator of a one-world government. Plagues, geopolitical machinations, and wars will ensue—the earth will be utterly devastated. Israel, God's chosen people and instrument for world redemption, will be seemingly on the verge of destruction, but a remnant will find supernatural preservation. At the climax of the seven years, the battle of Armageddon will see the victorious raptured church, led by Jesus himself, vanquish the forces of the antichrist. Satan will be bound for a thousand years; this is the same span of time that the millennial kingdom will reign in Jerusalem, its realm the entire globe, its rule one of peace and justice. A final confrontation with Satan after the thousand years will dispatch the devil forever into the lake of fire and prompt the final judgment of humanity.

This scenario has been expounded upon and analyzed by thousands of writers, pastors, and scholars, many to denounce rather than promote its teachings. In popular culture dispensational eschatology has been conflated with the second coming (a doctrine that virtually all Christians ascribe to in some form), yet it represents just one tradition of Christian thought and one version of end-times belief. On its own, the sequence of events does not carry the same meaning as when it is embedded within the broader theology of dispensationalism. Its features are largely the product of a "literal" reading of the Hebrew prophets and book of Revelation, meaning a biblical interpretative strategy, or hermeneutic, that assumes physical and observable fulfillments of prophecy in historical time that are not simply allegorical or spiritual. The "system" of dispensationalism employs this literal hermeneutic and combines it with a "historical grammatical" method that strives to discover original authorial intent by reducing allegorical readings of all biblical passages in favor of a single objective interpretation. This objectivity extends to prophecy, which dispensationalists anticipate as being fulfilled in a single, preordained way by God.

In addition to an eschatology, dispensationalism is also a theory of time. Dispensationalists divide history into discrete units, or "dispensations." Most commonly, dispensational authors teach that there are seven total dispensations. In this system, we live in the sixth, or second to last. The most crucial point, however, is not the number but the pattern. If human history is a story of dispensations, it is a history of human failure and God's persistent faithfulness. Whether it is the dispensation of innocence in the garden of Eden, or the dispensation of law as delivered to Moses, God does not cast away disobedient humanity but resolves to work through sin for redemptive purposes. The end-times scenario, for all its particularities, is the climactic episode in a pattern that unites the unformed earth of Genesis with the new heavens and new earth of Revelation.

Dispensationalism is as much a theory of the church as it is of dispensations. Or rather, dispensationalism divides humanity into three distinct groups: Israel, the church, and the nations. The first two are each in covenant with God. Israel has the starring role as God's direct partner for redemption. But because of the rejection of Jesus by both Rome and Israel, God is using the church as the current agent for world redemption, which will ultimately be taken up again and completed by Israel. The great masses of humanity not part of either Israel or the church constitute the nations, alternately the instruments and recipients of God's judgment, and the beneficiaries of blessings imparted by God through Israel and the church.

While offering a three-part anthropology of humanity, dispensationalism is fundamentally dualistic in its understanding of the relationship between God's two chosen peoples. As Darby wrote in 1839, "The church and the people of Israel are each respectively the centres of the heavenly glory and of the earthly glory, each of them has a sphere which is proper to itself, and in which all things are subordinate to it." Though the church is bound to this planet for now, its true purpose is otherworldly, with the "angels, principalities, and powers with all that belongs to heaven." In contrast, Israel's purview is this world and "the nations of the earth."[13] This separation of God's purposes into church-Israel, earth-heaven dualisms set the Brethren apart from virtually every other Christian tradition, suggesting a more complicated development than traditional supersessionism, which saw the church taking over the role of Israel in God's plans. Rather, the dispensational view was that God's promises to Israel in the prophetic literature awaited literal fulfillment in the future.

These teachings on the end times, dispensations, Israel, and the church were all derived from a particular reading of the Bible. And so, dispensationalism is also a unique biblical hermeneutic, or an approach to reading the Bible. Again, this story has changed over time, with Brethren deeply invested in symbolical, allegorical, and typological readings of Scripture, while later dispensationalists became the standard-bearers for "plain" and "commonsense" readings. What has been consistent is a "literal" or material interpretation of biblical prophecy, a genre that makes up more than a quarter of the Protestant Bible and can be found in passages stretching from Genesis to the Hebrew prophets to the Gospels to Paul's epistles (and, of course, the book of Revelation). The dispensational hermeneutic assumes the absolute inerrancy of the Bible and tends to equate nonliteral readings of prophetic passages with a rejection of inerrancy.

Lastly, dispensationalism offers a particular theory of salvation, or what it means to be "born again." Here, once again, later dispensationalists differed from Darby, who taught a rather high barrier of entry into the elect that included evidences of redemption such as personal piety and "sealing" by the Holy Spirit. Borrowing from the American revivalist tradition, dispensationalists were promoters of a less demanding "free grace" tradition that lowered the bar of salvation to little more than a onetime mental assent to the proposition that Jesus is Savior. This "free grace" understanding, often described colloquially as God's "free gift" of salvation, received intense scrutiny from fellow Christians (especially fellow fundamentalists), even as it won in broader American understandings of being "born again."

Alongside its theological teachings, dispensationalism also displays social influences that bear the marks of its unique history. These bring us closer to grounding the story of dispensationalism in cultural and not just theological concerns.

13. John Nelson Darby, "The Purpose of God," in *Collected Writings*, vol. 2, Prophetic No. 1 (reprint, Oak Park, IL: Bible Truth Publishers, 1971), 267.

Dispensationalism arose in the United States as a social critique, though one directed toward the post–Civil War American situation rather than the dynamics of Great Britain that exorcised the Brethren. American adopters beginning in the 1860s prioritized sectional white reconciliation between North and South, and they found Brethren teachings helpful toward this goal. They advanced a social project, in other words, even as it was couched in nonsocial language. That project has persisted (with adaptations) since the 1860s and deeply shaped broader evangelical and fundamentalist engagement with American politics and culture.

Dispensationalism also became a source of cultural production and consumption. If there is one characteristic that today sets dispensationalism apart from other Protestant theologies, it is its commercial viability. Popular interest has fueled dispensational growth since William Blackstone's *Jesus Is Coming* (1878) and the *Scofield Reference Bible* (1909), through Hal Lindsey's *Late Great Planet Earth* (1970) and the Left Behind novels (1995–2007). Dispensationalism has adapted to and been influenced by new consumer models, from mass distribution of printed tracts to apocalyptic memes online, not only making it resilient but also redirecting its historical development. Dispensationalists have straddled popular and scholastic cultures—sometimes in cooperation, often in rivalry. The instability of dispensationalism is not unique nor is it an indicator of reception—mass culture has shaped all of American religion—but rarely have the swings been so dramatic, and so dramatically significant to the fate of a theological tradition.

Finally, dispensationalism has always been a dissenter movement, and one with a populist bent. Even as dispensationalists systematized their theology, they traveled further away from the American intellectual mainstream. While exclusion from elite circles has sounded the death knell for many theological and intellectual movements, it fueled the popularity of dispensationalism. The movement carved out a space that took ideas seriously but did not directly engage with contemporary thought, displaying an anti-intellectual intellectualism that is a common feature of populist movements. Dispensationalism's skepticism of secular and religious institutions, its alternate tradition of rationality, its reordering of cosmic history, its deep interwovenness into the logic of consumerism—all make it a fascinating window into the workings of American religion.

Dispensationalism in Time and Space

But who were (and are) the dispensationalists? Dispensationalism was no static set of teachings handed down from generation to generation. Rather, it was adopted and taught by people who saw it as not only true but relevant to their broader commitments as Christians and Americans.

At its height, dispensationalism was a full-blown religious subculture embraced by millions of Americans. "American" is key—while dispensationalism has had life beyond the geographical borders of the United States, its most dramatic theater has remained there. While finding supporters across the country, the institutional centers of dispensationalism have shifted over time. Representing its origins in the Great Lakes basin, Chicago was at one time the hub of dispensational organizations, including churches, seminaries, Bible institutes, and mission agencies. In the twentieth century, Dallas and Southern California emerged as two other key areas—for reasons explored in the following pages and deeply tied to the broader social and cultural forces shaping the theology. No matter where people were, dispensationalism imparted a wide range of assumptions about how the world worked and how society was supposed to work. At its most potent, dispensationalism was learned not only through books and sermons but also through prayer and Bible reading, through hymns and conversations, and by living with people who shared similar beliefs.

The majority of this history is focused on the key historical actors who forged the dispensationalist theological and institutional movement, as well as those individuals who brought that movement into cultural and commercial success or oversaw its scholastic decline. This is a predominantly educated, white, male cast of characters. The institutional and theological structures of dispensationalism in the nineteenth century were forged by white evangelicals who privileged the goal of white reconciliation after the Civil War over the aims of Reconstruction. While the project of reconciliation achieved astounding success in creating a broad coalition of white evangelicals, it also killed a potential (if unlikely) future of a racially diverse dispensational tradition. Later generations exacerbated earlier decisions, and with few exceptions dispensationalists have never led in advocating for social or political equality. In many cases they actively supported such discriminatory measures as racial segregation. They often did so for expediency and for reasons unrelated to the specific theological commitments of dispensationalism. But sometimes they did connect social attitudes to their theology. It is in these examples, which span from responses to Reconstruction to Cold War anticommunism, that dispensationalism's social and political location is most visible.

The geographical spread of dispensationalism is tied to its demographics, too. A remarkable subplot in the story of dispensationalism is how its teachings originally gathered a regional following in the Great Lakes basin and then, over time, spread to the South and the West Coast while retreating from New England.

By and large, the South slowly and only haltingly adopted dispensationalism, and then in ways that accommodated other southern-specific factors. For the most part, dispensationalists were eager to gain new adherents in the South, even if that meant accommodating white southern attitudes on race and segregation.

The demographic and geographic dimensions of dispensationalism are also connected to its economic story. Who funded the expansion of dispensationalism? It is difficult to give one answer. In the nineteenth century, and stretching to the fundamentalism of the 1920s, the broader institutional complex that housed dispensational teachings was funded by industrial profits. For example, the oil money of Milton and Lyman Stewart funded the founding of the Bible Institute of Los Angeles and the publication and distribution of *The Fundamentals*. To take a less prominent example, the revival campaigns of J. Wilbur Chapman were funded by railroad tycoon John H. Converse, giving Chapman nearly complete autonomy from Presbyterian denominational oversight and allowing him to popularize dispensational teachings unfettered. This "old money" model gave rise to a particular institutional complex of Bible conferences, Bible institutes, publishing houses, and revival circuits that effectively created the dispensational subculture by the early twentieth century.

A second type of money fueled dispensationalism after World War II—namely, the vast profits that came from commercializing the theology itself. This "new money" was derived from book sales, movie tickets, and television donation drives, among other ventures. It was amplified in the modern megachurch movement and given a boost in the pop-dispensational-infused rhetoric of the New Christian Right. The accumulators of this wealth shifted focus from the old institutional complex to a new one governed far more by the drive for commercial expansion and transmedia viability than by theological education and global missions. The new money funded a new complex: Christian television, film, and music; megachurch platforms; political action groups; and online content. The shifting financial leadership of the movement inevitably altered its message, as well. Scholastic dispensationalism fell into steep decline while paperbacks and talk shows (focused almost exclusively on eschatology and politics) took advantage of consumer tastes and new markets.

In these areas and the many more that are discussed in the following pages, dispensationalism was a movement that changed significantly over time. It has never been a static set of beliefs or a fixed community, nor is its legacy easy to summarize. It bears mentioning that while this history will focus on those who constructed and deconstructed the theology of dispensationalism, the teachings themselves have been formative for millions of other Christians. Those who were introduced to Christianity by dispensationalists or were influenced by dispensational teachings are too numerous to list. Critics have conceded as much, dating to critical theologian George Eldon's Ladd's observation in 1952 that it was "doubtful if there has been any other circle of men [than dispensationalists] who have done more by their influence in preaching, teaching and writing to promote a love for Bible study, a hunger for the deeper Christian life, a passion for evangelism and zeal for missions in the history of American Christianity."[14] Similar sentiments have been voiced in every decade since, and dispensationalism has been formative for many Christians who no longer subscribe to its tenets but have been indelibly shaped by them.

The full scope of dispensationalism was lost even on Philip Mauro, who assumed that the theology's fruits were wholly rotten and that its ideas would be easy to dismantle. Mauro made sure to clarify in his many screeds against dispensationalism that his disagreement was "with the doctrine itself; and not at all with those who hold and teach it."[15] Yet in reality, such a distinction was not possible; dispensationalism not only supplied theological language and concepts but also gave spiritual sustenance and meaning to its adherents. Assembling the story of dispensationalism involves faithfully representing its allure and the explanatory power it provides to its followers. It also means acknowledging its limitations and weaknesses, all the while probing how dispensationalism waxed and waned over time.

14. George Eldon Ladd, *Crucial Questions about the Kingdom of God* (Grand Rapids: Eerdmans, 1952), 49.
15. Mauro, *Gospel of the Kingdom*, 3.

PART I

THE NEW PREMILLENNIALISTS
1830–1900

John Nelson Darby develops a new method of biblical interpretation as a critique of the Church of Ireland ◆ Darby's movement, the Exclusive Brethren, gains a smattering of American followers who adapt Darby's ideas to their own political and social situation in border states ◆ Early converts during the Civil War and Reconstruction are attracted to Brethren ideas of church and prophecy that support their bids for sectional neutrality ◆ The most important promoter of this new American subculture of new premillennialism is the revivalist Dwight Moody, whose religious movement builds a vast complex of institutions that perpetuates new premillennialism in the service of global missions ◆ The Moody movement nurtures new premillennial leaders and institutions, making its teachings integral to one of the most vibrant subcultures in American Protestantism at the turn of the twentieth century

Premillennialism is no barren speculation—useless though true, and innocuous though false. It is a school of Scripture interpretation; it impinges upon and affects some of the most commanding points of the Christian faith; and, when suffered to work its unimpeded way, it stops not till it has pervaded with its own genius the entire system of one's theology, and the whole tone of his spiritual character, constructing, I had almost said, a world of its own; so that, holding the same faith, and cherishing the same fundamental hopes as other Christians, he yet sees things through a medium of his own, and finds every thing instinct with the life which this doctrine has generated within him.

David Brown,
Christ's Second Coming: Will It Be Premillennial?
(1858)

David Brown, a Glasgow Free Church minister and onetime premillennialist, was one of the nineteenth century's foremost critics of the new premillennialism that John Nelson Darby helped popularize. To this quotation (from his book *Christ's Second Coming: Will It Be Premillennial?*), Darby responded, "This is thoroughly true, and shews how necessary it is, in all grace and patience, to see where the truth lies."

1

Across an Ocean

In 1825, at the age of twenty-five, an Anglo-Irish graduate of Trinity College Dublin, John Nelson Darby, became a curate in the Church of Ireland. Darby's parish was the District of Calary, just south of Dublin. He had no church to work out of, so he spent most of his time on horseback, visiting poor Irish Catholics with the message that the true church of God was the Church of Ireland. By 1826 he had begun to have some success, and a purported "Irish Reformation," of which Darby was one small agent, was believed by some Anglicans to be on the horizon.

But then, as Darby described later, the momentum was halted in its tracks. Indeed, the entire religious fate of Ireland suddenly darkened. Darby described the year 1827 as a time when "Roman Catholics were passing over to Protestantism many hundreds in a week" in a process that, given time and the movement of the Holy Spirit, would have sealed the British Isles as the global center of Protestantism. Then politics intervened. In an 1827 petition, Darby continued, "the Archbishop of Dublin insisted that the Protestant Establishment suited the State, made them take the oaths of abjuration and supremacy, and the work stopped."[1] The elites in the Church of Ireland, in other words, had abandoned their heavenly duty to win souls and had embraced a worldly political Protestantism subservient to the interests of the British Empire.[2]

The accuracy of Darby's account is debatable. There is only a sparse record of Protestant conversions in Ireland in the mid-1820s. The archbishop of Dub-

1. Quoted in Donald Harman Akenson, *Discovering the End of Time: Irish Evangelicals in the Age of Daniel O'Connell* (Montreal and Kingston, ON: McGill-Queen's University Press, 2016), 249.

2. Quoted in Timothy Stunt, *From Awakening to Secession: Radical Evangelicals in Switzerland and Britain, 1815–35* (Edinburgh: T&T Clark, 2000), 171.

lin, William Magee, did write a policy statement in mid-1827, one which Darby angrily responded to in an unpublished letter, but Magee hardly said what Darby thought he did. Moreover, just two years later the Roman Catholic Relief Act, part of the ongoing campaign of Catholic emancipation in the United Kingdom, removed most demands that Catholics renounce the authority of the pope in order to become full citizens. Catholic converts did not suddenly flood the Church of Ireland then, either.

Yet, in the Irish countryside, exactly one hundred years before Mauro coined "dispensationalism," the energetic Darby suddenly found himself with time to stew on his (and Ireland's) misfortune. In December 1827 he was badly injured by his horse. Bedridden for months, Darby would later recall that it was during this time that he came to realize the eschatological kingdom described in the Bible was entirely different from the Church of Ireland. As he remembered, the unpublished salvo against Magee was "the first germing of truth which has since developed itself into the Church of God."[3] The radical claim was the opening gambit for a new understanding of Christianity that would travel far indeed from the craggy hills of Calary.

Darby's voluminous writings from 1827 to his death in 1882, numbering some nineteen million words, would be remembered for their apocalyptic teachings, but his life's work was equally focused on his grievances with the Church of Ireland, and indeed all established churches. In his letter to Archbishop Magee, Darby wrote that his ministry was part of "the manifestation of the power of the Divine Spirit which has begun a work in this country," but which "is of no country, but of the power of that kingdom which shall fill the whole earth."[4] Established churches across Europe paid fealty to this monarch or that pope; all invested in the machinations of politics and riches. Darby, who cast a radical dualism between heaven and earth, church and nation, was driven by the perceived slights to the gospel he witnessed.

Darby developed a radical understanding of the church as a heavenly and lay-run body that informed his broader theological project. The implications of his thinking extended to reimagining the way Christians should understand the Bible, the structure of time, and the prophetic, or redemptive, ends of God's plans for humanity. While dispensationalism would come of age in North America a century later, its genealogy dates to this earlier era based in Ireland and Great Britain.

3. Quoted in Akenson, *Discovering the End of Time*, 251.
4. Quoted in Akenson, *Discovering the End of Time*, 254.

Prophetic House Parties

Darby's initial decades of theological creativity in the 1830s and 1840s were a time when he wrote prodigiously, traveled constantly, and sparked strong responses at every opportunity. His teachings were new, radical, and raw—they developed in real time and never quite settled into a discrete system.

Darby's lasting contribution was in bundling three theological innovations into an interlocking set of teachings: a new theology of the church, a new theology of the millennium, and a new dualism between heaven and earth that informed how he read the entire Bible. Outside of these areas, Darby could sound and read like a typical theologian in the broader nineteenth-century Reformed tradition, deeply indebted to Augustine and Calvin, among others. Like other Anglican (and later dissenter) radicals of his class and education, Darby was also immersed in the English Bible and its categories. "I do not care for novel interpretations of scripture," Darby wrote. "Cream lies on the surface."[5] But his innovations, which he insisted were recoveries rather than novelties, still set him in a different theological direction. His writings were highly complex, not entirely consistent, and could change over time. Even with his protestations, Darby spent most of his life explaining why his readings of Scripture were not heterodox and why, in fact, they were exactly the fresh insights Christians needed.

The Brethren movement that Darby led emerged out of a complaint with the Church of Ireland that blew up into an indictment of all existing organized religion. By 1835, Darby was aggrieved enough to attack the idea of apostolic succession (core to the Anglican understanding of church authority) and the entire notion of professional ministers. This line of thinking was brought to maturity in 1840 with his classic essay *Reflections on the Ruined Condition of the Church; and on the Efforts Making by Churchmen and Dissenters to Restore It to Its Primitive Order.* The title was notable for crystallizing the critique of the "ruined condition" of organized Christianity. The Brethren would become known for their aversion to a clergy class ("every man his own priest"), but Darby's focus on ruination revealed another crucial aspect to the Brethren's project. For the most part, the mission of the Brethren was aimed at nominal or otherwise cultural Christians who made up much of organized Christianity. As one friendly observer noted of Darby in 1835, "He says he feels his office

5. John Nelson Darby, *Pilgrim Portions: Meditations for the Day of Rest* (London: Morrish, n.d.), accessed May 10, 2022, https://www.stempublishing.com/authors/darby/Pilgrim_Portions.html#a3.

principally lies in urging believers to walk worthy of their high and holy calling."[6] The Brethren, like so many like-minded dissenter groups, were passionate to revive existing Christians as much as to make new converts.

Darby's view of the church was the foundation for his view of the future.
Reacting against the establishment ethos of postmillennialism, or the teaching that it was organized Christianity that would usher in the millennium of
peace, Darby adopted a premillennial eschatology that looked for the ruin of
the church as a precursor to the second coming. His first writing on the end
times came a year after his complaint against Magee. Until the early 1830s, he
promoted a premillennialism that assumed that a proper decoding of biblical
prophecy would reveal the exact date of Christ's return. The key symbols were
the "seventy weeks" of Daniel 9:24–27 (a cryptic prophecy that premillennialists read symbolically to mean 490 years) and an even more cryptic phrase
in Daniel 7 of "time, times, and half a time" that eventually landed most premillennialists on the number of 1,260 days, which, like "seventy weeks," they
translated to years. The "day-year" symbolism was just one example of how
premillennialists did not exactly read prophecy with a wooden literalism, but
they did expect that the prophecies would be fulfilled materially in observable
space and time. By the 1830s, the ascribed significance of 1,260 years was the
time between the reign of Justinian I (527–565) and the French Revolution
(1789–1799). Living at the close of that span, most premillennialists in the
early nineteenth century supplied dates for the second coming that ranged
from the 1840s to the 1860s.

At the time of Darby's rise to prominence, premillennialism lived on the
margins of Anglican life, and Darby was hardly its only radical proponent. Its
popularity grew in a novel series of gatherings, or "prophetic house parties,"
hosted by small circles of Anglo and Anglo-Irish social elites. Darby attended
the Albury Conferences (1826–1830), hosted by banker Henry Drummond,
who would go on to cofound a rival premillennialist sect to the Brethren
known as the Irvingites. In another breakaway prophetic house party, the
Powerscourt Conferences (1831–1833 at the Powerscourt Estate, and later
meetings through 1836 in Dublin) became the platform for Darby to not just
expound a premillennial scheme but to introduce a newer version of his own.
Here Darby offered two key novelties: that the prophetic timeline was stalled
in a "parenthesis" period, with the kingdom postponed at Daniel's sixty-ninth
week (leaving one "week" of seven years to completion); and that this parenthesis would be concluded by the rapture of the church into heaven, an event

6. Quoted in Akenson, *Discovering the End of Time*, 454.

that other premillennialists placed at the end of the prophesied "tribulations." In theological terminology introduced much later, "posttribulational" and "pretribulational" would distinguish the old from the new premillennialist views of the rapture.

The popularity of "old" premillennialism rose at the same time in the United States, where the day-year analysis of Baptist minister William Miller led to a raft of prophecy speculation that Jesus would return in 1843 or 1844. In his calculations, Miller afforded no indeterminate parenthesis. When the appointed times passed without incident, they were remembered as the "Great Disappointment" and sullied the premillennial reputation for at least a decade. There remained an old premillennial tradition even after the early 1840s, and indeed groups like the Seventh-day Adventists (the erstwhile disciples of Miller) continued the focus on prophecy. Other movements heralded radical critiques of established churches: the Church of Jesus Christ of Latter-day Saints, founded by Joseph Smith in 1831, indicted all of organized Christendom as ruinous. So, too, did Robert Matthews, a short-lived religious leader in New York who promised to be ushering in the kingdom of heaven, along with numerous other radicals exposing cracks in the edifice of organized religion during the Second Great Awakening.

The Anglo-American premillennial marketplace of the 1830s allowed Darby room for his own innovations. He rejected the "day-year" symbolism for 1,260 days and insisted that this period of tribulation lay in the near future. In later theological terminology, the new premillennialism Darby espoused was defined as "futurist," for its emphasis that most of biblical prophecy remained to be fulfilled in the near future, rather than "historicist," which correlated the historical reign of Justinian or the French Revolution to prophecy.

Like his grievance against established churches, Darby's new premillennialism shaped how he understood the Bible. Here was the third and perhaps most decisive innovation that Darby introduced in the 1830s. In simplest terms, Darby drew new lines of separation inside of traditional biblical categories. He separated ancient Israel from the church—the patriarchs and prophets were not proto-Christians, nor was the church the new Israel. He separated the church from the nations—Christians were citizens of heaven with no sanctioned role in the lives of empires. Like other Protestants, he separated the "true" church from the visible church—the established churches and "Christendom" were in ruins, while the invisible body of Christ persisted. More uniquely, he separated the "kingdom of God" from the "kingdom of heaven"—the former defined as God's universal dominion and the latter the prophesied reign of peace on earth that would only come in the future through Israel. And he separated the rapture from the second coming, creating room for complex scenarios of end-times events in between these two bookends. These distinctions were all governed by a foundational dualism between heaven and earth, which permeated everything Darby thought and wrote, from the most staid treatise to his Christmas devotionals, one of which embedded the dualism into the call for Christians "to be entirely heavenly, for the earth is far from God, and daily its darkness closes in, but we belong to the light, and await another day."[7]

These separations informed how Darby read the Bible: it was a book telling the story of God's redemption of all things through two chosen peoples, Israel and the church. Much of Scripture applied to one or the other, with very little applying to both. The concept of dispensations, or divisions of time, was not new to Christian thought, but Darby's twist was that these dispensations correlated with the church-Israel distinction and always ended in failure. The Bible told the story of successive dispensations involving Israel (mostly) or the church that each ended in tragedy, each "no sooner fully established than it proved a failure."[8] Such a test-fail cycle pervaded all aspects of Darby's vision of the Bible and Christian faith. "In every instance," he clarified in his classic 1836 formulation, *The Apostasy of the Successive Dispensations*, "there was total and immediate failure as regarded man." And yet all was not lost, because each dispensation, as recounted in the Bible, exhibited, too, that "the patience of God might tolerate and carry on by grace the dispensation in which man has thus failed in the outset."[9] The dispensations supplied a strong dose of Christian pessimism to the Brethren cause, mixed with an appreciation of God's "extraordinary grace."

Darby was not making entirely novel contributions on any of these points— by the 1830s the well of speculation and writing in Anglo-American Protestantism was already deep. But he was shaping a new type of Christian identity that bundled a condemnation of established churches, a premillennial eschatology, and a dualism between heaven and earth. His was a singular vision fashioned by and for disaffected Anglicans in the era of British empire.

From the outset, Darby's views divided the fledgling Brethren movement and the social elite that attended the early prophetic house parties. Fellow Brethren, even, couldn't stomach the introduction of the secret rapture or the novel divisions of Scripture. Tensions bubbled for more than a decade

---

7. Darby, *Pilgrim Portions*.

8. Darby, *Pilgrim Portions*, 448.

9. John Nelson Darby, *The Apostasy of the Successive Dispensations*, 1836, https://www.stempublishing.com/authors/darby/ECCLESIA/01009E.html.

before a clean break in 1848, ostensibly over methods of church discipline but also rooted in power rivalries and the influence of Darby's teachings. While the "Open" Brethren remained indebted to Darby on the ruined state of the church and on many other secondary issues, they rejected most aspects of Darby's new premillennialism and his hermeneutical schema. The Exclusive Brethren, the branch of the Plymouth Brethren that followed Darby, dedicated themselves to propagating his theological vision.

"Evangelising the Denominations"

The 1850s created new opportunities for religious ideas to gain a foothold in North America. Revivalism returned with a force not seen in a generation, beginning in Canada in 1857. Phoebe and Walter Palmer, two Methodist evangelists, held wildly successful camp meetings in what is now Ontario and Quebec, which spread southward. The Panic of 1857, the first financial crisis borne by telegraph, created an immediate economic depression in the United States. In New York City, businessmen began to meet in prayer, the first led by newly appointed Presbyterian lay missionary (and avid distributor of tracts) Jeremiah Lampier. The Businessmen's Revival, as it was soon named, quickly moved west toward Chicago and south along the Eastern Seaboard. Thousands converted or recommitted to pious living, equaling in one historical estimate 3 percent of the entire population of the United States. By 1858 the revival jumped east across the Atlantic and quickly spread throughout the United Kingdom.

Even though Methodists and Presbyterians were the chief beneficiaries of revival, smaller groups like the Brethren also thrived. "With the Brethren, as with all others, the work of the gospel was greatly revived in 1859," recounted Andrew Miller, an ally of Darby's, twenty years later.[10] The Brethren writer and evangelist C. H. Mackintosh, whose work deeply shaped Americans, recalled how in 1858 "the mighty tide of spiritual life and power rolled in upon us, and swept away for the time being a quantity of human machinery, and ignored all question of man's authority in the things of God and the service of Christ." Such "machinery" included "official and denominational channels" that, in the Brethren reading, exploited revivalism for the agenda of a postmillennial ideology of church and state, a doctrine of error that sought to realize God's kingdom on earth through empire. "This," Mackintosh concluded, "the Holy

10. Andrew Miller, *The Brethren: A Brief Sketch of Their Origin, Progress, and Testimony* (London: G. Morrish, 1879), 72.

Ghost would not sanction." Instead, "the work and the workman were lionized in all directions"—the Brethren were unleashed.[11]

The Holy Spirit was on the move in the 1850s, but what were its designs? For those caught up in the transatlantic revivals, the call was to individual holiness, to embody the "fruit of the Spirit," and to realize the promise of spiritual power to aid the believer in right living. These aims bridged the Reformed, or Calvinist, tradition that emphasized the sovereignty of God and authority of the Bible, and the Wesleyan tradition that placed its emphasis on personal faith and holiness. In the spirit of revival, both centered on the fate of the individual's soul. One Scottish Presbyterian testified in 1860 of "how terrifying a sight it is when the Holy Spirit is pleased to open a man's eyes to see the real estate of his heart."[12] The process of individual sanctification—of the Holy Spirit freeing the Christian from sin and making one like Christ—became a frequent fixation for Protestants for the next fifty years, spawning an emphasis on holiness not only in the Wesleyan churches but also in Reformed circles, the Keswick, or Higher Life, movement, which taught of the power of the Holy Spirit to shape human behavior.

For the Brethren, who were aggressive in their maintenance of Reformed theological boundaries, individual holiness was important primarily for its reform potential in the wider apostate church. In the 1850s, Brethren quickly grew concerned that the bulk of revival energy was being channeled into individualistic reform, based on faulty Wesleyan notions of sanctification, while ignoring the deeper ruination of the church. More important to them than entire sanctification was ecclesial revival from the bottom up, leading to the institutional renewal of the church and its return to the purity of the New Testament. Writing in 1863, the Brethren observer Henry Soltau described that his movement "has no parallel in the whole history of the Church of God, because in no other instance has the Word of God (freed from all tradition) been taken as the guide of those who have sought a revival in the Church of God."[13] The "Church of God," rather than the individual followers of God, was where revival had to do its most important work. Within the convulsing revivalism on both sides of the Atlantic, divergent emphases compounded

11. Charles H. Mackintosh, "Papers on Evangelization," in *The Assembly of God: Miscellaneous Writings of C. H. Mackintosh*, vol. 3 (New York: Loizeaux Brothers, 1898), 55–56.

12. Quoted in J. Edwin Orr, *The Fervent Prayer: The Worldwide Impact of the Great Awakening of 1858* (Chicago: Moody Press, 1974), 56.

13. Henry William Soltau, *"They Found It Written"; or, "The Brethren." Who Are They? What Are Their Doctrines?* (Glasgow: Pickering & Inglis, [1863]), 6–7.

theological differences. Brethren became some of the most outspoken opponents of revivalism in the English-speaking world.

Thus, while typical revivalists called upon "lost souls" and the nonreligious to turn from their sinful ways, Exclusive Brethren focused on "evangelising the denominations"—the apostate churches themselves, fellow Christians. Theirs was a revival within Christendom, that is, a calling out of Christians from worldly Christendom into the heavenly church. Brethren regarded the difference as one between evangelism and teaching, between introducing the gospel and reintroducing right faith—"teaching, or giving lectures on scripture to Christians." The "important distinction between preaching the gospel to the unconverted and teaching Christians, as thus enforced and illustrated by the Brethren, was altogether new," Miller claimed of the 1859 Ulster Revival. "The gift and work of the evangelist are perfectly distinct from those of the teacher; but the distinction has, always excepting the apostolic ace, never been acted upon in the church generally until very lately."[14]

These fault lines over the purpose and direction of revival, like the division between Open Brethren and Exclusive Brethren, motivated Darby and his followers to write and move more—to travel, preach, and print more. Long before Darby set foot in North America, Brethren used tracts to popularize their mode of defending "church truth" and ecclesial renewal. Their success lodged some key concepts in the religious culture of the day.

North America, in this schema, was a rich field for teaching. Brethren expansion was organized on this principle: focus on established clergy, preach against wrong belief, and unmask false religion within Christendom. This mission animated the Brethren popularizers who adapted Darby's teachings for the target audience of "worldly" Christians. Their message and tone included a dose of religious populism, driving to make accessible their complex theology for a wider lay audience and calling to task institutions and their leaders. Novel ideas like the rapture, and novel images like the prophecy chart indicating the dispensational progression of time, extended Brethren teaching far beyond the places they personally visited.

Popularizing Darby

Popularizing Brethren teachings was always a trade-off between accessibility and precision. It was a transaction that Darby himself rarely made but that his Brethren colleagues trafficked in constantly.

14. Miller, *The Brethren*, 36–37.

EIGHT

LECTURES ON PROPHECY,

DELIVERED IN

THE MERCHANTS' HALL, YORK,

DURING MARCH AND APRIL, 1851,

BY WILLIAM TROTTER AND THOMAS SMITH.

FROM SHORT HAND NOTES;

WITH CORRECTIONS AND ADDITIONS BY THE AUTHORS.

LONDON: J. K. CAMPBELL, HIGH HOLBORN;

AND

BRISTOL: E. GRANVILLE, 18, BROADMEAD.

1851.

CONTENTS.

Lecture I.—The importance of prophetic study, and the spirit in which it needs to be conducted; with a general outline of prophetic testimony.

Lecture II.—The second coming of Christ proved to be pre-millennial.

Lecture III.—The return and restoration of the Jews.

Lecture IV.—The millennial reign of Christ, and the univer-sal blessing of the earth, connected with the restoration of the Jews.

Lecture V.—The distinct calling and glory of the church, as bride and co-heir of Christ.

Lecture VI.—The predicted corruption of christianity, with its final results.

Lecture VII.—The times of the Gentiles: the character and doom of the great Gentile powers.

Lecture VIII.—The hope of the church; with concluding practical observations.

Appendix.—The church removed before the apocalyptic judg-ments.

Figure 1. Trotter and Smith's *Eight Lectures on Prophecy*, cover and table of contents, from 1851. The structure of this work, moving from general to particular doctrines, and from shared to contested premillennial theological territory, worked to disarm immediate rejections and to incorporate Darby's teachings into a much longer premillennial tradition, concealing the relative novelty of certain escha-tological teachings within the fold of a wider discourse.

William Trotter and Thomas Smith were a Brethren duo who wrote the first comprehensive distillation of Darby's eschatology to reach North America, *Eight Lectures on Prophecy* (1851). The book provided a manual for "the study of prophecy rightly conducted" that soft-launched a popular version of the dualism and literalism underlying Exclusive Brethren theology.[15] The intended audience was not lost souls but troubled saints. "These Lectures were deliv-ered, and are now printed, for the benefit of Christians almost or altogether unacquainted with the subjects of which they treat," the authors began.[16] The

15. William Trotter and T. Smith, *Eight Lectures on Prophecy* (London: J. K. Campbell, 1851), 14.

16. Trotter and Smith, *Eight Lectures on Prophecy*, 3.

lectures were framed within Protestant eschatological debates and arrayed against established church teachings. Postmillennial optimism corrupted the office of the prophet, they diagnosed, to flaccidly "prophesy smooth things, and cry peace, when there is no peace." Trotter and Smith instead warned that judgment was rapidly approaching, and only then would "a day of universal peace and blessedness" appear.[17]

In their lectures, Trotter and Smith presented a case for the new premillennialism while never mentioning Darby by name. This was strategic, as they presented their arguments as emerging directly from Scripture and not from "the reasonings and speculations of men."[18] Indeed, they blamed Irvingites and other sects, including Mormons and Millerites, movements in debt to the insights of charismatic leaders, for the general disrepute of prophecy study, insisting that the numerous examples of misinterpretation made their investigation more pertinent. "Instead of proving that prophecy should be neglected," they wrote, its past misuse "proves that it should be studied; calmly indeed, with prayer—in entire dependence upon the Spirit of God; but still studied."[19]

Yet, what was gained in Trotter and Smith's presentation was counterbalanced with what was lost. The eight lectures focused narrowly on prophetic study, unbundling Darby's views of the future from his separatist and anticlerical positions. The reader could agree with the lectures and adopt a premillennial reading of Scripture but remain entrenched in the churches. Darby's dualism worked behind the words of the lectures and could be detected by the initiated, but the outsider could easily miss the integral link between eschatology and ecclesiology. This was one of the bargains struck for popularizing Darby's teachings.

Another example was Charles Stanley, a popular itinerant Brethren evangelist who traveled the United Kingdom distributing thousands of his own tracts. Stanley was the unlikely progenitor of the most popular visual representation of Darby's eschatology: the prophecy chart. He was best known for his "Railway Tracts," short records of his preaching successes, many of which took place in railway carriages or living rooms. Many of the tracts, like the *Eight Lectures*, named as their intended audience fellow Christians. Stanley, too, pined for the day when Christians would look for Christ's return. "The invasion of England could not give greater surprise, or alarm, than would be the awak-

17. Trotter and Smith, *Eight Lectures on Prophecy*, 6.
18. Trotter and Smith, *Eight Lectures on Prophecy*, 6.
19. Trotter and Smith, *Eight Lectures on Prophecy*, 18.

ening of the slumbering church to the fact that the Lord was really coming," he complained. He likened the hollowness of contemporary Christian anticipation for the second coming to "the lamp without the oil"—gilded but darkened to reality. "Is this my reader's condition? Then, there is not a moment to be lost—no, not a moment; for it is Jesus who says, 'Surely, I come quickly.'"[20]

Yet, more than his tracts, Stanley provided an enduring visual representation of one aspect of Darby's teachings, the progression of dispensational time. While preaching in Llandudno, a coastal town in northern Wales, Stanley sketched what would become an icon of later dispensational culture. "I was speaking on the coming of the Lord," he later recalled. "And finding some difficulty in explaining the difference between the present gospel period and the millennium, or the period of the reign of Christ, I took up a piece of chalk, or lime, and made two circles on a garden door." He explained the two circles as the present and future ages, which prompted further questions from the crowd. He drew lines to indicate historical narratives—"the history of the Jews," "the ascension of Christ to heaven," "the coming of the Lord Jesus to fetch His saints," and so forth, until the line came to "the beginning of an endless circle, to show the eternal state." He reflected on this first diagram: "All these were crude marks, on the garden door, but [they] wonderfully helped the audience to understand dispensational truth." A colleague by the name of "Colonel B." copied it onto pasteboard, and it made its way into multiple publications.[21]

The "illustrative diagram" captured dispensational time in its most simplified, and therefore most viral, form. Brethren had visualized their teachings before—in the 1840s Sir Edward Denny and John Jewell Penstone produced an elaborate multipage chart and companion volume that was intricately made and daunting to the outsider.[22] A two-hundred-page companion to a pair of other charts by Denny, depicting the seventy weeks of Daniel, was a testament to how much exposition the creator felt was required to grasp his chart's meaning.[23] These works tended to include significant scriptural paraphrasing or full passages, illustrating in heavy-handed fashion the mediation between

20. Charles Stanley, "Awake! Awake! Behold the Bridegroom Cometh," in *The C. S. Tracts*, vol. 2 (London: G. Morrish, n.d.), 2.

21. Charles Stanley, *Incidents of Gospel Work: Shewing the Way the Lord Hath Led Me* (London: G. Morrish, 1889), 62–64.

22. Edward Denny, *Companion to a Chart, a Prophetical Stream of Time* (London: J. Nisbet, 1849). The chart itself was drawn by John Jewell Penstone.

23. Edward Denny, *Forgiveness Seventy and Sevenfold, Companion to Two Prophetical Charts* (London: J. Nisbet, 1849).

text and image. Often drawn in color and on large paper, these charts were to be displayed—to be "Mounted, either on Hollers, in Covers, on Frames, or otherwise"—for teaching or sacred decoration in the home.[24]

In contrast, Stanley's diagram was initially included in volume 1 of *The C. S. Tracts*. It also appeared in pamphlet form with the title *Coming Events, as Revealed in Scripture, Arranged with a View to Shew Their Order and Connection, with Illustrative Diagram*. The short pamphlet of sixteen pages listed passages from Scripture on the second coming next to each other, ordered as "a continuous chain of events," with Stanley's paraphrased interpretations down the center of each page. He instructed his readers to "read clause by clause, with all the passages referred to, seeking guidance from God to understand them." The illustrated diagram on the last page "will tend to fix the order of events on the memory."[25]

Like Trotter and Smith's *Eight Lectures*, Stanley's diagram held immense popularizing potential, but it also distorted Darby's intended bundling of ecclesiology, eschatology, and biblical hermeneutics. Dispensational time structured Darby's understanding of past, present, and future, but the diagram directed the viewer's interest distinctly toward the future. Of the nine labeled points, only the first three designated the past and present; the other six mapped out the series of events that would culminate in the Eternal State. While the original diagram included the dotted line signifying "the history of the Jews, cut out during the present period," and thus nodded to the central storyline of redemptive history, later versions excised that feature for even more simplicity, and in any case, the vertical dualism between heaven and earth was harder to detect in a drawing purposed to explain the horizontal advancement of time. While the diagram undoubtedly made the basic outlines of dispensational time more accessible, it did so at the cost of the principles that had led Darby to the dispensational concept in the first place, and, like Trotter and Smith, it dropped ecclesiastical separatism as a point of representation.

In the throes of transatlantic revival, these trade-offs made sense, even to Darby, who dabbled in outdoor preaching but preferred smaller gatherings. Brethren teachers, including Trotter, Smith, and Stanley, and others who would make a mark on North America, including William Kelly and C. H. Mackintosh, honed a popular style of teaching that offered modest numerical

24. Denny, *Companion to a Chart*, front matter.

25. Charles Stanley, *Coming Events, as Revealed in Scripture, Arranged with a View to Shew Their Order and Connection, with Illustrative Diagram*, 5th ed. (London: G. Morrish, n.d.), 2.

success in the United Kingdom. The process of transmission to North America would ensure that these ideas would spread widely and become even more disaggregated from their original source in Darby's writings.

Hymns of Doctrine

Brethren teachings became popular not only through theological writings. Hymns and poetry, inspired by Brethren separation and dissent, also drew outsiders to the distinctive teachings of the group. The music of Sir Edward Denny, the Anglo-Irish Brethren composer, was an early example. Denny created hundreds of hymns, some intended for Brethren worship and others for a wider Protestant audience. His staple "millennial hymns" often pondered the rapture within the broader Brethren critique of the Anglican Church:

> Like foolish virgins, ye have fail'd
> Your holy watch to keep;
> And lo, he comes, and almost finds
> Your languid souls asleep!
>
> Then wake, for, lo, the midnight cry
> Of warning in the air.
> Bids all his church to greet him now,
> Their dying lamps prepare.[26]

Other hymns embedded Darby's dualism into the experiences of each individual dissenter, whom Denny depicted in one of his most popular hymns, "A Pilgrim through This Lonely World":

> In tents we dwell amid the waste
> Nor turn aside to roam
> In folly's paths, nor seek our rest
> Where Jesus had no home
>
> Dead to the world, with Him who died
> to win our hearts, our love
> We, risen with our risen Head
> In spirit dwell above

26. Sir Edward Denny, *Hymns and Poems* (London: James Nisbet, 1848), 41.

The hymn was originally published in 1839. It was later included in numerous Church of England hymnals, but "its principal use," as one later dictionary of hymns described it, "is in America, where it is found in numerous collections."[27] In many cases the song was abbreviated and misattributed, but it nevertheless spread widely, and quickly. By the 1880s it could be found in Methodist, Lutheran, Baptist, and Seventh-day Adventist hymnals, among others.[28]

In typical Brethren fashion, Denny's hymns were created to be "a basis of truth and sound doctrine." He produced "millennial hymns" and other varieties that taught unique Brethren views, including the rapture. According to an early twentieth-century hymnologist, Brethren verse like Denny's tended toward themes "concerning the coming of Christ to raise His saints, and the millennium." Brethren hymns taught "the dreariness of this world and all belonging to it, the full assurance of faith, and the completeness of the Christian in Christ."[29] In no less exacting fashion than Trotter or Stanley, Denny fixed his creative output on conveying the core truths and implications of Darby's teachings for a lay audience.

Denny was joined by other Brethren hymnists and poets in his themes of pilgrimage and wilderness, loneliness and the all-sufficient grace of the cross. On the theme of alienation from the world and dualistic understanding of heaven and earth, Denny's work stood alongside Darby's similarly-themed contribution, "A Song for the Wilderness." But unlike other Brethren hymns, which were produced largely for the "little flock," as Darby's 1881 edition of the commonly used Exclusive hymnal was titled, Denny's verses gained a second life far removed from the concerns of Plymouth.[30] If the metropole of the Brethren empire of tracts was Paternoster Street in London, where each year millions of pages began their journeys into the English-speaking world, the Great Lakes basin in North America was the periphery region that would receive and reappropriate Brethren truth for its own purposes, and in doing so remake the legacy of the Brethren in America.

27. John Julian, ed., *A Dictionary of Hymnology: Setting Forth the Origin and History of Christian Hymns of All Ages and Nations*, 2nd ed. (London: J. Murray, 1907), 3.

28. See "A Pilgrim through This Lonely World," Hymnary.org, accessed May 11, 2022, https://hymnary.org/text/a_pilgrim_through_this_lonely_world/compare.

29. Darby, quoted in Julian, *A Dictionary of Hymnology*, 899.

30. John Nelson Darby, ed., *A Few Hymns and Some Spiritual Songs. Selected . . . for the Little Flock, Revised* (London: G. Morrish, 1881).

I am getting used to the Atlantic, if used one can.

John Nelson Darby, from New York City, 1865

*Poor Christendom! What a sovereign mercy to be out
of the camp!*

John Nelson Darby, from Boston, 1875

Can man restore the Church? Poor helpless worm, restore thyself!

John Jewell Penstone, Brethren poet, 1876

A scholar and poet, close friend of Darby's, and partisan of the Exclusive Brethren, John Jewell Penstone was among the first-generation Brethren writers who enjoyed a warm reception in North America. Both he and Darby counted it a blessing to stand apart from the established churches. It was a sentiment they failed to impart to most of their American admirers.

2

American Mission Field

There is a tradition of Europeans touring the United States and diagnosing the unique features of American society. No observer is more famous than Alexis de Tocqueville, the French diplomat who visited North America for nine months in 1831–1832 and published an instant classic, *Democracy in America*. Among Tocqueville's enduring observations was the religiosity of Americans. "On my arrival in the United States it was the religious aspect of the country that first struck my eye," Tocqueville wrote.[1] In one of his most famous assessments, he concluded that "there is no country in the whole world in which the Christian religion retains a greater influence over the souls of men than in America."[2]

A generation after Tocqueville, another European crossed the Atlantic for the first time but took a much less sanguine view of North American religiosity. In July 1862, John Nelson Darby disembarked near Toronto to visit a group of Brethren in Guelph, a town thirty miles inland. In his first venture south into the United States the following year, Darby found a dreary spiritual landscape wracked by the ongoing Civil War. "The church is more worldly in America than anywhere you would find it, that is, the professing bodies, the world—professedly such—inordinately wicked," he wrote a colleague in 1863.[3] What defined Americans was not their "religious aspect," as Tocqueville identified, but their preference for restless action that masqueraded as spirituality. Darby's impressions of American Christians were slight: "The Presbyterians, the Methodists, the Baptists, are minded to oppose" his teachings, he wrote

---

1. Alexis de Tocqueville, *Democracy in America*, trans. Harvey C. Mansfield and Delba Winthrop (Chicago: University of Chicago Press, 2002), 282.

2. Tocqueville, *Democracy in America*, 278.

3. Darby to Mr. Pollack, May 1863, in *Letters of J. N. Darby: Supplement from the French*, vol. 1 (Chessington, UK: Bible and Gospel Trust, 2014), 211.

from Boston. "But I let all these movements pass."[4] Of the fledgling city of Chicago, he speculated that "any true spiritual mindedness and devotedness (not mere outward activity) would be more despised there than anywhere."[5] Even though his ministry would focus increasingly on the United States, Darby's diagnosis barely improved with time.

In truth, Darby—like Tocqueville—did not visit "America" but particular regions and communities that formed deep impressions and the grist for generalizations. Darby's impressions helped to shape the Brethren strategy for gaining an audience in the United States; although the country largely failed to produce new Brethren, Brethren teachings did manage to gain traction in popular religious culture.

Darby's mission field was the Great Lakes basin, extending as far south and west as St. Louis and as far east as Boston. His work in Canada hugged close to the bodies of fresh water, along the St. Lawrence River to Montreal and Quebec. The American Midwest and New England were tied together through the Erie Canal, opened in 1825, and a rapid increase in railroad infrastructure bound the two regions more tightly in the 1850s. Darby never set foot south of Missouri, and he spent the majority of his three years on US soil in the areas of four American cities: Chicago, St. Louis, New York City, and Boston. While the American reception of Darby was haphazard, many of the first American champions of his ideas were Midwestern and East Coast urban evangelicals.

Darby's journeys could not be separated from his leadership of the Brethren faction increasingly known as Exclusive. A community entirely invested in the theological principles laid out by Darby, Exclusive Brethren tended to be skeptical of revival, outdoor evangelism, or mass preaching, preferring to grow their ranks instead through diligent discipleship. Darby himself viewed American revivalism as "shallow work"—always mixed with too much worldliness and too little rigor.[6] In his visits to American cities, he preferred to host Bible studies, show his methods and work through his teachings with individual clergy, distribute tracts, and stay at homes for weeks or months at a time. He would preach in pulpits, where his command of the Bible impressed Americans, but his most effective tools were directed on a smaller scale.

The same was true of the Brethren writ large in their work to North America. While they struggled to make true disciples, their ideas—and many of Darby's

4. Darby to Mr. Brockhaus, June 1877, in *Letters of J. N. Darby: Supplement from the French*, vol. 2 (Chessington, UK: Bible and Gospel Trust, 2014), 262.
5. Darby to Mr. Brockhaus, June 1877, in *Letters of J. N. Darby*, 2:262.
6. Darby to C. McAdam, February 1875, in *Letters of J. N. Darby*, 2:210.

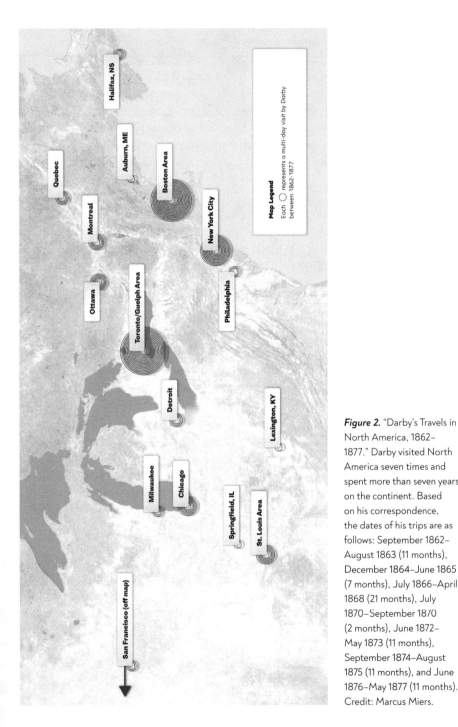

Map Legend

Each ○ represents a multi-day visit by Darby between 1862-1877

Figure 2. "Darby's Travels in North America, 1862–1877." Darby visited North America seven times and spent more than seven years on the continent. Based on his correspondence, the dates of his trips are as follows: September 1862–August 1863 (11 months), December 1864–June 1865 (7 months), July 1866–April 1868 (21 months), July 1870–September 1870 (2 months), June 1872–May 1873 (11 months), September 1874–August 1875 (11 months), and June 1876–May 1877 (11 months). Credit: Marcus Miers.

teachings in particular—gained a foothold in parts of the Great Lakes basin. Americans adopted Brethren ideas on their own terms and in their own ways, while Darby's original Irish and British context faded with the transmission of Brethren ideas in North America. The legacy of the founding generation of Brethren to the story of dispensationalism was less in transmitting their ideas wholesale than in loosening the ground for radical new religious ideas that would be picked up by Americans to form their own Christian subculture.

John Nelson Darby in America

As he spent time in North America, Darby developed an interpretation of its religious landscape that reflected his theological commitments. He wrote with concern about fledgling Brethren communities, that they "should be devoted, not conformed to this world," and should fix upon "our citizenship in heaven, and leading us to wait for the blessed Lord."[7] The American church, in contrast, was defined by an admixture of the worldly and the spiritual, by a quest for "activity" that was gilded, hollow, rotten in its work on the souls of a biblically aloof people. The Civil War and its effects merited only a few reflections in the hundreds of letters Darby wrote while in North America, and then only as a surface indicator of deeper problems. "The condition of the States spiritually—indeed, everyway except money making—is frightful," he wrote in 1866. Daily threats of assassination in American cities were so numerous, he speculated, that newspapers did not even report them. "But that they have had enough of it, there would probably be a war again, they speak of it openly," he mused. The whole country reinforced his claim to heavenly citizenship: "Thank God, I pass through as a stranger and a pilgrim . . . the Christian is not of the world at all."[8]

What religiosity did exist in America was "an impulsion to revival work everywhere" led by lesser Christians. Darby did not dismiss entirely the boom of revivalism in the 1870s—"I doubt not God's hand in it"—but at best the mass gatherings did preparatory spiritual work. "Conversions apart," he wrote of the revivals of Dwight L. Moody, "it strengthens the evil in the church, and the evil that is so sad now."[9] Darby was optimistic of influencing Moody, who was based in Chicago, and eventually met with him on multiple occasions. In his extended stays, Darby's objective was precisely to find leading clergy or other influential religious leaders to convert to his views, to "call them out" of

---

7. Darby to Pollack, September 1876, in *Letters of J. N. Darby*, 2:244.
8. Darby to A. B. Pollack, October 1866, in *Letters of J. N. Darby*, 1:274.
9. Darby to McAdam, February 1875, in *Letters of J. N. Darby*, 2:210.

their denominations and the comfort of Christendom, and to spark a growing exodus, led by leaders, into a purer form of Christian brotherhood.

Darby's hopes with Moody died slowly over the 1860s, while Brethren had to navigate an already crowded religious marketplace. The embarrassment of the Great Disappointment lingered over the land, and Darby made a point to differentiate himself from Millerite teachings when he could. The followers of Miller formed the Seventh-day Adventist Church in 1863 in Battle Creek, Michigan, in the very region Darby crisscrossed. The new church set the date of the second coming now in 1868 and taught Sabbatarianism and the mortality of the soul, or annihilationism. Growing through revivals, Adventism appeared as a clear threat to Darby's influence. He was particularly vexed by the Adventists' success among potential Brethren converts. The Adventists "picked up a large number of souls weary with the state of things, and pious," he lamented in 1865, though they drifted into heresy and now comprised only "godly scattered souls."[10]

Darby passed no less critical judgments on established Protestant leaders. Wesleyan perfectionism was his most consistent target. The revivals of Charles Finney and the growth of Methodism enflamed American passions for the teaching of John Wesley that through discipline and the power of the Holy Spirit individuals could attain a state of perfect sanctification. The fully sanctified person would become "so far perfect as not to commit sin," Wesley taught, and while such perfection was granted "by mere faith, and as hindered only by unbelief," Darby saw this teaching as cheapening basic Christian virtues.[11] "The perfectionists say I want people to be more perfect than they do," Darby wrote from Boston. "I said, Certainly I do. Their system denies (not willfully) the true Christian position, and thus lowers holy exercise." In particular, Darby detested the Wesleyan emphasis on personal experience as the marker of spiritual attainment. Wesleyan ministers of Boston exhibited "a good deal of pretension"; perfectionism trafficked in "wild exaggerations, and pretensions which its leaders disown, but which are the fruit of their principles."[12] Revivalism, on the model of Finney and now of Moody, blended with Wesleyanism, swamping American Christianity with a mix of cheap grace and impossible expectations disconnected from Darby's concern for right belief.

On his first trip in 1863, Darby shared the Tocquevillian insight that "it is a religious population, men would say: people join churches for respectability," but

---

10. Darby to G. V. Wigram, June 1865, in *Letters of J. N. Darby*, 1:247.

11. John Wesley, *A Plain Account of Christian Perfection: As Believed and Taught by the Rev. John Wesley, from the Year 1725 to the Year 1777* (New York: Lane & Scott, 1850), 22, 39.

12. Darby to McAdam, February 1875, in *Letters of J. N. Darby*, 2:204; Darby to E. R. Ulrich, February 1875, in *Letters of J. N. Darby*, 2:208.

he concluded that in America "Christian life is feebleness itself."[13] He did express hope for a brighter day, though not as frequently as he bemoaned the current situation. In St. Louis, on his fourth trip to North America, in 1872, he wrote of "a good many opportunities here, and the door open as it had not been."[14] The progress was especially clear among those in "the west," where, "several ministers among them, teach the Lord's coming, the presence of the Holy Ghost, that all sects are wrong." Even so, on Darby's call for separation from denominations, "as yet few move from their place."[15] The yield of the spiritual harvest was small. "I have met at the least a dozen ministers, one or two several times, but, with rare exceptions, they are the farthest from spiritual wants and spiritual intelligence of any."[16]

The truth is that Darby managed to convince few North Americans of the need to separate from their churches. He found more success in spreading awareness of "the Lord's coming," and especially of his distinctive teaching of the imminent rapture. But such a partial reception of his ideas was only a little better than rejection. His vision for a heavenly church was received incompletely and selectively; the Americans he met adapted his teachings—often a single insight—for their own ends, in ways he would never have approved of.

Darby's halting progress in North America was buoyed, however, with the flood of Brethren tracts into the United States. The Brethren were masters at publishing and distributing their own literature. On Darby's first visit to North America, he described "four tract depots in London" that printed Brethren materials, with single orders of up to two million tracts and selling "perhaps 800,000 a month." Writing from Toronto in 1863, Darby approvingly observed that this flood of paper was not confined to the United Kingdom, but that "the publications of the brethren, gospel tracts and those for edification, have been disseminated everywhere." He noted that "the works of Mackintosh are being disseminated also everywhere, even in the United States."[17] A decade later, he reported from the United States that the same commentaries were "supplying sermons for the ministers teachings for the Sunday schools."[18]

For the most part, the Exclusive Brethren employed their own stable of publishers clustered on Paternoster Row in London, the epicenter of British publishing, who brought to market the works of Darby, Kelly, and Mackintosh. George Morrish and George Wigram oversaw much of the printing in the 1850s, William H. Broom in the 1860s, and William B. Horner in the 1870s. In

13. Darby to G. F. Patterson, May 1863, in *Letters of J. N. Darby*, 1:212.
14. Darby to F. Rowan, n.d., in *Letters of J. N. Darby*, 2:108.
15. Darby to B. Slim, September 1872, in *Letters of J. N. Darby*, 2:110.
16. Darby to R. T. Grant, 1875, in *Letters of J. N. Darby*, 2:209.
17. Darby to Mr. Foulquier, February 1863, in *Letters of J. N. Darby*, 2:74.
18. Darby to Mr. Chièze, April 1873, in *Letters of J. N. Darby*, 2:289.

1876, Paul and Timothy Loizeaux, brothers who immigrated from France to Iowa, started their own publishing firm in New York and became a primary distributor of Brethren literature in the United States for the rest of the century, alongside smaller publishers in Boston and Philadelphia.

Brethren often relied on American boosters to circulate their teachings. James Inglis, a Scottish immigrant to Michigan, was the most important American popularizer of Brethren teachings in the 1850s and 1860s. A religious experimenter and Baptist minister, Inglis most likely encountered Brethren teachings during a stint in Canada and began to articulate his own views in public, though he did so anonymously, in a series of articles for the *Toronto Christian Observer* in 1853.[19] Inglis mixed old and new premillennial motifs, but on one issue in particular he aligned decisively with Darby: he rejected date setting. "How near or remote the coming of the Lord may be, is not for us to say," he cautioned. The year-day theory, which remained the predominant old premillennial assumption, "is fallacious and cannot be sustained . . . the general adoption of this notion has been injurious to the study of prophecy, and has derailed many from entering upon it."[20] Inglis's allergy to date setting and adoption of new premillennialism helped to redraw the premillennial community in North America to be favorable to Darby's teachings.

Inglis soon began his own journal, *Waymarks in the Wilderness*, which borrowed eclectically from across the premillennial spectrum. *Waymarks* facilitated a consistent flow of Brethren ideas into North America until Inglis's death in 1873 and introduced to Americans a comprehensive understanding of dispensational time.[21] Over the course of a year and a half, *Waymarks* ran a large portion of Brethren writer Henry Soltau's "Thoughts on the Tabernacle," an extensive study of the Israelite structure from a Brethren typological perspective.[22] While interspersing other writers, *Waymarks* tilted heavily toward the Exclusive Brethren. The J. Inglis and Company press promoted Exclusive Brethren writers along with Inglis's own tracts.

---

19. These appeared under the series title "The Prophetic Oracles" from April to December 1853.

20. "Parting Words on the Study of Prophecy," *Toronto Christian Observer*, December 1853, 183.

21. W. C. Baynes, "The Dispensations, Prophetically and Doctrinally Considered," *Waymarks in the Wilderness* 1 (1864): 440–63. Baynes's series was published through vol. 2, no. 5 (March 1865).

22. Henry William Soltau, "Thoughts on the Tabernacle," *Waymarks in the Wilderness* 3, no. 1 (May 1865): 17–41. Soltau's series was published through vol. 4, no. 1 (January 1866). For Inglis's introduction to Soltau's work, see James Inglis, "The Veil of the Tabernacle," *Waymarks in the Wilderness* 2, no. 6 (April 1865): 440–48.

In all this activity in North America, it is of immense importance that Darby, as the leader of the Exclusive Brethren, felt drawn to its shores. Darby continued to travel widely across the British Isles and western Europe, but his more than seven years in North America between the years of 1862 and 1877 revealed the potential he saw across the Atlantic. In his effort to secure distant converts, and in his conviction that the Spirit was moving among Americans, he fixed the attention of his colleagues on the land across the sea and led by example.

Interpretive Innovations

The very nature of Darby's journeys as faith missions meant that he did not work alone but depended on networks of Brethren and sympathetic ministers around the Great Lakes basin. He wrote appreciatively of "brother E." (elsewhere "R. E.," probably lifelong friend Ralph Evans), an evangelist working in North America prior to 1862, who also traveled with Darby on his first journey.[23] Darby may have been the font of a new theology, but his teachings were transmitted through popularizers who did not fully represent its complexity or feel the same aversion to mass evangelism.

Darby needed all the help he could get. In addition to an antipathy for large crowds and impatience with outsiders, Darby's millions of written words were a jumbled heap, delivered *ex animo*—from the soul. "He wrote rapidly, as thoughts arose in his spirit, and often with scarcely a word changed," recalled William Kelly, the longtime editor of Darby's papers and one of his best popularizers. This did not make for easy reading. "He delighted in a concatenated sentence, sometimes with parenthesis within parenthesis, to express the truth fully, and with guards against misconception," Kelly explained—a charitable characterization of a communication style that could hardly present more barriers to perspicuity. The truth was probably closer to Kelly's next description: because of Darby's tireless schedule, he "had not time to express his mind as briefly and clearly as he could wish." The most famous remark Darby made of his own writing was a playful quip to Kelly: "You write to be read and understood. I only think on paper." For the legacy of his work, the more fitting remark was that he "was but a miner." Kelly extended the metaphor: "He left it to others to melt the ore, and circulate the coin."[24]

23. Darby to G. Owen, December 1862, in *Letters of J. N. Darby*, 1:199; Darby to Mr. Chièze, March 1863, in *Letters of J. N. Darby*, 2:76.

24. William Kelly, *John Nelson Darby as I Knew Him* (Belfast: Words of Truth, 1986), https://www.stempublishing.com/authors/kelly/7subjcts/jnd_knew.html. This remembrance was likely written in the 1880s.

The "coin" of Brethren teachings already held a different value in the United States, where Americans prized the advances of modern science and pragmatic truths gleaned through experience over Darby's dualistic teachings and dense prose. Most Americans wanted to use the methods of observation, empiricism, and falsification to establish the authority and thematic unity of the Bible, much as the Newtonian laws of nature established the authority and unity of the created order.

American reception of Darby and his methods hinged on the practice of the "Bible Reading method" (which is how Americans referred to it). Its philosophical underpinnings lay in the commonsense tradition, imported from the Scottish Enlightenment, that posited a common or "plain" correspondence between words and their meaning that was accessible to all. Common sense provided the basis for optimism that the method would produce shared knowledge. Outside influences that dulled common or "plain" understandings of English terms were to be kept to a minimum. "Such a method is self-interpreting," one popular Bible-reading manual explained, "light is seen in light."[25] The method assumed that the most authoritative guide for the interpretation of the Bible was other Bible passages; as an infallible revelation, the Bible's only proper interpretive referent was itself. If interpretation was induction through the gathering of diffuse texts, then the process could not only be performed by every Christian but could be replicated to produce the same insights over and over, like a scientific experiment.

Though Americans based their reception of Darby's teachings on this Bible Reading method, Darby himself did not use it. He based his thinking not on a method of inductive reasoning but on a presuppositional dualism between heaven and earth from which he deduced biblical knowledge about the church, Israel, salvation, and the future. On the surface, both methods arrived at similar conclusions about many evangelical doctrines, but the distinctive Brethren and American foundations introduced a tension that helped set American receivers of Darby's teachings on a different trajectory than the Brethren.

While the Bible Reading method rejected the new methods of higher criticism, which investigated the origins of biblical texts, it had other strengths. Bible Reading not only made intuitive sense to many Christians steeped in commonsense republican ideals, but also supplied imaginative insights that higher criticism failed to match. If the realizations of higher criticism cast doubt on the unity of Scripture—with competing manuscripts, authors, and redactors—then it was Bible Reading that maintained a coherent unity and synthesis with

25. S. R. Briggs and John H. Elliott, *Notes and Suggestions for Bible Readings*, 2nd ed. (Chicago: Revell, 1879), 20.

accessibility to nonspecialists. A person using the method most often took a keyword in the English Bible and marked as many occurrences of the term as could be found throughout the text. This inductive Bible Reading created chains of verses assuming a biblical unity that was conveyed from expositors to audiences, from preachers to their congregations.

Two new interpretive tools democratized the Bible Reading method in the same years that Darby and the flood of Brethren tracts poured into North America. The first was Bagster's Polyglot Bible, originally issued in 1816. The English version of the eight-language polyglot Bible included sixty thousand parallel references (or cross-references) derived from the larger polyglot project, promising on the title page "a Copious and Original Selection of References to Parallel and Illustrative Passages; Exhibited in a Manner Hitherto Unattempted."[26] These references revealed connections and patterns across the text, allowing readers to chain together similar themes, words, events, or people. Situated in the margins of each page, these cross-references were tantamount to nineteenth-century text hyperlinks that created cross-reference chains to reveal fresh meanings of Scripture.

With Bagster's in one hand, proponents of Bible Reading held a second textual innovation in the other: Cruden's Biblical Concordance. Alexander Cruden, an eighteenth-century Scottish Presbyterian philologist, catalogued every word in the Bible in an alphabetized index and later added snippets of commentary, definitions of words, and cross-referencing to create a fully realized biblical concordance. No less than Bagster's references, Cruden's editions became widely used tools to catalogue, count, and connect key words across the Bible's sixty-six books.

Bagster's Bible and Cruden's concordance supplied Americans in the 1870s with an interpretive infrastructure to develop their own insights, especially in premillennial circles. Early American premillennialists endorsed both works as necessary tools, while the first American-made concordance by James Strong appeared in 1890. *Strong's Concordance* and the most popular British version, *Young's Analytical Concordance of the Bible* (first published in 1879), and *Thompson's Chain-Reference Bible* (first published in 1908) became mainstays for premillennial teachers. These tools were powerful aids to achieve a God's-eye view of Scripture, and to distill Darby's complex theological insights into something more easily consumable by Americans.

The Bible Reading method informed the emergent tradition of interpretation based on induction and literal meanings of words. Terms like "heaven,"

26. *The English Version of the Polyglot Bible* (London: Bagster & Sons, 1816), title page.

The Watchword.   11

truths not as yet tested by experience: such as resurrection and heaven, with all that is therein implied, but which are so confirmed *to* me and *in* me by faith, that it is all one as if God had revealed those things to me directly by his Spirit, and not mediately through His Word. Of these we can say, our eye hath not seen, our ear hath not heard, neither hath it entered into our heart, the things that God hath prepared for us, but He hath revealed them to us by his Word and Spirit (1 Cor. ii. 9, 10). These things comprise my Bible *within* the Bible; and daily this inner Bible is growing. This Bible I have marked out on the printed page of my study Bible. Let me say, that I think it well, also, to keep a Bible *free* from marks of any kind, to read in; that you may not be limited, or have the Word limited, by old thoughts. Our marking, important and helpful as I think Bible-marking is, should not be allowed to "bind the Word of God." You must adopt your own system of marking. Do not take somebody's else method. And yet, you may find many suggestions that will be helpful to you from the experience and work of others. For example: I have taken a camel's-hair brush, and dipping it into blue ink, I have passed it lightly over all those passages in the Word of God that speak of His love to man; such, for example, as John iii. 16: "God so loved the world," etc.; and with *red ink* and the brush, I have covered those passages that speak of the blood of Jesus Christ, in the New Testament: for example, 1 Pet. i. 19; 1 John i. 7, and the blood of atonement in the Old. It is surprising how *blue* and *red* your Bible will be, thus marked. And then, suppose you were to take some purple ink, and cover all those passages that are closely related to and are based on love and atonement; you would still further have your Bible interpreted to your eye at a glance. And then, for contrast, take your pen and run a deep line of *black* around those passages that expose and lay bare the depravity and sinfulness of the human heart, and the fact of the righteous judgment of God to come; and the perdition of ungodly men; such, for example, as Gen. vi. 5; Isa. i. 5; Matt. xv. 19; Rom. ii. 6–9. But I forbear any further suggestion in this line, being assured that a hint to the wise is sufficient.

ILLUSTRATION OF BIBLE MARKING.

1 Peter i.
Num. 3.46: 18.16

18 Forasmuch as ye know 'that ye were not redeemed with corruptible things, as silver and gold, from your vain conversation *received* by tradition from your fathers; *Jam. 1.2.3*
19 But 'with the precious blood of Christ 'as of a lamb without blemish and without spot:
20 'Who verily was fore-ordained before the foundation of the world, but was manifest 'in these last times for you,
21 Who by Him do believe in God, 'that raised him up from the dead, and 'gave Him glory; that your faith and hope might be in God. *John 15.3.*   John 7:7
22 Seeing ye 'have purified your souls in obeying the truth through the Spirit unto unfeigned 'love of the brethren, *see that ye* love one another with a pure heart fervently:
23 'Being born again, not of corruptible seed, but of incorruptible, 'by the word of God, which liveth and abideth for ever. *Gen. 6.12. II Pet. 1.4.*
24 || For 'all flesh is as grass, and all the glory of man as the flower of grass. The grass withereth, and the flower thereof falleth away:
25 'But the word of the Lord endureth for ever. 'And this is the word which by the Gospel is preached unto you. *Jam. 1.18*

(margin: Redemption · Regeneration)

MEEKNESS.
"Seek Righteousness, seek Meekness."—Zeph. ii. 3.

SEVEN NEW TESTAMENT PRECEPTS.	SEVEN OLD TESTAMENT PROMISES.
I. "*Put on* Meekness." Col. iii. 12.	I. "The Meek *shall increase* their joy in the Lord." Isa. xxix. 19.
II. "*Follow* after Meekness." 1 Tim. vi. 11.	II. "The Meek *shall inherit* the earth." Ps. xxxvii. 11.
III. "Be . . . gentle, *showing* all Meekness unto all men." Titus iii. 2.	III. "The Lord *lifteth up* the Meek." Ps. cxlvii. 6.
IV. "*Walk* . . . with all lowliness and Meekness." Eph. iv. 2.	IV. "The Meek shall He *teach His way.*" Ps. xxv. 9.
V. "*Receive* with Meekness the engrafted Word." James i. 21.	V. "The Meek shall *eat* and be *satisfied.*" Ps. xxii. 26.
VI. *Be adorned with* "the ornament of a Meek and quiet spirit." 1 Peter iii. 4	VI. "He shall *beautify* the Meek with salvation." Ps. clxix 4.

Figure 3. The *Watchword* on Bible marking. Edited by A. J. Gordon in Boston, the premillennial *Watchword* advocated for the plain reading of Scripture and the new method of Bible reading. This page from 1879 provides an example of "Bible marking," indicating how the Christian reader could develop a personal concordance and bring thematic organization to the text.

"earth," and "Israel" referred to the same thing, no matter where they were found in the Bible—as indicated by cross-referencing and concordances. Prophecy passages were no exception to this rule. The thousand years of Revelation 20 meant one thousand trips around the sun for the earth, while the coming of the Lord meant, in the common premillennialist language of the

1870s, "a real and bodily coming of Christ." The antichrist, too, "is a literal person, and not an ecclesiastical system, nor a succession of rulers."[27] This literalism, also described as a "plain" reading of Scripture, was not so facile as to negate any allegorical or symbolic meanings (when John the Baptist introduces Jesus as "the Lamb of God," this was not an invitation to reclassify the species of the Christ). But literalism did insist that such a passage directly corresponded to a historical event and represented it accurately.

The Bible Reading method provided an American substitute for Darby's more esoteric dualism. American premillennialist James Brookes assured readers in 1874 that "the language in which prophecy is written is as simple and as easy to understand as any other part of Scripture." This was a far cry from Darby's view. What made "every scripture fall into place" for Darby was not reading the Bible literally, but "a spiritual understanding by the Holy Ghost of things in heaven and our connection with them, and things in earth and our separateness from them."[28] Writing on the prophecies of Isaiah, Darby explained: "Although the subject of prophecy is not a figure, yet figures are not only largely used, but they are often intermingled with literal expressions; so that in explaining the prophetic books one cannot make an exact rule to distinguish between figure and letter."[29] This complicated parsing of plain and symbolic reading confronted Americans with, by their standards of common-sense realism, an unwieldy approach to reading the Bible.

Types and Antitypes

While later dispensationalists would follow a "consistent literal hermeneutic" to interpret the Bible, Americans in the 1870s who were drawn to Brethren teachings attempted to merge literal and typological methods. Types appealed to someone like Darby because they gave virtually every passage in the Old Testament a figural power and literal fulfillment in the New Testament or in the prophetic future. These types were no mere symbols, but the design elements that shaped God's dealings with humanity in every dispensation. They fit into a wider set of narrative elements, including "resemblances and differences, types and antitypes, shadows and body, times and seasons, peoples and

27. James H. Brookes, *Present Truth: Being the Testimony of the Holy Ghost on the Second Coming of the Lord . . . in the Study of the Word* (St. Louis: Wilson, 1877), 35, 38, 83.

28. James Hall Brookes, *Maranatha; or, The Lord Cometh*, 5th ed. (St. Louis: Edward Bredell, 1878), 35; Darby, quoted in Ronald M. Henzel, *Darby, Dualism, and the Decline of Dispensationalism* (Tucson, AZ: Fenestra Books, 2003), 79–80.

29. John Nelson Darby, *Synopsis of the Books of the Bible: Isaiah* (London: G. Morrish, 1877), https://www.stempublishing.com/authors/darby/synopsis/isaiah/isaiah.html.

dispensations, the eternal purpose, the varied preparation, and the final fulfillment."[30] In Darby's words, these types were "the counsels of God," the Lord's "eternal thoughts." They comprised ways for Christians to glimpse the deep structure of sacred history and how it manifested in the observable world.[31]

The need for types pointed to one of the shortfalls of a purely inductive method of Bible reading. Pursued in a vacuum, the inductive method produced competing meanings of the same text. Even under the optimistic rubric of commonsense realism, faithful Christians disagreed on what the plain meaning was. In order to function beyond the individual reader, the Bible Reading method had to be more than simply gathering chains of prooftexts. Though not the only check on inductive Bible Reading, types provided a framework for conducting Bible Reading methods and testing the results. By overlaying typological analysis with plain readings of the text, Americans created a new interpretive tradition that was neither wholly Brethren-influenced nor a homegrown American method. It was, rather, a new hermeneutic altogether.

Typological readings of the Bible were not unique to the Brethren, of course. Allegories, symbolism, and representational readings of Scripture are as old as Christianity. In the fourth century, Augustine famously distinguished the literal and figurative parts of Scripture on the basis of love and doctrine: "Whatever there is in the word of God that cannot, when taken literally, be referred either to purity of life or soundness of doctrine, you may set down as figurative."[32] Though further refined by later Christian thinkers, Augustine's dichotomy persisted into the nineteenth century.

God's salvation of the world through Jesus Christ was the lodestar that governed all Brethren and American typological thinking, structuring the Bible and revealing God's innermost plans. As Brethren writer C. H. Mackintosh explained in his commentary of Leviticus: "It is one and the same Spirit which records the ingredients of the type, and gives us the facts in the Antitype."[33] This insight displayed the divine and unified authorship of the whole Bible. In the two-layered interpretive community of plain and typological logic adopted by American readers of the Brethren, the unity of Scripture undergirded dispensational time. The "counsels of God," from the first pages of Genesis, were

30. Briggs and Elliott, *Notes and Suggestions*, 20.

31. John Nelson Darby, *On the Government of God and His Counsels in Grace* (London: R. L. Allan, 1870), https://www.stempublishing.com/authors/darby/MISCELLA/32010E .html; John Nelson Darby, "Mark's Gospel," (n.d.), accessed May 11, 2022, https://www .stempublishing.com/authors/darby/EXPOSIT/24029_32E.html#a10, 281–82.

32. Augustine, *On Christian Doctrine* (Edinburgh: T&T Clark, 1877), 90.

33. C. H. Mackintosh, *Notes on the Book of Leviticus* (New York: Loizeaux Brothers, 1880), 38.

pointing to the church as the heavenly people of God. Only the tools and guidance of the Holy Spirit were required to discover this truth.

As an example of the wide-ranging influence of this interpretive tradition, types also structured arguments around social relations, including gender roles and the family. Female types in the Bible were hardly uniform, nor did they predictably translate into particular social attitudes. In the prophetic sections of the Bible, women were portrayed most frequently as victims or recipients of God's blessings. Jesus prophesied: "Two women shall be grinding at the mill; the one shall be taken, and the other left" (Matt. 24:41 KJV). He further lamented: "But woe unto them that are with child, and to them that give suck, in those days!" (Luke 21:23 KJV). Gendered symbolism was common in apocalyptic texts like the Revelation of John—"Whore of Babylon," "Woman of the Apocalypse"— though in Brethren exegesis these signified evil men (the antichrist) or whole nations (Israel). The church as the "bride of Christ" was another feminine type largely fulfilled by men. Yet this typology drew from the brides of Scripture and romantic (even erotic) passages such as Song of Solomon, and infused Brethren theology with crucial metaphors for the mystery of the church. "When we view her [the Church] as the body, the Bride, the companion, the counterpart, of His only-begotten Son," Mackintosh explained in an exegesis of Genesis 24, "we feel that there was, through grace, wondrous reason for her being so thought of before the foundation of the world. . . . In the counsels of God she [the church] is necessary to Christ; and in the accomplished work of Christ, divine provision has been made for her being called into existence."[34]

This Brethren typology made its way across the Atlantic. Brethren writer William Kelly's commentaries on Daniel and Revelation began to appear in the early 1870s, while Mackintosh's four-volumes of "notes" on the Torah were published by the newly formed Loizeaux Brothers Press, based in New York City, in 1880. The prevalence of types was intended to check Bible Reading practices. For Brethren, types constituted a fundamental aspect of biblical interpretation that revealed the dualism between heaven and earth on every page. For Americans, the role of types worked in concert with the ideal of a plain interpretation of Scripture.

"A Difficult Field"

In truth, the gap between Tocqueville's positive views and Darby's negative impressions of American religiosity was not as wide as it first appeared. Writing

34. C. H. Mackintosh, *Notes on the Book of Genesis*, 4th ed., vol. 1 (London: Morrish, 1861), 229.

from New York to France in 1831, Tocqueville confided that what "the immense majority [of America] has faith in" was not Christian doctrine but "human wisdom and good sense, faith in the doctrine of human perfectibility." He concluded that much of American religiosity was superficial: "Either I am badly mistaken or there is a great store of doubt and indifference hidden underneath these external forms. . . . Faith is evidently inert; enter the churches (I mean the Protestant ones) and you hear them speak of morality; of dogma not a word, nothing that could in any way shock a neighbor, nothing that could reveal a hint of dissidence."[35] Darby could readily agree with these observations, writing decades later, on his last visit to North America in 1876, "the Colonies, and much of the States, are a difficult field, in this, that people come out to get on—own land—in a word, the world."[36] The common European refrain about American culture, that it was beholden to Mammon, bridged the personal impressions of the 1830s French Catholic and the 1870s English dissenter.

To an extent far less acknowledged than with Tocqueville, Darby, too, imparted to Americans a set of tools for self-understanding. Not Darby alone, but an entire wave of Exclusive Brethren whose writings and concepts rolled into North America through the 1870s. Like Tocqueville, the Brethren interpreted the New World in relation to developments and interests in Europe. Yet by the time of Tocqueville's journey in 1831, and certainly by Darby's first visit to the United States in 1863, both had come to see Americans as central protagonists in the drama of the church.

The American reception of Darby's radical message—of separation, rupture, and rapture—would be used in ways that disregarded its British creators' context or intentions. Darby had journeyed through a nation wracked by division, and it was those divisions that ultimately shaped his legacy in America.

35. Alexis de Tocqueville, *Selected Letters on Politics and Society*, trans. James Toupin and Roger Boesche (Berkeley: University of California Press, 1985), 46–48.
36. Darby to Mr. Pollock, September 1876, in *Letters of J. N. Darby*, 2:244.

It may be at morn, when the day is awaking,
When sunlight thro' darkness and shadow is breaking,
That Jesus will come in the fullness of glory,
To receive from the world "His own."

It may be at mid-day, it may be at twilight,
It may be perchance, that the blackness of midnight
Will burst into light in the blaze of His glory,
When Jesus receives "His own."

Oh, joy! oh, delight! should we go without dying,
No sickness, no sadness, no dread and no crying,
Caught up thro' the clouds with our Lord into glory,
When Jesus receives "His own."

H. L. Turner, "Christ Returneth" (1878)

Little is known of H. L. Turner. The music was composed by James McGranahan, a colleague of both Ira Sankey and Philip P. Bliss, some of the most prolific revivalist musicians of the 1870s (and new premillennialists). All three were based in Chicago, giving a possible location for Turner. By the year 1900, this song had appeared in more than a dozen hymnals and would go on to appear in ninety more.

3

Border-State Conversions

From Darby's journeys to Stanley's prophecy charts, Brethren ideas flowed into the Great Lakes basin. They were carried by paper and by song, transmitted in Bible studies and personal encounters. The radical nature of these teachings, and the various methods through which they were disseminated, increased the diversity of their reception and adaptations by Americans. The Brethren produced very few direct disciples, but they shaped a wider swath of American Christianity.

The logic of who selectively adopted Brethren teachings and when was complex, but one overriding factor was that both Brethren evangelization and American adoption were taking place in the years surrounding the American Civil War. The experience of white evangelicals in the border states, in particular, proved to be fertile ground for Brethren reception. The trauma of war made some Americans in the border states allergic to overtly nationalist conceptions of the church. This aversion was carried into the era of Reconstruction, when border-state Christians became some of the loudest proponents of sectional reconciliation between Northern and Southern whites.

By 1870, the outlines of a new radical subculture emerged that combined the priority of sectional reconciliation with key Brethren teachings about the heavenly nature of the church and the premillennial arrival of the kingdom of God. These radicals created a new interpretive community—first in the border states and then beyond—with its own ways of talking about the Bible, salvation, the church, prophecies, and the future. They ditched the old premillennial methods of date setting, making a break with the long-standing premillennial tradition in America. They also rejected key aspects of Brethren teachings, including anticlericalism (most of the early new premillennialists were professional pastors), ecclesiastical separatism (most remained in their denominations), and the Brethren resistance to the holiness movement (most embraced these teachings). Alternately, they offered a new hermeneutic for reading the Bible's prophetic passages that centered on a dualism between Israel and the church, producing an intricate scenario of the coming plans of world redemption and a narrower, heavenly mandate for the contemporary church. The new premillennial teachings privileged civil peace over racial justice, since the former facilitated the ability for global missions that drew from the full resources of American Protestant churches. White Christian unity, in other words, would more ably repair the damage wrought by the Civil War and empower the project of global missions.

Two pastors with backgrounds in the border states—James Hall Brookes in Missouri and Joseph A. Seiss from Maryland—spearheaded new premillennial thinking that soon spread throughout religious networks in the North. Brookes, a Presbyterian pastor in St. Louis, was attracted to Brethren teachings by way of concern for his local church and denomination. Seiss, a Lutheran from Maryland who pastored the largest Lutheran congregation in the country in Philadelphia, was more fixated on the moral and prophetic significance of the Civil War. They adopted Brethren teachings for different theological motivations—Brookes through a concern for the church and Seiss through a concern for the future. Both also became prolific boosters of post–Civil War sectional reconciliation between white Americans. Darby's teachings were unexpectedly suited for a time of civil war.

James H. Brookes and the Church

The St. Louis–based Presbyterian minister James Hall Brookes towered over the formation of new premillennialism for more than thirty years, beginning in the 1860s. In that span he empowered virtually every significant contributor to new premillennialism and mentored the next generation of institution builders. Yet he did not become attracted to Brethren teachings until he was a seasoned pastor, and even then his interest in new premillennialism was not focused on the end times as such but on the way the new teaching recontextualized the church as a heavenly community. To a pastor who was seemingly forced into taking positions on such earthly concerns as slavery and secession, the church as a heaven-bound body was especially attractive.

As a convert to premillennialism in the 1860s, Brookes typified a wider shift in American attitudes that helped to break up the widely shared expectation that America would usher in God's kingdom. For all the violent disagreements between Northerners and Southerners over slavery, Americans tended to agree on this postmillennial perspective, on a type of lockstep progressive march of the church and nation that idealized their unity and continuity. For centuries such confidence was supported by a shared postmillennial reading of the Bible. There were dissenters, of course, and differences of opinion within this postmillennial consensus, but most Americans assented in spirit, if not in mind, to the words of Jonathan Edwards, who was sure in 1742 that "the latter-day glory is likely to begin in America."[1]

The days of postmillennial consensus ended in the 1860s. The Civil War's violence and destruction helped shatter the image of the United States as the vanguard of the coming kingdom, but this was just the initial shock. Higher criticism of the Bible and Darwinian evolution, two academic discourses that permeated seminaries and universities after the war, began to unravel the biblical case for postmillennialism. While the nascent Social Gospel movement that applied Christian ethics to social problems saw the kingdom of God as righting the wrongs of industrialization, premillennialists regarded correcting modern social ills as too difficult an endeavor and, in any case, a secondary task to evangelization. Ultimately, many evangelicals who experienced the war and its aftermath simply did not see a reason to sustain the postmillennial vision.

No region of the United States felt the crosscurrents of sectional strife as powerfully as the border states that included Missouri. As the country divided over slavery, border communities understood themselves to occupy a neutral political position that combined Southern cultural sympathies (and legal chattel slavery) with a desire to avoid secession. For those Americans shaped by this border-state culture, a stark separation between church and state became the cherished ideal to maintain neutrality. On the western edge of this border region, in the nation's fourth-largest city of St. Louis, the ideal was put to a strenuous test.

Enter James Hall Brookes, born in Pulaski, Tennessee, in 1830, the son of a Presbyterian minister who died from cholera in 1833. The Brookes family was poor, and James worked as a farmhand, clerk, and teacher before the age of eighteen. He enrolled in Miami University (Ohio), United Presbyterian Seminary (Virginia), and finally Princeton Seminary (New Jersey) before being ordained a Presbyterian minister in 1854. Brookes was, in the words of his son-in-law, "a Southerner, born and bred," but also a creature of the border

---

1. Jonathan Edwards, "Some Thoughts concerning the Present Revival of Religion in New England," in *The Works of President Edwards*, vol. 4 (New York: S. Converse, 1830), 128–33.

region.[2] After a first pastorate in Dayton, Ohio, Brookes moved to St. Louis in 1858, where he would live for the rest of his life.

Though poor, the Brookes family continued to employ at least one African American servant when James was a young man, a "Mammy Hannah," who, while nursing him from sickness, prophesied that he would become a preacher.[3] While personally opposed to the institution of slavery, Brookes never agitated against it. The Old School Presbyterian statement of 1845, which refused to render judgment on slavery at all, became his guiding light. To the question: "Do the Scriptures teach that the holding of slaves, without regards to circumstances, is a sin, the renunciation of which should be made a condition of membership in the church of Christ?," the General Assembly refused to answer definitively. While "not to be understood as denying that there is evil connected with slavery," the statement refrained from attaching the word "sin" to slave ownership, which would have required church discipline. "Since Christ and his inspired Apostles did not make the holding of slaves a bar to communion, we, as a court of Christ, have no authority to do so," the Assembly decided.[4]

The years following 1845 only cemented Brookes's conviction that the church should remain silent on slavery. From St. Louis he propounded the doctrine of the spirituality of the church, teaching that the true church was a spiritual community with heavenly citizenship. The view held clear political implications; namely, it made the status quo acceptable. Credited most prominently to the South Carolinian Presbyterian pastor and theologian James Henley Thornwell, the spirituality of the church was deeply appealing to Southern Presbyterians in the lead-up to the Civil War. "Where the Scriptures are silent, she [the church] must be silent, too," Thornwell wrote in 1850.[5] Accordingly, slavery was a political issue, not a spiritual issue, due to the Bible's lack of an explicit condemnation.

It is hard not to see the spirituality of church as taught by Thornwell as a fig leaf for the perpetuation of slavery, especially as Thornwell himself, after Lincoln's election in 1860, advocated for the secession of his own state and became the leading architect of the Presbyterian Church in the Confederate States of

2. David Riddle Williams, *James H. Brookes: A Memoir* (St. Louis: Presbyterian Board of Publication, 1897), 97.

3. Williams, *James H. Brookes*, 19.

4. *Minutes of the General Assembly of the Presbyterian Church in the United States of America*, vol. 11 (Philadelphia: General Assembly, 1845), 15–17.

5. James Henley Thornwell, "The Rights and Duties of Masters" (May 26, 1850), in *Sermons in American History: Selected Issues in the American Pulpit, 1630–1967*, ed. DeWitte Holland (Nashville: Abingdon, 1971), 221.

America before his death in 1862. Thornwell then cast away entirely his nonpolitical veneer, designating chattel slavery as key to maintaining social order.[6]

Brookes may have been a Southerner by birth and culture, but he was against secession. "His sympathies were with his friends in the South, but he thought their course of action ruinous," his son-in-law explained.[7] Since secession constituted Brookes's breaking point with Southern Presbyterians, it is unsurprising that Thornwell's name hardly appears in Brookes's writings. Antebellum politics and denominational infighting produced a peculiarly Presbyterian spirituality of the church that was alluring to those seeking neutrality in the war. Border-state Presbyterians like Brookes, however, continued the tradition after Thornwell and Southern Presbyterians abandoned it to become Confederate partisans.

Brookes arrived at Second Presbyterian Church in St. Louis in 1858, perhaps briefly overlapping with James Inglis's stint in the city, though there is no evidence that they met at this time. Brookes's resignation after six years, and then appointment to nearby Walnut Street Presbyterian Church in the summer of 1864, was due to his unwavering neutrality during the war. Congregational strife at Second Presbyterian came to a head after elders voiced dismay that Brookes refused to publicly pray for the success of the Union army. Brookes resigned on July 3, 1864, but by the following day, more than one hundred parishioners who also believed in neutrality left to organize the Walnut Street Presbyterian Church. Brookes immediately accepted the invitation to the new pulpit and delivered his first sermon on July 9, a propitious and probably coordinated set of events for the thirty-four-year-old pastor.

Pressure to abandon neutrality increased during Reconstruction, in many ways outpacing the same pressure during wartime. Brookes signed the 1865 "Declaration and Testimony" protesting his denomination's conduct during the war. As with secession and schism, the General Assembly, too, sinned in joining the war effort. The fate of slavery was sealed, but still Brookes pined for the ideal of the 1845 statement. Signaling his willingness to join a short-lived Independent Missouri Synod of the Presbyterian Church beholden to neither North nor South denominational leadership, Brookes lambasted the General Assembly at its 1866 annual meeting. As he attempted another worn defense of the 1845 statement, he insisted that moving forward, the questions surrounding

6. James Henley Thornwell, "To All the Churches of Christ" (December 4, 1861), in *The Collected Writings of James Henley Thornwell: Ecclesiastical* (Richmond, VA: Presbyterian Committee of Publication, 1873), 448.

7. Williams, *James H. Brookes*, 97.

slavery be put to rest for the sake of spiritual purity and civil peace.[8] As the applause in the chamber made clear, Brookes channeled the feelings of a large swath of white Missourians. His stridency was shrewd in St. Louis, where he pastored congregants whose wartime identification with one or the other side, or insufficient support of either side, now threatened their church standing. In subsequent years Brookes relentlessly called for reconciliation throughout the state and for détente among white Protestants. He lamented the destruction and death without drawing moral distinctions between Union and Confederacy.

Brookes traveled the theological road to premillennialism by the route of his concern for church neutrality. The "premillennial truth" was a teaching that, he later recalled, "during the first years of my ministry . . . had never occupied my attention." His new beliefs became evident in the late 1860s, with his major premillennial announcement coming in 1875 with the the launch of his premillennial journal, *The Truth*. But Brookes did not narrate his conversion to premillennialism in terms of border-state neutrality. His own account focused on intense Bible reading and an individual conversion of the head and heart. He credited no outside source, "no single human book or comment, no exposition of any sort," save his unique method of study. "With a lead pencil in hand," he marked every passage that he deemed relevant to "the future of the church and the world," and, "having gathered up the marked passages and brought them together," he concluded that Jesus would return, bodily, to inaugurate the millennial kingdom.[9]

Accepting Brookes's account at face value that the Bible Reading method led to his premillennial conversion, we cannot rule out the role other factors may have played. His views bore the distinctive marks of Darby, who first visited St. Louis in 1862, then again in 1872 and 1875. Darby commented on the success he was having in the city, though never with names. One later account of the Brethren claimed that Darby preached in Brookes's pulpit, though there is not a primary source to verify.[10] The extent of Darby's direct influence on Brookes is unclear—certainly Brookes's own Presbyterian denomination had as much to do with the spirituality of the church as did Darby's dualism, especially before the Civil War. But Brookes adopted numerous aspects of Darby's thought that bolstered the spirituality of the church, with premillennialism

8. James Hall Brookes, *Argument . . . on the 31st of May 1866 in the Defence of the Louisville Presbytery* (St. Louis: George Knapp, 1866).

9. Williams, *James H. Brookes*, 147–52.

10. See Harry A. Ironside, *A Historical Sketch of the Brethren Movement* (New York: Loizeaux Brothers, 1942), chap. 8.

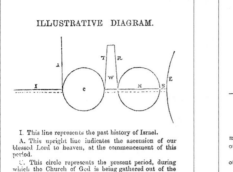
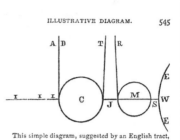

I. This line represents the past history of Israel.
A. This upright line indicates the ascension of our blessed Lord to heaven, at the commencement of this period.
C. This circle represents the present period, during which the Church of God is being gathered out of the world.
T. This line shews the coming of Christ to take the Church to meet Him in the air, which closes this period.
W. This short line, the period of judgment, betwixt the present period of grace and the millennium.
R. This line shews the glorious appearing, or revelation of Christ to the earth.
M. This circle represents the period of the millennium, or kingdom in power.
S. This short line, the letting loose of Satan again, after the thousand years.
E. This beginning of a circle points to the eternal state.
The dotted line represents the history of the Jews, cut off during the present period (c). Since the captivities Israel is "Lo Ammi" (not my people), but it shall be acknowledged again when repentant at the close of the tribulation as "Ammi" (my people). See Hosea i. to iii.; Zechariah xiii. 9.

This simple diagram, suggested by an English tract, may assist the reader in fixing and retaining the order of events as presented in the previous discussion:
I,I,I. Represents the history of Israel up to the time of our Lord's rejection.
A,D. Represents His ascension, and the descent of the Holy Ghost at the beginning of the present dispensation.
C. Is the Church age, during which the Holy Ghost is gathering out of all nations the body and bride of Christ.
T. Is the translation of the risen and changed saints at the coming of the Lord for His waiting people.
J. Is the short period of terrible judgments, described in the Apocalypse, chapters vi–xix, when the Antichrist shall reign and Israel shall be taken up again.
R. Is the revelation of Christ with all His saints here on the earth.
M. Is the millennial kingdom for a thousand happy years.
S. Is Satan loosed out of his prison for a little season.
W. Is the final judgment of the dead before the great white throne.
E,E. Is Eternity.

Figure 4. Comparison of Stanley's and Brookes's dispensational time charts. The Brethren Charles Stanley pioneered a visual representation of dispensational time in the 1850s (left) that American premillennialist James Brookes copied in his popular book on the second coming, *Maranatha* (1874). The diagram is one of the clearest American appropriations of Brethren theology. The genre of the prophecy chart later emerged as one of the defining visual markers of dispensationalism.

emerging as the larger edifice of his post–Civil War theology. Brookes began to write of the two peoples of God, Israel and the church, and the "earthly" mission of Israel as recorded in the Old Testament and the church's "heavenly" vocation as spelled out in the New. "In the one, therefore," Brookes concluded of the two halves of the Bible, "Israel received an earthly calling, but in the other, the church has a heavenly calling."[11] While Brookes championed "plain" readings of Scripture, especially of prophecy, he also adopted the typological logic of Darby. On the subject of humanity's judgment, Brookes taught typologies that made sense only through the lens of Brethren teachings. "We might argue from analogy that a heavenly people, the church, would be preserved from

11. James Hall Brookes, *Maranatha; or, The Lord Cometh*, 5th ed. (St. Louis: Edward Bredell, 1878), 522.

[judgment] like Enoch; and that an earthly people, the faithful remnant among the Israelites would be preserved through it, like Noah; while the ungodly who have despised His love would be overwhelmed by it, like the Antediluvian world."[12] This analysis of the three categories of humanity mirrored, line for line, Darby's commentary in his popular *Synopsis of the Books of the Bible*.[13]

Over the 1860s, Brookes became a champion of this new premillennialism. *Maranatha* (1874), a five-hundred-page treatise that he later described as "this little volume to the truth of His pre-millennial return," signaled a new era in American premillennialism when it appeared.[14] Brookes cited warmly the (non-Millerite) old premillennialists of prior decades and situated his conversation among the major theological and biblical minds of the nineteenth century, all the while making a case for a novel understanding of many of the details. Only once in *Maranatha* did Brookes mention Darby, whose English rendering of the rapture passage in 1 Thessalonians 4:14–18 was Brookes's preferred version.[15] But acknowledgment came in many other forms. Brookes highlighted the Brethren theologian William Craig Baynes of McGill University and his division of the dispensations, and made scattered references to Exclusive Brethren, including C. H. Mackintosh. He prioritized his needs as a border-state evangelical to mix and match. Brookes's eclecticism had clear Brethren influence, appealing to the survivors of an American Civil War who were grappling with the legacy of neutrality and dim prospects of sectional reconciliation.[16]

Joseph A. Seiss and the Future

While Brookes embraced premillennialism in his concern for the church, others were drawn to a prophetic critique of antebellum America, especially its democratic and egalitarian inclinations. Joseph A. Seiss, one of the most significant Lutheran ministers of the nineteenth century, typified the eschatologically inclined interest in Brethren teachings by border-state Christians

---

12. Brookes, *Maranatha*, 523.

13. See John Nelson Darby, *Synopsis of the Books of the Bible: Genesis* (London: G. Morrish, 1877), https://www.stempublishing.com/authors/darby/synopsis/genesis/genesis5 .html. See also Darby's *Hints on the Book of Genesis*, which has a more concise version of the same typology: "Enoch is a figure of those caught up, Noah of the remnant of the Jews that go through the tribulation." https://www.stempublishing.com/authors/darby /EXPOSIT/19002E.html#a5.

14. Brookes, *Maranatha*, 3.

15. Brookes, *Maranatha*, 102.

16. Brookes, *Maranatha*, 545.

and pointed to the ways new premillennialism became an attractive American alternative to old premillennialism in the 1860s.

Prophetic critiques of antebellum America were a mainstay of old premillennialism. David Lord, who edited the *Theological and Literary Journal* from 1848 to 1861, typified the old premillennial view when he bewailed the great American "error" of democracy, of the average American's overblown estimate "of his capabilities and dispositions to a safe, benign, and wise government of himself."[17] When the Civil War came in 1861, old premillennialists saw it as prophetically significant as well as a moral comeuppance. Seiss, a conservative in most every sense of the term, agreed and was himself an old premillennialist in 1861. But his evolving interpretation of prophecy and American society in the 1860s pushed him toward the new brand of premillennialism pioneered by the Brethren.

Born in 1823 on a Moravian settlement outside of Graceham, Maryland, Seiss decided as a sixteen-year-old to become a Lutheran minister. He attended Gettysburg College, a new preparatory school for the Lutheran Seminary at Gettysburg, but an outbreak of typhoid cut his time short. Just two years later he was commissioned by the Virginia Lutheran Synod to be a home missionary, essentially an itinerant preacher, and a year later he received his first pastoral calling in Virginia. Less than a decade later he returned to Maryland and became the president of the state's synod, and in 1858 he was called to Philadelphia, to St. John Lutheran Church, the largest Lutheran congregation in America at the time. There he helped found the General Council in 1867 in opposition to the movement led by Samuel Simon Schmucker to unite American Lutherans with other Protestants.

Seiss's premillennialism stands out as a major caveat to his defense of the historic Lutheran faith. The Augsburg Confession, adopted by Lutherans in 1580, explicitly condemned the teaching "that before the resurrection of the dead saints and godly men will possess a worldly kingdom and annihilate all the godless."[18] The original targets of refutation were apocalyptic Anabaptists, especially the followers of the radical German preacher Thomas Müntzer. In America, the condemnation extended to the Millerites and essentially silenced end-times speculation in the Lutheran church.

Seiss, however, was not a normal Lutheran. While the "Great Disappointment" of 1844 seemed to discredit premillennialism for a generation, it spurred Seiss to realize the second coming's "very great importance," albeit on terms

17. David Lord, "The Lessons Taught by Late Political Events," *Theological and Literary Journal*, no. 52 (April 1861): 662.

18. *The Augsburg Confession* (St. Louis: Concordia, 2001), 11.

other than Miller's faulty math. Seiss credited his conversion from a "quite settled" postmillennialism to discussions with a fellow Lutheran minister, as well as to exposure to a five-volume collection of British writings published from 1840 to 1842 titled *The Literalist*. These texts informed "months and months" of study in 1843 and 1844, amounting to "the most anxious and agonizing battle" of his life, which, he said, by the grace of God, he "fought through to some leading conclusions which have never since been shaken." Seiss's premillennialism became "the root spring" of all he subsequently wrote, preached, and published.[19]

And there was a lot that Seiss preached and published on prophecy. Until the 1860s, his sermons and tracts were steeped in depressing analysis of the current world and, like Brookes's works, shaped by the border-state anxiety of looming crisis. He lamented in *The Last Times and the Great Consummation* (1856), his first major contribution to premillennial theology, that "this world is a disjointed and dilapidated fabric," riven with natural disasters and humanity's "unholy deeds." What God created "to minister to our joy has become a disorderly servant, as if indignant to obey a convict sovereign." The world to come, organized not by humans but by divine fiat, will be "a vast improvement upon the present scene of things."[20]

All this before the Civil War, and before Seiss developed his views to reflect Brethren peculiarities. In January 1861, while states were actively seceding from the Union, Seiss spoke from his new pulpit in Philadelphia of "the threatening ruin," lamenting that lame-duck president James Buchanan was already "the last president of these United States."[21] The war was a morality tale of the wayward nation whose only hope was a miraculous reconciliation with God—not through revival (which Seiss regarded as pandering to America individualism) or separation—but through embracing moral reform that would taper God's wrath. Reconciliation was in fact too kind a word—Seiss held no illusions that Americans ever possessed a rightly ordered relationship with God. The Declaration of Independence was "essentially deistic"; the Constitution "entirely atheistic." The spirit of the pious "pilgrim fathers" was "about as intolerant as that from which they fled"; the supposed Manifest Destiny of territorial enlargement "has been effected, in a considerable measure, by the butchery and

19. Seiss, quoted in Samuel R. Zeiser, "Joseph Augustus Seiss: Popular Nineteenth Century Lutheran Pastor and Premillennialist" (PhD diss., Drew University, 2001), 38.

20. Zeiser, "Joseph Augustus Seiss," 62–63.

21. Joseph A. Seiss, *The Threatening Ruin; or, Our Times, Our Prospects, and Our Duty* (Philadelphia: Smith, English, and Co., 1861), 27.

forcible ejectment of its former proprietors."[22] The end was indeed soon, with the failure of the great American experiment as its great herald.

But when would the end come? In 1861 Seiss still stood with the old premillennialists, who for more than fifty years insisted that the end times would begin between 1864 and 1872. The calculation came from aligning the prophecies in Daniel and Revelation to mean that "a time, times, and an half" (Dan. 12:7 KJV) equaled three and a half periods of 360 days. Equating days with years, it appeared that antichrist powers would reign over the earth for 1,260 years, followed by another 75 years before the full restoration of Israel and return of Jesus. Correlating the antichrist's reign to the rise and fall of papal supremacy over Christendom, which these interpretations placed at the overthrow of the French monarchy in the 1790s, it seemed like the mid-1860s would usher in the onset of the apocalypse. The breakout of war in 1861 quickened these expectations.

Seiss was convinced that the final antichrist would be Louis Napoleon (Napoleon III, Bonaparte's cousin), emperor of France, closing the loop on the French Revolution as one of the decisive events in the prophetic timeline. Napoleon Bonaparte's dramatic reign from 1804 to 1815 inaugurated a prophesied "Napoleonic headship" that would lead to the revival of the Roman Empire and presage the return of Jesus. While it appeared that the headship was short-lived after the Battle of Waterloo, the rise of Louis Napoleon as emperor in 1852 confirmed that the Napoleonic headship was the "septimo-eighth head of the seven-headed and ten-horned Beast of the great Roman dominion."[23] Writing in 1863, Seiss resisted equating Napoleon III with "the personal Antichrist of the Last Days," but he inched as close as he could, assuring readers of the second edition of *The Last Times*, "we have no hesitation in saying that we are strongly inclined, with some of the most sober and learned of prophetic expositors, to believe that he is."[24]

What Seiss saw in the next few years disappointed him, with Louis Napoleon failing to fulfill any of the prophecies ascribed to him by old premillennialists. He did not extend his empire's reign to match that of ancient Rome, he did not resettle Jews in the Holy Land, he did not persecute Protestants. In fact, the 1860s were a disastrous decade for the French monarchy and ended

22. Seiss, *The Threatening Ruin*, 29–31.

23. Joseph A. Seiss, "The Antichrist: Will It Be Louis Napoleon?" *Prophetic Times* 1, no. 2 (February 1863): 17.

24. Joseph Seiss, *The Last Times and the Great Consummation*, revised and enlarged ed. (Philadelphia: Smith, English, and Co., 1863), 348–49.

in Louis Napoleon's exile to Britain, where he would die in 1873. France's debt ballooned under the emperor's public works projects, and his own health began to fail. When France declared war on Prussia in July 1870, it took less than eight weeks for the Germans to force Louis Napoleon, captured and his army broken, to capitulate.

Having constructed his premillennial edifice on a failing emperor, Seiss began to hedge even before Louis Napoleon's die was cast. In 1864 he wrote "The Difficulty Solved: Two Stages of the Advent," in which he adopted the basic eschatological framework of a new, Darbyite premillennialism distinguishing between Christ's first and second return. He now insisted that "the Scriptures plainly set for a coming of Christ FOR his Church, which he catches up 'in the air,' and a coming of Christ WITH His Church, surrounded by which He descends to the earth." This meant that the "watching and waiting" for the rapture would precede the geopolitical climax of the second stage. Though prophecies awaited fulfillment, "between us and Christ's coming for his saints," Seiss now taught, "the Scriptures locate nothing upon which we can find a solid argument that it shall not take place tomorrow."[25]

Seiss's evolution on the issue played out in real time in the pages of *Prophetic Times*, a self-styled elite journal founded in 1863 by Seiss, George Duffield, and a fellow Philadelphian old premillennialist, Episcopal minister Richard Newton. "Having no connection whatever with the erratic and irresponsible men usually claiming attention on these themes," the editors clarified in their first issue, "we come before the public as accredited ministers of orthodox Churches."[26] *Prophetic Times* began as an old premillennial journal, but under the leadership of Seiss, it began introducing new premillennial ideas. Seiss's proposal of a multistage second coming was accordingly met with resistance by readers. Seiss began a vigorous written defense and published selections from William Trotter, airing, under a different Brethren name, Darby's scheme.[27] A *Prophetic Times* series, "Israel and the Church," in 1869 relied on Darby's definitions of these terms, bringing to the fore Seiss's increasing indebtedness to the Brethren.[28] He warned his readers, perhaps as a public reminder to himself, that "'Napoleonism' has exerted a wider influence than

25. "The Difficulty Solved: Two Stages of the Advent," *Prophetic Times* 2, no. 10 (October 1864): 157–58.

26. "Our Enterprise," *Prophetic Times* 1, no. 1 (January 1863): 12.

27. "The Judgment Not Simultaneous, from 'Plain Papers on Prophetic Subjects,'" *Prophetic Times* 3, no. 3 (March 1865): 39–43.

28. "Israel and the Church," *Prophetic Times* 7, no. 1 (January 1869): 1–5. This series continued through *Prophetic Times* 7, nos. 6 and 7 (June and July 1869).

PROBABLE DATES OF THE SEVEN LAST VIALS. 863

VIAL.

IV. *The scorching and blasting career of Napoleon I.*, from his appointment as First Consul to his abdication of the empire:—A.D. 1799–1814.

V. *Judgments upon the throne and kingdom of the Beast*, from the overthrow of Napoleon I. to the revolutions of 1848, the overthrow of the Orleans dynasty, and the rise of Napoleon III.:—A.D. 1814–1849.

VI. *Wane of Babylon's resources and supports, and mustering of the nations for their final overthrow*, from the rise of Louis Napoleon to the emperorship to the coming of Christ as the thief to remove the Church of the first-born, or wise virgins, from the earth to meet him in the air:—A.D. 1850—

VII. *The great tribulation, unexampled earthquake, and judgment of the nations*, from the full development of the personal Antichrist—most likely Napoleon III.—to the manifestation of Christ for his final destruction and the binding of Satan; estimated by numerous interpreters to date from A.D. 1865–6—1869–70.

These vials, however, are to have their literal and *complete* fulfilment only within the last months before the descent and manifestation of Christ and his grand saint-army, which ushers in the time of blessedness for those who wait and come to that day—the day for which the earth has been sighing for wellnigh six thousand years.

CHRONOLOGY OF THE BIBLE. 863

best, the disagreement is still such as to prove that the present data on the subject is not such as to secure perfect accuracy, even within a considerable number of years. Nor can it now be seen by what means the clouds can be lifted, and the actual truth ascertained. Perhaps a better astronomy, and a full understanding of the meaning of the constellations, which evidently date back to the early history of our race, may serve to settle and make clear what is in so much mist and dispute.

The value of chronology to history, and our dependence upon it for the understanding of events and their relations to each other, is so great, that we would naturally expect more definiteness than appears to be possible. But there is doubtless a providence in the matter. It is not for us accurately to know the times or the seasons. Some of the great ends of the divine counsels would be interfered with, if we could forecalculate definitely what has been predetermined; and hence all the foundations on which to proceed are more or less veiled in uncertainty. Especially with regard to the return of our Savior and the great consummation, the intention is that we should watch and pray continually, not knowing what hour the Lord may come.

As far as we can see, the 6000 years have about expired. The signs are, that the day of judgment is now near at hand. There are no signs, no dates, no years, no foretold points or particulars first to be reached, which can now be put between us and the fulfilment of what the Savior has predicted in Luke xvii. 34–37, or what Paul has so graphically set forth in 1 Thess. iv. 15–17. The next great prophetic event to be awaited on earth, is the sudden recall of the sleeping saints from their graves, and the equally sudden seizing away from earth to their Lord in the air, of all such waiting and watching ones as are ready when the day arrives. It may be any one of these passing hours. "Blessed is he that watcheth."

Figure 5. Comparisons of two editions of Joseph Seiss's *The Last and Great Consummation*. Seiss's conversion from old to new premillennialism can be seen in his writings, which he continued to update throughout his life. On the final page of the sixth edition of this book (left), published in 1863 while he was still an old premillennialist, he concluded with a list of "probable dates" of prophecy fulfillment, culminating in the date range of "1869–70." The next time he revised the text, in 1878 (right), he removed the "probable dates" and finished instead with a more sedate assessment.

'Millerism'" in prophecy circles in recent years and warped the conversation. The solution was simple: "We should, therefore, learn to interpose no event before the coming of the Lord to receive his waiting Church"—in other words, teach the any-moment-rapture to guard against date setting.[29]

The drama of Seiss's changing eschatological commitments unfolded as he toured Europe, the Near East, and North Africa, including the Holy Land, in 1864. Upon his return, he produced his magnum opus, the three-volume *Lectures on the Apocalypse*, which was written mostly in 1865 and published from 1870 to 1884. The lectures reflected Seiss's new multistage system of premillennialism. He would also revise his old works, writing in the third edition of *The Last Times*, in 1878, "When this book was last touched by the author, fifteen years ago [in 1863], he did not so clearly apprehend the distribution of events involved in the momentous occurrences as his subsequent studies have

29. "Prophetic Time," *Prophetic Times* 8, nos. 10 and 11 (October and November 1870): 146.

made plain to him."[30] A public *mea culpa* won Seiss few new Lutheran friends, but it endeared him to the new premillennial community.

Where James Brookes appealed to the spirituality of the church as a gateway to premillennialism, Seiss took the opposite path and adapted his views of the church as a result of his changing eschatological commitments. He now counseled that it was an error to confuse "the coming of the Lord and the removal and rapture of the Church" with "events solely pertaining to the present existing world—kingdoms of earth," replicating the dualism at the heart of Darby's teachings.[31] Seiss began to think in terms of dichotomies, bringing new assumptions to his understanding of the Bible and the world, and reshaping how he saw himself—and his church—in relation to the future.

A Wider Interpretive Community

During his sixty-year tenure as a pastor, from 1844 to 1904, Seiss deepened his appreciation for the dual destiny of humankind. Reflecting late in life, he speculated that the renewed earth, after Christ's return, would be no place for the church. "It will not be the home of the elect and glorified; for they shall be like the angels, and in the same sort of supernal life in which Jesus is." The new earth would instead "be the home of righteousness, and of a redeemed race, such as would have been if Adam had never sinned."[32] The new earth would be a ministration for a different people; the church would commune in its heavenly abode for eternity, far away from the particularities of this terrestrial plane.

The pastoral reflections of an aging Seiss revealed a changed premillennialist, who looked for the Lord's day at any moment, who dreamed of union with his Savior across a distant sea, who was tasked by his creator to wait, to watch, and to, above all, "look forward to the closing of this present world."[33] The differences between Seiss-the-old-premillennialist and Seiss-the-new-premillennialist were subtle on the surface, but they worked their way into his sentiments, his theological and intellectual interests, and the influence he ultimately exercised on American Christianity. For both James Brookes and Joseph Seiss, converting to new premillennialism when they did, where they

30. Joseph A. Seiss, *The Last Times; or, Thoughts on Momentous Themes*, 7th ed. (Philadelphia: Lippincott, 1878), 341.

31. "Prophetic Time," 150.

32. Joseph A. Seiss, *Beacon Lights: A Series of Short Sermons* (Philadelphia: Board of Publication of the General Council of the Evangelical Lutheran Church, 1899), 537–38.

33. Seiss, *Beacon Lights*, 539.

did, redirected their careers and their ministries in new directions as they channeled once-obscure Brethren voices into American evangelicalism.

And their work drew in unexpected followers. James Robinson Graves was another creature of the same Civil War tensions—born in Vermont but a resident of Nashville, Tennessee, until the war, when he enlisted as a Confederate soldier, fled to Mississippi in 1862, and then moved to Memphis after the war. He, too, became drawn to new premillennialism. Like Seiss, Graves converted to a version of old premillennialism before the war, which he promoted in his popular periodical *The Baptist.* By the 1880s he was reprinting articles from Brookes's journal *The Truth* and Seiss's journal *Prophetic Times.* It was Seiss whom Graves in 1887 commended to his readers as "doubtless the ablest expounder of the Book of Revelation that has written in this country or this age."[34] The version of premillennialism Graves taught possessed its own peculiarities, adapted to his commitments of a true and visible local church in the Landmark Baptist mode, and to his Southern interests that saw a worldly, as much as a heavenly, role for the church.

The new premillennial conversions of Brookes and Seiss—and Graves—took place in the shadow of the Civil War and Reconstruction. In reconciling with the seismic changes to American society wrought by the war, each man embraced already-circulating Brethren teachings that made sense of his particular sectional and denominational setting. There was no single pathway into new premillennialism—no one argument or doctrine that immediately resonated with a wide swath of Americans—and the growth of this new interpretive community was slower, but stronger, because of it. The multiplicity of new premillennialism's appeal would advance along the trajectories set by these first American converts.

34. Graves, quoted in Danny Eugene Howe, "An Analysis of Dispensationalism and Its Implications for the Theologies of James Robinson Graves, John Franklyn Norris, and Wallie Amos Criswell" (PhD diss., Southwestern Baptist Theological Seminary, 1988), 103.

Suppose the dark ages were again upon us, and to all human ap-
pearance the entire church were apostate, this need not prevent the
humble believer with an open Bible in his hand from receiving and
holding firmly the great truth, so fully and clearly set forth in the
word of God, that Christ is coming back to our earth, and that He
may come at any time, no conversion of the world being predicted
as antedating His personal return. . . . Then whether with many or
few, he would know the unspeakable value of "that blessed hope"
to separate him in life from the defiling scene around him, to solace
him in sorrow, to sustain him in weakness, and to shine like the
golden rays of the Morning Star across the deepening darkness set-
tling down into blackest night over an ungodly world.

James H. Brookes, "The Coming of Christ:
Personal and Pre-Millennial" (1885)

The new premillennial position was not just an abstract theological commitment. As Brookes related in this sermon at an 1885 prophecy conference, knowledge of the "blessed hope" of the imminent rapture and second coming gave adherents a resilience that, they contended, was absent in other Christians. For Brookes and his circle of teachers, the values of separation, solace, and sustenance were cultivated through ceaseless practices of prayer and Bible study that revealed God's truths.

4

Numbers and Structures

In the 1860s, James H. Brookes and Joseph A. Seiss embraced Brethren teachings on dispensational time, the heavenly nature of the church, and the imminent rapture, remolding their own understanding of the Christian faith. But as loyalists to their denominations, they made no blanket endorsement of the Brethren. Unique concerns ensured that the American new premillennial tradition would develop in its own direction. Yet in the 1870s, new premillennialists still lacked their own class of theologians, and Brethren writers—John Nelson Darby, William Kelly, C. H. Mackintosh, and Frederick W. Grant—continued to shape their thinking. Americans spent these years navigating the multiple influences on their community: the longer history of old premillennialism, the Brethren writers, and the more immediate American influences of inductive Bible reading, commonsense realism, and revivalism. They hoped to reconcile competing theological influences just as they sought to reconcile competing sectional interests.

The emerging premillennial tradition emphasized two areas of biblical analysis that gave it added shape. Borrowing from the Brethren, new premillennialists were interested in the overarching narrative structure of the biblical story (the progression of dispensational time) and the unified perspective of the biblical text itself. These interests were expressed in structural analysis of the Bible's organization, in typological analysis that reinforced the test-fail cycles of dispensations and the centrality of Israel to prophecy, and in numerology, or the significance of biblical numbers. In each case Americans marked their fledgling new premillennial tradition with idiosyncrasies. What Darby understood to be American spiritual "mud"—defined by "activity," revivalism, denominationalism, individualism, and democratic impulses—was also the stuff that made American Christianity dynamic and open to radical ideas.

64

THE TRUTH.

BOOK DEPOSITORY.

At the office of THE TRUTH will be found, for sale, a carefully selected assortment of English and American publications, designed to bear testimony to the truth as it is in Jesus. It is our purpose to add to this stock such books as we can safely commend, of which notice will be given in future issues of THE TRUTH. Below we give a partial list, with the prices at which we can supply the Books. Address,

CHAS. B. COX,
212 North Fifth Street, St. Louis.

NOW READY.

By THE EDITOR.—MARANATHA: or the Lord Cometh.

The table of Contents is as follows: Chap. I, The Question Stated; II, Importance of the Subject; III and IV, Christ's Coming Literal; V, Post-millennial Testimony; VI, Prominence of the Doctrine; VII, Scriptural use of the Doctrine; VIII-XVI, No Millennium till Christ Comes; XVII, History of the Doctrine; XVIII, Power of the Doctrine; XIX, Return of the Jews; XX, The Two Resurrections; XXI, The Hope of the Church. Sent postpaid on receipt of the Price, $1.25.

BAGSTER'S POLYGLOT BIBLES.
With complete Index of Subjects, Cruden's Concordance, and much other valuable matter.

OXFORD BIBLES.
In various styles and prices. We have a neat Bible for presents, bound in roan, with gilt edges; $5 per dozen, or 50 cts. per single copy.

AMERICAN BIBLE SOCIETY
Being the Depository of the St. Louis County Bible Society, we can supply all the publications of the American Bible Society.

CRUDEN'S CONCORDANCE, at $1.50, $2, $2.75, $3.50.

BIBLE DICTIONARIES, from $1.50 to $26.

By Prof. GAUSSEN.
Canon of the Holy Scriptures, $4.
It is written; or the Scriptures the Word of God, $1.50.

EXPOSITORY THOUGHTS ON THE GOSPELS, by Rev. J. C. Ryle.
We do not hesitate to say that these are the best practical Commentaries on the four gospels known to us. We hope the author will find lleisure to furnish Explanatory and Critical Notes on Matthew and Mark, such as he gives on Luke and John, thus greatly adding to the value of his Thoughts on the two former, and making them uniform in arrangement with the two latter. Seven volumes $1.50 per volume.

BIBLE THOUGHTS AND THEMES, by Dr. H. Bonar.
In five volumes, viz: Vol. 1, Old Testament, $2. Vol. 2, The Gospels, $2. Vol. 3, The Acts and the Larger Epistles, $2. Vol. 4, The Lesser Epistles, $2. Vol. 5, The Revelation, $2. No Christian who reads either of these admirable volumes can fail to be profited by the rich expositions of Scriptural truth it contains.

NOTES ON GENESIS, EXODUS, LEVITICUS AND NUMBERS, by C. H. McIntosh.
Most cordially do we recommend these Notes to the Christian reader, as worth far more to the soul than any of the more learned and pretentious Commentaries on the same precious portion of God's word. 4 vols., $1.15 per vol.
Things New and Old; for the Lambs and Sheep of the Flock of Christ; 60 cts. per volume—volumes sold separately.
Life and Times of David, 50 cts.; Practical Reflections on the Life and Times of Elijah the Tishbite, 50 cts.

THE TABERNACLE AND THE PRIESTHOOD, by Rev. H. W. Soltau.
This book is a wonderful compilation of the most precious Gospel truth, and we wish it could be thoroughly studied by every child of God, and especially by every minister of Jesus Christ.

By C. H. SPURGEON.
The Saint and his Saviour, $1.50.
Morning by Morning, $1.75.
Evening by Evening, $1.75.
Sermons. Eight volumes, $1.50.
The writings and Discourses of this honored servant of the Lord are too well known to need commendation.

JUST RECEIVED.
Joshua and His Times, by Thornly Smith, $1.25.
Joshua and his Successors, by W. H. Groser, $1.
The Class and The Desk, by J. C. Gray, $1.50.
The Golden Fountain, by J. H. Wilson, Edinboro, $1.25.
All of these books will be helpful particularly to the Sunday School Teacher.
Prize Essay on Infidelity, by Pearson, $1.50.
Discussion of the Millennium, by Dr. Litch.
Although we do not agree with the Author in all of his views, we are glad to see that his work is a thorough refutation of Dr. David Brown.

By J. G. BELLETT.
The Moral Glory of the Lord Jesus Christ, 75 cents.
The Son of God, $1.
The Patriarchs—Enoch, Noah, Abraham, Jacob, Joseph, $2.25.
Introduction to the Book of Job.

By ANDREW JUKES.
The Law of the Offerings, $1.50.
Characteristic Differences of the Four Gospels, $1.15.

By Dr. W. P. MACKAY—Grace and Truth, $1.

By WILLIAM LINCOLN—Lectures on the Epistles of St. John, $1.

By J. R. MACDUFF.
Healing Waters of Israel, $1.25.
Morning and Night Watches, 50 cts.
Mind and Words of Jesus, 50 cts.

By THE EDITOR.
How to be Saved, paper, 20 cts; cloth, 50 cts.
May Christians Dance; paper, 25 cts; cloth, 60 cents.
Gospel Hymns; containing 675 hymns in harmony with The Truth, $1.50 and $2.
The Way Made Plain; third edition, $1.25.
Maranatha; or the Lord Cometh; $1.25.

DUBLIN TRACTS.

The Dublin Tracts are gratuitously furnished by the proprietor of this paper, to all persons who love to work for the Master, and who will faithfully distribute them. Application may be made in person, or by letter.

The following small books and tracts are for sale at the prices named.
Charles Stanley Tracts, 2 vols. 60 cts each.
The great Truths of the Bible are set forth in a striking and instructive manner.
Words of Truth; 6 vols., 75 cts. per vol:
God's Record, 50 cts.
Asleep in Jesus, 40 cts.
Life Truths. Every Christian should have a copy of this book, 55cts.
The Lord's Hosts, 60 cts.
Jesus the Way, by E. P. Hammond, 50 cts.
The Blood of Jesus, by Rev. Wm. Reid, paper, 15cts., cloth, 30 cts.
Immortality of the Soul; by Rev. N. L. Rice D. D., 70 cts.
Stories of Old—Old Testament, New Testament, and Stories of the Apostles; 3 volumes 75 cts. per volume.
A most instructive book for children.
Ruin Utter, and Redemption Complete, 25 cents.
By JAS. INGLIS—School of God, 10 cts; Secret of Abiding Peace, 5 cts.
By C. H. McINTOSH—Regeneration, Forgiveness of Sins, Sanctification, Christian Perfection, Wells of Sychar, each, 10 cts.; Work of God in the Soul, 20 cts.
By J. G. BELLETT—Waiting for the Son from Heaven, 6 cts.; Return of the Lord Jesus, 25 cts.
Notes on Scripture, by J. N. D., 25 cts.
Eternity of Punishment and Immortality of the Soul, 50 cts.
Gospel Truth, 20 cts.
Daily Trials and How to bear Them, 5 cts.
What must I believe to be Saved, 10 cts.
The Little Pilgrim in verse, 10 cts.
The Blessed Hope, by Alex. McCaul, 10 cts.
By ANNIE SHIPTON—Tell Jesus, 25 cts.; Saved Now, 15 cts.
Glasgow Series of Gospel Tracts, 12 kinds, 80 cts. per package.
Call of God—Reflections on the Life and character of Abraham and Lot, 20 cts.
Future Punishment; by Jos. C. Stiles, 10 cts.
The Coming Glory—a series of brief discourses on the Coming and Kingdom of Christ, 20 cents.
Can I be assured of salvation.
Edinburg Tracts, 40 cts. per package.
Come to Jesus, by Newman Hall, 5 cts.
Only One Way of Salvation, by Rev. J. C. Ryle, 5 cts.
The Elder Brother, 5 cts.
The Siege of Samaria, 5 cts.
Jehosaphat: a word on Church Bordering, 10 cts.
Pronouncing Dictionary of Scripture Proper Names, 25 cts.
The Righteousness of God, by W. Kelly, 25 cents.
Call to Prayer, by Rev. J. C. Ryle, 5 cts.
Quench not the Spirit, by Newman Hall, 5 cents.

Figure 6. The Truth magazine book depository listing. James Brookes's prophecy journal, *The Truth*, may have been published in St. Louis, but it was indebted to the thought world of Brethren in the United Kingdom. A back-page "Book Depository" boasted "a carefully selected assortment of English and American publications" (pictured here from the March 1875 issue). The entire third column featured "Dublin Tracts" by Brethren, including Darby ("J.N.D."), Charles Stanley, and William Kelly. Courtesy of Wisconsin Historical Society.

The American process of reconciling with Brethren theology was messy. Americans preferred merging Brethren techniques with their own tools of interpretation to read and organize the Bible afresh; to pull it apart and put it back again; to discover hidden connections revealed in their new methods of analysis. Americans also pursued a different social and religious agenda than the Brethren. They wanted to recast the role of the church after the Civil War. The theology taking shape supplied a framework to mold a new type of Christian, and a new type of Christian community that could stand erect in the mud of American Christianity.

Premillennialism, Old and New

Premillennialists claimed a distinguished lineage of interpretation that dated to church fathers Justin Martyr, Irenaeus, and Lactantius and stretched to the twelfth-century Italian monk Joachim of Fiore (1135–1202), who looked forward to a new "age of the spirit" in the year 1260 based on numerological analysis. The tradition continued in the wake of the Reformation and took form in the "old premillennial" school in the eighteenth and early nineteenth century. The new premillennialism introduced by the Brethren and adopted by a growing movement of Americans rivaled this older tradition. The continuity and tension between the two are visible in the shared interest in the study of numbers, or numerology.

The significance of numbers was part of the longer history of premillennialism. For old premillennialists, numerology was one of the chief sciences of biblical interpretation and the key to decode the connection between biblical texts and real historical events. The "year-day" theory, in which a day spoken in prophecy represented a year, and many days implied many years, was older than the nineteenth century and thus was able to withstand the embarrassment of the Millerite "Great Disappointment."

Yet others regarded the year-day theory as poor exegesis and a limitation to the premillennial tradition. Brethren rejected the year-day theory and insisted that prophetic days meant literal days. Subsequent new premillennial focus shifted away from correlating the long arc of historical events with prophecies and numbers, and toward determining in real time where the prophetic timeline was headed in the future. This was a key distinction in new premillennial circles, which were largely uninterested in tracing God's activity in history, since prophetic events were understood to happen in a dramatic and contracted period of time in the near future. Instead of decoding historical correlations to prophetic events, new premillennialists were more interested in the pattern or structure of God's activity in history. If there were predictable designs to God's work, the future would undoubtedly conform to the past.

In contrast to the older numerology, new premillennialists employed a new symbolism, as well. While invoking the sense of materiality and realism of prophecy interpretation shared by all premillennialists, they interpreted symbols and imagery differently. Old premillennialists made allowances for allegory, poetry, and symbolism—it all just needed to correlate to historical events. Brethren, believing that most of prophecy remained unfulfilled, applied culturally contextualized meanings to symbols in order to make them immediate and directly connected to the present. Both "schools" of premillennialism were hardly rigid literalists—neither demanded that the beast in Revelation 13:1 literally rise "out of the sea" or denied the poetic quality of the Psalms. Both trafficked in Romanticist longing and Enlightenment rationalism, deploying a mix of allegorical and literal hermeneutics to support their commitment to prophetic materiality. But while for old premillennialists that commitment was to historical correlation, for new premillennialists the agenda was to anticipate future fulfillment.

Old and new premillennialists in fact shared many commitments that allowed for the construction of a common tradition stretching to the early church. Brookes traced "the doctrine of the Millennium as now believed substantially by the Pre-millennialists" to the first centuries of Christianity, claiming that chiliasm—the belief that the millennium would soon be established by Christ's return—was so prominent in the second and third centuries that it was hard to find another perspective.[1] "Every one of the Apostolical Fathers, who says anything at all on the subject, is a Chiliast," he explained, and even in statements like the Nicene Creed (325), the councils "found it everywhere existing, and they did not condemn it."[2] Nathaniel West, representing old premillennialism in one of the defining works to come from that school, *The Thousand Years in Both Testaments* (1889), declared that "the Pre-millennial Coming of Christ" was, "for 300 years, 'the test of orthodoxy,' and formed a chief article of faith and hope."[3]

Premillennialists agreed that disaster came from the innovation of "spiritualized" and allegorical understandings of the millennium, introduced by

1. James Hall Brookes, *Maranatha; or, The Lord Cometh*, 5th ed. (St. Louis: Edward Bredell, 1878), 334.

2. Brookes, *Maranatha*, 336.

3. Nathaniel West, *The Thousand Year Reign of Christ: The Classic Work on the Millennium* (Grand Rapids: Kregel, 1993), xiii. This is a reprint of Nathaniel West, *Studies in Eschatology: The Thousand Years in Both Testaments* (Chicago: Revell, 1889).

church fathers such as Origen, Jerome, and Augustine of Hippo. In the premillennial telling, this allegorical tradition continued into the modern era under the guise of postmillennialism or amillennialism. The latter, the position taught by the Catholic Church and many Protestant denominations, rejected a literal future millennium altogether and understood the church itself to be the symbolical millennial kingdom.

Premillennialists did not entirely reject the teachings of such luminaries as Augustine, but they did not mince words, either. The "great investigators" who spiritualized the millennium and therefore prophecy, West summarized, trafficked in a "fundamental error which vitiates their otherwise matchless and meritorious work."[4] The preference to see the millennium, and all of the associated prophetic texts, as elaborate images with no direct correlation to material or historical realization sent the church into centuries of bad theology, premillennialists maintained, and coincided with the thorough political domination of Europe by the Catholic Church. Investment in worldly power went hand in hand with spiritual and symbolical biblical hermeneutics, creating a relationship of convenience that read the symbols to justify the power.

This was no surprise to a Lutheran like Seiss, who maintained that during the long "dark age" from Augustine to Luther, "there was hardly any doctrine of the gospel which did not suffer a like eclipse." New premillennialists, because of their orientation toward the future, may not have regarded the Catholic Church as the antichrist (which old premillennialists did), but their views on Catholicism were hardly less critical. "The Church had become corrupt and vastly apostate, and the peculiarities which were most prominent in the primitive faith were overlaid and thrust out of sight." A narrative of recovery bolstered premillennial confidence: "It is enough to know that the doctrine of the Millennium and personal reign was the orthodox and catholic persuasion of the primitive Church," Seiss wrote. The errors in the nineteenth century were much the same as those in the fifth: to "Platonize, allegorize, and explain away the scriptures" in order to find comfort in the world.[5]

With the Reformation, the premillennial genealogy began to revive and branch out. The exegesis of Thomas Brightman, the hymns of Isaac Watts, and the writings of John Gill and Joseph Mede all brought the tradition of English premillennialism into the nineteenth century. It was crucial for new premillennialists to also claim this tradition, and indeed there was significant over-

4. West, *The Thousand Year Reign of Christ.*

5. Joseph A. Seiss, *The Last Times; or, Thoughts on Momentous Themes*, 7th ed. (Philadelphia: Lippincott, 1878), 396–97.

lap. Commitment to the "literal" reading of prophecy, even if interpretations diverged, bound them and the old premillennialists against "spiritualization." Commitment to the regathering of the Jewish people in the Holy Land, even if the details remained contested, bound them in a fixation on Jewish missions and proto-Zionism. Commitment to the conviction that God was bringing his epic plan for world salvation to a close bound them in a confidence and hope to witness the second coming (or the rapture) in their lifetimes. And commitment to the declension of human civilization as a testament to the all-sufficiency of Christ, even as prophetic timelines differed over past and future fulfillment, bound them toward a skepticism of social reform and progress. These commitments could be found in the old premillennialism of the 1860s and 1870s, which was more vibrant in Great Britain—in the sermons of Charles Spurgeon and Henry Gratton Guinness, in the music of Horatius Bonar and William Pennefather, in the periodicals of David Lord and George Duffield, and in the massive tomes of Edward Bishop Elliot and George N. H. Peters.

American new premillennialists, though, also tried to bolster their historical pedigree with quotations from great men—many of which were poorly sourced or dubiously applied. One common quotation attributed to Sir Isaac Newton had the scientist, who also wrote voluminously on biblical prophecy, saying: "About the time of the end, in all probability, a body of men will be raised up who will turn their attention to the prophecies, and insist on their literal interpretation, in the midst of much clamor and opposition."[6] This fabricated quotation was probably introduced into American circles through British writings in the early eighteenth century, ironically by opponents of the premillennial "literal interpretation" who were conscripting Newton to their cause.[7] Another common, dubiously applied quotation was by Augustine of Hippo, who wrote: "Distinguish the ages, and the scriptures harmonize" (*Distribute tempora, et concordant Scriptura*). Uttering it in a sermon

6. See, for example, A. J. Gordon, "The Relation of the Baptists to the Doctrine of the Lord's Coming," in *Primitive Paths in Prophecy: Prophetic Addresses Given at the Brooklyn Conference of the Baptist Society for Bible Study*, ed. George C. Needham (Chicago: Gospel Publication Co., 1891), 44. Thank you to Cornelis Schilt, of the Newton Project (University of Oxford, http://www.newtonproject.ox.ac.uk/), for help with this point and confirmation that the quotation is not part of Newton's known writings.

7. The earliest example of this quotation I have found is in William Thorpe, *The Destinies of the British Empire, and the Duties of British Christians at the Present Crisis*, 2nd ed. (Philadelphia: Orrin Rogers, 1841), vi. Thorpe paraphrased Newton as part of a lament for how literal interpretation of prophecy is dividing British Christians.

on "New Testament lessons," Augustine was distinguishing between when it was proper to rebuke a fellow Christian in public and when it was proper to do so in private (on Matt. 18:15). Yet this quotation made its way into the new premillennial lexicon and was ultimately found in the introduction of the *Scofield Reference Bible* (1909) as support for "the progressive order of the divine dealings of God with humanity."[8] Later commentators admitted the inappropriate application, but the quotation was already fixed as proof of Augustine's dispensational sympathies.[9]

All of this historical jockeying played a key role in harmonizing the novel parts of new premillennialism with tradition. Moreover, new premillennialists showed a predilection for Higher Life piety, an embrace of interdenominational activism, and sympathy for revivalism, popular religion, and grassroots institution building. These new premillennial commitments flowed from the growing American internalization of the message of Brethren popularizers in the late nineteenth century even as new premillennialists themselves claimed roots that went much deeper into the past.

Frederick Grant and the Structure of Scripture

Supplying a theory of the structure and organization of the Bible was one of the most significant Brethren contributions to new premillennialism, and a lasting influence on dispensationalism in the twentieth century. Brethren influence among new premillennialists was deeply felt in just this area: in the numerological and structural analysis of Scripture. For Brethren writers, and especially for Frederick W. Grant, the most important North American Brethren in the late nineteenth century, numbers also revealed the dispensational structure of history and the divinely ordained dual purposes of Israel and the church. Grant's contribution to new premillennial thinking was by offering a highly deductive framework for the Bible's structure within which later new premillennialists undertook inductive theological reasoning.

The "numerical structure of Scripture" was first made visible to Grant in his study of the Psalms. It occurred to Grant, laboring in New Jersey on behalf of Exclusive Brethren sometime in the 1860s, that the five sections of the book

---

8. Introduction to *Scofield Reference Bible* (Oxford: Oxford University Press, 1909), front matter.

9. See, for example, Arnold D. Ehlert, *A Bibliography of Dispensationalism* (Grand Rapids: Baker, 1965), 27. Ehlert admits the misapplication but seeks other grounds on which to define Augustine as a dispensationalist.

of Psalms imitated the five books of the Pentateuch and were structured for narrative and thematic coherence, from the first section illustrating God as the source of all blessing (paralleling the book of Genesis) to the final psalms illustrating the "moral conclusion" of God and humanity united (paralleling Deuteronomy). The outlines of this structure were already being promoted by Lutheran premillennialist and Old Testament scholar Franz Delitzsch, but Grant's belief in the divine inspiration of biblical structure drove him to probe the possibility more thoroughly than any other theologian at the time. He soon concluded that "not only a few opening psalms, but the books in every part corresponded, book with book," in these "two pentateuchs"—that is, the five books of Moses and the book of Psalms, the "Pentateuch of David."[10]

Grant's conclusion on the structure of the Psalms was only the beginning of his thinking. Awareness of parallel structure led him to investigate specific psalms, especially Psalm 119, the longest in the Hebrew Bible, divided into twenty-two sections, each under the heading of one of the twenty-two letters of the Hebrew alphabet. "Why, then, this strange peculiarity?" he asked, especially if, as higher criticism scholarship increasingly assumed, the Psalms was organized by human, not divine, will. "But if this be of God, and the Spirit of God has written an acrostic, can we afford to pass it lightly by? Is there not— must there not be—meaning in the very form?" The acrostic structure of the psalm, nested within the narrative structure of the book of Psalms, compelled him to go "beyond the book of Psalms itself." In every corner of Scripture, in every method of numerical and patterned organization in the sixty-six books of the Bible, potential meaning was hidden. "I began to see that there was a methodical structure throughout, and that this had to do with the meaning that was there."[11]

This was the inciting insight of Grant's magnum opus, the seven-volume *Numerical Bible*, with the helpful subtitle *Being a Revised Translation of the Holy Scriptures with Expository Notes Arranged, Divided, and Briefly Characterized according to the Principles of Their Numerical Structure*. First published in 1882, extending to a fourth edition that completed its print run in 1904 (two years after Grant's death), the *Numerical Bible* included cross-references, Grant's own section headings, and extended annotations at the bottom of the page. To further his thesis, Grant dropped traditional verse numbers in favor of his own system that divided books into narrative divisions, subdivi-

---

10. Frederick W. Grant, *The Numerical Structure of Scripture* (New York: Loizeaux Brothers, 1887), 8–10.

11. Grant, *Numerical Structure of Scripture*, 11.

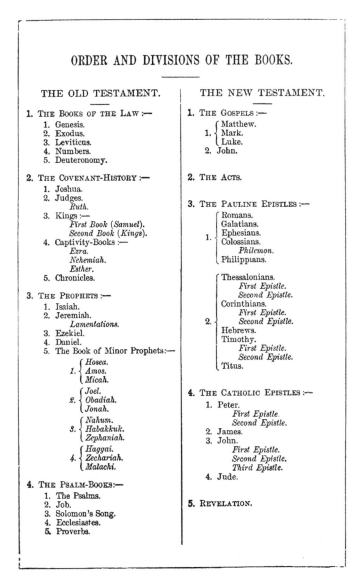

ORDER AND DIVISIONS OF THE BOOKS.

THE OLD TESTAMENT.

1. THE BOOKS OF THE LAW :—
    1. Genesis.
    2. Exodus.
    3. Leviticus.
    4. Numbers.
    5. Deuteronomy.

2. THE COVENANT-HISTORY :—
    1. Joshua.
    2. Judges.
       Ruth.
    3. Kings :—
       First Book (Samuel).
       Second Book (Kings).
    4. Captivity-Books :—
       Ezra.
       Nehemiah.
       Esther.
    5. Chronicles.

3. THE PROPHETS :—
    1. Isaiah.
    2. Jeremiah.
       Lamentations.
    3. Ezekiel.
    4. Daniel.
    5. The Book of Minor Prophets:—
       1. { *Hosea. Amos. Micah.*
       2. { *Joel. Obadiah. Jonah.*
       3. { *Nahum. Habakkuk. Zephaniah.*
       4. { *Haggai. Zechariah. Malachi.*

4. THE PSALM-BOOKS:—
    1. The Psalms.
    2. Job.
    3. Solomon's Song.
    4. Ecclesiastes.
    5. Proverbs.

THE NEW TESTAMENT.

1. THE GOSPELS :—
    1. { Matthew. Mark. Luke.
    2. John.

2. THE ACTS.

3. THE PAULINE EPISTLES :—
    1. { Romans. Galatians. Ephesians. Colossians. *Philemon.* Philippians.
    2. { Thessalonians. *First Epistle. Second Epistle.* Corinthians. *First Epistle. Second Epistle.* Hebrews. Timothy. *First Epistle. Second Epistle.* Titus.

4. THE CATHOLIC EPISTLES :—
    1. Peter.
       First Epistle. Second Epistle.
    2. James.
    3. John.
       First Epistle. Second Epistle. Third Epistle.
    4. Jude.

5. REVELATION.

Figure 7. Grant's *Numerical Bible* (1903) table of contents. Frederick W. Grant divided his *Numerical Bible* into five narrative units spanning the Old and New Testaments that mirrored the structure of the Pentateuch. "The dispensational types seem to be scattered through these books," he explained of the original Pentateuch, "coming out here and there into unmistakable prominence, and then disappearing, always linked with, and apparently dependent upon, the individual ones, which seem to extend throughout each book and the whole series of books, and to be the thread upon which all else is strung." A plain literal hermeneutic this was not.

sions, and sub-subdivisions, so that, for example, the story of Joseph began not in Genesis 37 but in Genesis 2.7.1.[12] These divisions emphasized that, like a fractal, the pentateuchal structure held the same shape at the micro as well as the macro level. Grant's willingness to rearrange the order of books and reassign textual divisions was more evidence that a "plain" reading was more complicated than a flat literal or commonsense interpretation of the text. In any case, the *Numerical Bible* became an indispensable reference for new premillennialists until the introduction of the *Scofield Reference Bible*, which relied heavily on Grant's notes, in 1909.

Grant and his followers believed they could obtain insight into God's intentions through the study of structure and numbers. In an appendix to the volume on the Psalms, Grant summarized "the numerical symbolism of scripture." Each number contained a set of fixed signifiers—one being a number of "soleness," "unity," and "primacy," while two signified "difference," "relation," and "division." The math got complicated with the introduction of addition, subtraction, multiplication, and division. The number four "divides thus in two ways; either as 3+1, the number of manifestation and that of divine sovereignty (and this is the good sense, when the creature reveals the divine hand that is over it); or else by true division, 2x2, which seems to be invariably significant of evil." Moreover, these "lower" (single-digit) numbers also "entered into" the significance of "higher" numbers, so that ten was better understood as 5x2 and forty as 4x(5x2). Grant realized that this all meant very little if there was not "a Mind behind it, which has arranged these marvellous harmonies." He was at pains to bring the reader back from the edge of the numerological rabbit hole and reiterated that "every division, subdivision, section, verse, must more or less contribute" to the meaning of the whole. "The numerical harmony must be the key to a spiritual harmony which emphasizes everywhere the distinctive features of each part in such a way as to combine them into an intelligible and intelligent whole."[13]

Grant's Bible annotations included much more than considerations of numbers—he was interested in structures of all types. His extensive notes provided a full-fledged Brethren theology, exhibiting deep engagement with Brethren writings, typological analysis, and the dualistic understanding of Israel and the church. Pharaoh's dreams in Genesis 41, which Joseph interprets as seven years

12. See Frederick Grant, *Numerical Bible*, vol. 1, *The Pentateuch*, 4th ed. (New York: Loizeaux Brothers, 1903), 120.

13. Frederick W. Grant, "Appendix II: A Study of the Numerical Symbolism of Scripture," in *Numerical Bible*, vol. 3, *The Psalms*, 4th ed. (New York: Loizeaux Brothers, 1897), 1–30.

of plenty before seven years of famine, gave Grant an opening for a lengthy digression on the "plenteous years" of the current dispensation and "the time of famine which is nevertheless not far off." Joseph himself was a sort of supertype, "the Christ-life developed in full 'image.'" His ascension to power in Egypt and his marriage to an outsider typified Christ and the gentile church. Joseph's Egyptian name, Zaphnath-panneah, meant "Revealer of Secrets," according to Grant—an obvious link to the New Testament references in Matthew and Ephesians of the "mysteries of the kingdom" and "the mystery of His will." The entire narrative arc of Joseph was the drama of Christ and Israel in miniature: Joseph "is Christ as we know Him, once rejected and suffering, now exalted"; Benjamin, Joseph's younger brother, is Christ as suffering servant; the other ten brothers are the people of Israel, who reject the former and abandon the latter before their hearts, represented by Judah, "are stirred, and in [their] agony for Benjamin, [they are] met and overwhelmed by the revelation of Joseph"—a type of the future recognition by the Jewish people that Jesus is their Messiah. Every narrative beat held structural significance beyond the scope of Genesis.[14]

Grant regarded this intricate numerical and typological structure of the Bible as not only generative of new insights but also an exercise in interpretive control. The connectivity, unity, and wholeness that his analysis afforded the Bible put "a wholesome restraint upon the imagination in the things of God, and assure[d] to our hearts the full inspiration of His entire Word."[15] This optimistic view was harder to maintain in practice, and Grant's own project was plenty creative itself.

Grant's insights into the Bible's structure contributed to his break with the Exclusive Brethren. Darby, who would die in 1882 in the middle of a transatlantic exchange of tracts on the issue, maintained a distinction between a person being "quickened," or recognizing one's sinful nature, and being "sealed by the Spirit," or actually entering into the state of being a Christian. Darby narrated his own spiritual journey as a long sequence of first being "quickened" and then "sealed"—and he anticipated that many people (especially nominal Christians) existed in the middle. Grant, alternately, took on a view far more amenable (and popular) in the American context, that there was "practically no middle class" of Christians "that have not yet received [the Holy Spirit]."

The breakdown in relations between Grant and Darby on this seemingly minor theological issue resulted in the "Montreal Division" in 1883 and the cre-

14. Grant, *The Pentateuch*, 112–20.
15. Grant, *Numeral Structure of Scripture*, 23.

ation of the "Grant party" in the already deeply fractured Brethren movement. Beyond the jockeying of the Grant and Darby parties for influence, the break revealed how types and structures informed such debates. For Grant, a key type to understand an individual's salvation journey was Israel's deliverance from Egypt. The blood atonement of the Passover story, Grant insisted, saved the people of Israel: "They are taken out of Egypt, type of the fleshly state, through the sea of death, its limit, and outside of the territory of Pharaoh, the sin that reigns there." Applying this type to the New Testament passage in Romans 7 and 8, one of Paul's classic descriptions of conversion, Grant could clarify the simultaneity of being made aware of one's sinful nature and being born again. Alternately, the Darby faction deployed a different type, that of Israel crossing over the Red Sea and needing to look upon the bronze serpent, a type of Christ, to receive life. This episode, as one of Darby's allies wrote in response to Grant, comes after the Passover and "at the very end of the wilderness journey. It is the lesson over again of Rom. vii., viii."[16]

This particular issue of the meaning of being "born again" would have a unique career in the history of dispensationalism. Grant's view, which was the assumption of virtually every popular revivalist and gospel tract writer in the late nineteenth century, was taken up with special verve by later dispensationalists, who would amplify its insights into a "free grace" tradition that further simplified the meaning of being "born again." The free grace tradition was widely popular in American religious culture but was only taught in a systematized form in later dispensational seminaries.

In this and many other issues, the *Numerical Bible* set patterns in biblical interpretation that would be used for generations by the new premillennial tradition then in ascendance. As Grant's testimony makes clear, it was hard for readers to unsee the deeper structures of the Bible once they were pointed out.

Joseph A. Seiss and Numerological Premillennialism

Grant's numerology and typology were tame in comparison with that of some of his contemporaries who mixed the influences of Brethren theology and commonsense induction. The resulting theological insights pushed in often radical (and contradictory) directions and showed a destabilizing tendency rather than Grant's hoped-for "wholesome restraint." Interpreters often

16. Quoted in Ronald V. Huggins, "Romans 7, Conversion, and Sanctification from Arminius to Ironside (1591–1928)" (PhD diss., University of Toronto, 2015), 386, 395–98.

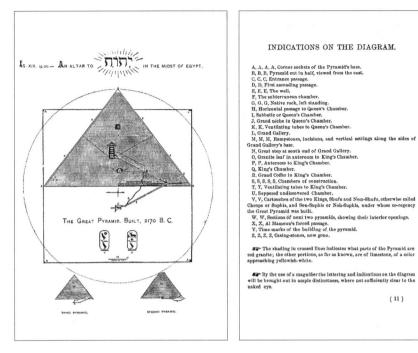

Figure 8. Seiss's pyramidology. Joseph Seiss's theory of the Great Pyramid rested on measuring the surfaces and distances of the structure in metric inches and equating those inches to years. For example, the Grand Gallery (corresponding to "L" in the diagram) symbolized "the Christian era—the grandest section in all the scrolls of human history. It begins at the inch which marks the Saviour's birth. Thirty-three inches from that beginning bring us to the startling symbol of death, burial, descent into hell, and resurrection from the dead." The "startling symbol" was a well that originally had a stone covering that, in subsequent centuries, had broken. For Seiss, the Great Pyramid, like the Bible, contained an entire system of prophetic truth that gestured to the premillennial second coming.

treated premillennial numerology as an entryway into hidden truths that could reshape Christian theology to its very foundations.

The innovative potential of numerological analysis was shown by Joseph A. Seiss in the 1870s, when he was at the peak of his influence as a theologian. The Lutheran premillennialist was, to put it simply, transfixed with numerical patterns. His focus lingered on the pseudoscience of pyramidology, a logical site for numerological study of the mind of God. Seiss was convinced of the worth of a deeper knowledge of the pyramids, especially the Great Pyramid of Giza, as a "sort of key to the universe—a symbol of the profoundest truths of science, of religion, and of all the past and future history of man." Led to this conclusion by a rash of technical writings on the pyramids from Great Britain and France—"the researches and studies of mathematicians, astronomers, Egyptologists, and divines"—Seiss saw the same inner logics of numbers in the Bible at work in the Great Pyramid, the "miracle in stone."[17]

Legends of the Great Pyramid's origins and deeper spiritual significance existed for millennia, but Seiss was convinced that a "modern scientific theory," based on precise spatial measurements and new archaeological discoveries, would unearth new truths. The English lawyer John Taylor floated the theory in 1859 that the true builders of the pyramid were the Israelites. Seiss gravitated toward an even more unorthodox theory, to wit, that the chief builder was the biblical character Job; he pointed to Job 38:1–7, which uses architectural language to describe "the foundations of the earth." This supposition alone alienated many of Seiss's Christian colleagues, but he was convinced. He summarized that it was not the Egyptians but "men of quite another faith and branch of the human family" who "induced and superintended the erection of that mighty structure." God's purpose in commissioning this structure fit into Seiss's premillennial understanding of world history. The Great Pyramid stood "as a memorial for long after times, to serve as a witness of inspiration, and of the truth and purposes of God, over against the falsities and corruptions of a degenerate and ever degenerating world."[18]

Seiss's analysis of this theory stretched for hundreds of pages, connecting every measurement of the Great Pyramid to biblical events and types. "The Scriptural signs of the end have appeared," he assured his readers. "Every method of computation points to the solemn conclusion that we are now on the margin of the end of this age and dispensation." Never able to shed entirely his old premillennial roots, he speculated about specific dates: "Measuring off one thousand eight hundred and seventy-seven inches from the beginning of the Grand Gallery for the one thousand eight hundred and seventy-seven years since the birth of Christ, there remain but a few inches more to bring us to its end," he wrote in 1877.[19] This was a double confirmation of the premillennialist hermeneutic: there were now two revelations—the Bible and the Great Pyramid—which confirmed each other.

A later premillennialist called Seiss's *Miracle in Stone* "the most unfortunate book he ever wrote," and most new premillennialists found pyramidology a

---

17. Joseph A. Seiss, *A Miracle in Stone; or, The Great Pyramid of Egypt* (Philadelphia: Porter & Coates, 1877), 3.

18. Seiss, *A Miracle in Stone*, 32–33.

19. Seiss, *A Miracle in Stone*, 152.

bad application of their developing set of hermeneutical tools.[20] Novelties were still expected to conform to the constructed history of premillennial tradition dating to the church fathers. Yet the unstable grounding of new premillennial theology, as well as the decentralized structure of evangelicalism and the diffuse adoption of new premillennialism, offered few external restraints to interpretation. The new premillennial tradition was more recently constructed and more potentially radical than many new premillennialists wanted to admit.

The tradition's instability extended beyond the outer limits of socially acceptable Protestant belief and practices. Charles Taze Russell, founder of the Watch Tower Society, admired Seiss and cited him as one of his few influences. To many outsiders, Russell appeared to be yet another premillennial prophet. Russell rejected all confessional statements, but, like Seiss, he found in the Great Pyramid "the Plan of the Ages."[21] On its surface, Russell's analysis followed Seiss, yet as Russell weaved pyramidology into his own doctrines and those of the developing Millennial Dawn movement (later Jehovah's Witnesses), including that Christ already returned in secret in 1874, the typologies and numbers accommodated his expectations rather than Seiss's. Subtracting the length between a broken well covering in the pyramid and the entrance passage (1,542 years-inches) from the length between the entrance passage and "the Pit" (3,457 years-inches), which represented "the great trouble and destruction with which this age is to close," one came up with the answer 1915. "Thus the Pyramid witnesses that the close of [the year] 1914 will be the beginning of the time of trouble such as was not since there was a nation—no, nor ever shall be afterward," Russell prophesied. "And thus it will be noted that this 'Witness' fully corroborates the Bible testimony on this subject."[22] Reading the measurements of the pyramid confirmed the practice of date setting for Russell, while this was the very practice that Seiss rejected in his own premillennialism.

In the new premillennialist community developing in the late nineteenth century, numerology represented a valuable tool when used within certain limited parameters. While pyramidology fell out of favor, and Grant's *Numerical Bible* was surpassed by later annotated Bibles (especially the *Scofield Reference Bible*, which bore his influences), the emphasis on structure provided inductive Americans with dynamic directions of interpretation that made it

20. Wilbur M. Smith, *Egypt and Israel Coming Together?* (Grand Rapids: Baker, 1957), 148.

21. Charles Taze Russell, *Studies in the Scriptures*, vol. 3, *Thy Kingdom Come* (Brooklyn, NY: Peoples Pulpit Association, 1917), 328, http://www.pastor-russell.com/volumes/V3/vo3s10.php.

22. Russell, *Thy Kingdom Come*, 342.

far livelier than a simple "plain" reading of Scripture. Structure and numerology remained integral to new premillennialists as they began to develop their own tradition in America—indebted to Brethren but in pursuit of a different project for different ends.

Meaning Making

The intricate ordering of the biblical narrative and the role of numbers extended much deeper than apocalypticism or speculation about end times. In a pattern that mirrored the border-state appropriations of Brethren teachings and the embrace of dualistic and numerical structures of the Bible, new premillennialists also used their theological insights to make sense of the regular rhythms of life and death.

A funeral sermon in 1890, held in Dallas, Texas, is a case in point. The new premillennial preacher spoke on 2 Corinthians 5:8: "We are confident, I say, and willing rather to be absent from the body and at home with the Lord." These twenty words, he declared, "seem to me to express more fully than any others of equal brevity the whole Christian doctrine of death." They neatly juxtaposed earthly mortality ("absent from the body") with heavenly reward ("at home with the Lord"), yet there was at least one bridge laid across the gap. Death was no undiscovered country. "Voices have spoken to whom that country is as familiar as the roads and fields about the old farm are familiar," the preacher pondered. "The 'frontier' exists only in our crass, material, five senses, and suffers violence every day—the benign violence of angels, the sinister violence of demons."

Death was, in the new premillennialism of 1890, a type of the future snatching-up of heavenly citizens from the earth. Previews of the rapture happened hundreds—thousands—of times every day, as the Lord gathered to himself his followers absent in body but now at home. The preacher delighted in the sudden translation to heaven of "a beggar, covered with sores" who "dies at a rich man's gates," a reference to the parable of the rich man and Lazarus the beggar in Luke 19. The story of the beggar inhabited the same typological role as the rapture. "One instant a despised beggar with only the dogs to pity him," the preacher continued, "the next, erect, regnant, with the splendid angels his willing servitors! And then the word comes falling down, down from highest heaven like clearest, sweetest music: 'Lazarus is comforted.'"

Here the structure of the Bible supplied the preacher with resonate insights to minister in a time of grief. Certain texts (2 Cor. 5; Luke 19) and certain typologies (dualism and rapture) were interwoven into the most formidable and regularly confronted challenges of death and grief.

In the years following the Civil War and Reconstruction, themes of death and reconciliation were on the hearts of white evangelicals across the country. The preacher of the 1890 sermon was a forty-seven-year-old pastor of First Congregational Church in Dallas named Cyrus I. Scofield. A native of Michigan and an ex-Confederate soldier, Scofield converted to Christianity in the late 1870s under the influence of James H. Brookes in St. Louis. The church he founded in Dallas started with more northern transplants than southern natives, when the cause of white sectional reconciliation was smoldering. Scofield's personal life, and his emerging ministry, were each bound to the cause of sectional and theological reconciliation, when not in name, then in practice. And Scofield was also bound to the greatest reconciler of the age, Dwight L. Moody.

Some people say, "I believe Christ will come on the other side of the millennium." Where do you get it? I can't find it. The Word of God nowhere tells me to watch and wait for the coming of the millennium, but for the coming of the Lord. . . .We are not to wait for the great white throne of judgment, but the glorified Church is set on the throne with Christ, and to help to judge the world.

Dwight L. Moody, "Our Lord's Return" (1877)

Based in Chicago beginning in 1856, Moody was the foremost revivalist of the late nineteenth century. His premillennialism helped to popularize some of the key points as taught by Brethren and early American converts, including the imminent rapture and the heavenly nature of the church.

5

Revival

Through the ministries and revivals of Dwight L. Moody, the most famous post–Civil War evangelist in the English-speaking world, a distilled version of new premillennialism washed over hundreds of thousands of Americans in the later decades of the nineteenth century. Moody was no theologian, and he was uninterested in doctrinal specifics. He spoke of the second coming with less flourish than Brethren writers and with more laxity than the exacting sermons of James Brookes. His passion was not for the second coming as such, but for how belief in it could spark new religious practices—of conversion and personal piety, of reconciliation and cooperation, of ministry to the poor, and of global evangelization.

These goals galvanized evangelicals, who organized under the growing Moody movement—the vast network of Christian workers and institutions influenced by Moody's revivals. Moody was equally passionate about a more immediate problem in the wake of the Civil War: sectional reconciliation. The revivalist faith he fashioned in the 1870s, and which spread throughout his sprawling network, carried with it a powerful call to address the social tensions of the Reconstruction era by suppressing disruptive efforts for racial justice. Rather, it was reconciliation, in Moody's eyes, that better advanced the goal of Christian unity and global evangelization. New premillennialism, forged in a radical dissenter Brethren community, then appropriated by border-state evangelicals, found its most successful adaptation in this Northern, reconciliationist revivalism of the 1870s. The theology became a critical tool to encourage reconciliation—especially across sections and denominations—in the service of fulfilling the Great Commission to "make disciples of all nations" (Matt. 28:19). Moody and the network he built moved new premillennialism to the center of Northern evangelical culture, which it would continue to occupy for the next century.

Dwight Moody, a Premillennial Revivalist

Born in 1837 in Northfield, Massachusetts, Moody spent his childhood in and around the Boston area. As a sixteen-year-old, he sold shoes before heading west in 1856 on the hopes of better opportunities. A middling student who later admitted he "knew nothing of the Bible" when he attended his first church service, Moody could hardly have differed more from the studious personalities of Brookes and Seiss. "I was not acquainted with the Word," Moody reflected about his early faith. "I do not think there were a dozen passages in the whole Word of God that I had committed to memory, and that I could quote."[1] This lack of theological training meant that his adoption of premillennialism, and one with Darbyite peculiarities, was always inconsistent. Nevertheless, it proved to be a potent mix when Moody preached on the revival circuit.

Moving to Chicago was a propitious choice for Moody, who immediately found his calling as an organizer. A wildly successful day school for poor children became the basis for the Illinois Street Church, established just north of the Chicago River, and his first pastorate. The church became the epicenter of Moody's ministry. He had begun working with the YMCA in Chicago during the 1858 Businessmen's Revival and eventually became the Chicago organization's president. By 1860 Moody had quit the shoe business, which had made him a small fortune, and dedicated himself to full-time ministry.

With the outbreak of war in 1861, Moody became "a staunch Union man," according to one biographer.[2] At least once before the war he protested the Fugitive Slave Act of 1850, which compelled Northerners to help slave catchers apprehend runaway slaves. In Illinois, Moody joined the new Civil War Christian Commission as a chaplain and dedicated most of his time to Camp Douglas, one of the largest Union prisoner of war camps. Notorious for its poor conditions and high death rate of Confederate prisoners, the camp was both a mission field and a field of death. The horrible setting undoubtedly shaped Moody's concern after the war for reconciliation between North and South.

In the aftermath of the war, Moody idealized sectional reconciliation. During Reconstruction he minimized the political issues and moral stakes of the conflict and instead called for overcoming division through forgiveness and

---

1. Dwight Moody, *New Sermons, Addresses, and Prayers* (New York: Goodspeed, 1877), 634.

2. W. H. Daniels, *D. L. Moody and His Work* (Hartford, CT: American Publishing Co., 1875), 172.

common religion. The reconciliation he spearheaded after the war cannot be separated from his repudiation of the radical goals of social reform proposed by victorious Republicans. For Moody, a Unionist as much as Brookes was a neutralist, this historical moment made interdenominational networking on the basis of separating churchly from political issues—race and Reconstruction in particular—deeply appealing.

Moody and Brookes may have crossed paths as early as 1865, when Moody was invited, on the basis of his outsider status, to moderate the State Christian Convention of Missouri, hosted in St. Louis by interdenominational clergy with divided wartime loyalties. It is unclear if Brookes attended, though as a prominent pastor of a city with a history of neutrality, he had good cause to be there. Moody "seemed to hold the Union men by one hand and the ex-Confederates by the other, thus constituting himself a tie of Christian brotherhood between them," one biographer reported.[3] Crucially, Moody intervened to stop the constant arguments and recriminations from getting too heated; he moved the assembly to prayers or hymns at a moment's notice. The goal of the convention, at least for Moody, was precisely to transcend the issues of the Civil War, including secession, slavery, and the fate of freed African Americans. His highest ideal was "Christian brotherhood," which he preached fervently everywhere he went.

Moody's approach to reconciliation was connected to his premillennial eschatology, which regarded sectional and denominational differences as temporary barriers to the work of Christian brotherhood. Moody's son dated his premillennialism to 1867, coinciding with the year he first visited the British Isles.[4] Moody's son-in-law claimed that Moody first heard "dispensational truth" in 1872, the year he met with Darby in Chicago.[5] In either case, his proximity to the Brethren was close. True to his aversion to denominational divisions, Moody befriended and praised both Open and Exclusive Brethren, from Henry Moorhouse, whose itinerant career took off after speaking in Moody's Chicago pulpit in 1870, to C. H. Mackintosh, one of Darby's foremost American popularizers, whose work Moody was so indebted to that he said he would rather part with his entire library, excepting the Bible, than with Mackintosh's collected works.[6] By the time Moody had become a transatlantic

3. Daniels, *D. L. Moody*, 171–72.
4. W. R. Moody, *D. L. Moody* (New York: Macmillan, 1930), 101–4.
5. Arthur Percy Fitt, *Moody Still Lives: Words and Pictures of D. L. Moody* (Chicago: Revell, 1936), 55.
6. Dwight Moody, *Heaven; Where It Is; Its Inhabitants; and How to Get There* (Chicago: Revell, 1880), back-matter advertisements.

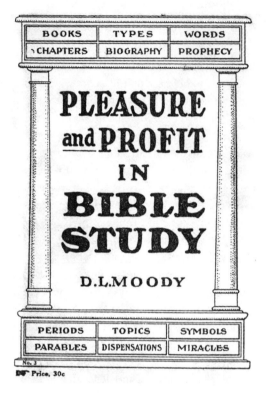

Figure 9. The cover of Moody's *Pleasure and Profit in Bible Study.* As illustrated by the cover to this 1895 collection, "types," "symbols," "prophecy," and "dispensations" were important building blocks for a larger edifice of biblical truth.

phenomenon, he had already taught new premillennial doctrines such as the imminent rapture in his sermons even as he criticized the Brethren as fractious. Eclectic and unsystematic, Moody entertained influences much broader than the Brethren, but his haphazard inclusion of their teachings meant that new premillennial concepts circulated widely.

Moody adopted Brethren eschatology in the same years he embraced a new language of sanctification, the Higher Life movement, which was also gaining popularity in the United States. Though these two teachings stood in tension for many Christians, in Moody they combined into a potent message of revival. The Higher Life teachings reached Moody through the Keswick Convention, which he visited while in Great Britain; they were indebted to William Edwin Boardman's *The Higher Christian Life* (1858), which proposed to merge Lutheran, Calvinist, and Wesleyan holiness theology into one grand

"Harmony in the Great Object" of full sanctification. Boardman's book was so influential that its title became the flagship name of the new movement.[7] The Keswick Convention, an annual gathering that attracted a wide array of Protestant leaders, gained influence throughout the Anglo-American world. Moody adopted the Higher Life movement in the same way he did premillennialism—haphazardly and impressionistically—but his bigger contribution was to provide its teachers a platform in Chicago and in his hometown of Northfield to spread the word.

A great uptick of religiosity in America ushered in by Moody's massive 1875–1877 revival circuit transformed the spread of Brethren teachings in two ways. The first was that Moody popularized premillennialism to the masses, integrating its doctrines into his gospel message. Far from the careful and complex theology of Darby, Moody's premillennialism was simple: Jesus could come at any moment, and you don't want to be left behind. The second coming was assumed in his sermons, and dispensational time was referenced but rarely explained. Moody conveyed these teachings to listeners uninitiated in eschatological schemes, which is to say, most Americans.

The second way Moody fused new premillennialism to his revival messages was by merging premillennialism and Higher Life teachings to unite Northern and Southern whites, sacralizing the reunited republic in the language of grace, forgiveness, and reconciliation. Moody's goal was to turn the country's Christians away from the past and the world, and toward the future and heaven. In practical terms, Moody encouraged Americans to abandon political analyses of the country, which in the mid-1870s meant dropping the polarizing issues of blame for the war and Black civil rights. He routinely described the war in general terms of lament, absolving blame and citing just one count of the deaths that included Union and Confederate soldiers. "The nation was deluged in blood, and half a million men laid down their lives. . . . It was a great calamity, and came right home to the heart of the nation," he preached in 1877.[8] In a typological application of Noah's flood, he wrote that before the Civil War "there was the great revival, in which there was a tide of salvation that swept over this land and brought many people into the Church of God. Right after that came our terrible war, and we were baptized in blood. Now we are again living in a glorious day. . . . Is not to-day a day of mercy and grace?"[9]

7. William Edwin Boardman, *Higher Christian Life* (Boston: Hoyt, 1858), 63.
8. Dwight Moody, *New Sermons*, 240.
9. Quoted in Edward J. Blum, *Reforging the White Republic: Race, Religion, and American Nationalism, 1865–1898* (Baton Rouge: Louisiana State University Press, 2005), 132.

While urging a turn away from politics and toward "mercy and grace," Moody's passion for reconciliation held inescapable political consequences. He broke down barriers between white Christians—between denominations and confessions, between sections, between classes—which came at the expense of racial reform and integration. Judged by his sermons, the Black church lay outside Moody's vision of reconciliation. As the most consequential religious leader in late nineteenth-century America, Moody played an outsized role in depoliticizing the Civil War and bridging divides between North and South during Reconstruction. But this program of forgiveness was narrow and narrowly conceived, premised on bracketing existing racism and discrimination, ignoring the rise of racial segregation regimes in the South, and rekindling fellowship and brotherhood with secessionists and advocates of Jim Crow. This deal was one that premillennialists not only tolerated but, in later decades, embraced. The benefits to shared missionary efforts and Christian unity were too important to pass up.

These two implications of Moody's ministry—the popularization and fusion of new premillennialism with revivalism—could hardly be separated. They worked together to form a potent and wildly successful message. Moody's ministry spearheaded an interdenominational evangelical ethos shot through with the influences of new premillennialism.

Sectional Reconciliation and Interdenominationalism

Moody's revival circuits were powerful shapers of American culture not only for their message of personal salvation and sectional reconciliation but also for their vision of Christianity that transcended denominations. This created a wider base for the reception of the new premillennial teachings. Interdenominational cooperation, which Moody championed in all his ministries, rejected both Brethren sectarianism and the ecumenical movement of the post–Civil War era. His brand of revivalism pursued large-scale cooperation, which his followers would expand into a movement of institutions, schools, and churches that became the primary vehicles for the promotion of new premillennialism and, eventually, dispensationalism.

While Moody promoted sectional reconciliation primarily in his revival sermons, interdenominational energy was most visible in the accompanying music. For most of his career, Moody partnered with musician Ira D. Sankey, whose lyrics and melodies shaped the spirituality of generations of Americans. Born in 1840 and raised a Methodist, Sankey served the Union in the war and lived in the small town of New Castle, on the western edge of Pennsylvania, until moving to Chicago as an adult. Sankey's voice was unique—one admirer described it as "a marvel of sweetness, flexibility, and strength"—but his legacy as a composer and editor of hymns loomed even larger.[10] His hymnal, *Sacred Songs and Solos*, first published in 1873, popularized an American gospel canon that combined the works of eighteenth-century English divines such as Isaac Watts (Congregationalist) and William Cowper (Anglican) with the popular hymns of Fanny Crosby (Methodist), Elizabeth Clephane (Scottish Presbyterian), and Robert Lowry and W. H. Doane (both Baptist). Sankey blurred in song the denominational divisions that Moody transcended in his revival sermons.

Wartime experience introduced Moody and Sankey to the possibilities of working across denominational lines. After the war, the drive to cooperate was especially powerful among urban revivalists and preachers, who shared common religious sensibilities (including revivalism and gospel music), a common experience of war, and a common desire to build new organizations that bypassed old bureaucratic structures and divisions for the sake of global evangelization. By 1870, Moody and Sankey were at the head of a sprawling movement of interdenominational evangelicalism that included dozens of organizations and thousands of pastors and churches. This network of associates cooperated to organize and expand the causes of evangelization and reconciliation.

With rapid expansion, the most useful points of interdenominational commonality were connections to Moody and Sankey. Their network was a sprawling web of revival and conference circuits, independent mission agencies, urban churches, Bible institutes, social service organizations, publishing houses, and periodicals—many invented in the late nineteenth century to accommodate cooperation. The movement's leaders, beginning with Moody, tended to pastor large, urban congregations, many becoming "institutional churches" that combined preaching, evangelization, education, and poverty relief. These institutional churches were worlds unto themselves, occupying blocks of major downtown areas—in Philadelphia, New York City, and Chicago—with pastors more comfortable asking their denominational overseers for forgiveness than permission. In the nineteenth century, the Moody network remained rooted in the Great Lakes basin and New England, though success attracted a smattering of Southern white pastors, too.

More than a doctrine or creed, interdenominationalism offered its promoters a template for action. James Brookes's periodical *The Truth* proudly declared that it was "entirely free from sectarian control, having for its sole

---

10. Robert Boyd, *The Wonderful Career of Moody and Sankey* (New York: Goodspeed, 1875), 570.

object the glory of God in the salvation of sinners and the comfort of saints, without the slightest regard for denominational peculiarities or preferences."[11] Moody made it a central aim of his ministry to "lay aside all difference, all criticism, all coldness and party feeling."[12] "Talk not of this sect and that sect, of this party and that party," he enjoined his fellow Chicagoans, "but solely and exclusively of the great comprehensive cause of Jesus Christ."[13] Arthur T. Pierson, a newer convert to premillennialism in 1878 and editor of *Missionary Review of the World*, wrote a piece titled "The Exemplification of True Christian Unity" and described the ideal missionary effort as "both unsectarian and undenominational. No lines of division appear between workers, and no 'tribal standards' are unfurled."[14]

As Pierson suggested, interdenominational work was most often in the service of revivalism and global missions. The philanthropist John V. Farwell, one of Moody's patrons in Chicago, described Moody as driven by "the all-absorbing idea of making the world feel the power of Christian union in active work for the masses."[15] Pierson himself, who helped to launch the Student Volunteer Movement in 1886 at Moody's summer conference in Northfield, popularized the goal of "the evangelization of the world in one generation."[16] If sectional and denominational divisions hobbled the work of Christians, this new age of cooperation promised brighter days. And light was needed because the task of evangelization was never more daunting. Writing in 1887, Pierson asked the perennial question: "How are we to bring every soul of this seven hundred and fifty millions of mankind to the knowledge of a crucified Christ?"[17] Interdenominationalists saw their new levels of cooperation as the only viable path.

Besides ties to Moody and Sankey, interdenominationalists emphasized a shared set of religious interests. Though counting prominent Methodists, including Sankey (who later converted to Presbyterianism), Moody's interdenominational network generally drew its leaders from Presbyterian, Baptist,

11. James H. Brookes, *Maranatha; or, The Lord Cometh*, 5th ed. (St. Louis: Edward Bredell, 1878), back page.

12. Quoted in Barbara Dobschuetz, "Fundamentalism and American Urban Culture: Community and Religious Identity in Dwight Moody's Chicago, 1864–1914" (PhD diss., University of Illinois–Chicago, 2002), 182.

13. Dwight Moody, *New Sermons*, 14.

14. Arthur T. Pierson, *Evangelistic Work in Principle and Practice* (New York: Baker & Taylor, 1887), 283.

15. *Christianity Today*, November 23, 1962.

16. Quoted in Dana L. Robert, *Occupy until I Come: A. T. Pierson and the Evangelization of the World* (Grand Rapids: Eerdmans, 2003), 150.

17. Pierson, *Evangelistic Work*, 15.

and Congregationalist ranks. They generally embraced Higher Life theology, which emphasized spiritual discipline and the power of the Holy Spirit to multiply efforts and serve the church. The very nature of the movement de-emphasized church hierarchy. Moody set the tone and others followed: unity of Christians in common cause took precedence over unity of the churches.

New premillennialism was woven into interdenominationalism. Moody and his acolytes did not expect a mass conversion of the world in these days, but they did feel the burden of presenting the gospel to as many humans as possible, in the quickest ways possible. Pierson called for all peoples to receive "the knowledge" of the gospel, not for all humankind to respond to it. As one prophecy conference speaker explained in 1878: "We have failed [at missions] simply because we have been aiming at universal conversion and not at universal evangelization. We have been trying to convert patches and not evangelize the whole."[18] To civilize as well as Christianize—the long-standing order of denominational missions work—was foolhardy and ineffective, based on a triumphalist postmillennial eschatology of an earlier age. Interdenominational efforts, on the other hand, focused solely on presenting the gospel.

Interdenominationalists also distinguished themselves by rejecting the modernist "new theology," which articulated the Reformed tradition in the language of modern science and the ambitions of modern society in the language of Christianity. Responding to biblical higher criticism and new theories of evolution popularized by Charles Darwin's *Origin of Species* (1859), Moody rejected these as distractions from the gospel message. While proponents of the new theology called for "interchurch" unity and focused on ecumenical, denominational partnership as necessary responses to modernity, interdenominationalists preferred to work outside of church hierarchies and dismiss rather than engage new academic findings in science and theology.

For a time, ecumenists and interdenominationalists overlapped, sharing the same webs of social connections, the same expectation of eschatological fulfillment (whether pre- or postmillennial), and the same diagnosis of a great need for Christian work. But eventually the two visions of cooperation would be rivals for the future of American Protestantism. In the 1880s this was the will of very few—certainly not of Moody or Sankey, or Brookes or Joseph Seiss, or the emerging ranks of interdenominational evangelicals who hoped their work would revitalize the denominations rather than rip them apart.

18. William P. Mackay, "The Return of Christ and Foreign Missions," in *Premillennial Essays of the Prophetic Conference Held in the Church of the Holy Trinity, New York City*, ed. Nathaniel West (Chicago: Revell, 1879), 459.

Nevertheless, Moody's brew of new premillennialism, Higher Life teachings, sectional reconciliation, and interdenominational activism carved out a new space in American Christianity. For the Moody movement, the events of the Civil War and Reconstruction shaped how those ideas were received. Had the popularization of Brethren teachings begun a decade earlier, or a decade later—or had Darby wandered the Deep South rather than the Midwest—the career of new premillennialism, and later dispensationalism, may have taken a very different route, or none at all.

Therapeutic Premillennialism: It Is Well with My Soul

Premillennialism infused interdenominational activity and also helped to shape the lives of individuals. The famed hymn writer Horatio Spafford was one example. In the devastating Great Chicago Fire of 1871, Spafford's real estate fortunes burned up, and as a result he leaned ever more heavily on his Christian faith. Two years later he planned to join Moody in his revival tour of the British Isles. But Spafford was too weighed down with work to travel with his wife, Anna, and four daughters, who boarded the SS *Ville du Havre* in New York City to sail to Wales. On the morning of November 22, in the middle of the Atlantic Ocean, the SS *Ville du Havre* collided with a Scottish iron clipper, sinking in twelve minutes and leaving more than two hundred drowned. When Anna arrived in Cardiff, Wales, she telegrammed Horatio, "Saved alone what shall I do."[19] Horatio quickly left to reunite with his wife, sailing by the area where his children died and, as legend has it, penning the lines to his famous hymn:

> When peace like a river attendeth my way
> When sorrows like sea billows roll
> Whatever my lot Thou hast taught me to know
> It is well, it is well with my soul.[20]

Put to music by friend and hymnist Philip P. Bliss, the poem became "It Is Well with My Soul," a staple song of Moody revivals, an anthem of Higher Life faithfulness, and one of the most popular hymns in the world.

The Spaffords—not to mention Bliss and Moody—were new premillennialists, believing in an imminent rapture and waiting for the kingdom to come.

19. Anna Spafford to Horatio Spafford, telegram, December 2, 1873, Library of Congress, https://www.loc.gov/item/mamcol000006.

20. Horatio Spafford, *Waiting for the Morning and Other Poems* (Chicago: Revell, 1878), 44.

"It Is Well with My Soul" first appeared in Horatio's 1878 collection of poems, *Waiting for the Morning*, an extended meditation on his grief and hope for the Lord's return. The original poem included the final verse:

> And, Lord, haste the day when the faith shall be sight
> The clouds be rolled back as a scroll
> The trump shall resound and Thy kingdom shall come!
> "Even so"—it is well with my soul![21]

Back in Chicago, Anna worked alongside Emma Dryer, who oversaw much of Moody's work in the city, as they crafted a premillennial-informed philosophy of education that would lay the foundation for the Moody Bible Institute. The couple's biggest statement, however, came in 1881, after the death of yet another child, this time from scarlet fever. Despondent and destitute, the Spaffords (with their two remaining daughters) sailed to Jerusalem to await the second coming. The American Colony they founded soon became a fixture of the ancient city, though the small commune's millennial fervor dimmed with the death of Horatio in 1888 and was transformed by Anna into a personal fiefdom, which she controlled until she died in 1923.

The Spaffords are one example of how new premillennial ideas worked their way into the lives of urban, Northern, white evangelicals during the period of Reconstruction. The Spaffords became committed premillennialists in the early 1870s, in the same years as James Brookes and Joseph Seiss and, more importantly for them, Dwight Moody. Individually, their circumstances, more heartrending than most, formed a crucible that swung from existential to cosmic crisis, in which the "blessed hope" of the rapture was reason for personal perseverance. The Spaffords may have ultimately chosen an extraordinary way to enact their faith—few premillennialists contemplated moving to Jerusalem—but they acquired those beliefs quite ordinarily for Americans in the late nineteenth century, through the influence of Dwight Moody.

---

21. Horatio Spafford, *Waiting for the Morning*, 45.

The Saviour who loves me and suffered the loss
Of heavenly glory to die on a cross
The Babe of the manger, though born without stain
This Jesus is coming, is coming again

O hearts that are weary, and sinful, and sad
We carry the tidings that make us so glad
We publish the Saviour o'er mountain and plain
The Lord who redeemed us is coming again

James M. Gray,
"Jesus Is Coming, Is Coming" (1905)

Written by the popular preacher and hymnist James M. Gray a year after assuming the presidency of the Moody Bible Institute, these verses elucidated typical summaries of both the gospel and the rationale for global missions among Moody movement activists. The life of Jesus and the second coming were often paired together.

6

The Premillennial Complex

The Moody movement grew outside the structures of denominations, and this fact deeply shaped its development. Untethered from a central controlling authority, the movement possessed no formal hierarchy, no headquarters, no shared institution around which to organize. Rather, it created its own structures emergently—not exactly from scratch but oriented around a novel constellation of cultural, social, and theological markers of identity—a chief one being the new premillennialism preached by Moody himself.

One indicator of the influence of new premillennialism was that the Moody movement's basic activities—revivals, conferences, missions, and publishing—were hardly conducive to long-term institution building. While these could be powerful shapers of religious identity, they were also transient. In 1877 Moody preached that he "felt like working three times as hard," ever since he had come to understand that Christ's return was imminent. Others shared the sentiment, but what work deserved such exertion? "I look on this world as a wrecked vessel," was Moody's answer. "God has given me a life-boat, and said to me, 'Moody, save all you can.'"[1]

The answer Moody offered, and which most of his movement embraced, was the cause of global missions. This ambitious agenda became the organizing principle for Moody, and for new premillennialism, too. Without the binding commitment of global evangelization—the conviction that only through new bonds that transcended historic divisions could the gospel reach all humanity—new premillennialism may have remained a curiosity of Old School Presbyterians and eccentric Lutherans. Instead it became integral to a new

---

1. Dwight Moody, *New Sermons, Addresses, and Prayers* (New York: Goodspeed, 1877), 535.

religious community aimed at global missions that, all together, formed something of a premillennial complex—a set of cooperative and interdependent institutions that perpetuated new premillennialism.

New premillennialism's fortunes could have been more fleeting. The Higher Life teachings, while influencing later holiness movements, suffered something of this fate. But for new premillennialism, precisely the opposite happened: its teachings accrued great weight in the eyes of its adherents and became the subject of intense scrutiny, discourse, and debate. New premillennialism was of such importance that its converts built cultural institutions for its protection and propagation: regular conferences for its exposition, schools for its transmission, missions for its dissemination. Three organizational forms in particular—the Bible conference, the Bible institute, and the independent mission agency—were created in the late nineteenth century by new premillennialists as pipelines for a new generation of Christian laborers equipped and motivated to work "three times as hard" in light of the imminent rapture. This was the start-up phase of the premillennial complex, a movement that would structure the religious life of millions of American Christians for the next century and more.

The Bible Conference

Bible conferences were the lifeblood of the growing Moody movement and the fledgling base of new premillennial belief. In simplest terms, a Bible conference was a regular gathering where biblical exposition focused on core theological themes that united attendees and stirred them to action. Such meetings had a deeper history in premillennialism, dating at least to the prophecy meetings of the 1820s and the formative Albury (1826–1830) and Powerscourt (1831–1836) meetings that helped shape early Brethren thinking. Later in the century, the Keswick Convention, beginning in northern England in 1875, became the font of Higher Life theology. Another annual English gathering, the Mildmay Conferences, promoted premillennial and Higher Life interests in Britain and featured both American and British speakers through the 1870s.

The Moody movement's Bible conferences were linked to this history. By the 1880s, yearly conferences had formed around several themes including premillennialism, global missions, Higher Life living, and Christian education. Moody's own Northfield Bible Conference was the most celebrated, held every summer at Mount Hermon School in Northfield, Massachusetts, beginning in 1882.

The most important Bible conference shaping premillennialism had roots that extended across the Moody movement. In 1868, on the advice of an Irish

Brethren-turned-Baptist, George Needham, a small group met in the publishing office of James Inglis in New York City. In Needham's recounting, the intent of that first "Believers' Meeting for Bible Study" was to combat "the ancient heresy of a sentimental higher life"—Wesleyan perfectionism—which had conditioned Christians toward "boasted sinlessness."[2]

The Niagara Believers' Meeting for Bible Study, or Niagara Bible Conference, transformed from an anti-Wesleyan-perfectionism group into the most consequential Bible conference for new premillennialism. In 1870, the still-private gathering met at James Brookes's church in St. Louis, where it was joined by Charles Campbell, editor of a small premillennial magazine, *Grace and Truth*, and William J. Erdman, a Presbyterian premillennialist who became the conference's longtime secretary. When Inglis fell sick and died in 1873, the meetings stopped until a group of Chicago-based new premillennialists approached Brookes about restarting them. The new meetings reflected Moody's network and were rooted in the same geographic and cultural borders of new premillennialism.

Under Brookes's leadership, gatherings took place annually until 1900. From 1883 to 1897 they convened every summer on the southern shore of Lake Ontario, at the mouth of the Niagara River. Upon assuming control of the gatherings, Brookes opened them to the public and anchored them in extended explorations of premillennial themes. At the 1878 meeting, inside a sanatorium in Clifton Springs, New York, Brookes unveiled fourteen "Articles of Belief" as "the bond of union with those who wish to be connected with the Believers' Meeting for Bible Study."[3] The articles defined the creedal boundaries of the Bible conference—a difficult task for a group of denominationally diverse individuals that met only once a year. But they shared a broadly evangelical theology and were enlivened by Higher Life teachings. Article 10 defined the interdenominational ethos, to "keep the unity of the Spirit in the bond of peace, rising above all sectarian prejudices and denominational bigotry, and loving one another with a pure heart fervently."[4] They were also unflinchingly premillennial. Article 14 described a broad premillennialism without dividing new from old, in the "blessed hope set before us in the Gospel for which we should constantly be looking," which was defined as the "personal and premillennial advent" of the Lord.[5]

2. George C. Needham, "Bible Conferences," *Watchword* 13, no. 3 (March 1891): 60.

3. See reprint of "Articles of Belief," in *Report of the Believers' Meeting for Bible Study Held at Niagara-on-the-Lake, Ontario, July 18–25, 1888* (Toronto: Toronto Willard Tract Depository, 1888), 13–16.

4. "Articles of Belief," 15.

5. "Articles of Belief," 16.

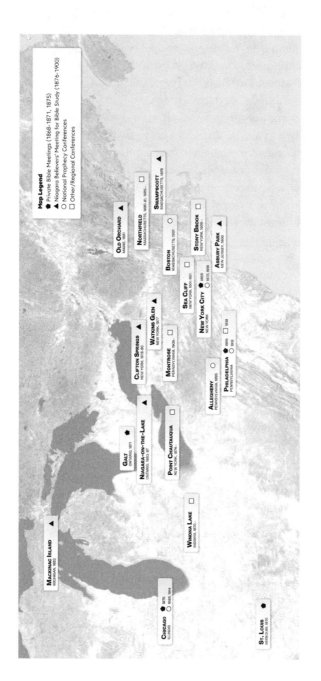

Map Legend
● Private Bible Meetings (1868–1871, 1875)
▲ Niagara Believers' Meeting for Bible Study (1876–1900)
○ National Prophecy Conferences
□ Other/Regional Conferences

MACKINAC ISLAND
MICHIGAN, 1882

GALT
ONTARIO, 1871

NIAGARA-ON-THE-LAKE
ONTARIO, 1883–97

POINT CHAUTAUQUA
NEW YORK, 1874–

WINONA LAKE
INDIANA, 1870–

CHICAGO
ILLINOIS
● 1875
○ 1886, 1914

ST. LOUIS
MISSOURI, 1870

CLIFTON SPRINGS
NEW YORK, 1876–80

WATKINS GLEN
NEW YORK, 1877

MONTROSE
PENNSYLVANIA, 1908–

ALLEGHENY
PENNSYLVANIA, 1895

PHILADELPHIA
PENNSYLVANIA
● 1899
○ 1918
□ 1918

SEA CLIFF
NEW YORK, 1890–1891

NEW YORK CITY
NEW YORK
● 1868
○ 1878, 1899

OLD ORCHARD
MAINE, 1881

NORTHFIELD
MASSACHUSETTS, 1880–85, 1885–

SWAMPSCOTT
MASSACHUSETTS, 1878, 1878

BOSTON
MASSACHUSETTS, 1901

STONY BROOK
NEW YORK, 1909–

ASBURY PARK
NEW JERSEY, 1900

Figure 10. "Niagara Bible Conference and Others, 1868–1920." Bible conferences were the engine of the premillennial complex. While many of these gatherings—including six National Prophecy Conferences between 1878 and 1918—purported to be national in scope, their locations remained bound to the Great Lakes basin and the Northeast. Over time, Bible conferences settled in established retreat areas, with many meeting into the late twentieth century. Credit: Marcus Miers.

The Niagara Bible Conference revealed the outlines of a formative subculture of new premillennialism. Brookes joked to the 1888 attendees that they "know they are not 'popular,' and they do not wish to be. They are fully aware of the fact that they are not in harmony with 'the spirit of the age,' and in this they rejoice."[6] The narrow interests of the conference, which ranged not far beyond articulating Higher Life and premillennial doctrines for the purpose of global missions, set the gatherings apart from denominational meetings concerned with ecclesial matters. The speakers and organizers often became each other's closest friends, lending their gathering the feeling, in George Needham's words, of a "quiet informal family reunion in the home, where all is love and peace."[7]

The regular Niagara attendees came to identify themselves as a new Christian community. The "beautiful spirit of unity" that eluded them in their local churches and denominations could be found at Niagara. Needham enumerated the group's common convictions: "Looking, all of them, for the speedy personal return of the Lord Jesus, makes its members unworldly. Recognizing the blood as the only ground of redemption, makes them distinctly evangelical. Discerning their common standing as sons of God, suppresses all show of denominationalism. And realizing their call out from the world, to walk in Christ in separation, hinders them from following and of the carnal ways of modern conventicles, or resorting to any worldly devices for capturing the masses."[8] The Niagara people would be known by their attributes—unworldly, evangelical, interdenominational.

The 1890 meeting exhibited a growing sense of ecclesiastical significance with the introduction of the sacrament of communion. "We believe that 'the time is short,'" Brookes preached that year before distributing the elements. "We are nearing the harbor after a long and stormy voyage, and can almost hear the voice of the approaching Bridegroom on the shore."[9] The "we" in Brookes's telling were the "elect," the invisible church identified by no denomination or institution but in gatherings like the Niagara Bible Conference. As Elizabeth Needham described the meeting a few years later, "the Niagara company are simply aiming to manifest the primitive, New Testament idea of an ecclesia."[10] By this time the Bible conference had grown to be something of a shadow church existing alongside denominations.

6. "Historical Preface," in *Report*, 10.
7. George C. Needham, "Bible Conferences," 60.
8. Mrs. George C. Needham, "Niagara Bible Conference," *Our Hope* 4 (July 1897): 67.
9. James Brookes, "Communion Address," in *A Week of Blessing, Being a Full Report of the Believers' Meeting for Bible Study Held at Niagara-on-the-Lake (Ontario), July 10 to 17, 1890* (Toronto: Toronto Willard Tract Depository, 1890), 92.
10. Mrs. George C. Needham, "Niagara Bible Conference," 69.

With the momentum from Niagara, new premillennialism began to extend its influence. The first self-styled national prophecy conference was held in late October 1878 at the recently constructed Episcopal Church of the Holy Trinity in Manhattan. More than one hundred pastors joined the official call for a conference to boost "the precious doctrine of Christ's second personal appearing" and to reverse "a sad decline in our times from the clear, vivid, ardent faith of the early church in regard to this doctrine."[11] The conference organizers, headed by Brookes and other Niagara regulars, presented to the public an inclusive premillennial movement featuring old as well as new premillennialists, Reformed and also Wesleyan holiness teachers, American and also British evangelicals—from "the Church of God in all its branches" to "teachers and pastors, expositors and lay workers, evangelists and missionaries." The gathering was most critical of other Christians who shrunk the eschatological hope to one of individual destiny, who regarded "the coming of Christ as equivalent to their own death," or, alternately, who presumed a triumphant "diffusion of Christianity" across the globe that would transform humanity on its own.[12]

The 1878 conference was pitched by its organizers as an outgrowth of the Niagara meetings and a counterpart to recent British gatherings.[13] In 1877, a group of Exclusive Brethren gathered at the Freemasons' Hall in London to discuss *Sixteen Addresses on "The Blessed Hope"* that articulated the dispensational divisions of time and Scripture and an imminent rapture. The previous year a group of theologically diverse premillennialists began a series of Second Advent Conferences at the historic hall at Mildmay Park, just north of London. These meetings included old premillennialists Horatius Bonar (hymnist and editor of the *Quarterly Journal of Prophecy*) and William Freemantle (president of the Prophecy Investigation Society).[14] The theological center of gravity of the American conference more resembled the Freemasons' Hall meeting, but the coalition-building work more resembled the Mildmay meetings. Both were cited by later premillennialists as important signs of growing international strength.[15]

---

11. "Call for the Conference," in *Premillennial Essays of the Prophetic Conference, Held in the Church of the Holy Trinity, New York City*, ed. Nathaniel West (Chicago: Revell, 1879), 11.

12. "Call for the Conference," 11.

13. "Call for the Conference," 12.

14. See *The Coming of the Lord: Sixteen Addresses on "The Blessed Hope"* (London: Hawkins, 1877); *Our God Shall Come: Addresses on the Second Coming of the Lord at Mildmay, February, 1878* (London: Shaw & Co., 1878).

15. William E. Blackstone, *Jesus Is Coming* (Chicago: Revell, 1898), 206.

The publicity success of the 1878 conference was clear from the start. New York's *Tribune Extra* republished a selection of the addresses, selling as many as fifty thousand copies, while the *Chicago Tribune* covered the proceedings on its front page. The following year, Nathaniel West edited the conference papers for the publisher Revell, which, in addition, also published William Blackstone's *Jesus Is Coming*; this gained an immediate foothold with premillennialists. The almost simultaneous publications—a popular collection of conference addresses and a popular tract-turned-book—helped not only to elevate the social stature of premillennialism but also to announce the arrival of a new premillennial subculture.

If success could be measured in criticism, the conference succeeded here, too. The display of premillennial solidarity provoked concern from those who, in the words of one Baptist magazine, "look with some anxiety upon the spread of the view represented at the so-called Prophetic Conference held in New York."[16] The Presbyterian iconoclast and voice of the new theology Charles A. Briggs compared the 1878 conference to "Anabaptists of the Reformation, and the Fifth Monarchy men of the English Revolution. . . . We see their culmination in the Zion of Münster"—none of which were meant as compliments. Briggs elsewhere prophesied that premillennialists would break away and become a "heretical sect."[17] One Congregationalist magazine described Revell's volume as "absurd and self-contradictory."[18] As the outlines of the premillennial constituency became clearer, the prospect of a struggle between premillennialists and their opponents looked more likely.

Periodic large gatherings continued, with a second national premillennial conference hosted in Chicago in 1886, and a third in Allegheny, Pennsylvania, in 1895. A fourth conference was held in Boston in 1901, but by this point James Brookes was dead and the bonds uniting old and new premillennialists had frayed. Boosters called these gatherings American Bible and Prophetic Conferences and then, later, International Prophetic Conferences, but the attendees were drawn overwhelmingly from the Great Lakes basin and Northeast.[19] These conferences were effective primarily as showcases for the movement.

16. Quoted in Ernest Robert Sandeen, *The Roots of Fundamentalism: British and American Millenarianism, 1800–1930* (Chicago: University of Chicago Press, 1970), 152.

17. Quoted in George N. H. Peters, *Theocratic Kingdom*, vol. 1 (New York, 1884), 481.

18. Quoted in Daniel Vaca, *Evangelicals Incorporated: Books and the Business of Religion in America* (Cambridge, MA: Harvard University Press, 2019), 43.

19. See preface in *Prophetic Studies of the International Bible Conference (Chicago, November, 1886)* (Chicago: Revell, 1886), 1.

Their purpose was communal and social, in the service of expanding a new subculture nurtured by the Bible conference format.

The Bible Institute

If the Bible conference pumped energy into a fledgling new premillennialism, the institution that solidified its gains was the Bible institute. Beginning in the 1880s, new premillennialists went on a building spree, creating centers to educate and commission Christian workers, based in the same Great Lakes basin but sending graduates into every region of the globe. Bible conferences appeared but then dispersed; their organizers died. Institutes, in theory, could last until the moment of the rapture and multiply through infrastructures for growth.

The earliest American Bible institutes were born out of European inspirations. Albert B. Simpson, a Canadian preacher who converted to new premillennialism in the early 1870s, encountered training schools in Europe, such as the East London Institute for Home and Foreign Missions led by Irish (Open) Brethren revivalist Henry Gratton Guinness. Disaffected with the strictures of his Presbyterian pulpits in Kentucky and New York City, Simpson took the radical step in 1881 to begin an independent ministry. He founded a new church, a new healing ministry, a new periodical, and, the year following, a new school—the Missionary Training Institute, headquartered in New York City and later relocating to the suburb of Nyack. Simpson's institute was replicated by a handful of others: the interdenominational Union Missionary Training Institute of Brooklyn in 1885, A. J. Gordon's interdenominational Boston Bible and Missionary Training School in 1889, and the Northwestern Bible Training School in St. Paul, Minnesota, also in 1889.

While Simpson could claim to have started the first American missionary training school, the foremost such institution was the Chicago Bible Institute, founded in 1889, which would be renamed Moody Bible Institute in 1899. While Moody fund-raised and secured its early stability, the school's formative influences were Emma Dryer, who had overseen Moody's educational work in Chicago since the early 1870s, and its first superintendent, Reuben A. Torrey, who moved to Chicago after undergoing a conversion to premillennialism.[20] Dryer, a schoolteacher and evangelist who converted to premillennialism while visiting Chicago in 1870, experimented with different educational models for training ministry workers over the previous fifteen years, including the

---

20. Reuben A. Torrey, *The Return of the Lord Jesus* (Los Angeles: Bible Institute of Los Angeles, 1913), 20.

May Institute, which equipped lay ministry workers in the city. Torrey would become one of the central figures of new premillennialism for the next thirty years upon his move to Chicago. He arrived to lead the Chicago Evangelistic Society, created in 1889 with the ascent of Dryer, Moody, and a number of Moody's core financial backers, including the McCormick family (founders of the McCormick Harvesting Machine Company) and John V. Farwell (a department store magnate). The society formed the basis for the Bible institute, which held its first classes that same year.

As superintendent at Moody until 1904, Torrey exercised an outsized influence in the nascent Bible institute scene. The 1890s witnessed several additional school openings—in Toronto; Providence, Rhode Island; Cincinnati; and Minneapolis—and Torrey's *What the Bible Teaches for Greatest Profit* (1898) was indicative of what this experimental educational model would convey to students. The textbook wove together premillennialism, Higher Life theology, and modern business strategies—all in the service of training Christian workers. Torrey's students in Chicago exemplified the school's interdenominational pull, representing some thirty-six denominations, and he described his approach as "a careful, unbiased, systematic, thorough-going, inductive study and statement of biblical truth."[21] Each of the book's fifty sections employed the Bible Reading method, with a list of all relevant verses and a series of propositions developed from harmonizing the verses. The entire study was steeped in a managerial and self-described "scientific" language that reflected Torrey's confidence in bridging biblical and modern knowledge.[22]

One area where Torrey departed with modern science was in his embrace of physical healings by the Holy Spirit. The early Bible institutes were awash in the Higher Life teachings, of which healing by means of the Spirit was one of the most visible and controversial manifestations. Yet among the Bible institutes the teaching was widely accepted. A. J. Gordon wrote an early defense in *The Ministry of Healing* (1882), followed by Simpson's *The Gospel of Healing* (1885). Pierson's *Acts of the Holy Spirit* (1895) and Torrey's *Baptism with the Holy Spirit* (1895) recalled the full gamut of the gifts of the Spirit in the early church as a model for the modern church. The Dutch South African revivalist and preacher Andrew Murray, who built his own missionary training school in Wellington, South Africa, and was a frequent speaker in North America, collated a series of sermons into a work titled *Divine Healing* (1900). These books were but a sampling of material on holiness, prayer, healing, and Bible

21. Reuben A. Torrey, *What the Bible Teaches* (Chicago: Revell, 1898), 1.
22. Torrey, *What the Bible Teaches*, 1.

reading produced and consumed by Bible institutes. It would not be until the 1900s that healing and premillennialism were pitted against each other in interdenominational circles. Nothing was further from the reality in the 1880s.

The dozen separate Bible institutes across the Great Lakes basin in 1900 reflected a loose cooperative network connected through personal relationships and shared commitments to new premillennialism. In an 1888 reflection on "missionary training colleges," Simpson summarized Bible institutes as "less technical and elaborate than the ordinary theological seminary" but "designed to afford the same specific preparation for direct missionary work."[23] Often founded by charismatic leaders, Bible institutes were usually appendages to larger ministry complexes. The schools were lay oriented, enrolling women as well as men, and expected students to attend for only one or two years before entering ministry work. The curricula focused on a basic knowledge of the Bible and church history, theology and practice of missions, and practical skills including singing or playing musical instruments and teaching.

The first Bible institutes were founded in the same decades as higher education began a new wave of expansion across the country. Johns Hopkins (founded in 1876) and the University of Chicago (1892), and a host of other private colleges and universities, were erected to address the pressing needs of modern society. Most new private universities were funded by the immense coffers of a few benefactors, who were clear winners in the struggles between capital and labor. Each school embodied, at least in its early years, the particular interests of its founder, from Johns Hopkins's exclusive focus on graduate training to the University of Chicago's Divinity School training ministers in the liberal Protestantism that its funder, John Rockefeller, cared so much about.

The early Bible institutes were founded alongside these universities but with far less financial backing. Most institutes rented space and moved frequently, with graduating classes in the dozens, many of the instructors working for free. The Panic of 1893 affected the entire country but especially the Great Lakes basin, where Michigan, New York, and Pennsylvania suffered unemployment rates above 25 percent. The American Sunday School Union, a vast enterprise headquartered in Chicago with deep ties to Moody, was forced to appeal for relief funds amid "the long continued financial depression."[24]

---

23. Quoted in Virginia Brereton, *Training God's Army: The American Bible School, 1880–1940* (Bloomington: Indiana University Press, 1990), 55.

24. J. M. Crowell, "An Appeal from the American Sunday School Union," *Record of Christian Work* 13, no. 12 (December 1894): 384.

These economic realities shaped the Bible institutes. Moody claimed his students would be "gap-men" between the laity and ministers. Graduates would serve the poor, preach to the masses, and coordinate the work of the church outside denominational structures.[25] This was his vision, developed through his understanding and ability to gather resources for the cause. His institute supporters included the merchant Robert Scott and Henry Parsons Crowell (founder of the Quaker Oats Company), who had their own ways to influence the growth of the institute. These men, successful as they were, occupied a strata of wealth below the railroad and oil tycoons founding new universities—and it showed.

The nonelite status of Bible institutes fueled their self-image as correctives to a declining Christian education system in America. Institutes shared a commitment to work "outside of the regular channels," as Arthur Pierson wrote in 1900, by which he meant denominations and established schools of higher education. Pierson compared Moody to the German Lutheran pastor and missionary Louis Harms, who established an independent venture in 1849 in Hermannsburg, Lower Saxony. Harms "not only had his own society and missions," Pierson recalled, "but his own mission ship, mission magazine, and mission training-school." The model, Pierson reported, was being replicated on a larger scale in Chicago—tailored to fit the demands of expanding global missions.

The Mission Agency

Bible conferences and Bible institutes supported the premillennial complex's centerpiece: global missions. *Forward Movements in the Last Half Century* (1900), written by Pierson as a look back on the growth of global missions since the Civil War, was one popular account of the effort. Pierson argued that with the growth of "Bible schools and conventions," a third organizational type, the interdenominational mission agency, would disseminate the gospel to the entire globe.[26] His account charted a globe-spanning network of ministries that were the end points for Bible institute graduates. His examples included George Müller's orphanages, Jerry McAuley's rescue missions, Samuel Fisk Green's medical missions, and the work of Andrew Murray (South Africa), Hudson Taylor (China), and Pandita Ramabai (India), among many others.[27]

25. Quoted in Paul Dwight Moody and Arthur Percy Fitt, *The Shorter Life of Dwight Moody* (Chicago: Bible Institute Colportage Association, 1900), 2:14.
26. Paul Dwight Moody and Fitt, *The Shorter Life*, 154.
27. Paul Dwight Moody and Fitt, *The Shorter Life*, 389, 409.

The 1890s witnessed a plethora of experimental "faith missions"—modeled especially on the examples of Hudson and Maria Taylor, who had decided to become independent missionaries to China with financial support provided solely "as answer to prayer in faith."[28] They adopted this idea from the Brethren, whose leaders, Darby among them, pioneered the "faith principle" of independence from a single church or denomination for financial support. By the 1880s, the role of philanthropy—especially of individual large benefactors—aligned with this theological principle, providing expansive growth based on personal relationships rather than denominational affiliations.

Along with the "faith principle," the Brethren practice of lay ministry also influenced these new faith missions. Hudson Taylor's China Inland Mission, founded in 1865, was the model. Taylor, a British nonconformist, was deeply influenced by Open Brethren practice of faith missions. Like his Brethren colleague George Müller (and Darby), he did not require ordination of missionary workers. China Inland Mission empowered laity to assume any leadership position. This expansion of lay leadership was a profound expression of Brethren values. Missionaries squared the egalitarian impulse through the premillennial conviction that global missions were a feature of the last days, requiring new tactics to achieve their goals.

Taylor's mission inspired other agencies, too. Albert B. Simpson, a long-time follower of Hudson's work, founded the Evangelical Missionary Alliance in 1887 on similar principles; a decade later it merged to form the Christian and Missionary Alliance. The up-and-coming disciple of James Brookes, Cyrus I. Scofield, helped to found Central American Mission on the faith principle in 1893. Arthur Pierson helped to found Africa Inland Mission in 1895, while a combination of Canadian and New York missionaries were inspired by A. J. Gordon to found the Sudan Interior Mission in 1901. These agencies, all of which lasted in various forms into the twenty-first century, channeled thousands of Christian workers—most trained at Bible institutes—into missions work across the globe.

The experimental nature of faith missions was also evident in how missionaries reimagined the role of women in the mission field. James Brookes and the Niagara Bible Conference represented a more traditional Victorian attitude of separate spheres for men and women that afforded no opportunity for women as teachers of the Word, let alone as ordained ministers. While the second

28. Quoted in Klaus Fiedler, *Interdenominational Faith Missions in Africa: History and Ecclesiology* (Mzuzu, Malawi: Mzuni Press, 2018), 23.

chapter of Joel envisioned that "sons and daughters shall prophesy," Brookes insisted that "this prophecy will be witnessed only after the second coming of our Lord, and it has nothing to do with a woman preaching now."[29] But while Brookes reigned over one segment of new premillennialism, others more directly engaged in global missions promoted women as missionaries to teach, especially where institutional structures were emergent and Christian workers in short supply. Pierson and Gordon interpreted the growing presence of women in ministry as a sign of revival, while Simpson listed "the ministry of women" as a core institutional value for his new mission agency in 1887.[30]

New premillennialists distinguished their work from other Christian efforts with their ceaseless focus on Jewish missions. More than forty Jewish mission agencies were founded from 1880 to 1920. Arno C. Gaebelein, a Methodist new premillennialist and copious writer, led one of the largest in the Hope of Israel Movement, which grew out of his mission to immigrant Jews in New York City. In 1893, Gaebelein received permission from the Missionary Society of the Methodist Episcopal Church to separate his work from the denomination and embrace the faith principle; he was "free to develop on such lines as will prevent all denominational narrowness."[31] A theological innovator in his own right, Gabelein owed his early success in part to his novel claim that Jewish converts to Christianity did not need to join existing churches but could form separate communities and retain Jewish religious practices. "From the very start of my work among the Jewish people," Gaebelein wrote in his autobiography, "I felt that they should not be Gentilized and that the attempt to make Methodists, Baptists, Lutherans or Presbyterians out of them would be a mistake." The church-Israel distinction reinforced his view, even though most new premillennialists cautioned against separate congregations for Jewish converts. Indeed, by 1899 Gaebelein recognized his error and explained that in the church "there is neither Jew nor Gentile; all are one in Christ."[32] Even so, he left the Methodist fold the following year, as his now-interdenominational work attracted the attention of Brookes, Simpson, and Pierson, among others.

29. Brookes, quoted in Margaret Bendroth, *Fundamentalism and Gender, 1875 to the Present* (New Haven: Yale University Press, 1996), 46.

30. Simpson, quoted in Bendroth, *Fundamentalism and Gender*, 25.

31. Arno C. Gaebelein, *Half a Century: The Autobiography of a Servant* (New York: Our Hope, 1930), 37.

32. Gaebelein, *Half a Century*, 52–53.

Blackstone's Jesus Is Coming: *The First Premillennial Best Seller*

Amid the institution building by premillennialists in the late nineteenth century, there remained the need for cultural productions to rally the faithful and define new premillennialism for the masses. New premillennialists tended to promote popular rather than scholarly ideas and build institutional rather than theological edifices. In this fledgling stage of growth, social and institutional capital went further than scholarly credibility.

The closest thing to a shared new premillennial text was the best-selling book by William E. Blackstone, a Chicago businessman-turned-evangelist, an early Christian Zionist, and a frequent speaker at Moody revivals, titled *Jesus Is Coming* (1878). His original tract of some ninety pages, written at the behest of James Brookes, sold 10,000 copies in its first year, and, by 1904, with a new edition, sales had reached nearly half a million.[33] It was one of Fleming H. Revell's most successful publications, and by 1932 it had sold more than 800,000 copies.

In the original 1878 edition, Blackstone adapted the traditional format of Brethren popularizers, offering "seven arguments" for Christ's premillennial return that moved from general to more specific teachings such as the rapture.[34] The second edition, which was released into a mature premillennial complex at the end of the century, retained an earthy apologetical tone but doubled in length and ditched the simple structure for a confident presentation of new premillennialism. To many readers, Blackstone had accomplished more than any previous American writer in synthesizing and making accessible the complex Bible-reading methods and prophetic passages that informed new premillennialism. While removed from Protestant scholarly conversations, *Jesus Is Coming* found deep resonance among the new class of Bible conference speakers, Bible institute graduates, and Christian workers of all types engaged in global missions.

Later editions of Blackstone's book included dozens of testimonies from pastors, evangelists, and missionaries who said the book's presentation prompted their conversions from childhood postmillennialism to premillennialism. Familiar names included Arthur Pierson, William J. Erdman, and Albert Simpson. There were also less prominent names who were building yet more

33. See the advertisement in the front matter of William E. Blackstone's *The Millennium* (Chicago: Revell, 1904), which claims *Jesus Is Coming* sold its "495th thousand" copy.
34. See "Religious Miscellany," *Inter Ocean*, September 28, 1878, 6.

institutions: John Willis Baer, president of Occidental College in Los Angeles, founded in 1887; D. W. Potter, a popular evangelist based in Chicago; and William G. Moorehead, the lone scholar cited, teaching at Xenia Theological Seminary. An oil businessman in Los Angeles, Giles Kellogg, represented the donor class. "The first reading of 'Jesus is Coming' marked a distinct epoch in my own life," Kellogg wrote. "I am sincerely anxious that the book may have a broadcast distribution."[35] And so it did—in the premillennial institutions erected in the late nineteenth century and beyond.

---

35. Blackstone, *Jesus Is Coming*, 246–48.

PART II

The Dispensationalists
1900–1960

New premillennialism expands to the West Coast and
South ◆ The dual developments of expansion and
division between old and new premillennialism spurs a
first major effort at theological standardization, resulting
in the *Scofield Reference Bible* ◆ At the height of their
organization and influence, new premillennialists suffer
the first of a string of setbacks during World War I,
sparking the formation of fundamentalism ◆ Dispensationalists obtain their name and their discrete identity in
the heat of organizing and infighting among fundamentalists ◆ Dispensationalism's identity is formed in the
heat of religious competition, spurring its theological
and institutional growth ◆ The success of dispensationalism as a theological identity reaches a highpoint
in the late 1950s ◆ Dispensationalism contributes
to a distinctive brand of conservative politics during
the early Cold War era

A hundred thousand souls a day
Are passing one by one away
      In Christless guilt and gloom
Without one ray of hope or light
With future dark as endless night
         They're passing to their doom
         They're passing to their doom

The Master's coming draweth near
The Son of Man will soon appear
      His Kingdom is at hand
But ere that glorious day can be
The Gospel of the Kingdom, we
         Must preach in every land
         Must preach in every land

Albert B. Simpson, "A Missionary Cry" (1897)

One of the hundreds of hymns written by the famed preacher and evangelist to convey the mix of passion and concern for evangelization by turn-of-the-century premillenni-alists. Simpson's own faith was buoyed by expectations of radical interventions by the Holy Spirit—in the forms of signs, wonders, healings, and gifts bestowed on Christians to advance the spread of the gospel.

7

Sprawl

By 1900, the premillennial vision of global missions had drawn together a diverse assortment of white Christians: bookish Presbyterians and revivalist Congregationalists, holiness Methodists and Reformed Episcopalians, Spirit-filled members of the Christian and Missionary Alliance and a smattering of high-church Anglicans. Shared institution-building "outside of regular channels" had created the infrastructure for a new premillennial subculture that emerged as a force in the early twentieth century.

Yet, in the same decades that new premillennialists achieved some institutional coherence, they also experienced a new type of chaos. Their teachings spread rapidly, especially toward the West Coast and the South—with growth buoyed by the long project of sectional reconciliation. In these regions, Christians with few direct connections to new premillennial institutions began adopting core teachings such as the rapture and dispensational time. By the early 1900s, new premillennialism had begun to reach more far-flung interpretive communities, including the new Pentecostal movement.

The premillenial sprawl traveled through the channels of transmission and institutions pioneered by Brethren and then Moody movement evangelicals. The next generation of new premillennialists in America matured and eventually outgrew the Moody movement. Premillennial sprawl, while growing the ranks and influence of the established leadership of premillennial institutions, redistributed the movement's sources of power toward the West and South.

Biola and West Coast Premillennialism

The Bible Institute of Los Angeles (later Biola University), founded in 1908, marked a watershed in the history of new premillennialism, representing the biggest extension yet of the Moody movement's base of operations outside the Great Lakes basin. Thousands of miles west, Biola inhabited at once familiar and foreign territory. The school was founded by new premillennialists and was deeply tied to the existing Moody movement. Its focus on training missionaries for Asia was well in line with the goals of other Bible institutes. At the same time, the culture of Los Angeles was a mix of unique influences, and its economy was driven by citrus and other fruit agriculture, new energy sources such as petroleum, and, by the 1910s, a burgeoning film industry.

The differences between the Midwest and the West Coast influenced the founding of the institute in 1908. The school, which became known by its initials, BIOLA, was playing catch-up to the institutes out east. Unlike the older Bible institutes, Biola's seed money and early funding came from the fortunes of a successful oil magnate, Lyman Stewart, whose drilling interests accounted for 15 percent of all oil production in California by 1886. A Pennsylvania-born wildcat oil driller, Stewart cofounded Union Oil Company with his brother Milton, both of whom moved to California in 1882.

Independent in religion as well as business, Lyman detested his rival John D. Rockefeller and the monopoly of Standard Oil. The near hegemony of Rockefeller's crude empire, often working in league with the US federal government, alarmed not only committed free marketeers like Stewart but also interdenominational evangelicals who watched Rockefeller mount a massive philanthropic offensive in support of modernist Protestant denominational cooperation. As a committed liberal, Rockefeller favored religious institutions that tended to support "interchurch" projects, including broad ecumenical cooperation and a new center of liberal Baptist theological training, the University of Chicago. The Rockefeller Foundation, founded in 1913, ensured a permanent presence for the family's already significant largesse in civic and religious institutions for the cause.

Stewart founded Biola for the same reason he championed the independent Union Oil Company: to stall a looming liberal Protestant monopoly. In his view, new premillennialism was a battering ram to break up the postmillennial hold on nineteenth-century Protestantism. With the growing popularity of theological modernism, which adjusted Christian teachings to the intellectual climate of the late nineteenth century, Stewart had identified his main rival. As early as 1884, as a lay attendee of the Niagara Bible Conference, Stewart contemplated underwriting a massive circulation boost of James Brookes's magazine *The Truth*. He later funded the printing of thousands of copies of Blackstone's *Jesus Is Coming* and boosted the circulation of Gaebelein's new premillennial successor magazine, *Our Hope*.

With the success of the Moody movement and consolidation of oil money, Biola emerged as Lyman's most ambitious plan to keep the religious market free from a modernist monopoly. Lyman spoke of his desire to "radiate streams of influence which will be a great blessing" locally and globally, through religious channels carved between the mountains of modernist institutional advantage.[1] Lyman and his brother Milton became Biola's chief early benefactors, as the regular cast of interdenominational donors farther east—Henry Parsons Crowell in Chicago and John Wanamaker in Philadelphia, among others—were already committed to causes closer to the Great Lakes basin.

The story of Biola's founding is entangled with the larger history of Midwestern evangelicals moving west at the turn of the century. Biola drew its inaugural leadership from the old stock, with William E. Blackstone of Chicago its first academic dean. In 1912, Stewart and Biola's first superintendent, Thomas C. Horton, a onetime YMCA director and assistant to Arthur Pierson in Philadelphia, enticed Reuben A. Torrey to move from Chicago to become Biola's second superintendent (and its first at the school's own property). For more than a decade (1912–1924), Torrey implemented the same institutional and pedagogical methods that had underpinned Moody Bible Institute. Biola was deeply invested in the surrounding community, promoting evangelistic outreach to farmers, laborers, and fishermen; connecting with white-collar workers in Los Angeles; and emphasizing the role of service and experiential learning in its curriculum. Its official organ, the *King's Business*, first published in 1910, quickly became an important paper in the wider Moody movement. In 1914 Torrey founded a new nondenominational church, the Church of the Open Door—with a four-thousand-seat sanctuary located on the same downtown block as Biola's campus—which became one of the most influential churches in the region for the next fifty years.

In addition to "setting in motion streams of real truth" that flowed into American Protestantism, as Lyman Stewart articulated the school's mission, Biola was to be "inter-denominational in its organization and character" and committed to "training men and women who could be depended upon to preach and teach the truths of redemption in such dark places of the world as God, in His providence, might call them."[2] Missions were vital to the school's purpose, and the centrifugal tendencies toward sprawl inevitably brought new opportunities—from training "its Bible women, its Fishermen boys, its

1. Stewart, quoted in James O. Henry, "History of Biola University since 1908" (unpublished manuscript, 1996), 53.
2. Stewart, quoted in Henry, "History of Biola University," 40, 46–47.

Lyceum girls" (all LA-based ministries) to sending dozens and eventually hundreds of missionaries to China.[3] Like Brethren faith missions in a previous generation, the new imagination of gender roles that included women as teachers and missionaries was seen as a stopgap measure to meet the immense challenge of global missions.

Biola sat firmly in the Moody movement tradition, even as that tradition was diffusing along geographic and other lines. The school's growth as a center of premillennial education, and as an institution opposed to modernist theology, created free-flowing lines of influence both to and from the older Bible institutes of the Midwest and East Coast. At the same time, Biola's relative geographic isolation meant its mission would develop differently. While Moody Bible Institute was founded to accommodate a robust premillennial infrastructure in Chicago, Biola was generative of a new premillennial culture in Southern California. The diverging paths were subtle and would take decades to become distinct. But by the mid-twentieth century, Biola was not just a proponent of new premillennialism but a champion of dispensationalism, eclipsing in importance many of the eastern institutions that had spawned it.

Premillennialism and Pentecostalism

Less than one mile from Biola's thirteen-story central campus building (erected in 1913) in downtown Los Angeles stood the Apostolic Faith Mission on Azusa Street. Though both would become centers of national, even global, religious activity and shared significant theological overlap, including premillennialism, the two communities reflected how racial and class differences, alongside divergent theological commitments, shaped the sprawl of new premillennialism to reflect the contours of existing American social divides.

The Apostolic Faith Mission was the epicenter of a religious awakening, the Azusa Street Revival, which helped to spur the new global movement of Pentecostalism. Revival came with the preaching of William J. Seymour, a Black holiness preacher whose distinctive marks were the insistence on speaking in tongues as evidence of the Holy Spirit and the practice of charismatic gifts as evidence of the sanctified Christian life. For almost a decade after Seymour's arrival in Los Angeles in 1906, thousands of visitors flowed through the Apostolic Faith Mission, experienced the power of the Holy Spirit, and fanned out across the globe, bringing the teaching of tongues and the practice of gifts

3. Stewart, quoted in Henry, "History of Biola University," 55.

to every region of North America and linking with similar Spirit-centered revivals in Wales, India, Chile, and Korea.

Moody movement leaders interpreted Spirit-centered revival in multiple ways. Theology, culture, and race each bonded the Moody movement's leadership to particular expressions of faith, even as many of the Spirit-filled revivals linked to Azusa Street were led by Moody-influenced Christians. The overlap in teachings of divine healing, sanctification, and premillennialism between the Moody movement and the early Pentecostals was hard to miss, even as collaboration went largely unrealized. In fact, some of Pentecostalism's harshest critics were the luminaries of the Moody movement. A potential spirit of unity dissipated in the face of difference. Ironically, all this disagreement fueled more sprawl, as both groups employed a common lexicon of new premillennialism.

The theological roots of Pentecostalism extended far deeper into the Methodist-led holiness movement and the Black church than did those of new premillennialism. Methodists were important members of Moody's leadership group when he was alive, but they remained guests in a movement directed along broadly Reformed theological commitments, a situation dating to Moody's earliest revival connections and the influence of Reformed theology through groups such as the Brethren. Northern racism and Moody's commitment to North-South white reconciliation meant that Black Americans were apportioned no place in the Moody movement leadership, and this remained the case after his death in 1899. Pentecostalism, combining the Methodist revivalist tradition, speaking in tongues, divine healing, and premillennialism, was similar enough to draw from interdenominational evangelicalism, and yet different enough to create real fractures within the Moody movement. The appeal of Pentecostalism among Black and working-class whites ensured that these fractures would widen.

This was nowhere truer than in the early Pentecostal adoption of premillennialism. Many of the leading lights of early Pentecostalism converted to premillennialism in the 1890s—showing a similar inflection point in Methodist holiness circles as that among border-state evangelicals in the 1860s. The southern evangelist George Watson, the minister Martin Wells Knapp, and Pentecostalism's first systematic theologian, D. Wesley Myland, all adopted belief in an imminent rapture along with a premillennial view of the kingdom. Yet they were not disciples of James Brookes or Joseph Seiss, and rejected the finer points of new premillennialism as often as they embraced them. Instead, they elevated the doctrine of the baptism of the Holy Spirit in place of dispensational time, situating at the center of their theology the themes of rupture, divine intervention, and the individual believer's charge to "Watch ye therefore, and pray always" (Luke 21:36 KJV) in anticipation of the Lord's judgment.

Early Pentecostals did preach familiar new premillennial themes about a "rapture," a "first resurrection," and a "marriage feast" that looked expectantly for the imminent return of Jesus, but few adopted the Brethren-turned-new-premillennial understanding of dispensational time, test-fail cycles, or an absolute church-Israel distinction. Types and antitypes ran rampant in early Pentecostalism, but there was far less interest in systematic or comprehensive typology. Experiential testimony worked to bind prophetic sequences into coherence—visions, earthquakes, and reports of wonders helped make sense of Scripture. Myland's *Latter Rain Covenant and Pentecostal Power* (1910) was the first systematic theology of Pentecostalism, merging literal, figurative, and prophetic (dispensational time) interpretations of the Bible. Among other innovations, Myland pointed to the increasing rate of rainfall in Palestine as direct evidence of the increase of Holy Spirit power in the form of Pentecostalism.[4] Such an interpretive move, especially in the service of an imminent rapture, found no precedence in existing premillennial teachings.

To the broader Moody movement, Pentecostal emphasis on signs like rain, divine healing, and baptism of the Holy Spirit were both intriguing and alarming. Shared theology and spirituality was obvious. Arthur Pierson, Reuben Torrey, Albert Simpson, and other new premillennialists either made theological allowance for or personally practiced divine healing. As a group, they expected a spiritual deluge as a sign of the times.[5]

Yet common ground dissipated when it came to Pentecostalism's most strident teachings on the power of the Holy Spirit. Few Moody movement leaders experienced or endorsed speaking in tongues. Their early responses to the outpouring of tongues in California were tentative and skeptical, often based on secondhand reports. In 1907 Arno Gaebelein published a positive assessment of a Pentecostal revival in Denver, declaring that the local revivalist believed in the "second and near coming of Christ" and affirming that "what we need most among our people is a heartfelt and Holy Spirit religion, instead of so much 'head religion.'" Mere months later, though, he denounced any idea of a

---

4. D. Wesley Myland, *The Latter Rain Covenant and Pentecostal Power*, 2nd ed. (Chicago: Evangel Publishing House, 1911), 178–79.

5. Arthur Pierson, *The New Acts of the Apostles; or, Marvels of Modern Missions* (New York: Baker & Taylor, 1894), 13–14.

"personal Pentecost" and took issue with the way speaking in tongues empowered women to exercise spiritual authority over men.[6] In another example, the new pastor of Moody's historic church in downtown Chicago, Amzi Clarence Dixon, was forced to confront an outbreak of the Spirit in 1908, which he did by ejecting its leader, Andrew Urshan, an Iranian Christian immigrant who would go on to found a Pentecostal mission nearby.

Early tensions contributed to the fracturing of premillennial culture in the heartland of the Moody movement. Myland delivered his lectures that became *The Latter Rain Covenant* at the Stone Church Convention in 1909, a few miles south of Moody Bible Institute. Pentecostal periodicals, including the *Latter Rain Evangel* (1908–1939) and *Pentecostal Testimony* (1909–1912), were printed in Chicago. Other important presses were also located in the Great Lakes basin: Plainfield, Indiana, and Springfield, Missouri; along with Cincinnati and New York City. The West Coast, too, began to teem with Pentecostal activity, with Seymour's magazine the *Apostolic Faith* issuing from Los Angeles until moving to Portland.

Pentecostalism split the Moody movement, but it also contributed to a new wave of premillennial sprawl. In many cases, new premillennial visions of the future influenced Pentecostal understandings of prophecy, even as new premillennial hermeneutics, dispensational time, and church-Israel distinctions (what would become integral parts of the entire dispensational "system") were dropped. The shared roots of early Pentecostalism and the Moody movement meant that for decades they would be grouped together by external observers even as they regarded each other with suspicion.

Amzi C. Dixon and the Cause of Sectional Reconciliation

If Los Angeles represented new premillennialism's geographic expansion and Pentecostalism its translation into new religious movements, Chicago remained its bustling metropolis. A magnet for migrants from across the continent after the Civil War, Chicago was, by 1900, the second-largest city in the country, behind New York City. From this urban center of the Midwest, the cause of sectional reconciliation had many advocates. Among evangelicals this advocacy bore fruit, with the consequence that, among other North-South exchanges, new premillennialism began to make its first inroads south.

---

6. Gaebelein, quoted in Gerald Wayne King, "Disfellowshiped: Pentecostal Responses to Fundamentalism in the United States, 1906–1943" (PhD diss., University of Birmingham, 2009), 68.

In his massive Northern revival circuit of 1875–1877, Moody had invited select Southerners, such as evangelist William Swan Plumer of South Carolina, to share the podium and enact a microcosm of white Christian fellowship. Moody was welcomed in the South with thronging crowds; his meetings were segregated; he prayed for the Confederate dead; and he signaled his desire that Christian unity take precedence over racial equality. Moody won praise as a unifier and embodied the prevailing mood among white Americans. Over the following decades, even as Southerners embraced the "Lost Cause" and implemented Jim Crow segregation, Northerners like Moody pursued fellowship for the sake of reconciliation.

In the wake of Moody's death, Southern involvement in the movement increased. At Moody's own Chicago Avenue Church, Amzi Clarence Dixon, a Southern Baptist born in North Carolina, ascended to the pulpit in 1906. An opponent of the new theology, biblical higher criticism, and the Social Gospel movement, Dixon viewed racial difference through the lens of his Southern roots. He was no zealous segregationist like his brother, Thomas Dixon, who was one of the South's most popular novelists. Thomas's *The Clansmen* (1905), about the victimhood of the South at the hands of the North during Reconstruction, was adapted into *The Birth of a Nation* (1915), the first American blockbuster film and a cornerstone of white supremacy in the twentieth century. While Thomas proudly promoted Jim Crow segregation, his brother (who preferred to be called Clarence) conveyed a more paternalistic attitude toward nonwhites in a Northern evangelical culture committed to global missions.

The difference was one Clarence was at pains to articulate. As a pastor in Boston before he was called to Chicago, he was pressured into responding to charges that he was "the son of a slave owner" (which was true) by speaking at a ministers' conference in 1905 on "the racial problem in the South." In reference to a recent White House dinner between President Theodore Roosevelt and Booker T. Washington, Dixon explained that his personal approval or disapproval of the meeting had no correlation to public policy. He clarified that he personally approved of racial reconciliation but doubted its "political sagacity."[7] He already lamented in 1899 that immediately awarding suffrage to freed slaves was "the blunder of the age."[8] To his Yankee audience he explained the Southern fear that "social equality means inter-marriage, which would

---

7. Dixon, quoted in Helen C. A. Dixon, *A. C. Dixon: A Romance of Preaching* (New York: Putnam's Sons, 1931), 151.

8. Dixon, quoted in Matthew Avery Sutton, *American Apocalypse: A History of Modern Evangelicalism* (Cambridge, MA: Belknap Press of Harvard University Press, 2014), 134.

portend the extinction of the Anglo-Saxon race, and its transmutation into a race of mulattos." Dixon carried this concern himself, saying elsewhere that though he wished political rights extended "to all educated and moral men" regardless of race, a change in social relations was out of the question. "I am free to confess that I do not want the negro, or the Mongolian, to marry my daughter nor my son to marry his daughter."[9] Dixon understood "the feeling of the South" as unmovable, suggesting the only recourse was for each person to individually follow Christ's command "by love to serve one another."[10]

The distinction between individual and social agency, and between spiritual and corporeal brotherhood, allowed Dixon to wax about spiritual equality while ignoring social racism in his midst. Northerners as well as Southerners inhabited cities stratified by race and material inequality, yet Dixon was muted on why such a situation existed. The "solidarity of the race" was God's intention, Dixon preached, but sin broke it. "Now God is making a new solidarity which begins at Calvary and is based upon the new creation," and yet the plane of transformation was narrowly spiritual. "Only the cross can make the confusion of Babel give way to the fusion of Pentecost," he taught, referencing God's act of dispersing humanity into separate tribes and language groups, and the latter coming of the Holy Spirit to diverse early followers. "Only in this fire of God's love can races be molded into one family with the spirit of true brotherhood."[11] Clarence was no Thomas, yet the distinctions he made fueled new premillennialist views of racial difference.

At this moment of sectional reconciliation in the early 1900s, Southerners like Dixon were guests in the Northern world of the Moody movement. Dixon "had not lost contact with the South," his niece recalled, as he moved from pulpit to pulpit in the North, "although the personal links were snapping one by one."[12] The handful of Southerners leading Northern congregations adapted to their surroundings even as they contributed to the culture of Northern evangelicalism. Dixon was one of the most prominent Southern transplants, but he was not alone in the Moody movement. Others included gospel singer and Tennessee native Charles McCallon Alexander and the longtime Reformed Episcopal bishop and Mississippi-born William Nicholson (both were also counted as new premillennialists).

9. Dixon, quoted in Donald Lewis Martin, "The Thought of Amzi Clarence Dixon" (PhD diss., Baylor University, 1989), 219.
10. Dixon, quoted in Helen C. A. Dixon, *A. C. Dixon*, 151.
11. Dixon, quoted in Martin, "The Thought of Amzi Clarence Dixon," 221.
12. Helen C. A. Dixon, *A. C. Dixon*, 151.

Northern evangelicals also began reaching southward. Michigan-born Cyrus Scofield was living with relatives in Tennessee when he enlisted in the Confederate army and later settled in the border-state metropolis of St. Louis, and later in Dallas, Texas. Indiana-born William Bell Riley, later famous for his fundamentalist empire in St. Paul, Minnesota, was trained at Southern Baptist Theological Seminary in the late 1880s. Ohio-born Leander Whitcomb (L. W.) Munhall, a Methodist evangelist and constant presence at the Niagara Bible Conferences, was educated at the racially segregated Chattanooga University and the University of New Orleans. These examples pointed to new possibilities of white sectional cooperation. They aggregated into a pattern of exchange that solidified Moody's sectional reconciliation agenda and would shape the future of dispensationalism as a largely white but transsectional theology, too.

While the priority of reconciliation muted criticism of Jim Crow segregation and racial discrimination in the North, there were exceptions. The influential *Missionary Review of the World*, which Arthur Pierson edited from 1892 to 1911, highlighted acts of lynching and connected the plight of Southern Blacks to black South Africans oppressed by the British and Boers. Pierson's journal praised the early work of W. E. B. Du Bois, publishing one of his stories on prison labor in 1901. In 1905, with Du Bois founding the Negro Niagara Movement (predecessor to the National Association for the Advancement of Colored People), which was hosted mere minutes from where the Niagara Bible Conference met until 1897, the *Missionary Review* endorsed the gathering, quoting Du Bois's condemnation of white churches who exhibited a willingness to "bow [t]o racial prejudice, to narrow the bounds of human brotherhood, and to segregate black men in some outer sanctuary."[13] Like many Northern evangelicals, Pierson tended to favor the gradualist approach for Black economic progress promoted by Booker T. Washington, but he also demanded that political change happen quickly in light of racism's undermining influence on global missions. "The Christian missionary makes slow progress in Africa," Pierson wrote in 1887, "because he can offer the negro no true brotherhood except in another world."[14]

Still, Pierson's opposition to racism in America operated within dominant racial categories as defined by the three sons of Noah: Ham (African), Shem (Asian), and Japheth (Occidental). In 1910 Pierson outlined the familiar judg-

13. "The Negro Niagara Movement," *Missionary Review of the* World, o.s., 29, no. 9 (September 1905): 708.
14. Arthur T. Pierson, *Evangelistic Work in Principle and Practice* (New York: Baker & Taylor, 1887), 219.

ments by white Christians: "Of the Hamitic races the dominant characteristic is servility; of the Semitic, nomadic conservation; and of the Japhetic, commercial enlargement and enterprise. It is so even to-day." These categories worked just like biblical types. In the Bible, "Japheth is represented as going to Shem for his knowledge of the Lord God, for his religious faith; and it is remarkable that there has not been one great religion that has not come from the Semitic races, or been mainly espoused by them. Even the Christian religion had its birth among Semitic people." Pierson concluded: "Noah thus outlined the whole history of these races, and we see that the providence of God is behind all national history."[15]

With examples like Dixon and Pierson, the social reality of racism hardly registered in the writings of most new premillennialists. For the most part, they eagerly accommodated reconciliation with Southern evangelicals. Individual leaders kept personal records of tolerance and opposed the harshest examples of Jim Crow segregation, but few gave sustained attention to pervasive social racism as experienced by nonwhites. As Southerners joined the ranks of premillennial leadership and as Midwesterners developed closer ties to the South, the balance of power in the community reflected this shift.

Imagining the Kingdom in Racial Terms

The racial dynamics of reconciling Northern and Southern whites played out in new premillennial constructions of the coming kingdom. A deep tension existed between the obvious divisions of church and society along racial lines in the United States, and the Bible's millennial vision of a united humanity in the kingdom of God. According to Revelation 7:9, "A great multitude, which no man could number, of all nations, and kindreds, and people, and tongues, stood before the throne, and before the Lamb" (KJV). New premillennialists used their eschatological speculations to imagine how the racial categories of their world would translate into the next.

The anthropological categories introduced by the Brethren supplied new premillennialists with one template for imagining the kingdom. In their schema the earth would be governed by a renewed national Israel of converted Jewish Christians, which would rule the nations. The raptured church would play various mediating roles between heaven and earth, but its time for earthly activity will have passed. While mapping imprecisely onto American racial

15. Arthur T. Pierson, "The Incredible Facts of Modern Missions," *Record of Christian Work* 29, no. 10 (October 1910): 675.

lines, Israel, the church, and the nations—which new premillennial writers called "races"—shaped the new premillennial imagination. "Two races shall occupy the Millennial earth," Albert Simpson explained in 1912, representing one popular view. Jews would reign in their historic land, while "the Gentile peoples shall also be left on earth." At this point, both "races" would be Christian "and raised to all the immunities, privileges, and blessings of the highest Christian civilization."[16] A third race of humans, the raptured church, would exist above and rule over the earth as helpers to Jesus. They would, in Simpson's speculation, "reign upon the earth and yet possess a heavenly life and a spiritual body" and "shall have free and constant access to the material world and the whole system of human life, visiting men, visible to them, and oft engaged in conflicts with them but living on a far higher plane."[17]

American racial categories often underpinned these otherworldly speculations, however. For G. Campbell Morgan, who directed the Northfield Bible Conference upon Moody's death, the rapture would take white people only. "Should He come soon," Morgan wrote in 1907, "I do not think any of His angels would go into the interior of China. I do not think they would go into the heart of Africa. I think these angels would be in the great centres, all about the parts where white men congregate." This echoed an observation by Moody more than twenty years earlier that heaven's diverse inhabitants would not be "the Scotchman or the Englishman only," but also "the Frenchman, the German, the Italian, the Russian"—a spectrum relegated to contemporary white or white-adjacent ethnic identities.[18] Taken together, these speculations cast the vision of the kingdom of God as something like a benevolent European empire, the saints acting as representatives of the monarch, enjoying the benefits of mobility and power, reporting to the king who sits on his throne in the new Jerusalem, hovering between heaven and earth as a "metropolis of immensity," a "metropolis of the world."[19]

Yet, resisting a complete capitulation to twentieth-century racism, new premillennialists did allow for a less Western-centric, albeit still racist, vision of the kingdom. The radical discontinuity that new premillennialists expected between this and the coming age countered any monolithic translation of Amer-

16. Albert B. Simpson, *The Coming One* (Nyack, NY: Christian Alliance Publishing, 1912), 164.

17. Albert B. Simpson, *The Present Truth* (Nyack, NY: Christian Alliance Publishing, 1898), 130.

18. Dwight Moody, *Heaven: Where It Is, Its Inhabitants, and How to Get There* (Chicago: Revell, 1884), 30.

19. Simpson, *The Coming One*, 178; G. Campbell Morgan, *Jesus Is Coming to That Great Meeting in the Air* (n.p., 1917), 131.

ican racial hierarchy into the kingdom. Some new premillennialists insisted that white Christians themselves would be the source of the great rebellion at the end of the thousand years of peace. It is significant, Morgan explained, "that the Japhetic races rule the world. The great princes, potentates, millionaires, gold-bugs, and railroad kings are white men." When Satan is loosed, he will play on this "hereditary depravity." The white men will "muse much on their illustrious ancestry, who possessed the money and ruled the world," and the Deceiver will lead them back to a desire to dominate. In contrast, the races of Ham and Shem, who, Morgan speculated, would after a thousand years of living in the kingdom number some "three thousand millions" in Africa and "eight thousand millions" in Asia, constitute the vanguard of God's chosen people. Morgan looked into the future to see the rise of African Christianity, albeit tinged with Western stereotypes. "When all the negroes in Africa have shouted full salvation a thousand years, the Dark Continent checkered with railroads and illuminated with Holiness camp-grounds and colleges, those grand old Ethiopians will stand flatfooted, throw their big mouths open and shout the devil out of countenance, till he will be glad to retreat crestfallen from the land of Ham, without a single follower."[20] The final destruction of Satan and his white followers will come at the hands of more than one billion nonwhite Christians, led by Jesus.

The inversion of racial categories suggested by Morgan and other new premillennialists portended a more radical potential of their theology had sectional reconciliation not come to animate the Moody movement's social agenda. In this example, contemporary white racial essentialism shaped imaginings of the kingdom far more than did biblical categories. New premillennialists reflected the common racial attitudes of the North compounded by reconciliation efforts with Southern evangelicals. Yet new premillennialists were also capable of being unsettled by the implications of their theological commitments.

20. Morgan, *Jesus Is Coming*, 128–31.

In the crimson of the morning, in the whiteness of the noon,
In the amber glory of the day's retreat,
In the midnight, rob'd in darkness, or the gleaming of the moon,
I listen for the coming of His feet.

Down the minster-aisles of splendor, from betwixt the cherubim,
Thro' the wond'ring throng, with motion strong and fleet,
Sounds His victor tread, approaching with a music fair and dim—
The music of the coming of His feet.

He is coming, O my spirit! with His everlasting peace,
With His blessedness immortal and complete.
He is coming, O my Spirit! and His coming brings release—
I listen for the coming of His feet.

Lyman Whitney Allen,
"The Coming of His Feet" (1900)

Allen (1854–1930) was a Presbyterian pastor, first in St. Louis, and then in Newark, New Jersey. The hymn does not necessarily refer to Christ's imminent second coming. It was, however, appropriated for that meaning in Clarence Larkin's popular book *Dispensational Truth* (1918).

8

Standard Text

When it incorporated under Canadian law in 1890, the Niagara Bible Conference had given vital energy and structure to new premillennialism. For its organizers, the future looked promising. The 1890 annual meeting was "the best and largest yet held," according to its annual report; the conference had designs to expand the summer meetings into summer school for young Christian workers.[1]

But the future of the Niagara Bible Conference was tempered with concern for theological drift. "In order to guard against future apostasy, (if the Lord should tarry), the statement of doctrinal belief, adopted some years ago, will be embodied in the act of incorporation," the conference's doctrine committee explained in 1890. Deviating from the articles would act as a kill switch on the entire conference. "Of course no human measure can wholly prevent the inroads of error and the wiles of the devil," they admitted. "But it is a comfort to know that if there comes any departure from these articles of faith, the Conference will cease to exist, as it ought to cease."

As it turned out, the primary fear that this statement of belief was intended to alleviate—the encroachment of new theology and modernism—never materialized. The conference should have been more attentive to dissension in its own conservative ranks. By 1901 the Niagara Bible Conference had ceased to exist because of internal disunity over premillennialism. Its members, while sharing many theological and cultural convictions, split into old and new premillennialist factions that increasingly defined themselves against each other.

1. Preface to *A Week of Blessing, Being a Full Report of the Believers' Meeting for Bible Study Held at Niagara-on-the-Lake (Ontario) July 10 to 17, 1890* (Toronto: Toronto Willard Tract Depository, 1888), front matter.

The torchbearer of new premillennialism became Cyrus Scofield, who grew convinced that the teachings he learned from his mentor James Brookes were distinct not only from those of modernists but also from those of old pre-millennialists. Growing awareness that he was a *new* premillennialist spurred Scofield to undertake a massive project: the *Scofield Reference Bible*. Conceived in 1902 and published in 1909, by Oxford University Press, Scofield's magnum opus immediately became the standard text for new premillennialism. More than anyone else, Scofield transformed new premillennialism into a full-blown religious identity for millions of Christians.

Old and New Premillennialists Divide

Before the 1890s, old and new premillennialists coexisted at Niagara-on-the-Lake by focusing on the beliefs they held in common. The spirit of unity in the face of the new theology and postmillennialists was refreshed every year, where the pattern of prayer, preaching, and worship energized attendees in the cause of global missions. Yet with numerical growth came increasing tensions. Divisions that once appeared minor now widened and took on added importance. The theological differences that separated old and new premillennialists were evident not just in the surface teachings like the timing of the rapture— old premillennialists placed the rapture after the tribulation, while new pre-millennialists insisted it was imminent—but extended to the deeper structures of theological reasoning and biblical interpretation.

Tempers reached such a fever pitch by 1897 that even the sanguine Eliza-beth Needham admitted that the year's attendees "may not, and do not see eye to eye in all minor points of truth, particularly prophecy." The "brotherhood" did agree on a host of issues, including a "literal and pre-millennial return of Jesus Christ," "the restoration of the Jewish Commonwealth," and especially the need for "missionary zeal."[2] But when Brookes, the most important new premillennialist of his generation and president of the conference, died that same year, so too did clarity on the future of these differences. The dream of a robust premillennial movement that united old and new premillennialists in massive resistance to modernism was becoming less clear—and premillenni-alists had no one to blame but themselves.

In the early 1890s, Brookes had observed a growing dissension about the timing of the rapture. Nathaniel West, one of the country's most respected premillennial writers, broke with new premillennialism in favor of an older

2. Mrs. George C. Needham, "Niagara Bible Conference," *Our Hope* 4 (July 1897): 69.

view that placed the rapture after the tribulation. While this shift might have seemed minor to outsiders, the rhetoric quickly grew heated. West concluded in an 1893 salvo that "the Darby-Doctrine has nothing new in it that is true and nothing true in it that is new."[3] He was allied with Robert Cameron, a Canadian Baptist minister who wanted to turn the conference over to old premillennialists. Others followed, including William G. Moorehead and Charles Erdman, two of the original organizers who were both lapsed new premillennialists. When Cameron argued a couple of years after West that the early church had not taught an imminent rapture, Brookes realized the threat of division was imminent. "It is a sad fact that pre-millennialists, notwithstanding their knowledge of the truth, are going to pieces," he wrote in his magazine in 1895.[4]

Late that summer, Brookes, now in declining health, invited Cameron to his home. Only Cameron's version of the meeting remains, and it portrays Brookes as a troubled soul. "That article on the Lord's coming," Brookes was said to have confessed, "it seems to me unanswerable." In the late afternoon sun he turned to Cameron and pleaded, "Even if the apostles did not expect a secret meeting in the air, can't you leave me the hope, after all these years have passed away that I may live to see my Lord come, and escape the clutches of that awful enemy, death?"[5] Friendship won out—this time. "I only muttered in broken accents something like the following," Cameron recalled: "'Oh Dr. Brookes that is quite another matter—some will surely be alive and escape death at the coming of the Lord.'"[6] The answer admitted nothing, theologically speaking, and would not be offered in less intimate settings.

Cameron had his own reasons for portraying Brookes's faltering faith in the any-moment rapture. Partisans for Brookes, including his wife, denied that he ever wavered, and indeed there is little extant evidence outside of Cameron's recollection that he did. But the story was revealing all the same. Divisions had threatened to split apart the new premillennial network before, but never were the stakes so high, and the doctrines so central to the future of the movement. Brookes had been holding the cause together, but with his passing the teeming energy of premillennialism lost its steady hand.

The divide between the followers of Brookes and followers of Cameron only widened after the final meeting of the Niagara Bible Conference in As-

3. Quoted in Ernest Robert Sandeen, *The Roots of Fundamentalism: British and American Millenarianism, 1800–1930* (Chicago: University of Chicago Press, 1970), 210–11.

4. Quoted in Sandeen, *The Roots of Fundamentalism*, 209.

5. Quoted in Sandeen, *The Roots of Fundamentalism*, 211.

6. Quoted in Sandeen, *The Roots of Fundamentalism*, 211–12.

bury Park, New Jersey, in 1900. At that modest gathering, divisions were more apparent than ever. The successors to Brookes held no hope for a grand premillennial alliance, no shared experiences of war, no memory of a world before interdenominational activity was a matter of course. Two of the younger new premillennialists in attendance, Scofield and Arno Gaebelein, left the meeting so unsatisfied that they organized a separate conference that was intended for new premillennialists only. The Sea Cliff Bible Conference, held on Long Island, New York, occurred every year from 1901 to 1911 and excluded the old premillennialists.

Yet the breakup of the Niagara Bible Conference did not entirely dash the dream of a premillennial consensus. The existential pressures felt by the movement's leaders spurred them toward their most ambitious effort yet to unite premillennialists under one theological banner. That project, the *Scofield Reference Bible*, became the definitive articulation of fifty years of new premillennial thinking and organizing, solidifying the movement's successes and delineating its theological boundaries. The annotated Bible accomplished something neither old nor new premillennialists could previously claim: it embedded premillennialism into a full presentation of evangelical Christianity and standardized its teachings on terms that millions of Christians would embrace as their own.

The Scofield Reference Bible

Cyrus Ingerson Scofield's early life was difficult and hardly pointed to the wide influence he would exercise on American religion. He was born in Michigan in 1843, but as a teenager he moved to Tennessee to live with relatives. At seventeen years old, he enlisted in the Confederate army. He fought at Antietam in 1862 and was discharged later for being underage. Lacking passion to rejoin the war, he took a Union loyalty oath and settled in St. Louis with extended family. After having trained as a lawyer, he managed an appointment as the US district attorney for Kansas in 1873—but resigned the same year after allegations of bribery. A heavy drinker, he abandoned his wife and two daughters while under the same cloud of scandal.

At this low point in his life, Scofield had a conversion experience and came under the mentorship of James Brookes. By 1880 Scofield had begun to preach at the local YMCA and circulate among local Moody revival networks. He began imbibing new premillennialism, Higher Life teachings, and the cause of sectional reconciliation all at once, merging them into what would become the definitive presentation of new premillennialism in the early twentieth century. He

HOW TO USE THE SUBJECT REFERENCES.

THE subject references lead the reader from the first clear mention of a great truth to the last. The first and last references (in parenthesis) are repeated each time, so that wherever a reader comes upon a subject he may recur to the first reference and follow the subject, or turn at once to the Summary at the last reference.

ILLUSTRATION
(at Mark 1. 1.)

> *b Gospel.* **vs.1,**
> **14,15; Mk.**
> **8.35. (Gen.**
> **12.1-3; Rev.**
> **14.6.)**

Here *Gospel* is the subject; vs. 1, 14, 15 show where it is at that particular place; Mk. 8. 35 is the next reference in the chain, and the references in parenthesis are the first and the last.

Figure 11. Instruction page in *Scofield Reference Bible*. In addition to the hundreds of notes and "helps" offered in the *Scofield Reference Bible*, the extensive system of subject references created a vast internal architecture of biblical meaning. This instruction page was inserted more than a dozen times in the Bible, preceding each grouping of books (Pentateuch, Historical Books, Poetical Books, etc.).

was ordained as a Congregationalist minister in 1884 as part of his move to Dallas under the aegis of the Council of Congregational Ministries and Churches.

Scofield's first pamphlet was *Rightly Dividing the Word of Truth* (1888), which previewed his reference Bible's suggestion of a seven-dispensation structure. In the core passage of the pamphlet, Scofield explained that there were "seven unequal periods, usually called dispensations, although these periods are also called ages." Following the new premillennial pattern, each dispensation "may be regarded as a new test of the natural man, and each ends in judgment, marking his utter failure in every dispensation." He located his readers in the midst of the story: "five of these dispensations, or periods of time, have been fulfilled; we are living in the sixth, probably toward its close, and have before us the seventh, and last: the millennium."[7]

The short pamphlet, which quickly gained classic status in the Moody movement for its winsome and concise presentation, previewed the much larger project that would become the *Scofield Reference Bible*. Scofield's stature increased throughout the 1890s as a constant presence on the Bible conference circuit. His name grew synonymous with Scofield's Bible Correspondence Course, a distance-learning curriculum hosted by Moody Bible Institute starting in 1890. In 1895 he was called from Dallas to pastor Moody's church in

7. Cyrus I. Scofield, *Rightly Dividing the Word of Truth*, 11th ed. (Chicago: Revell, 1897 [1888]), table of contents, 1, 10.

East Northfield, Massachusetts, which placed him at the epicenter of global missionary activity. Four years later he officiated at Moody's funeral.

The idea of developing a comprehensive set of Scofield's notes for an annotated Bible was first broached at the second Sea Cliff Bible Conference in 1902. Arno Gaebelein, who recounted the origin story decades later, encouraged Scofield in his interactions with the Sea Cliff conference's chief benefactor, New York–based printer Francis Emory Fitch. Scofield and Gaebelein also spoke with New York real estate broker Alwyn Ball Jr. and department store owner John Pirie, longtime supporters of premillennialism in New England. Fitch, Ball, and Pirie were all Exclusive Brethren, and it was significant that Scofield's notes would reflect key Brethren teachings, including the imminent rapture and the church-Israel distinction, alongside the more widely shared evangelical emphases on biblical authority, missions and evangelism, conversion, and personal piety. With a ready author and abundant financial support, the group decided that "the time for definite action had come."[8]

With financial support secured, Scofield worked full time on his notes for four years while traveling in North America and Britain. One of his most valuable encounters abroad was with Henry Frowde, the manager of Oxford University Press, who was known for such feats as shipping one million copies of the Revised New Testament in twenty-four hours. Frowde was also a lifelong Exclusive Brethren. He oversaw Oxford's expansion into North America with its first office in New York City in 1896. Scofield's prospective Bible notes aligned with Frowde's desire to reach a popular audience, and the *Scofield Reference Bible* did not disappoint when it was released on both sides of the Atlantic in April 1909. In less than a decade it sold one million copies. By most accounts it remains the best-selling book in the history of Oxford University Press. It was both a culmination of the two generations of new premillennial thought and a popular tool for modern "Christian workers" in mission fields, urban areas, and church pulpits.

The *Scofield Reference Bible* presented new premillennialism as a religious framework of estimable pedigree that could be accessible to clergy and laypeople alike. The years of sustained work allowed Scofield to present a vast amount of material as if he were merely transmitting scholarly consensus, even as the notes conformed to his own distinct perspective. He wrote in the preface that the "modest if laborious task" was "summarizing, arranging, and condensing" a "vast literature, inaccessible to most Christian workers." Yet this

---

8. Arno C. Gaebelein, *The History of the "Scofield Reference Bible"* (1943; reprint, Edinburgh: CrossReach Publications, 2017), 38.

statement undersold Scofield's own role as arbiter of not only the thousands of notes that he created but also the thousands of subheadings and topical references, book introductions, and outlines to each section of the Bible. Scofield's first reference of "dispensations" came in the introduction, where he summarized them as "the majestic, progressive order of the divine dealings of God with humanity."[9] His formal definition came as a section subheading and note for Genesis 1:28, the famous passage in which God gives humanity dominion over the earth. "A dispensation is a period of time during which man is tested in respect of obedience to some specific revelation of the will of God. Seven such dispensations are distinguished in Scripture," the note read.

Scofield's count of seven dispensations pointed to his preference for Scottish Brethren Walter Scott's version of Darby's scheme. In the 1880s, Scott became involved in a Brethren debate over the extent of Christ's atonement and eventually sought "occasional communion" with Open Brethren, becoming something of a pariah among Exclusives. Scofield, happily innocent of internal Brethren politics, drew on Scott's dispensational writings along with Frederick Grant's *Numerical Bible*, Darby's *Synopsis of the Books of the Bible*, and Brethren Andrew Jukes's typological analysis, *The Characteristic Differences of the Four Gospels*.[10] Scofield did not just inherit the teaching of dispensational time but also inherited the structural and typological concerns of these earlier writers, which included hundreds of "types" and "antitypes" discernible only by way of the hermeneutical framework of the Brethren. He offered a seven-stage division of time that bridged Brethren teachings with the concerns of Americans for a commonsense biblical interpretation that rejected higher criticism.

Scofield claimed to have consulted "a very wide circle of learned and spiritual brethren in Europe and America," including faculty at the University of Lausanne, Oxford University, and Princeton University. He assembled seven "editorial consultants," all premillennialists and familiar names. Their role in the notes was left vague. Scofield acknowledged elsewhere his indebtedness to Gaebelein on the prophetic portions of Scripture, which may be what Scofield was referencing when he marveled in the Bible's preface at "the modern results of the remarkable study of the Prophets."[11] Whatever the role of scholars and fellow premillennial expositors, Scofield presented his notes not as novelty or

9. Introduction to *Scofield Reference Bible*, ed. Cyrus I. Scofield (Oxford: Oxford University Press, 1909), front matter.
10. John Reid, *F. W. Grant: His Life, Ministry, and Legacy* (Plainfield, NJ: John Reid Book Fund, 1995), 27–28. In *The Fundamentals*, vol. 12 (Chicago: Testimony Publishing Co., 1915), 122, Scofield lists Jukes as one of his top nine recommended books.
11. See introduction to *Scofield Reference Bible*, front matter, and David A. Rausch,

revision but as securing into place received insight and wisdom, fit for both learned and novice Christian alike. Though the notes would always be attached to his name, he did succeed in presenting them as an accessible version of a scholarly consensus that was modern in its emphasis on precision, classifica tion, and logical organization.

The Scofield Reference Culture

In addition to fixing a new premillennial framework around the Bible, Sco-field's notes taught readers to disregard threats to understanding the Bible in commonsense terms as an inerrant text. He used the language of scholarship to dismiss competing brands of scholarly authority, especially biblical higher criticism and modern scientific theories of evolution.

The reference Bible opposed higher criticism, except for a mention of "the field of textual criticism" in the preface used to reinforce that the Authorized (King James) Version remained accurate to a "remarkable degree."[12] In other venues, Scofield described the biblical text "as absolutely inerrant in every statement of fact."[13] This would become a sticking point. In the 1917 updated edition, more than in the original 1909 edition, Scofield squarely defended himself against the findings of higher criticism by emphasizing the unity of the text and its themes, counting the harmony of more than forty biblical writers as "the unanswerable proof of the divine inspiration of the Bible."[14]

Scofield also weighed in on the compatibility between modern science and biblical knowledge. To the questions of creation and humanity, the Bible supplied "words of matchless grandeur, and in an order which, rightly under-stood, is absolutely scientific." While Scofield relied at times on the cosmo-logical chronology of seventeenth-century bishop James Ussher, he rejected a recent date for the origin of the universe. He distinguished multiple "creative acts." The first, God's creation of heaven and earth in Genesis 1:1, "refers to the dateless past, and gives scope for all the geologic ages." He separated in time this act from Genesis 1:3, which described God's first declaration of light

Arno C. Gaebelein, 1861–1945: Irenic Fundamentalist and Scholar (Lewiston, NY: Mellen, 1983), 73.

12. Introduction to Scofield Reference Bible (New York: Oxford University Press, 1909), front matter.

13. Cyrus I. Scofield, Things Old and New: Old and New Testament Studies (New York: Our Hope, 1920), 112.

14. "A Panoramic View of the Bible," in Scofield Reference Bible, ed. Cyrus I. Scofield, rev. ed. (Oxford: Oxford University Press, 1917), v.

and darkness. Scofield endorsed the "gap theory" popularized by Exclusive Brethren George H. Pember, which posited an indeterminate amount of time between Genesis 1:1 and Genesis 1:3, opening a gap between God's "original creative act" that produced a "primitive order" that was then ruined and the seven days of creation detailed in the rest of Genesis 1. "Relegate fossils to the primitive creation," Scofield explained, "and no conflict of science with the cosmogony remains." Scofield's subheadings in the text were decisive to how readers understood the periodization. While Genesis 1:1 was titled "The Original Creation," Genesis 1:2 received its own subheading: "Earth made waste and empty by judgment." A further division at Genesis 1:3 indicated that what followed was "The New Beginning," taking place aeons later.[15]

While Scofield harmonized biblical and scientific timelines, he rejected the theory of Darwinian evolution. "Man was created, not evolved," he wrote in his note to Genesis 1:26, the verse in which God says to "make man in our image." Conscripting a line from Thomas Huxley, one of the early champions of Darwinian evolution, Scofield argued that "'an enormous gulf, a divergence practically infinite,'" existed between "the lowest man and the highest beast" and that "science and discovery have done nothing to bridge that 'gulf.'"[16]

Scofield's rejection of evolution did not flow from a literal reading of the Genesis account. He proposed that the word "day" held three potential meanings, only one of which was "the solar day of twenty-four hours," and concluded that the use of "days" most likely meant "a [longer] period of time marked off by a beginning and an ending."[17] Rather, Scofield opposed Darwinism to protect the high status of humans over the rest of the created order. The "image of God," Scofield explained in one of his longest notes to Genesis, "is found chiefly in man's tri-unity, and in his moral nature." Evolution, or what Scofield categorized in biblical language as science "falsely so called," ruptured the "triunity" of humanity that reflected God's Trinitarian nature.[18]

Scofield also advanced a biblical anthropology rooted in the Brethren-inspired trio of Israel, the church, and the nations. In his 1917 revised notes, he included a brief essay, "Panoramic View of the Bible," meant to shore up criticisms that dispensational time unnecessarily divided the biblical message, suggested multiple paths to salvation, or severed the coherence of the biblical story. Even so, Scofield insisted that following Pentecost, "the division of the [human] race now becomes

---

15. *Scofield Reference Bible* (1909), 3, 3n2, 4n3.
16. *Scofield Reference Bible* (1909), 5n3.
17. *Scofield Reference Bible* (1909), 4nn1 and 2.
18. *Scofield Reference Bible* (1909), 944n1.

threefold—the Jew, the Gentile, and the Church of God."[19] Peppered through the notes, this "threefold" division performed a basic hermeneutical work that enfolded the novel implications of Brethren teachings for each category of humanity. As he warned in the introduction to the Gospels, readers needed to "exclude the notion—a legacy in Protestant thought from post-apostolic and Roman Catholic theology—that the Church is the true Israel." He concluded: "Do not, therefore, assume interpretations to be true because they are familiar."[20]

The *Scofield Reference Bible*'s success as a commercial and religious product created a robust Bible-reading community. Its impressive sales were a testament to the strength of new premillennialism, and new premillennial embrace of the Bible shaped an exegetical tradition that transcended denomination and section. While Bible institutes, mission agencies, and seminaries actually structured the subculture of new premillennialism, the *Scofield Reference Bible* helped to bring the teachings into the pulpits and pews of churches, the songs and hymns of revivalism, and, eventually, the commercial and mass consumer productions of popular culture.

A Republic of Scofield's Notes

If Brethren seeded North America with new premillennial teachings, Scofield was the one to reap the harvest. The *Scofield Reference Bible* created the cultural context for the adoption of dispensationalism in the 1920s by introducing millions of readers to some of its foundational concepts. Unlike modernist or higher-critical approaches to the Bible, Scofield's presentation did not force readers to reappraise basic inherited evangelical theology. Rather, he integrated new premillennialism, dispensational time, and other distinctive teachings into the shared American Protestant culture that emphasized personal piety, conversion, and activism on behalf of religion. This strategic conservatism for presenting relatively new teachings in annotated form helped to propel the *Scofield Reference Bible* to levels of success beyond any previous new premillennial publication.

The popularity of Scofield's Bible after 1909 was so great that it became a common marker of right belief in Moody movement circles, signaling fidelity to the same values Scofield espoused: the Bible's perfect and absolute authority over all aspects of life, its inerrancy, and the believer's duty to rightly divide its contents in order to identify the underlying harmony and unity of its teachings. While these values were most pointedly contrasted with teachings of higher

19. "A Panoramic View of the Bible," *Scofield Reference Bible*, rev. ed., vi.
20. "The Four Gospels," in *Scofield Reference Bible*, rev. ed., 989.

critics and modernists, Scofield's notes also marked lines among closer subsets of Christians. Confessionally Reformed theologians, steeped in the writings of Calvin, found little to laud in Scofield's notes, which adhered only loosely to Reformed themes and evidenced foreign influences, including new premillennialism, revivalism, Higher Life teachings, and Exclusive Brethren concepts.

Likewise, Scofield's divisions were insufficient for a smaller band of new premillennial followers that gathered around Anglican clergyman Ethelbert W. Bullinger in Britain, who insisted that the current dispensation (and therefore the church itself) did not begin until late in the apostle Paul's ministry. The "Bullingerite" position taught that most of Paul's epistles were written not to the church but to the Jewish people, to be applied in the future Israelite kingdom of heaven only. Water baptism and communion were among the casualties of Bullingerite practices that were redefined as Jewish. Arriving at the peak of Bullinger's influence, the *Scofield Reference Bible* confronted this more radical deduction of dispensational time (what would later be termed "ultradispensationalism") and ensured that it would only attract a marginal following in the United States.

From the Great Lakes basin to China, from Los Angeles to the Sudan, Scofield's notes were exported alongside, and were often inextricable from, the gospel message itself. By the 1920s, missionaries in Korea, East Africa, and Guatemala introduced Christianity through the Scofield Bible, and Scofield's goal of offering a one-stop resource for "Christian workers" bore immediate fruit. Horace G. Underwood, one of the earliest British missionaries to Korea, translated Scofield's notes into Korean as early as 1912. Watchman Nee, one of the most significant indigenous leaders of Chinese Christianity in the twentieth century, translated Scofield's correspondence course and notes into Chinese in 1926. The British missionary John Edward Church met with East African Christians in the late 1920s; he sparked the East African Revival after spending days in fellowship with them "tracing chain references in Church's Scofield Bible."[21] The spread of new premillennialism continued unabated, and the standardizing work of Scofield was now its most potent propellent. In fewer than fifty years, a new tradition of premillennialism managed to rally Christians across North America and, as a result of the institutional infrastructure erected to meet the urgency it posited, soon spanned the globe.

---

21. Quoted in Brenden Pietsch, *Dispensational Modernism* (New York: Oxford University Press, 2015), 207.

*Business is organized on a vast scale; the unit counts for nothing—
the mass for everything. The hours of the day are not enough for
toil, business burns up the nights as well. God's rest day is ruthlessly
appropriated; men are worn out, burnt out rather, and left behind
without thought or mercy.*

Cyrus I. Scofield,
"Busy about the Wrong Things" (1905)

*It is evident enough to those who will but give themselves a chance
to think, that something* is vitally wrong with the system. *Death
is entrenched at its heart. Crime and cruelty and misery in many
forms pervade it. Nothing is permanent. "Change and decay in
all around we see." The presence of those grim advance agents of
destruction is detected in all things wherein man has a part. Yet
somehow the presiding genius of this world system contrives to keep
men busy in one way and another, and to keep alive the delusion
that, as a general proposition, "things are getting better." Thus do
the sons of Adam continue to exhibit their inherited predisposition
to the acceptance of that pleasing doctrine: "Ye shall not surely die;
ye shall be as God."*

Philip Mauro,
The World and Its God (1908)

Premillennialists entered the twentieth century with a comprehensive social critique that
identified consolidation of the "world system" as its chief ailment. This meant they tended
to see similarities between the accrual of capital, the centralization of government, and
ecumenical Protestantism. Scofield and Mauro supplied their many readers with tools to
critique the present state of the world on premillennial terms—a role Mauro would later
regret when he rejected premillennialism.

9

The "World System" and War

When Moody Bible Institute hosted a massive prophecy conference in February 1914, most of the four-day gathering was dedicated to theological topics. But there were a few venues for more personal reflections, including a symposium entitled "How I Became a Premillennialist." In this conversational setting, presenters recounted their conversion stories. William L. Pettengill, a YMCA worker and editor of the magazine *Serving and Waiting*, recalled the day that "transformed" his life: "somebody handed me a copy of Dr. Scofield's 'Rightly Dividing the Word of Truth.'" This little text, he said, "made the Bible an open book to me, like a beautiful rose, or a beautiful fruit." Charles Gallaudet Trumbull, editor of the *Sunday School Times*, quoted a friend who described premillennialism as a theme that came to him "like a second conversion." Himself converted to the position after reading Blackstone's *Jesus Is Coming*, Trumbull now "simply marveled that anyone who ever read the Bible could see anything else in it than the Lord's Coming!"[1] Nearly every attendee had been born before new premillennialism had been adopted by Americans; by 1914, it was a formidable force on the American religious scene. Decades of institution building, standardization, and expansion transformed new premillennialism into a fully fledged religious movement that was supercharged with the recent publication of the *Scofield Reference Bible*.

The religious scene, however, was heading for a deep and permanent rupture. Lines of division between Protestants were widely noted at the time,

---

1. *The Coming and Kingdom of Christ: A Stenographic Report of the Prophetic Bible Conference Held at the Moody Bible Institute of Chicago, February 24–27, 1914* (Chicago: Bible Institute Colportage Association, 1914), 134, 65–66.

though few knew exactly how the breakup would occur. Modernists and their opponents were marching in opposite directions theologically, socially, politically. They were polarizing into rival factions, each claiming the mantle of true Protestantism.

While opposition to modernism had yet to cohere into a single oppositional movement, alternatives to Protestant modernism flourished in the 1900s, including the holiness and Higher Life movements, Pentecostalism, and new premillennialism. These separate yet overlapping alternatives could rival modernist Protestantism together, perhaps, but none could marshal comparable resources, cultural capital, or institutional heft. How these alternative communities navigated the next decade would reshape Protestantism and lay crucial groundwork for forming the dispensational system in the 1920s.

New premillennialists approached the growing fractiousness in American Protestantism by relying on the same tools that had made the Moody movement so successful. Their response was not to form a political party or to court politicians, nor, in the wake of the break between old and new premillennialists, was it to rally around a single theology. Rather, new premillennialists joined other conservative Protestants to use their interdenominational networks to develop a religious response to "consolidation," or growing modernist power, that they identified in economic, political, and religious spheres. Through the 1910s, new premillennialists remained united on their diagnosis of the problems they faced, and in their prescriptions for right belief. This unity allowed them to continue to steward the leadership of the Moody movement. The tumultuous years of World War I would be the last time that premillennialists could claim to do so.

Philip Mauro and the World System

In their anticipation of the coming kingdom, new premillennialists frequently documented the depraved state of the world, which they understood to be under the rule of Satan in this dispensation. "He is expressly called the 'prince of this world,'" Brethren writer Frederick Grant reminded readers in 1894. "To dwell where Satan's throne is, is to settle down in the world, under Satan's government, so to speak, and protection."[2]

2. Frederick Grant, *The Revelation of Christ to His Servants* (New York: Loizeaux Brothers, 1894), 60.

The
King's Business

VOL. 1   JANUARY, 1910   NO. 1

THE BIBLE IS ALIVE.

"The Word of God is Living and Active" (Heb. 12:4, R. V.).

"The Gospels possess a secret virtue and mysterious efficacy, a warmth which penetrates and soothes the heart * * * * The Gospel is not a book, it is a living being, with vigor, a power that conquers everything that opposes."—Napoleon.

"When we read: 'The Word of God is living' we are to understand thereby that it lives with a spiritual, an inexhaustible and inextinguishable life—in a word, a Divine life. If the Word of God be indeed living in this sense, then we have here a fact of the most tremendous significance."—Philip Mauro.

Published Monthly by the BIBLE INSTITUTE
LOS ANGELES, CALIFORNIA.

Figure 12. King's Business first issue covers. Philip Mauro's influence as a new premillennial social critic peaked around 1910. In the first issue of the King's Business, January 1910, the periodical of the recently founded Bible Institute of Los Angeles, Mauro appeared on the front and back covers next to other luminaries prized by new premillennialists.

The belief that Satan, not God, temporarily ruled the world fueled a pre-millennial critique of society and church that was both populist and separatist. At the center of the social critique was the idea of the "world system," the interlocking institutions, organizations, and structural powers helmed by elites that ran the world. "The present world-system, organized upon the principles of force, greed, selfishness, ambition, and sinful pleasure is his work," Scofield wrote of Satan in his notes on the climactic chapter of the millennium, Revelation 20. "The notion that he reigns in hell is Miltonic, not biblical. He is prince of this present world-system, but will be tormented in the lake of fire."[3]

New premillennialism soon had its own leading theorist of the "world system": Philip Mauro, author and St. Louis lawyer. Mauro's pen blazed with the energy of recent religious conversion, which he experienced during a long night of the soul in 1903 after attending Albert Simpson's Gospel Tabernacle in New York City. By the end of his first decade as a Christian, Mauro was arguably the movement's foremost social critic. His books—Mauro published five between 1905 and 1913—sold well, and he was a frequent speaker on the Bible conference circuits.

A system was by definition closed with its own loops of cause and effect. The "world system," Mauro explained in 1905, was nothing less than "the consequences of the acceptance by the human family of Satan's programme and leadership" in all dimensions of life.[4] Mauro's analysis was expansive; he wrote that the world system "has worlds within worlds," ranging from business to politics, from fashion to sport. The world system encompassed nothing less than "civilization" and was "marvelous in its complexity and detail, as well as in the character and variety of its activities." While it had been a fixture of human society since the fall of Adam, the world system "has been gradually taking more and more definite shape during the present age," Mauro explained in 1910. The overwhelming force of the system as currently constructed lay in its economic might. "Trade, secure investment of capital, business interests, and 'spheres of influence,' are now the prime concern of governments and diplomacy. Business is a sacred thing; and the test of the merit of any measure or event is the question, 'How will it affect business?'"[5]

3. *The Scofield Reference Bible*, ed. Cyrus I. Scofield (Oxford: Oxford University Press, 1909), 1350.

4. Philip Mauro, *The World and Its God*, 2nd ed. (New York: Gospel Publishing House, 1905), 32.

5. Philip Mauro, *Man's Day*, 2nd ed. (New York: Gospel Publishing House, 1910), 174.

New premillennialists, like progressive reformers of the era, saw industrialization as a double-edged sword. The wealth generated by capitalism fueled global missions, while advances in communication and transportation linked Christians in new ways. Yet capitalism also led to the unprecedented consolidation of power and manifested materially the "powers and principalities" of the Prince of the World. Scofield lamented that "business is organized on a vast scale; the unit counts for nothing—the mass for everything."[6] Arno C. Gaebelein wrote in 1915 of "the utter destruction of the present imposing world-system by a crushing blow" as the view of the biblical prophets, and a decade later affirmed the Bible's prophecies of "the destruction of the great world-system" that would be lamented by "the kings, the merchants, the shipmasters, the company in ships and sailors."[7]

The urge to halt consolidation united world-system premillennialists. They all claimed to be witnessing a capitalist-fueled collapse of diversity and autonomy, a movement toward global unity and homogeneity in all areas of life, including the church. Mauro wrote worryingly of "the ideal of the Consolidation or Federation of all human affairs and interests," while Isaac M. Haldeman, a premillennialist with a pulpit in New York City, preached with alarm of the emerging "kingdom of commerce," the "titanic struggle for commercial supremacy" pushing the world to adopt "unity of measure, unity of speech and unity of commerce."[8] A worldwide drift into materialist oligarchy seemed inevitable. Writing in *Record of Christian Work*, Frederick B. Meyer, one of Moody's first British champions and a frequent Keswick speaker, lamented that "Capitalism is having its hour. Mammon is the idol of the age." He berated "iron kings and capitalists" whose "course is destructive of all smaller concerns" that did not enhance money or power.[9]

The upshot for new premillennialists was that the world, including much of organized Christianity, was beholden to an industrial consolidation that made a heretical promise to bring heaven to earth. "The modern world of business has to a large extent imposed its standards, ideals, and aspirations upon the professing Church, and this process has been going on unobtrusively for some

6. Cyrus I. Scofield, *In Many Pulpits with Dr. C. I. Scofield* (New York: Oxford University Press, 1922), 290.

7. Arno C. Gaebelein, *The Revelation: An Analysis and Exposition of the Last Book of the Bible* (New York: Our Hope, 1915), 107.

8. Isaac M. Haldeman, *Signs of the Times* (New York: C. C. Cook, 1910), 341.

9. Frederick B. Meyer, "Devotional Studies in the Sunday-School Lessons," *Record of Christian Work* 27, no. 9 (September 1908): 668.

time past," Mauro wrote in 1909. Centering on the "modernists"—proponents of the new theology, Social Gospel, modern science, and ecumenism—Mauro detected that the market ideology was at work in the church, too, "merging smaller into larger aggregates" with the bleeding effect of the capitalist's penchant "to substitute for many concerns which at one time competed fiercely and destructively therein, a single concern or monopoly."[10]

No development crystallized the concern of world-system premillennialists more than the founding of the Federal Council of Churches of Christ in 1908, which represented thirty-two denominations and more than twelve million Protestants. The new organization intended "to secure a larger combined influence for the churches of Christ in all matters affecting the moral and social condition of people"[11] and was underwritten by capitalist monopolists, the liberal Protestant ecumenist John D. Rockefeller chief among them. To new premillennialists primed to see the machinations of Satan behind consolidation efforts, all signs pointed to a conspiracy of religious and business elites whispering to each other: "We have come to dream of a GREAT UNIFICATION."[12] World-system analysis was the first self-consciously premillennial social criticism to emerge in the twentieth century, supplying premillennialists with a simple and yet multilayered understanding of the changes in geopolitics and economics on the cusp of World War I.

The Fundamentals

In the 1910s, new premillennialists continued to extend their influence through the religious networks built by Moody and the global missions movement. The most ambitious and consequential project of the decade was *The Fundamentals*, a twelve-volume publication from 1910 to 1915 that offered a robust—and final, as it turned out—expression of the wider Moody movement forged fifty years earlier. Conceived and led by new premillennialists, *The Fundamentals* drew from the same broad Anglo-American evangelical culture that Moody helped to create in the 1870s. And yet *The Fundamentals* also started a new chapter in the story of premillennialism, laying the outlines of a narrower

10. Philip Mauro, *The Number of Man: The Climax of Civilization* (Boston: Hamilton Bros., 1909), 62–63.

11. "The Constitution of the Federal Council," in Elias Benjamin Sanford, *Origin and History of the Federal Council of the Churches of Christ in America* (Hartford, CT: S. S. Scranton Co., 1916), 466.

12. Mauro, *The Number of Man*, 63.

and more concentrated appeal that was distinct from the holiness tradition, Pentecostalism, and other antimodernist movements.

The compilation and editing of *The Fundamentals* put on display all the gains and drawbacks of recent organizing. The project was funded by new premillennialists Lyman and Milton Stewart, who were acknowledged on the front of each volume as "Two Christian Laymen." The volumes were published by the Testimony Publishing Company, a new entity founded by Milton solely for this purpose. Operations were initially based in Chicago, where the Great Lakes basin leadership centered at Moody Bible Institute shaped the early volumes. Like the *Scofield Reference Bible*'s seven-person editorial committee, the Testimony Publishing Company was led by a seven-member "executive committee" of new premillennialists. Clarence Dixon, still pastor of Moody Memorial Church, and Reuben Torrey, former president of Moody Bible Institute, were joined by Louis Meyer, an Ohio-based evangelist; Elmore Harris, founder of the Toronto Bible Institute; and Methodist evangelist D. W. Potter. The final two spots went to Moody Bible Institute overseer Henry Parsons Crowell (of the Quaker Oats Company) and businessman Thomas S. Smith.

This Chicago-centric leadership set about to produce a series of volumes that displayed the breadth and respectability of not just premillennialism but also the interdenominational, revivalist evangelicalism of the Moody movement. Channeling the irenicism of Moody himself, Clarence Dixon, the first of the three editors of *The Fundamentals,* resisted the wishes of Milton Stewart for religious muckraking that would draw stark theological divisions across the American scene. Stewart's idea was for a series of short essays to root out heresies including Darwinism and biblical criticism, expose sects like the Millennial Dawn (Jehovah's Witnesses) and the Church of Latter-day Saints, and shore up teachings on the atonement and biblical inerrancy. Dixon, meanwhile, held grander hopes of rallying Anglo-American evangelicalism to a renewed agenda of missions, revivals, and Bible training.

The first five volumes under Dixon's editorship disappointed Stewart, but they featured other strengths. By tapping mainstays of the Moody movement including Mauro, Torrey, and Pierson (who died in June 1911), Dixon covered topics that were consonant with longtime Moody movement priorities. Published in 1910–1911, these first volumes argued for a high view of Scripture, rebutted higher criticism, and restated traditional Protestant doctrines such as the incarnation and justification by faith. While popular, the project's early effect was to repeat themes that most evangelicals already shared.

In 1911 Dixon took the prestigious pastorate of the London Metropolitan Church, leaving *The Fundamentals* without an editor. Louis Meyer, a messianic Jew and friend of Stewart's, took over and moved the editorial offices to his hometown of Cincinnati. The next five volumes, under Meyer's editorship, hewed closer to Stewart's original vision and included attacks on evolution, higher criticism, and groups including Mormons, Christian Scientists, and "modern spiritualists."

Meyer collapsed from exhaustion in 1912 and was diagnosed with tubercular meningitis. He revealed in his final edited volume that he had been "seriously ill since the beginning of November [1912] and [was] writing these lines while being under treatment in a sanatorium"—an expense funded by Milton Stewart.[13] Meyer died in July 1913, and it fell to Stewart's new ally in California, Reuben Torrey, to fill out *The Fundamentals* with two final volumes. Volumes 11 and 12 were the narrowest in appeal and most marked by the influence of Stewart. Scofield contributed the essay "The Grace of God," which drew a sharp distinction between the dispensations of law and grace and made salvation in the current dispensation a benefit of God's "free unadulterated grace" with nothing but a mental assent required by the sinner.[14] This view went unopposed in *The Fundamentals*—even as many of its contributors from Reformed backgrounds found it insufficient.

Other premillennialists filled out the final volumes. Arno C. Gaebelein offered an analysis of prophecy fulfillment as proof of the Bible's authority. His essay, by far the longest of volume 11, made the case for the literal fulfillment of "hundreds of Divine predictions written in the Bible."[15] Gaebelein was balanced by a follow-up from theologian Charles Erdman (professor at Princeton Theological Seminary and son of William J. Erdman), who insisted on an old premillennialist "literal, visible, bodily, return of Christ" but otherwise offered a far less strenuous approach to particular prophecy or end-times sequences.[16]

One development that spanned all three editors was the rise of an emergent reading community around *The Fundamentals*, referred to in the volumes

13. Foreword to *The Fundamentals*, vol. 10 (Chicago: Testimony Publishing Co., 1913), front matter.

14. Cyrus I. Scofield, "The Grace of God," in *The Fundamentals*, vol. 11 (Chicago: Testimony Publishing Co., 1915), 48.

15. Arno C. Gaebelein, "Fulfilled Prophecies a Potent Argument for the Bible," in *The Fundamentals*, 11:57.

16. Charles Erdman, "The Coming of Christ," in *The Fundamentals*, 11:87.

as the "Circle of Prayer." The circle became a visible measure of the project's reception during its years of publication. Introduced in a note at the end of volume 3, Dixon suggested that "a Circle of Prayer be organized for the express purpose of making this entire movement an object of definite prayer—that God will guide in every detail and entirely fulfill His purpose in the existence of this movement."[17] He referred to the thousands of encouraging letters sent to the offices in Chicago, and indeed, over the course of 1910–1915, some 300,000 pieces of mail were processed. The purpose of the Circle of Prayer was articulated in volume 5, which announced its official formation with "several thousand persons." Prayer would be directed "to the end that [*The Fundamentals*] may result in a world-wide revival in the study of the Word and in the deepening of the spiritual life of believers."[18] Meyer relocated announcements about the "Circle of Prayer movement" to the front of each volume and reframed the mission of *The Fundamentals* to strengthening "true religion"—language that Torrey maintained for the later volumes.[19]

There is scant evidence in the historical record to measure the Circle of Prayer's impact, but it typifies the kind of action the creators of *The Fundamentals* hoped to inspire. There was no call to effect an ecclesial separation, organize political or social energies, or construct an institution to continue the cause, though readers of the volumes edited by Torrey were pointed to his new magazine in Los Angeles, the *King's Business*. The "Circle" was an effort to organize readers of *The Fundamentals*, but one that was consciously counterpolitical and united around spiritual practices (prayer and revival) and dedicated to a narrow theological platform (the "fundamentals of the faith").

Some three million copies of *The Fundamentals* were eventually distributed, with one-third leaving the United States. Prayer and revival remained the preferred tools that could span the diversity and institutional sprawl of Moody movement evangelicalism. To new premillennialists, the encroaching world system could be resisted only by a concerted effort of spiritual action, simultaneously engaging "men and women from across the world" in prayer

17. "Publisher's Notice," in *The Fundamentals*, vol. 3 (Chicago: Testimony Publishing Co., 1910), 128.

18. "Publisher's Notice," in *The Fundamentals*, vol. 5 (Chicago: Testimony Publishing Co., 1911), 126.

19. Foreword to *The Fundamentals*, vol. 6 (Chicago: Testimony Publishing Co., 1911), front matter.

and petition that "the truth may have new power and that a world-wide revival of religion may result."[20]

More historically significant than the Circle of Prayer was the Prophetic Bible Conference held at Moody Bible Institute in February 1914, which featured speakers and organizers that mirrored the executive committee and author list of *The Fundamentals* and was intended to be a show of force. Yet more than any previous national prophecy conference, this one reflected a split between old and new premillennialism. Of the twelve signers to the conference call, eight were new premillennialists and eight published (or would publish) in *The Fundamentals*. James Gray, president of the Moody Bible Institute, situated the gathering in Moody Church's Farwell Hall, where other national prophecy conferences dating to 1878 had been held. The list of speakers showed the strongest presence yet of new premillennial influence at the top of the Moody movement, stretching from Charles A. Blanchard, president of Wheaton College, to Charles G. Trumbull, editor of the *Sunday School Times*. A handful of prominent southerners were present, as well. Along with transplants William Bell Riley and L. W. Munhall were E. Y. Mullins, president of Southern Baptist Seminary; L. E. McNair, pastor in Nashville; and Bob Jones Sr., evangelist from South Carolina—though these leaders remained largely beholden to old premillennialism. A list of more than four hundred "exponents of premillennialism" closed the volume of conference addresses, even as many of the names were deeply suspect when it came to premillennialism, including William Occam, Martin Luther, and John Calvin.[21]

In the end, *The Fundamentals* was helmed, indisputably, by new premillennialists. The most frequently printed authors of the twelve volumes were Pierson (five articles), Scottish Presbyterian minister James Orr (four), Mauro (three), and the geologist George Fredrick Wright (three). Of those, Pierson and Mauro were new premillennialists, and of the ninety essays, fully one-third were written by new premillennialists—and most on topics not directly related to eschatology or prophecy.

Volume 12 included book recommendations from nine movement leaders—six of whom were new premillennialists. The most common recommendations were books by Torrey, Pierson, James M. Gray, and South African revivalist

20. Foreword to *The Fundamentals*, vol. 12 (Chicago: Testimony Publishing Co., 1915), 7.

21. *The Coming and Kingdom of Christ*, 242–49.

Andrew Murray.[22] Viewed through the prism of *The Fundamentals*, new pre-millennialism had ascended to the predominant position of antimodernist evangelicalism by the time the final volume appeared in 1915.

Wartime Volatility

The world system seemed to have reached its inevitable conclusion in the summer of 1914 when fighting broke out across Europe. As Western powers destroyed each other, premillennialists watched and waited. Clarence Dixon, still pastoring the London Metropolitan Tabernacle, was more war-ready, and closer to the action, than most Americans, and urged the United States to aid the British side. Yet most premillennialists exhibited only tepid interest in joining the war.

Prophetic speculation ran rampant, of course, and for a time it appeared that the machinations in Europe would produce the prophesied confederation of nations, which would then lead to the antichrist and one-world government. Yet from the start, the Great War was seen more as a preparatory conflict than the end of days. In new premillennialist prophecy analysis, Germany lay outside the boundaries of the expected new Roman Empire. In any case, the decisive prophetic theater of action was expected to be the Holy Land, not France. When British forces under the command of General Allenby marched into Jerusalem in December 1917, the "times of the Gentiles" (Luke 21:24) appeared to be nearing its end—especially in combination with the Balfour Declaration pronounced earlier the same year promising British support for a "Jewish national homeland." But much more prophecy remained unfulfilled, so the most common premillennial view was that the war served as empirical validation of the accuracy of world-system analysis. Gaebelein, writing in 1916, captured the sentiment when he advised: "the only thing a Christian can safely say about these unprecedented conditions among the nations is that these events fully confirm the characteristics of the age and its predicted end as revealed in the Bible."[23]

As war pressure mounted in the United States, new premillennialists showed a mix of patriotic obligation and theological hesitancy toward the

22. "The Fifteen Books Most Indispensable for the Christian Worker," in *The Fundamentals*, 12:120–23.

23. Gaebelein, quoted in Timothy Weber, *Living in the Shadow of the Second Coming: American Premillennialism, 1875–1925* (Grand Rapids: Zondervan, Acadamie Books, 1983), 115.

increasingly ambitious (and postmillennial-inflected) rhetoric of the Wilson administration. In the debate over war preparedness, leading premillennialists lamented the resort to military expansion. The *King's Business* went so far as to republish a sermon by the liberal Protestant pacifist Henry Sloane Coffin that connected militarism with business interests—an insight that fit into world-system analysis but carried with it social risks when aired in the fever of wartime.

Among other premillennialists, however, the mood was more patriotic. James M. Gray, president of Moody Bible Institute, made sure the school promoted war bonds and was sufficiently supportive of national mobilization, while the evangelist George F. Pentecost, in the pulpit of Arthur Pierson's old church in Philadelphia, preached dozens of sermons on the need to defeat Germany. Mark Matthews, a premillennial pastor in Seattle, campaigned for Wilson in 1916 on a platform of preparedness (though Wilson maintained his goal of neutrality through the election). And a rising minister, William Bell Riley, who had pastored the large First Baptist Church in Minneapolis since 1897 and led the Northwestern Bible Training School, grouped the war, the Bolshevik Revolution, higher criticism, Darwinism, and the threat of world government into a unified "menace of modernism" as he increasingly called for "the rise of a new Protestantism" that would stand athwart these threats.[24]

The revivalist and premillennialist Billy Sunday, whose massive rallies popularized "walking the sawdust trail," was an unrepentant partisan for America and advocate of German defeat, preaching of the need to "flay 'Kaiser Bill' and 'his dirty bunch of pretzel-chewing, limburger-eating highbinders'" and, on one Atlanta stage, delivering an uppercut to a German American who confronted him about his Teutophobia.[25] A baseball-player-turned-revivalist from Iowa, Sunday eschewed theologians and rarely cited any of the premillennialists from whom he borrowed language about the imminent second coming. Like Dwight Moody, Sunday did not so much preach precisely as he did evocatively, which in the end helped premillennial sentiments lodge

24. William Bell Riley, *Menace of Modernism* (New York: Christian Alliance Publishing Co., 1917); William Bell Riley, "The Great Divide, or Christ and the Present Crisis," in *God Hath Spoken: Twenty-Five Addresses Delivered at the World Conference on Christian Fundamentals, May 25–June 1, 1919* (Philadelphia: Bible Conference Committee, 1919), 27.

25. Sunday, quoted in Matthew Avery Sutton, *American Apocalypse: A History of Modern Evangelicalism* (Cambridge, MA: Belknap Press of Harvard University Press, 2014), 61.

themselves in the "old-time religion" of the sawdust trail. "No man can be true to his God without being true to his country," he preached in the intoxicating days of mobilization in 1918.[26] The confluence of Christianity and nationalism that Sunday channeled into his ministry remade his brand of premillennialism into one that Brethren thinkers a half century before would have found unrecognizable.

One reason the Great Lakes basin may have contained more patriotic premillennialists than other regions was that it was where suspicion of nationalist loyalties ran highest. Centered at the University of Chicago Divinity School, wartime criticism of "premillennialism," by which critics mostly meant new premillennialism, reached fever pitch. In his 1918 book *Patriotism and Religion*, Social Gospeler and recent president of the Federal Council of Churches, Shailer Mathews, warned that "American churches are dangerously full" of the expectation of "supernatural intervention."[27] Mathews's colleague at Chicago, Shirley Jackson Case, dedicated his editorial energies at the prestigious journal *Biblical World* to root out the "premillennial menace" in the body politic. "The American nation is engaged in a gigantic effort to make the world safe for democracy," he began his most well-known essay on the topic. "While pledged to give unreservedly of its blood and treasure for the attainment of this ideal, there are those in our midst who declare that the undertaking is foredoomed to failure."[28] George P. Eckman, editor of the *Christian Advocate* in New York, joined the fray, releasing his own book that catalogued the "fancies and fallacies" of premillennialism, while James H. Snowden, of Western Theological Seminary in Pittsburgh, described premillennialism as "a survival of Judaism" and "Judaistic in its method of interpreting scripture," by which he meant literal in its expectation of a kingdom of Israel.[29]

In the war years, the mudslinging grew frenzied, with each side claiming the other was in league with the Germans. Modernists charged that premillennialists secretly hoped for a German victory because it would validate their interpretation of prophecy, and Case even charged (without basis) that German money funded premillennial literature. Premillennialists responded that

26. Sunday, quoted in Sutton, *American Apocalypse*, 61.

27. Shailer Mathews, *Patriotism and Religion* (New York: Macmillan, 1918), 101.

28. Shirley Jackson Case, "The Premillennial Menace," *Biblical World* 52, no. 1 (July 1918): 16–23.

29. James H. Snowden, *The Coming of the Lord: Will It Be Premillennial?* 2nd ed. (New York: Macmillan, 1919), 196.

liberal indebtedness to German theology made modernism suspect, and that the imperial war state of Germany, with its intent to expand "kultur" abroad, was the inevitable outworking of postmillennial theology. This eschatological standoff took place in the waning days of a fifty-year-old interdenominational evangelical order, and in the emergent days of the fundamentalist-modernist confrontation that defined the next fifty years. Differences over World War I hinged on rival conceptions of the kingdom, the millennium, and the church's relation to the state.

The strongest public display of premillennialists during the war was a pair of prophecy conferences in 1918, one held in Philadelphia's Academy of Music in May, and the other in New York City's Carnegie Hall in November—both following a successful "Advent conference" with American participation in London in 1917. In Philadelphia, the program was shaped by local business-men and the *Christian Herald* magazine, while in New York the planning fell mostly to Gaebelein and Brethren businessman Alwyn Ball Jr. (the same who funded the *Scofield Reference Bible*). The earlier gathering, taking place during the war, pondered its outcome; the latter, taking place just two weeks after the armistice, cast a dim view over elite "dreaming, and planning" of "permanent peace."[30]

An aging Scofield, who spoke at Carnegie Hall in November, was forced to send a note of regret to Philadelphia earlier in the year while convalescing from illness. Perhaps it was the forced brevity of a telegram, or the immediacy of his decision not to make the trip, that gave his words a special clarity of the purpose of the conference. He encouraged the three thousand in attendance that their gathering offered "a fearless warning that we are in the awful end of the Times of the Gentiles, with no hope for humanity except in the personal return of the Lord in glory," and at the same time he called the conference committee to make a "statement of the fundamentals of Christian belief, which may form a clear basis for Christian fellowship in a day of apostasy."[31] The dual purposes helped to crystallize new premillennial priorities during the war years, even as many leaders, including Scofield, who died in 1921, would not see the full implications of the work.

30. Reuben Torrey, "That Blessed Hope," in *Christ and Glory: Addresses Delivered at the New York Prophetic Conference, Carnegie Hall, November 25–28, 1918*, ed. Arno C. Gae-belein (New York: Our Hope, 1919), 21–22.

31. *Light on Prophecy: A Coordinated, Constructive Teaching Being the Proceedings and Addresses at the Philadelphia Prophetic Conference, May 28–30, 1918* (New York: Christian Herald, 1918), 32.

Philip Mauro's Discontent

Conspicuously absent from these wartime prophecy conferences was Philip Mauro, the popular world-system premillennialist, religious critic with three essays in *The Fundamentals*, and part of a thriving law practice that argued in front of the US Supreme Court.

Mauro was unsettled during the war. His confidence in the premillennial teachings he adopted fifteen years earlier had begun to erode. Writing in 1918 from his home in Burlington, Iowa, he wondered what would happen "after this"—the title of his first of many books breaking with the new premillennial understanding of the future kingdom of God. "Especially in the present era of unprecedented 'destruction and misery,' in which human progress and civilization have eventuated," Mauro reflected, what the Bible said about the future was more important than ever.[32] Jesus told his disciples, "After this I will return" (Acts 15:16 KJV), but as Mauro well knew, the devil was in the prophetic details as much as he was at the helm of the careening world system.

Mauro's unease began when he first picked up the *Scofield Reference Bible*. He was anticipating its arrival after years of hype and the high esteem in which he held "the editor and his co-workers." But Mauro did not make it past Scofield's notes on Genesis 1, which allowed for a nonliteral reading of "days" of creation. "I found to my surprise and disappointment that these notes made room for, and indeed rather favored, the absurd notion that the 'days' of Genesis 1 were long periods—ages—of time." A passionate advocate of a literal reading of the creation account, Mauro could not brook difference on this issue. "I was so grieved at the editor's note that I put the volume aside," he said, and did not open it again until 1918, when a missionary friend called his attention "to some of the notes on the Kingdom"—a topic the war years had brought to the center of Mauro's attention.[33]

From 1918 to 1920 Mauro unleashed a torrent of criticism on what he first identified as the "modern postponement theory" of the kingdom of God.[34] *"After This"* established the present reality of the kingdom, while subsequent books, finishing with a collection of essays he wrote in the fall of 1919, *Bringing*

32. Philip Mauro, *"After This"; or, The Church, the Kingdom, and the Glory* (1918; reprint, n.p.: Philip Mauro Library, 2008), 3.

33. Philip Mauro, *A Kingdom Which Cannot Be Shaken* (1919; reprint, n.p.: Philip Mauro Library, 2008), 10–11.

34. Mauro, *A Kingdom Which Cannot Be Shaken*, 9.

Back the King (1920), increasingly took aim at his onetime premillennialist friends. The tone of the works vacillated from regretful to accusatory. In one passage Mauro could express sympathy for fellow Christians who were "true to the fundamentals of Christianity" but mistaken on the kingdom. He could simply call for "the duty of the people of God to look most carefully into" the true teachings about the kingdom. Yet, in the next passage he could feverishly describe his "duty to spare no effort to deliver our fellow believers from a theory so dangerously erroneous, wherein we were ourselves at one time ensnared."[35] In *God's Present Kingdom* (1919) Mauro attempted to save the legacy of Darby and the Exclusive Brethren by arguing that "postponement theory" was a view concocted by Scofield, never seen before 1909—an argument he would drop in later books.[36]

Mauro's concerns with new premillennialism were many. Scofield's distinctions between the kingdom of God, the kingdom of heaven, and the church appeared to Mauro to diminish the universality of key ethical teachings, such as the Sermon on the Mount, to apply to just a portion of humanity. Moreover, the new premillennial teaching that the kingdom of heaven of the Gospels was in fact the "earthly" kingdom of Israel—a realization that Mauro apparently did not make until his thorough study of Scofield's notes in 1918—weakened the power of Jesus. Scofield's teaching of "free grace" allowed Christians to keep sinning, all the while claiming salvation. In each of these cases Mauro raised the alarm that "the builders of the elaborate postponement theory" had made great strides in the decade after the *Scofield Reference Bible* to establish their views "far and wide," to the detriment of "orthodox Christians" everywhere.[37]

In these same years, Mauro was wracked by personal tragedy and deep depression, with the death of his wife in August 1918 compounding his woes. Yet, amid both religious and personal trials, this was no crisis of faith. In a second edition of his theology of divine healing, *Sickness of the Saints*, which was reissued in 1919, he affirmed that even as his wife's health gave way, his faith in God "has been fully tested both in living and in dying; and that it has more than stood the test."[38] Mauro's crisis, and his understanding of the

35. Philip Mauro, *Bringing Back the King* (1920; reprint, n.p.: Philip Mauro Library, 2008), 6.

36. Philip Mauro, *God's Present Kingdom* (1919; reprint, n.p.: Philip Mauro Library, 2008), esp. 101–4.

37. Mauro, *Bringing Back the King*, 2.

38. Quoted in Gordon P. Gardiner, "Champion of the Kingdom: The Story of Philip Mauro" (1961; reprint, n.p.: Philip Mauro Library, 2008), 33–34.

world crisis, led him not to a loss of faith but to a change of faith. The crisis moment directed him into a new phase of activism on behalf of a kingdom of God that he now believed existed in the midst of the imploding world system. Mauro's new thinking stood in contrast to the new premillennial leadership, still deeply influential in the vast Moody movement, which taught the future kingdom as a cardinal doctrine. Mauro was becoming a new thing himself: a fundamentalist.

I am standing on the Word of God,
Which came to men of old;
The Holy Book our fathers love,
And treasured more than gold.

I am standing, standing on the Word,
Tho' the earth change and decay,
It shall never, never pass away;
I am standing on the Word of God.

I am standing on the Word of God,
And thus I am secure;
Tho' blows the tempest wild and hard,
'Twill evermore endure.

J. Wilbur Chapman, "The Judgment" (1911)

Chapman's musician partner Charles M. Alexander oversaw music at the Northfield Bible Conferences and also toured with revivalist Reuben Torrey until 1908. All three—Chapman, Alexander, and Torrey—were new premillennialists. This hymn, which foreshadowed some of the rhetoric of the fundamentalist movement a decade later, first appeared in 1911 but was included in a special preview edition of *Alexander's Hymns No. 3* (1915), a portion of which was issued, much like a highly anticipated movie today, in teaser preview form months before the official release.

10

Factions

In the summer of 1920, the Northern Baptist editor of the *Watchman Examiner*, Curtis Lee Laws, called for a new faction in his denomination that he named the "fundamentalists"—those "who still cling to the great fundamentals and who mean to do battle royal for the faith."[1] Though the coining of "dispensationalism" took another seven years, the two terms would become inextricably linked by the end of the decade.

From the start, the relationship between fundamentalism and premillennialism was one of tension as much as symbiosis. Laws wanted to distance his group, which organized in 1920 in the Northern Baptist Convention, from a narrow identification with "premillennialism," a doctrinal position he did not hold, and which won only partial adherence among Northern Baptists. He chafed at the "false impression" that his movement was "a premillennialist movement." It counted premillennialists among its ranks, "because premillennialists are always sound on the fundamentals" that Laws cared about, but the term was "too closely allied with a single doctrine and not sufficiently inclusive." The other terms Laws contemplated were "conservative," which he decided was too broad and signaled allegiance with "reactionary forces in all of life," and the Baptist-specific "Landmarkers," which, like "premillennial," signaled just one particular Baptist faction and hence was too narrow. He settled on the neologism "fundamentalists" and clarified that when he used the word, it would be meant "in compliment and not in disparagement."[2]

The name stuck and came to identify a range of Protestants in the 1920s far larger than Laws had originally intended. Each of the two parties of the

1. Curtis Lee Laws, "Convention Side Lights," *Watchman-Examiner*, July 1, 1920, 834.
2. Laws, "Convention Side Lights," 834.

emerging fundamentalist-modernist controversy coalesced through bitter debates and exoduses that began in the early 1920s and lasted for more than a decade, with consequences to the makeup of American religion and society that continue to reverberate today.

In its early years, fundamentalism looked more like a faction of factions than a unified movement. Some fundamentalists wanted to seize control of the denominations, while others cared more about leaving the denominations altogether. Still others ignored church structures and advanced into the public square with a set of cultural values they believed were integral to pure Christianity and pure Americanism. While there were definite internal differences, there was also no clean separation between these rival visions for fundamentalism, which is what allowed the factions to cooperate at all. But the different priorities mattered deeply to how the movement developed.

People who called themselves "fundamentalists" united in identifying themselves as the true inheritors of primitive and Reformational Christianity. They saw themselves as an antimodernist front within and across denominational lines opposed to biblical higher criticism, Darwinian evolution, and what they continued to call the "new theology." They confessed to five theological fundamentals—the divinity of Jesus, the virgin birth, the resurrection, the second coming, and biblical inerrancy—though on each of these there were multiple fundamentalist perspectives.

Fundamentalists also tended toward a shared cultural and political perspective. They opposed centralization and institutional consolidation in economics, politics, and religion. Many advocated a racially and religiously narrow American nationalism, and a public pietism shaped by prohibition and urban moral reform movements. In many of these positions they were hardly alone—Protestants of all types were nationalistic, pietistic, and racially segregated in the 1920s. Yet fundamentalists based their arguments on unique theological and historical claims, and increasingly fused their attitudes with an explicit opposition to modernism.

Among the patchwork of fundamentalist factions that emerged after World War I, two shaped the movement's early fate. The role of premillennialism in both was instructive to how the tradition of new premillennialism would both advance and suffer renewed scrutiny in the early years of fundamentalism.

Laws was a denominational fundamentalist, someone who prioritized denominational institutional power. Among Northern Baptists and Northern Presbyterians, denominational fundamentalists attempted to amass enough followers to unseat the modernist leadership of their churches. A second fundamentalist party eschewed denominations entirely and was animated instead by a Christian nationalist vision of American society. The nationalist fundamentalists were the most popularly identifiable faction in the 1920s, advancing their cause not in denominational meetings but in the most heavily trafficked civic spaces: the antivice crusades of John Roach Straton in New York City, the prohibition politics of Billy Sunday, and the antievolution campaigns of William Jennings Bryan. These nationalist fundamentalists, among whom Philip Mauro counted himself, based their activism on upholding biblical authority as the basis for right religion and right citizenship, and their agitation pioneered a new fusion of Christianity and American civic life that influenced later traditions of Christian nationalism.

Adherence to new premillennialism did not define the identity of either denominational or nationalist fundamentalists. Rather, it was a fault line in the broader fundamentalist movement. This reality deeply shaped the fate of premillennialism in the 1920s. As fundamentalist organizing matured, the peculiarities of new premillennialism attracted attention, which ensured two things: that new premillennialism would become permanently associated with fundamentalism, and that it would become a sticking point among fundamentalists themselves.

Laws, Fosdick, and Macartney: Denominational Fundamentalism

As the example of Laws illustrated, one origin story of fundamentalism emerged from the thick of denominational politics, especially among Northern Baptists and Northern Presbyterians, where new premillennialism was an ambiguous factor. In the case of the Northern Baptists, new premillennialists had only tentative connections to the fundamentalists then in ascendance. Laws, who had no particular interest in eschatology, partnered with Jasper C. Massee, who led the Baptist "Fundamentalist Fellowship" and was an old premillennialist. Another denominational organizer, Augustus H. Strong, who raised concerns about liberalism in the mission field, was president of Rochester Theological Seminary and a committed postmillennialist. Frank M. Goodchild, pastor in New York City and president of the Baptist American and Foreign Bible Society (and an amillennial fundamentalist), described the attitude of the early leadership as "not a 'premillennialist' movement.... Fundamentalists are in no way committed to vagaries concerning the second coming, nor to fanatical propaganda for a particular view of the Lord's return."[3]

3. Frank M. Goodchild, "The Spirit and Purpose of Fundamentalism," *Watchman-Examiner*, March 2, 1922, 268.

Frequent protestations, however, pointed to the popular perception that in fact one of the animating energies of Baptist fundamentalism was premillennialism. Upon organizing in 1920, Laws, Massee, and Goodchild were pressured by other Baptists who did espouse the centrality of new premillennialism. These Baptists were led by William Bell Riley of Minneapolis, one of the most influential pastors in the country, with his own church, Bible institute, and media empire. In the critical years of 1920–1925, the Laws party and the Riley party vied for control over the Baptist fundamentalist movement—to the detriment of both sides. Riley's efforts often went against those of Laws, Massee, and Goodchild, and in 1923 he created his own faction called the Baptist Bible Union. This union provided an organizing space for Baptist premillennialists, though even it did not make premillennialism a prerequisite for membership because doing so might alienate other Baptists. The split among Baptist fundamentalists proved disastrous. Laws's inability to steer Baptist fundamentalism became clear as early as 1922, and premillennialism had contributed to the movement's failure to take control of the denomination.

Fundamentalist agitation continued among Northern Baptists through the 1920s, but the fate of the denominational leadership was never really in doubt. Opposition to fundamentalism coalesced in the same year of 1922, led from the pulpit of a Presbyterian church in Manhattan manned by a Baptist pastor, Harry Emerson Fosdick. His famous sermon "Shall the Fundamentalists Win?" paid special attention to "the second coming of our Lord."[4] He cast premillennialism as a "Hebrew" influence on the faith, a conception of Christianity "that leaves the idea of progress out." At the same time, of the teaching that "Christ is literally coming, externally on the clouds, to set up his kingdom here," Fosdick declared, "I never heard that teaching in my youth at all." The second coming was best thought of not as "an external arrival on the clouds" but as a modern recognition that "the most desirable elements in human life have come through the method of development." Of the premillennialists, Fosdick had little to commend: "They sit still and do nothing and expect the world to grow worse and worse until he comes."[5]

Fosdick's sermon sparked a torrent of fundamentalist reactions. The most important critical response was from Clarence Macartney, pastor of Phila-

4. Harry Emerson Fosdick, *Shall the Fundamentalists Win?* (New York: First Presbyterian Church in the City of New York, 1922), 5.
5. Fosdick, *Shall the Fundamentalists Win?*, 10–11.

delphia's Arch Street Presbyterian Church. A loyal Presbyterian, Macartney seemed as aggrieved by Fosdick's broadside being lobbed from a Presbyterian pulpit as he was about what Fosdick said. In "Shall Unbelief Win?" Macartney responded to Fosdick point by point and minimized premillennialism's importance to the battle for the denominations. "In any recent controversy between rationalists and evangelicals," Macartney complained, using his preferred descriptors for modernists and fundamentalists, "there has been a tendency on the part of the former to use 'chiliasm' as a sort of smoke screen and raise the cry of 'premillenarian,' whereas they know that the strongest and most influential currents of thought in conservative Protestantism run in an altogether different direction."[6] "I do not adhere to the premillennial school of theology," he explained, and he pondered if the premillennial "defense of historic Christianity is not altogether a helpful one."[7]

The story in Macartney's Northern Presbyterian denomination after 1922 was strikingly similar to the Northern Baptist saga before 1922. The chief organizers of Presbyterian fundamentalism were only tangentially related to premillennialism. Besides Macartney, the most visible Presbyterian fundamentalist was J. Gresham Machen, professor of New Testament at Princeton Theological Seminary. Machen too was not a premillennialist. In his most famous book, *Christianity and Liberalism* (1923), Machen took space away from contending with the modernists to raise the warning of "the recrudescence of 'Chiliasm' or 'premillennialism' in the modern Church." Its "increasing prominence in recent years," he worried, "causes us serious concern; it is coupled, we think, with a false method of interpreting Scripture which in the long run will be productive of harm." Yet Machen was caught in the now-familiar bind shared by Macartney, Laws, Massee, and Goodchild: without the support of premillennialists, overtaking denominational leadership faced impossible odds. Subordinating concerns about premillennialism's long-term evils to gain political advantage against modernists in the present, Machen affirmed, "how great is our agreement with those who hold the premillennial view!" In the battle against modernists, Machen concluded that the premillennialists' error, "serious though it may be, is not a deadly error."[8]

6. Clarence Macartney, *Shall Unbelief Win? A Reply to Dr. Fosdick* (Philadelphia: Wilber Hanf, 1922), 6.

7. Macartney, *Shall Unbelief Win?*, 16.

8. J. Gresham Machen, *Christianity and Liberalism* (New York: Macmillan, 1923), 49.

Nevertheless, courting new premillennialists did not gain Northern Presbyterian fundamentalists the victory they sought. As in the Baptist struggle, premillennialists sunk the hopes of Presbyterian fundamentalists in their quest to take over the denomination. Charles R. Erdman, professor of theology at Princeton Seminary and son of William J. Erdman, was an old premillennialist and a moderate who wanted to diminish the importance of eschatology to the formation of Presbyterian fundamentalism. Erdman's campaign for moderator of the 1924 General Assembly was pitted against the platform of Macartney precisely on the level of militancy or, in Fosdick's words, "intolerance" that would be pursued in the denomination. Erdman won, dealing a blow to the militant wing of the fundamentalist party and making permanent a deep rift in the movement.

Name	Year Died	Occupation
J. Wilbur Chapman	1918	Revivalist
Charles M. Alexander	1920	Musician
George F. Pentecost	1920	Revivalist/Pastor
Cyrus I. Scofield	1921	Theologian/Writer
Robert McWatty Russell	1921	Seminary president
Joseph Kyle	1921	Seminary president
John Wanamaker	1922	Businessman
Lyman Stewart	1923	Businessman
William J. Erdman	1923	Theologian
W. H. Griffith Thomas	1924	Theologian
Clarence Larkin	1924	Theologian/Artist
Amzi C. Dixon	1925	Pastor
Reuben A. Torrey	1928	Revivalist/Bible Institute president
John Roach Straton	1929	Pastor

Figure 13. "Deaths of New Premillennial Leaders, 1918–1930." A remarkable number of new premillennialists died on the cusp of or during the organizing of the fundamentalist movement. Losses spanned the new premillennial networks and included pastors, seminary presidents, major donors and businessmen, and theologians. Many were Northern Baptists or Northern Presbyterians, so the losses depleted premillennial representation especially in those groups.

In the leadership contests for the Northern Presbyterian denomination, as with the Northern Baptists, new premillennialists were absent from the highest levels of denominational leadership, even as "premillennialism" was a constant topic of discussion. Where premillennialists were more numerous in the ranks of clergy and laity, they were divided on separating from the denomination. Many followed the lead of Machen, who eventually left in

1929 to create the Orthodox Presbyterian Church. But others stayed. Donald Grey Barnhouse, a graduate of Biola College and Princeton Seminary but too young to personally take part in the controversies of the 1920s, assumed the pastorate of Philadelphia's Tenth Avenue Presbyterian Church in 1927, remaining in the Northern Presbyterian denomination and retaining a new premillennial eschatology alongside a broader Reformed theology. His success as a pastor, radio host, and magazine publisher until his death in 1960 carved out a small, idiosyncratic subculture of new premillennialism in Northern Presbyterianism.

Laws, Fosdick, and Macartney each illustrated how new premillennialism had become a toxic label for fundamentalist and modernist leaders alike. Each side disavowed the errors of "chiliasm" and "premillennialism," although denominational fundamentalists made the pragmatic move to affirm rank-and-file premillennialists where they could. By 1925, at the elite levels of the power struggle for Northern Baptist and Northern Presbyterian denominations, premillennialism lost whatever sheen of respectability it had retained in these circles. Leaders across the theological spectrum associated it with heresy.

Bryan, Norris, and Straton: Nationalist Fundamentalism

If new premillennialists were largely absent from the elite circles of denominational fundamentalism, they were more prevalent among nationalist fundamentalists. Engagement in the public square on political, cultural, and legal issues was in many ways the most popular expression of the fundamentalist movement in the 1920s. Issues like antievolutionism attracted massive attention both within fundamentalism and outside of it. Not only did antievolutionism fit into the concern for Christian Americanism spearheaded by fundamentalists, but it also attracted a constituency that extended beyond northern denominations. Nationalist fundamentalism involved people in the North, South, and West, middle and working class, college educated and not, rural and urban, Reformed and Wesleyan, those with Pentecostal leanings and those with none, premillennialists, postmillennialists, and amillennialists all.

By the 1920s, Philip Mauro was one of the latter. His dissent from new premillennialism during World War I did not slow his advancement in fundamentalist circles—in fact, his staunch amillennialism brought him closer to Reformed theological circles where antievolutionism was the cause of the decade. By 1922, Mauro had become a leading antievolution activist, penning a popular pamphlet, *Evolution at the Bar* (1922), a mock indictment of evolution as unchristian and unscientific. He had also become a legal adviser for efforts in southern and midwestern states to pass antievolution bills that would ban teaching evolution in public classrooms.

Many fundamentalists joined Mauro in prioritizing nationalist activism. Fellow fundamentalist William Bell Riley, himself an arch opponent of the teaching of evolution in schools, worked behind the scenes to involve the most public face of the movement, William Jennings Bryan, the three-time Democratic presidential nominee, lifelong Northern Presbyterian, and, after World War I, dogged antievolution campaigner. It was Riley who helped to convince Bryan to travel to Dayton, Tennessee, to act as special prosecutor in the momentous Scopes trial of July 1925. Riley also founded the Anti-Evolution League of Minnesota in 1923, which spawned the Anti-Evolution League of America the next year, led by two famed nationalist fundamentalists, John William Porter and Thomas Theodore Martin.

The field of nationalist fundamentalist leaders was crowded. John Roach Straton, Baptist preacher in New York City, partnered with Riley against evolution but also railed against urban vices and sexual sin closer to his pulpit, calling for the closure of New York's theaters, dance halls, and brothels. In a series of debates in 1923–1924 with fellow Manhattanite and Unitarian minister Charles Francis Potter, Straton made national news for his defense of fundamentalism. Another nationalist leader was J. Frank Norris, who emerged in the early 1920s as an antievolution firebrand, haranguing "that hell-born, Bible-destroying, deity-of-Christ-denying, German rationalism known as evolution" in his home state of Texas before taking his message national.[9] Straton and Norris were early pioneers of radio and gained national platforms through the new medium, extending their influence far beyond their pulpits. All three were alumni of Southern Baptist Theological Seminary, with Norris a native of the region and Riley and Straton both culturally tied to it. Along with evangelist Billy Sunday, who was past his prime in the 1920s but still active, this cadre of leaders would also work in 1928 against the election of Democrat and Catholic presidential candidate Al Smith, whom they associated with the vices of "Rum and Romanism" (alcohol and Catholicism).

In the early 1920s, Riley, Straton, Norris (and Sunday) all subscribed to new premillennialism, which informed their energetic, frantic, and compre-

9. Norris, quoted in Darren Dochuk, *From Bible Belt to Sunbelt: Plain-Folk Religion, Grassroots Politics, and the Rise of Evangelical Conservatism* (New York: Norton, 2010), 30.

hensive critique of American culture. Yet it would be a mistake to limit nationalist fundamentalism to these figures; the movement was broader than new premillennialists. Bryan, the foremost antievolutionist in the country, had no use for dispensational time or associated teachings. Methodist preacher Bob Schuler, a presidential candidate in 1932 on the Prohibition Party ticket, despised end-times speculation and distanced himself from premillennialism, which he associated with Pentecostalism. The same allergy to premillennialism was true of Toronto-based Baptist pastor Thomas Todhunter Shields, who was deeply engaged in Canadian Baptist denominational fundamentalist efforts in the 1920s, joining nationalist efforts in the United States, too. Shields not only failed to subscribe to premillennialism, but he insisted, as president of the Baptist Bible Union, that a certain view of the millennium not be required as a condition of membership.

Nationalist fundamentalists sometimes policed doctrinal purity, but they cared more about defending Christian culture. They frequently redrew the boundaries of their movement to make allies on that quality alone. The inclusion of Seventh-day Adventists on the basis of shared antievolutionary beliefs was a case in point. By the early twentieth century, Adventists had developed a sophisticated literal interpretation of Genesis that posited an earth only thousands of years old. The foremost champion of this view was George McCready Price, a Canadian-born Adventist who began writing a steady stream of young-earth creationist literature. His magnum opus, *The New Geology* (1923), made "flood geology," establishing the historical reality of Noah's flood, a defining mark of young-earth creationist focus.[10]

Toiling for decades in relative obscurity, Price found a reception among antievolutionist fundamentalists in the 1920s who otherwise followed their Brethren forebears by regarding his Adventism as heretical. When William Jennings Bryan took the stand in Dayton to defend his views of creation, Price was one of only two scientists he cited favorably (the other being George Fredrick Wright, author of three essays in *The Fundamentals*). The novelty of Price's theories was lost on virtually all fundamentalists—including Bryan—who continued to equate the days of Genesis 1 to undetermined ages. In his reference Bible, Scofield had privileged older creationist understandings over a literal reading of the six days of creation. None of Price's chief fundamentalist champions subscribed to a young dating of the age of the earth or to the idea that

10. George McCready Price, *The New Geology* (Mountain View, CA: Pacific Press, 1923), 691–92.

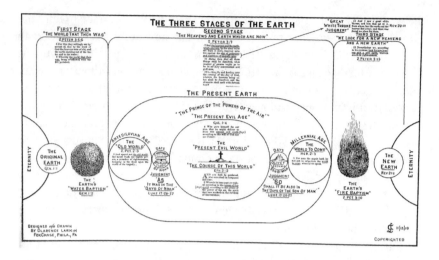

Figure 14. Clarence Larkin's "The Three Stages of Earth." While some fundamentalists adopted young-earth creationism in the 1920s, many others—including the vast majority of premillennialists—initially followed some version of Northern Baptist Clarence Larkin's "gap theory," which posited an indeterminate amount of time between Genesis 1:2 and 1:3. Here Larkin bases the stages of the earth on 2 Peter 3, a favorite chapter because of its teaching that "The Day of the Lord will come as a thief in the night" (3:10).

the Genesis flood was global in scope, yet they championed him as a partisan in the cause of antievolution all the same.

Like Adventists, Pentecostals were welcomed as allies by fundamentalists on the basis of shared cultural rather than theological positions. Aimee Semple McPherson, the pastor of Angelus Temple in Los Angeles and one of the most well-known preachers in the 1920s, was received warmly by the nationalists, including J. Frank Norris and William Bell Riley. In the early days of Angelus Temple—founded in 1923—she identified with fundamentalism by preaching sermons like "Trial of the Modern Liberalist College Professor versus the Lord Jesus Christ" (1923).[11] McPherson opposed teaching evolution, but her main concern was maintaining the Bible's authority in American culture.

The Scopes trial in July 1925 provided a rallying point that united nationalist fundamentalists of all stripes, if only for a moment. The prosecutors of teacher John T. Scopes won a legal victory, proving that Scopes had broken the

11. Quoted in Matthew Avery Sutton, *Aimee Semple McPherson and the Resurrection of Christian America* (Cambridge, MA: Harvard University Press, 2007), 50–51.

recently passed Butler Act that prohibited the teaching of evolution in public schools, but fundamentalism lost the public relations battle that was in many ways the real point of the trial. In the months afterward, the fate of nationalist fundamentalist organizing took a dramatic turn. Bryan died a week after the verdict, and his loss dealt a significant blow to the stature of the movement. His absence was compounded by the popular depiction of fundamentalists that emerged from the trial as uneducated, rural, and southern—an image perfected by journalist H. L. Mencken in his reporting from Dayton, but which was inaccurate on all three counts. While many nationalists conformed to the popular image (for there were increasing numbers of southern fundamentalists as the decade progressed), the leaderless movement began to decentralize as quickly as it had rallied.

The outcome of the Scopes trial and Bryan's death scattered antievolution energies into multiple competing directions. Leaders close to Bryan vied for the throne of the movement in the months following his death. Boston-based real estate developer George F. Washburn claimed to be Bryan's successor and founded the Bible Crusaders of America, winning a quick victory in securing antievolution legislation in Mississippi; Gerald B. Winrod, a radio preacher in Wichita, Kansas, founded Defenders of the Christian Faith in the same year; and California evangelist Paul W. Rood's Bryan Bible League also claimed to be an heir, organizing against evolution and "defending the historic position of evangelical Christianity."[12] Each organization curated its own member lists, extracted its own member dues, and competed for influence over the nebulous constituency of nationalist-oriented fundamentalism. They all initially focused on antievolution activism, but as legal wins and losses tallied, they turned to other issues: upholding Prohibition, opposing Bolshevism, supporting racial segregation, and opposing Catholicism.

By the end of the 1920s, both denominational and nationalist fundamentalists could identify with the experience of setbacks and infighting. Denominationalists had been thoroughly defeated in the Northern Baptist and Northern Presbyterian denominations, while nationalists had spun off in separate directions and largely lost on the substance of their issues. Winrod lamented in 1928 that fundamentalists agreed "on our name and statement of faith, but beyond that it is bedlam."[13] J. Oliver Buswell, president of the fundamentalist Whea-

---

12. "Bryan's Benediction," *King's Business*, December 1925, 535.

13. Quoted in Leo Ribuffo, *The Old Christian Right: The Protestant Far Right from the Great Depression to the Cold War* (Philadelphia: Temple University Press, 1983), 86.

ton College, soberly concluded in 1930 that "we have had so many battles to fight against modernism that it is hard for us to cooperate with one another."[14] The fate of premillennialism and the emergence of "dispensationalism" were deeply tied to this breakdown within fundamentalism.

Philip Mauro Coins "Dispensationalism"

By 1928, Philip Mauro had also concluded that something was wrong with fundamentalism. The movement had fractured, and he had identified one of the chief culprits in its own camp: the spread of "dispensationalism."[15] "The time is fully ripe," he wrote, "for a thorough examination and frank exposure of this new and subtle form of modernism that has been spreading itself among those who have adopted the name 'Fundamentalists.'" Mauro wanted to prosecute wrong beliefs within the fundamentalist movement and recapture the optimism of a few years earlier. "Evangelical Christianity must purge itself of this leaven of dispensationalism ere it can display its former power and exert its former influence," he urged in one of his first uses of the neologism. He alleged that dispensationalism—the theological bundle that included new premillennialism, dispensational time, and the church-Israel distinction—had come "into existence within the memory of persons now living" and was "more recent than Darwinism." Dispensationalism eroded the very basis of fundamentalism and "the truly 'fundamental' truths of Scripture," which the new "system" had "either completely obliterated or at least greatly obscured."[16]

It is noteworthy that "dispensationalism" was coined by a fundamentalist searching for the cause of fundamentalism's decline as a nationwide movement in the late 1920s. Rather than premillennialism equipping fundamentalists with a shared theology—the original vision of new premillennialists in the 1910s—this fundamentalist had singled out "dispensationalism" as the source of division. This interpretation of the recent past charged a wide swath of new premillennialists with having failed to join either the struggle for denominational power or the struggle for cultural power. Their theology, Mauro's

14. J. Oliver Buswell, "Prospects for Christian Education," *King's Business*, November 1930, 511.

15. Philip Mauro, *The Gospel of the Kingdom: An Examination of Modern Dispensationalism* (Boston: Hamilton Brothers, 1928), 5.

16. Mauro, *Gospel of the Kingdom*, 8–9.

analysis concluded, directed them onto a different path; their mix of quiescence and dissension had scuttled the boat of fundamentalism. These new premillennialists were instead beholden to a new type of modern heresy that now, thanks to Mauro, had a permanent name.

Whose are the whispers stealing
Out of the South and the North?
"Lo, from the secret chambers
The Christ is coming forth."
Whose are the voices crying
Out of the East and the West?
"Far in the desert hidden
Messiah takes his rest."
And one saith, "He is yonder,"
And one saith, "He is near,"
And one at the door is calling,
"Behold Him! He is here."

But as the terrible lightning cometh—
Terrible, swift, and bright,
Cleaving the heavens asunder
Searing earth with its light
Out of the storm-cloud leaping
Like a fiery sword-blade's flash
To the sound of the mighty waters
And the sevenfold thunders' clash
A vision of flaming glory
That every eye shall see—
Lo, as the lightning cometh
So shall His coming be.

Annie Johnson Flint,
"So Shall His Coming Be" (1917)

Poet Annie Johnson Flint (1866–1932) was popular in holiness and premillennial circles and published this poem immediately after the US entry into World War I (April 1917). Flint suffered from chronic arthritis for most of her life and spent her later years in the sanitarium at Clifton Springs, New York, the same site that hosted the Niagara Bible Conference in 1878–1880 and the unveiling of the Niagara "Articles of Belief" in 1878.

11

Scholastic Dispensationalism

In May 1927, hundreds of fundamentalists constituting the World Christian Fundamentals Association (WCFA) gathered in Atlanta, Georgia, in the main auditorium of North Avenue Presbyterian Church. This particular body was meeting in the South for only the third time in its nine years of existence. The main attraction was undoubtedly William Bell Riley, the association's founder and president—a man who had been in the thick of fundamentalist organizing since the beginning. In his address, "What Is Fundamentalism?," he claimed the movement's origins for himself.[1] Though coined in 1920 by Curtis Lee Laws, the term "fundamentalism," Riley insisted, began with the first annual meeting of the WCFA in 1919. Riley admitted that some who were outside the bounds of the WCFA could call themselves fundamentalists, but that most fundamentalists would be found under his leadership.

The WCFA was in many ways the most direct successor to pre–World War I premillennialism. Sitting uneasily alongside denominational and nationalist fundamentalism, the WCFA comprised interdenominationalists who fell through the fundamentalist cracks, who were less concerned with the contest for denominations or culture but were still focused on the theological and cultural identity of the church, broadly construed to include local churches, small denominations, parachurch organizations, and mission agencies. They worked through loosely organized affiliations like the WCFA and the American Conference of Undenominational Churches, and later creations such as the Independent Fundamentalist Churches of America. A lack of preexisting institutional structures meant that shared markers of

1. William Bell Riley, "What Is Fundamentalism?" *Christian Fundamentalist*, July 1927, 5–14.

belief, especially premillennialism, became central to interdenominational fundamentalist identity.

While some interdenominationalists followed Riley's lead into antievolution and other nationalist campaigns, a smaller group led by Lewis Sperry Chafer (Scofield's most distinguished disciple) formed a scholastic community that was less immediately concerned with winning back the denominations or the nation. They had a longer view of the purpose of fundamentalism. The scholastics began to form their own institutions to advance their theology, anchored in new premillennialism. They would make up the core of early dispensational theologians. Tied to the Bible institutes and global mission agencies, scholastic dispensationalists worked to create a theological tradition less interested in serving fundamentalism than in perfecting their species of premillennialism and constructing a full systematic theology to establish the credentials of dispensationalism.

By weaving new premillennialism, Higher Life teachings, and shared fundamentalist teachings into an original theological tapestry, early dispensationalists strengthened their interlocking system of teachings. Their theology surpassed in sophistication, popularity, and longevity Brethren and new premillennial predecessors, as well as rival fundamentalist varieties. Scholastic dispensationalists gave shape to both a highly technical theological conversation and a popular expression of fundamentalist theology. This tradition came into full bloom in the midst of deep fundamentalist infighting and was deeply shaped by its outcome.

The Rise and Splintering of the World Christian Fundamentals Association

The great organizer of interdenominational fundamentalism was William Bell Riley, the Northern Baptist partisan, pastor, and Bible institute president based in Minneapolis who was more or less ubiquitous in all three branches of early fundamentalism. A tireless institution builder, Riley had been active in premillennial circles for decades by the onset of World War I. Yet it was only in wartime, where he developed a pointed concern for a Christian presence in American geopolitics, that he started his project of rallying like-minded Christians against modernism.

In 1917 Riley published *The Menace of Modernism*, which decried the theological drift of universities, denominational schools, and seminaries, and offered the "modern Bible school" as the best "antidote to skepticism."[2] Channeling

2. William Bell Riley, *The Menace of Modernism* (New York: Christian Alliance Publishing, 1917), 130.

other new premillennialist writers, Riley called for a "Christian Confederacy" (borrowing from a passage in Isaiah 8) to counter the looming "consolidation" of religion headed by the Federal Council of Churches that cornered the market on "close interdenominational cooperation." Where the Federal Council channeled modernist theology, Riley wanted to base a "close fellowship, yea, even an organization, of true and evangelical conservatives" on "loyalty to Biblical precepts" and "evangelization of the globe." The basis for unity was in the alarming threat of modernism. Riley hoped to rally "churches, schools, and other Christian institutions" to stake their existence on the proposition that "the Bible is the very Word of God, and is, therefore, and must forever remain, the only rule of faith and practice."[3] His plans for a national movement began as early as 1909, following the creation of the Federal Council, but it was only a decade later that the possibility for creating one seemed realistic.

In May 1919, Riley called the first World Conference on Christian Fundamentals, a gathering that he claimed would form a "new Protestantism" that was rid of modernist influences.[4] The group that assembled came from a wide range of backgrounds and motives. Some chose to emphasize interdenominational activism as the primary expression of fundamentalism; these included Riley and other Bible institute leaders from the Philadelphia School of the Bible, the National Bible Institute (NYC), and Biola. Many other names were recognizable from the prewar period: William E. Blackstone and L. W. Munhall were Methodist evangelists; Cyrus Scofield, Charles Trumbull, and Lewis Sperry Chafer were Southern Presbyterians; James M. Gray counted himself a Reformed Episcopalian; and Arno C. Gaebelein was closely associated with the Exclusive Brethren. Other names, however, were new: William Evans, the first graduate of Moody Bible Institute and a British Lutheran Bible conference organizer; Paul Rader, a Chicago-based pioneer of radio ministry and second president of the Christian and Missionary Alliance; evangelist and onetime pastor of Moody Memorial Church, Harry A. Ironside, was an Exclusive Brethren; and J. Frank Norris, a Southern Baptist from Fort Worth, Texas, who became famous in 1922 for breaking with his own denomination over the teaching of evolution.

The conference led to the creation of the Christian Fundamentals Bible Conference Association, later renamed the World Christian Fundamentals Association (WCFA). The nine-point creedal statement adopted at the 1919 conference resembled the fourteen-point Niagara Creed from 1878, even as it

3. Riley, *The Menace of Modernism*, 156.
4. William Bell Riley, "The Great Crisis, or Christ and the Present Crisis," in *God Hath Spoken: Twenty Five Addresses Delivered at the World Conference on Christian Fundamentals, May 25–June 1, 1919* (Philadelphia: Bible Conference Committee, 1919), 27.

was less than a quarter the length, signifying a narrowing of core doctrines and simplification of what those doctrines entailed. The Niagara Creed had come largely from the mind of one person—James H. Brookes—and represented his attempt to channel new premillennial and Higher Life energies into a Bible conference network. The 1919 statement, on the other hand, was drafted by a committee reacting to the perceived inroads of modernism. It proclaimed the historicity of the virgin birth, the resurrection, and the doctrine of sub-stitutionary atonement, and, in a final article, it elevated premillennialism alongside these other issues: "We believe in 'that blessed hope,' the personal, premillennial and imminent return of our Lord and Savior Jesus Christ." Of-fering a fraction of the detail of the Niagara Creed's correlating article—which included "the present dispensation," "millennial age," and the restoration of Israel—the 1919 statement simply added the keyword "imminent" to signal the preference of the any-moment rapture as a marker of right belief.[5]

Premillennialism functioned for the WCFA much as antievolutionism did in allowing cooperation between otherwise opposed fundamentalists. Early on, the WCFA leadership explored the possibility of collaborating with Pentecos-tals and found common ground on the basis of premillennialism. Norris, on the WCFA board, reached out to Aimee Semple McPherson in 1923 and eventually published an article in McPherson's *Pentecostal Evangel.* Thomas C. Horton, still at Biola, encouraged the rapprochement, as did Riley. The next year L. W. Mun-hall spoke at McPherson's Angelus Temple. This friendship between McPherson and the WCFA held the potential to shift the wider balance of power in Protes-tant circles, especially as other Pentecostals, including leaders in the Assemblies of God denomination, also publicly decried "modernism" in their midst.[6]

WCFA leaders eager to partner with McPherson found her appealing largely because of her eagerness to contend for biblical truth not just in the pulpit but also in the public square. The contest with modernists was pitched as a battle, a fight, a struggle for the faith that demanded harsh words, clear enemies, and stark boundaries. Many WCFA leaders followed the lead of re-vivalist Billy Sunday, who had perfected a fundamentalist style of rhetorical pugilism. For these fundamentalists, premillennialism was true in a doctrinal sense, but it was more importantly a position of dogma that differentiated them from modernists. This allowed them to overlook a myriad of theological differences for the sake of their bigger contest against modernism.

5. "Report of Committee on Resolutions," in *God Hath Spoken,* 11–12.

6. Quoted in Matthew Avery Sutton, *American Apocalypse: A History of Modern Evan-gelicalism* (Cambridge, MA: Belknap Press of Harvard University Press, 2014), 106.

This cooperation, however, had limits. Reimagining the boundary lines of the movement to include Pentecostals did not meet with the approval of everyone in the interdenominational fold. Lewis Sperry Chafer, one of the speakers at the 1919 conference and prominent disciple of Scofield, privately chastised Norris in late 1923, declaring that McPherson's teaching of the second baptism of the Spirit was "one of the greatest errors of our time."[7] The following year Chafer used Gaebelein's magazine *Our Hope* to urge fundamentalist leaders to disassociate from Pentecostals.

While the WCFA worked to expand its constituency along narrow premillennial lines, Chafer and Gaebelein created a splinter group of dissenters. Writing to Gaebelein in 1923, Chafer speculated that in the "public mind" the fundamentalist movement "has been reduced to the influence of about four men: Dr. Riley, Dr. Munhall, Tom Horton, and J. Frank Norris." To be "coupled" with these controversialists worked against Chafer's personal temperament and his focus on deepening a tradition of fundamentalist theological education. "Just what these four plunging men will do before they are checked remains to be seen," he worried, "but it certainly is a great embarrassment to the rest of us."[8]

Chafer was not alone in his assessment. As these "plunging men" dominated the WCFA, there continued a steady exodus from the organization. By 1925, Chafer, Gaebelein, Reuben Torrey, and James M. Gray had distanced themselves from previous affiliation. "Saner ground" for the organization, in their estimate, was quickly vanishing.[9] They were joined by British evangelists G. Campbell Morgan and F. B. Meyer, and Canadian evangelists Alexander B. Winchester and Sydney Smith—all new premillennialists alienated by the WCFA leadership, its nationalist rhetoric, and its courting of Pentecostals.

The WCFA's most consequential years were 1919–1925, yet it continually faced defections even at the height of its influence. While Riley's leadership increasingly saw fundamentalism's purpose as waging a nationalist culture war, the scholastic faction led by Chafer began to plan for schools that would expand the educational reach of fundamentalist theology, namely, new premillennialism. Those who joined Chafer in distancing themselves from the WCFA and its pugilistic style of culture war were increasingly becoming, and being seen by other fundamentalists, as partisans of premillendialism more than of fundamentalism.

7. Quoted in John D. Hannah, *An Uncommon Union: Dallas Theological Seminary and American Evangelicalism* (Grand Rapids: Zondervan, 2009), 328n63.
8. Chafer, quoted in Hannah, *An Uncommon Union*, 92.
9. Quoted in Daniel W. Draney, *When Streams Diverge: John Murdoch MacInnis and the Origins of Protestant Fundamentalism in Los Angeles* (Colorado Springs: Paternoster, 2008), 137.

		Moment of Mobilization	Climactic Event	Representative Leadership	Anti-modernist Causes	Sectional Reach	Relationship to Premillennialism
Denominationalists	Baptist	1920: Northern Baptist Convention Annual Meeting in Buffalo, New York	1922 Northern Baptist Convention Annual Meeting in Indianapolis	Curtis Lee Laws; Jasper C. Massee	Biblical inerrancy; denominational confessional purity	Centered in Northern urban areas	Some old premillennialists; most leadership amillennial
Denominationalists	Presbyterian	1922: sermon by Harry Emerson Fosdick, "Shall the Fundamentalists Win?"	1924 Northern Presbyterian General Assembly in Grand Rapids, Michigan	Clarence A. Macartney; J. Gresham Machen			
Nationalists		1921–22: William Jennings Bryan antievolution rallies at public universities in the Midwest	1925 Scopes Trial in Dayton, Tennessee	William Jennings Bryan; Aimee Semple McPherson; John Roach Straton; J. Frank Norris	Antievolution; prohibition; anticommunism	Northern and Southern reach; largest antievolution success in South	Mixed with premillennialist majority
Interdenominationalists	Nationalists	1919: World Conference on Christian Fundamentalists in Philadelphia	1924 World Christian Fundamentals Association Conference in Minneapolis	William Bell Riley; Thomas C. Horton	Biblical inerrancy; premillennialism; antievolution; anticommunism	Centered in the Midwest and West Coast	Majority new premillennialist
Interdenominationalists	Scholastics			Lewis Sperry Chafer; Arno C. Gaebelein	Biblical inerrancy; new premillennialism	Centered in the Midwest and Dallas, Texas; New York City; itinerant	Majority new premillennialist

Lewis Sperry Chafer and the Origins of Scholastic Dispensationalism

If Riley was the undisputed leader of the WCFA, it was the dissenting Lewis Sperry Chafer who most successfully undermined his leadership that led to the breakaway of a scholastic faction. Contra the WCFA's current issues posture, Chafer envisioned training a new generation of ministers in the theology of premillennialism and placing them in the existing denominations to turn the tide of modernism over the coming decades. Prioritizing theological education instead of culture war, Chafer's approach was the first sign that more bookish fundamentalists might organize on their own. In this sense, Riley and Chafer represented two divergent impulses. From a distance, the two men appeared to be cobelligerents, and yet a closer look reveals competing priorities that would shape the future of fundamentalism.

Riley and Chafer came from similar Midwest backgrounds. Riley's father was a farmer who wished to be a minister, while Chafer's father was in fact a Congregationalist minister. Both decided by age twenty to work in ministry, with Riley training for the pastorate and Chafer training as a musician. Both came to their premillennial beliefs, and new premillennial distinctives, as adults, with Riley adopting his views sometime in the early 1890s and Chafer in the early years of the next decade. These dates coincide with when each entered the orbit of the Moody movement. Riley met Moody during his time at Southern Baptist Theological Seminary in 1887 and worked with him in revival settings for the next decade. Chafer, too young to personally know Moody, briefly attended voice classes at the Chicago Evangelistic Society in 1893 and, in 1900, moved to Northfield, Massachusetts, where he came under the tutelage of Cyrus Scofield.

At this point, the two men's stories began to diverge, pointing to the ways their fundamentalist organizing in the 1920s would take different shapes. Riley landed the pastorate of First Baptist Church in Minneapolis in 1897 and modeled its expansive reach and services on Moody's church in Chicago. Riley's congregation grew to thousands of members and offered a Bible institute, social services, and Sunday schools to attract a growing middle class in the Twin Cities. In these same years, Riley became increasingly disturbed by the growth of modernism—of biblical higher criticism, evolution, and the new theology—and began to orient his work toward its defeat. Premillennialism was a natural

Figure 15. "The Three Parties of Organized Fundamentalism, 1920–1925." From the perspective of new premillennialism, the fundamentalist movement of the early 1920s had distinct parties that related to eschatology differently. The formation of these parties shaped the sociological and theological makeup of fundamentalism for decades.

outgrowth of Riley's other cherished doctrine of biblical inerrancy, the belief
that the Bible's original manuscripts contained no error (a view popular among
Bible Reading method advocates). Riley preached in 1897 that "the plain language of the Holy Writ ought to be the end of the controversy for a Christian"
when it came to which millennial view to adopt.[10]

Chafer's experience of the same decades was quite different. After moving
to Northfield in 1900, he continued to travel as an evangelist, setting up the
Southfield Bible Conference in Crescent City, Florida, as a complement to the
work in Northfield. At the same time, Chafer developed a close relationship
with Scofield, under whom he apprenticed, and was tutored in the ways of defining, categorizing, and interpreting Scripture. Scofield's "remarkable power
of condensation" of Scripture, Chafer later reflected, contributed to unveiling
Chafer's "ignorance of the fundamental truths of the Bible."[11]

In Chafer's first books he exhibited a deep indebtedness to Scofield, dif-
fering only in the slightest of details from his mentor's exposition and teaching. Scofield charged Chafer, who continued to evangelize up and down the
Eastern Seaboard, with responsibilities at his new educational institutions,
including the New York Night School of the Bible (founded in 1911) and the
more ambitious Philadelphia School of the Bible (founded in 1914). During
this same period Chafer's ties to the South deepened to the point that he followed Scofield in joining the Southern Presbyterian Church, where aversion
to theological modernism ensured that, for the time being, teachings on free
grace and dispensational truth would be uncontroversial.

By World War I, Chafer had transformed himself into an interdenominational Bible teacher and promoter of dispensational time. Yet, unlike Riley,
whose attention was fixed on combating modernism in American churches and
culture, Chafer turned his talents toward systematizing his theology. The same
year that Riley published *The Menace of Modernism*, Chafer published *Salvation*
(1917), a work with not one reference to current events that was "in no way
intended to be a contribution to [contemporary] theological discussion."[12] The
terms "liberal" and "modernist" made no appearance, and besides the indebtedness to Scofieldian concepts of free grace, the book would be hard to date
to 1917 rather than thirty years before. Chafer fashioned his work to ignore its
historical moment, while Riley's writings were a direct response to it.

10. Quoted in William Vance Trollinger, *God's Empire: William Bell Riley and Midwestern Fundamentalism* (Madison: University of Wisconsin Press, 1990), 28.
11. Quoted in Hannah, *An Uncommon Union*, 62.
12. Lewis Sperry Chafer, *Salvation* (Chicago: Moody Press, 1917), vii.

Bibliography

Theocratic Kingdom	*Peters.*
Israel and the Church	*Brookes.*
Maranatha ; or, The Lord Cometh	*Brookes.*
Scofield Reference Bible	*Scofield.*
Scofield Correspondence Course	*Scofield.*
Addresses on Prophecy	*Scofield.*
Annotated Bible	*Gaebelein.*
Matthew	*Gaebelein.*
The Prophet Daniel	*Gaebelein.*
Hath God Cast Away His People ?	*Gaebelein.*
Harmony of the Prophetic Word	*Gaebelein.*
The Revelation	*Gaebelein.*
Zechariah	*Gaebelein.*
God's Oath	*Ottman.*
Unfolding of the Ages	*Ottman.*
Imperialism and Christ	*Ottman.*
The Evolution of the Kingdom	*Riley.*
Lectures on the Apocalypse	*Seiss.*
The Second Coming of Christ	*Haldeman.*
Signs of The Times	*Haldeman.*
God's Method with Man	*Morgan.*
Sunrise ; or, Behold, He Cometh	*Morgan.*
Christianity and Antichristianity	*Andrews.*
What the Bible Teaches	*Torrey.*
The Coming Prince	*Anderson.*
Synthetic Bible Study	*Gray.*
Christian Workers' Commentary	*Gray.*
The Revelation	*Scott.*

158

Bibliography 159

The Revelation	*Grant.*
Second Coming of Christ	*Moody.*
Ecce Venit	*Gordon.*
History Unveiling Prophecy	*Guinness.*
On This Rock	*Guinness.*
Even So Come	*MacNeil.*
The Great Prophecies	*Pember.*
The Coming of the Lord	*Pierson.*
Twelve Sermons on the Second Coming of Christ	*Spurgeon.*
Addresses of Chicago Prophetic Conference.	
Man's Day	*Mauro.*
The Number of Man	*Mauro.*
Jesus is Coming	*Blackstone.*
The Revelation	*Kelly.*
Christ Coming Again	*Kelly.*
Light on the Last Days	*Blanchard.*
Outline Studies in the Books of the Old Testament	*Moorehead.*
Plain Papers on the Lord's Coming	*C. H. M.*
Synopsis of the Bible	*Darby.*
Plain Papers on Prophecy	*Trotter.*
Wonders of Prophecy	*Urquhart.*

Figure 16. Bibliography of Chafer's *The Kingdom in History and Prophecy* (1915). This bibliography reveals the formidable theological edifice in which some fundamentalists could source their new theological system of dispensationalism.

By 1922 Chafer had grown disillusioned with Riley's leadership of the WCFA, with its constant antagonizing over timely, rather than timeless, issues of concern. Not content to simply bow out of fundamentalist organizing, Chafer undertook his most ambitious project yet to chart a different way. At a meeting in March 1922 in the Piedmont Hotel in Atlanta, Chafer hatched an idea with two like-minded fundamentalists—Canadian pastor Alexander B. Winchester and British Anglican theologian W. H. Griffith Thomas—to create "a high-grade theological school" on par with Princeton Theological Seminary, but one that would train pastors in the English Bible and impart the theology of dispensational time and new premillennialism.[13] The idea was not entirely unique: the WCFA had bandied about the idea of a "premillennial theological seminary" since 1919, with Riley claiming that the future of seminary education amounted to the most "important question" put "before the church since Acts 15."[14] Yet, because of WCFA priorities, infighting, and lack of funds, the idea had died in committee by 1923.

Chafer, on the other hand, had helped found the Philadelphia School of the Bible in 1914 on the Bible institute model and was ready to take on a more sophisticated academic venture. A more rigorous institution was needed if pastors were to be fundamentalist Bible expositors rather than rabble-rousers. As planning for the ambitiously named Evangelical Theological College proceeded (reflecting the British understanding of "college" shared by Winchester and Thomas), the actions of the WCFA only confirmed Chafer's desire to create an independent venture. "It would be too bad if the new school was linked in any way with fundamentalism," Gaebelein wrote Chafer, announcing elsewhere in late 1923, "I believe the days of the fundamentalist movement are numbered."[15]

The institution that Chafer envisioned opened its doors in October 1924, in downtown Dallas, near where Chafer was pastoring the newly renamed Scofield Memorial Church. With the library donated by recently deceased W. H. Griffith Thomas and land purchased in 1926, the school, which was renamed Dallas Theological Seminary in 1936, became the center for advanced new premillennialist education. The school celebrated its first commencement in 1925, awarding two degrees, and boasted a graduating class of twenty-five by 1936. The majority of early faculty and students were Presbyterian (Northern, Southern, and Canadian), with seven of the first eleven faculty ordained as

13. Quoted in Hannah, *An Uncommon Union*, 324n8.
14. Quoted in Nathan Lentfer, "A History of the World's Christian Fundamentals Association (1919–1952)" (PhD diss., Bob Jones University, 2011), 103.
15. Quoted in Hannah, *An Uncommon Union*, 92.

Southern Presbyterian clergy. None of the original faculty held PhDs, and because Chafer subscribed to the same faith principle as many missions agencies (that there should be no direct solicitation of funds), the early years of the school were mired in financial distress, faculty unrest, and institutional reorganization. In this, the early years of Dallas Theological Seminary mirrored fundamentalism writ large.

Independent from the WCFA and the band of fundamentalist irritants that Chafer loathed, the seminary articulated its purpose in a different register. As Chafer's brother and seminary administrator Rollin T. Chafer explained, the school aimed "to train men in the truth from various denominations and send them back to their own denominations as qualified ministers." Lewis Chafer described the school as "denominationally unrelated" rather than inter-denominational (which might imply a desire to affiliate with denominations) or undenominational (which might imply hostility to denominations).[16] He argued that only a denominationally unrelated school could avoid the heated controversy of fundamentalism and pursue theological truth unfettered. "No theological institution today can be under denominational control and not be a battleground for contending forces and doctrinal opinions," he explained to a friend in 1926. "We cannot maintain a united testimony and come under denominational control. This is why we are an independent institution."[17]

As a model for effecting immediate change in the contest against modernism, Chafer's plan proved to be no more effective than Riley's. A degree from Dallas Seminary carried hardly any cachet outside of the same fundamentalist circles that prized Bible institute graduates. Over the course of the 1920s and 1930s, the seminary gradually became a magnet for separatist and independent churches (and later megachurches), leaving the fight for denominational power to others. But for stitching together a different Christian identity steeped in the theology of dispensational time and new premillennialism, the founding of Dallas Theological Seminary would turn out to be one of the most consequential events in the history of dispensationalism.

Norris, Rice, and Jones: Separatist Fundamentalists

In its early years, Dallas Seminary operated on the margins of Southern Presbyterianism and fundamentalism. But it also grew alongside, and overlapped with, another, less defined religious subculture: the fledgling world of inde-

---

16. Quoted in Hannah, *An Uncommon Union*, 94.
17. Quoted in Hannah, *An Uncommon Union*, 95.

pendent and separatist fundamentalism. Dallas was itself independent, though Chafer remained a committed Southern Presbyterian and was willing to affiliate with denominations and leaders who could send students to the school and place its graduates. At the same time, independent fundamentalists took notice of the growth of new premillennialism and became an important conduit for its dispersion in ways that alternately strengthened and undermined Chafer's project of scholastic education.

By 1930, most fundamentalists were in some measure "separatists," in that they wanted to separate themselves from liberal denominations, regarding fellowship or direct affiliation with modernists as anathema to "Bible-believing Christianity." Fundamentalist exoduses from the denominations were steady throughout the 1920s, assuring that most observers, and most fundamentalists, would come to regard separatism as a marker of fundamentalism, even as the intentions of denominational fundamentalists (or those of Chafer) were originally far from this goal.

For the most committed separatists, a twofold separation entailed breaking ties not just with modernists but also with other fundamentalists who associated with modernists (such as Chafer). Claiming the mantle of true separatism, these double separatists were creators of their own religious subculture. Separatist fundamentalism was a world stitched together with some of the same threads as other fundamentalist factions: magazines, Bible conferences, revival circuits, and influential pulpits. It was a community bound by shared professions of biblical inerrancy and antimodernism, and to a large degree by new premillennial eschatology. But it was also a culture of infighting and discord on a scale that far outpaced even the other, already riven fundamentalist circles. Separatist institutions were almost uniformly headed by leaders boasting charismatic personalities and a strong sense of independence.

Because it was present at the creation of fundamentalism, new premillennialism quickly took on the trappings of the "old-time religion" that independent fundamentalists claimed was theirs to steward. Yet, crucially, independent leaders including Bob Jones Sr., J. Frank Norris, and John R. Rice, among others, were unaffiliated with the scholastic project of Chafer and the new Dallas Seminary. Independent fundamentalists often taught key features of new premillennial eschatology, such as the rapture and the encroaching reign of the antichrist, but just as often they neglected the teachings of dispensational time, the church-Israel distinction, free grace, and the spirituality of the church. In short, they were uninterested in adopting a theological system but preferred to adopt some features of the emerging system of dispensationalism.

While independent fundamentalists suffered from acute infighting, they were often eager to bridge North-South sectional differences, giving premillennial teachings a powerful conduit into the South. No one embodied this bridgework better than J. Frank Norris, who in 1935 assumed dual pastorates of First Baptist Church in Fort Worth, Texas, and Temple Baptist Church in Detroit, Michigan, with a combined membership in the tens of thousands. The latter church, originally comprised of white southern migrants to automobile-industry jobs, became one of the largest congregations in the Detroit area. Other separatists could tell of similar transsectional connections. Norris's one-time ally and later rival John R. Rice was a Texas native who spent decades leading his ministries from Wheaton, Illinois. The evangelist and Kentucky-born Mordecai Ham developed deep ties to Chicago and Minnesota even as his ministry spanned the South and Great Plains. Like Scofield and Chafer, these fundamentalists broke with geographic boundaries in the service of a new form of fundamentalist identity. Unlike Scofield and Chafer, who elevated scholastic authority above personal charisma and harbored hope that the denominations could renew themselves, independent fundamentalists adopted populist styles that ensured that dispensational concepts would find a broad audience among fundamentalist churchgoers, and that those concepts would be transmitted unevenly.

Norris and Rice were each unbending new premillennialists. Norris treated premillennialism as a marker of true fundamentalism, going so far as to debate other fundamentalists on the doctrine's merits. At one three-day debate in 1934 with Church of Christ amillennialist Foy E. Wallace, a crowd of more than six thousand witnessed ninety-minute speeches in which both men debated the historical views of Alexander Campbell (founder of the Churches of Christ) on the millennium. Later, Norris created a group of independent Baptist churches under the name of the Premillennial Missionary Baptist Fellowship. Rice was equally committed to new premillennialism. His flagship magazine, *Sword of the Lord*, declared in the banner of each issue the list of nonnegotiable theological fundamentals, including "the premillennial return of Christ."

Yet Norris and Rice each diverged from the emerging scholastic project of dispensationalism. Norris ditched the division of dispensational time and would later declare the dispensational system anathema to Bible-believing Christianity. "This dispensational business has been the most overdone thing. . . . And they have dispensationed out many of the great truths," he wrote of Scofield and his disciples.[18] Norris's complaint was that scholastic dispensationalism as practiced by Scofield, Chafer, and his disciples led to a Bible that was "all outlined," "divided up," and "talking about God's plan of the ages," rather than compelling

18. Quoted in Barry Hankins, *God's Rascal: J. Frank Norris and the Beginnings of Southern Fundamentalism* (Lexington: University Press of Kentucky, 1996), 75.

"sinners" to prepare themselves to "meet God in the day of Judgment."[19] Rice, for his part, criticized past new premillennialists, including Blackstone and Torrey, for their geopolitical analysis of the signs of the times. He also broke doctrinally with the *Scofield Reference Bible*'s teaching that the Pentecost event of Acts 2 inaugurated the church. This "false meaning for Pentecost," he insisted, diminished it as the ongoing source of "soul-winning and revival power" needed in the present. Rice's divergences from Scofield (and later Chafer) amounted to a repudiation of the emerging dispensational theology as insufficiently focused on evangelism. "It is time for us to go back to the fundamentals and essentials," Rice would later write, as opposed to "spend[ing] more time chopping the Scriptures up into artificial dispensations."[20]

Separatist pragmatism in the deployment of new premillennial eschatology extended to Bob Jones Sr., one of the most divisive of the independent fundamentalist leaders. An Alabama-born Methodist evangelist and later independent Baptist, Jones founded his own college in 1927 from the proceeds of his wildly successful itinerant preaching. Bob Jones College espoused, like the founder, various new premillennial concepts while rejecting key parts of emerging dispensational theology. Eschatology was a secondary concern to the standard of double separation, which Bob Jones Jr., who succeeded Bob Jones Sr. as president of the school, enforced in an even more draconian fashion. The school's statement of faith strategically made no mention of premillennialism and allowed for postmillennialism among the faculty.

The shadow of the Jones family was large. Jones Sr. was the most popular revivalist in all the country in the 1920s, and his separatist credentials allowed him to market himself and his college in Greenville, South Carolina, as the "ultrafundamentalist" option. His lackluster embrace of dispensationalism was no hindrance to this label nor to his strident criticism of fundamentalists he deemed insufficiently rigorous on issues he prioritized, including separation, biblical inerrancy, racial segregation, and anticommunism. Through the 1930s, dispensationalism spread through independent and Baptist circles but never became a marker of right belief.

Separatist mastery of mass media, including magazines and radio, ensured that premillennialism continued to shape southern religious culture. Norris

19. Quoted in Danny Eugene Howe, "An Analysis of Dispensationalism and Its Implications for the Theologies of James Robinson Graves, John Franklyn Norris, and Wallie Amos Criswell" (PhD diss., Southwestern Baptist Theological Seminary, 1988), 180.

20. Quoted in Matthew Lee Lyon, "John R. Rice and Evangelism: An Essential Mark of Independent Baptist Fundamentalism" (PhD diss., Southern Baptist Theological Seminary, 2019), 100.

and Rice each published weekly magazines, each attaining circulations in the tens of thousands by the mid-1930s. The term "dispensationalism" hardly ever appeared in these magazines, but the fixtures of new premillennial eschatology were frequent: the imminent rapture, an encroaching one-world government, the dangerous prospect of a one-world religion. These same themes were beamed across the country's radio waves. Norris and Jones each hosted shows that played on hundreds of stations across the country, often combining biblical exegesis with topical reflections on news and events. In the midst of 1920s culture wars over evolution and gender norms, separatists almost uniformly supported socially conservative candidates and the Ku Klux Klan, embedding themselves not just in the new fundamentalist identity but in the mainstream white southern culture, as well.

Dozens more midlevel evangelists and pastors populated the independent and separatist networks that crisscrossed the North and South, often working in support of one of the handful of nationally known separatist personalities. In these settings and relationships, theological divergence—even on particulars of eschatology—could lead to rifts. The heightened role of theological fidelity in the social cohesion of separatist fundamentalism meant that separatists themselves organized countless Bible and prophecy conferences, open-air campaigns, and tent revivals on premillennial themes. In these settings they harangued modernism, which set the backdrop to their religious and cultural identities, but most of all they agreed with or bickered with each other. Their theological confessions were carefully enumerated but less carefully constructed. Very little was systematized, and even less was intended as scholarly contribution to the education of future pastors. The separatists would play an important role in giving dispensationalism a wider receptive audience and in fusing premillennialism to a conservative, even right-wing, politics. But what separatists would not do is engage in scholastic theological discourse or seek in any systematic way to educate fundamentalists on a particular doctrine of eschatology.

Lewis Sperry Chafer Embraces "Dispensationalism"

In 1936, the same year he renamed his school Dallas Theological Seminary, Lewis Sperry Chafer was forced to contend with a growing chorus of critics from seemingly all sectors of fundamentalism. Using the pages of the seminary's newly acquired journal, *Bibliotheca Sacra*, Chafer identified himself publicly for the first time as a "dispensationalist." The term, having been coined by Mauro less than a decade earlier, had become common parlance among fundamentalists critical of the theology. Dispensationalism distinguished a particular lineage of biblical interpretation and theological reasoning in the fundamentalist fold, one that Mauro insisted was foreign to the movement's true aims. To outside observers, including most modernists, the distinction between a premillennialist and a dispensationalist was inconsequential. To Chafer, however, the differences dogged him daily, as other fundamentalists attacked his teachings as "modern," "illogical," and "extreme."[21] Finally, in October 1936, Chafer published a sixty-page, twenty-five-thousand-word rejoinder titled simply "Dispensationalism."

He wrote in exacting detail against the criticisms leveled at the "complete religious system" he unofficially led (409). All Christians were at least "partial dispensationalists," he mused, if they acknowledged the "Old" and "New" Testament and did not follow ancient Israelite sacrificial practices. Many Christians settled for "dimly observing a few obvious distinctions," but "a worthy and scholarly research of the Bible" had been revived "during the last century by J. N. Darby, Charles H. Mackintosh, Wm Kelly, F. W. Grant, and others who developed what is known as the Plymouth Brethren movement" (448, 392). These men had not deviated from the historic faith, Chafer clarified, but recovered the core "dispensational distinctions" propounded by the biblical writers and church fathers (392).

By 1936 the term "dispensationalism" had accumulated such ill repute among fundamentalists that Chafer used the term "reluctantly." He "suffered" its use, but he wanted to steal the epithet away from his fundamentalist opponents and turn it into a positive position. To that end, his reflections in the heat of controversy laid the groundwork for what would become his crowning achievement, an eight-volume defense of dispensationalism titled simply *Systematic Theology* (1947). By outlining a dispensational anthropology, soteriology, and exegetical theology to establish his orthodox credibility, Chafer made the case for dispensationalism's improvement over older Protestant traditions. In the "recovery of vital truth in the Reformation," Chafer wrote of church history in 1936, "dispensational distinctions, like various doctrines, were not emphasized. The truths thus neglected in the Reformation have since been set forth by devout Bible students, but against the opposition of those who assume that the Reformation secured all that is germane to Systematic Theology" (392). The recovery mission, waged especially against fellow fundamentalists, would dominate his life until his death in 1952.

The criticisms of dispensationalism that Chafer rebutted were not much different than the ones Mauro made to define the theological system a decade

21. Lewis Sperry Chafer, "Dispensationalism," *Bibliotheca Sacra*, October 1936, 394. Hereafter, page references from this work will be given in parentheses in the text.

earlier. Chafer nevertheless enumerated those criticisms: dispensationalism was of recent origin; it resembled modernist higher criticism in its willingness to "divide biblical truth"; it produced passive Christians and a cheap doctrine of salvation and grace; it was a bastardized form of premillennialism. The points and rhetoric resembled earlier attacks on new premillennialism but sharpened in the context of movement polarization and offered far more precision on what "dispensationalism" claimed to be and, conversely, how those who were arrayed against it differed.

The term "system" appeared more than twenty times in Chafer's article, though "premillennialism" appeared only once. Chafer was more interested in identifying the systemic differences between "conservative dispensationalists" (himself and his allies) and "partial dispensationalists" (everyone else). He concluded: "The [conservative] dispensationalist believes that throughout the ages God is pursuing two distinct purposes: one related to the earth with earthly people and earthly objectives involved, while the other is related to heaven with heavenly people and heavenly objectives involved" (448). The "two distinct purposes"—a concept indebted by Brethren dualism—was the crux of Chafer's dispensationalism, and in both his and Mauro's estimation the source of fundamentalist disagreement. Key theological inferences flowed from this difference in "premise," according to Chafer. At stake was the nature of salvation (especially the "free grace" position) and the purpose of the church—some of the very fundamentals in the wider controversy with modernists (396).

For the scattered leaders of fundamentalism, the demons of discontent were everywhere in 1936. The fundamentalist-modernist controversy had cooled as fighting among fundamentalists heated up. Dispensationalism, now attached to a particular subset of fundamentalists, survived the early attempts at its marginalization. It was now poised to be a key contender in the coming struggle for the soul of fundamentalism.

O weary one, on time's rough sea
Lift up thy heart and voice
Eternal shores are beck'ning thee
Arise, thou, and rejoice

Angelic music fills the breeze
Behold the gates ajar
And Eden's lovely fruits and trees
We soon shall cross the bar

Farewell to sorrow and pain
Farewell to sin and its reign
We'll soon be at home
Never more to roam
We're almost—almost home.

Jessie F. Moser, "We're Almost Home" (1928)

Written by a member of the Biola community and appearing in the *King's Business*, the poem channeled the angst of dispensationalists at the low point of fundamentalist organizing. As the accompanying commentary explained, "The omens of our Lord's coming are everywhere prevalent. We seem to be in the very midst of THE apostasy. . . . It is not strange that many of the Lord's anointed grow weary of the conflict." The struggle described was not only with modernists, but also, by the late 1920s, increasingly with other fundamentalists, as well.

12

The Great Rift

For Charles Gallaudet Trumbull's entire adult life he had traveled through the worlds of premillennialism, fundamentalism, and, finally, dispensationalism. An editor of the *Sunday School Times* from 1903 to 1941, Trumbull had two great passions in his long career: new premillennialism and the Higher Life teachings. Like Cyrus Scofield, about whom he wrote a glowing biography in 1920, and Lewis Sperry Chafer, a close friend, Trumbull disliked the style and rancor of the antievolution activists and World Christian Fundamentals Association. Paraphrasing 1 Corinthians 13:13, which lists the greatest gifts of the Spirit as faith, hope, and love, Trumbull wrote—for the first time in 1930 and many times thereafter—an appeal to his fellow fundamentalists: "And now abideth fundamentalism, premillennialism, and love, these three. But the greatest of these is love."[1]

Trumbull's repeated petitions for love illustrate how there was no period when dispensationalism was spared scrutiny. Debates took place in pulpits and seminary classrooms; the argumentation was both popular and technical in style. The stakes of disagreement were often obscured to outsiders, who associated dispensationalism with apocalyptic speculation rather than the "two distinct purposes" of God that Chafer placed at the center of his theology. "Love" would be a fleeting feature of the fundamentalist discourse around dispensationalism in its early years.

The struggle over dispensationalism and the theological identity of fundamentalism starting in the 1930s created a shared language of identification for conservative Protestantism that would last for the better part of a cen-

---

1. Originally published in the *Sunday School Times* and here quoted in an editorial response: "The Greatest of These Is Love," *King's Business*, October 1930, 451.

tury. Fundamentalists developed lasting loyalties based on their acceptance or rejection of dispensationalism. Polarization over theology helped to produce, in the span of little more than a decade, three distinctive fundamentalist subcultures. The dispensationalists organized in competition to an oppositional school of "covenantalism," so called for its emphasis on the historically Reformed categories that emphasized that God's covenants did not vary according to what "dispensation" history had reached. By the 1940s, a third faction of neo-evangelicals had triangulated between dispensationalists and covenantalists, engaging in some of the very same theological contestations. The factional divisions became, by midcentury, the permanent divisions of a fundamentalism that reflected the fallout of internecine battles as much as the larger contest with modernism.

Pink, Mauro, and Allis: The Covenantalists

Scholastic debates over dispensationalism in the 1930s may have looked different than fundamentalist organizing in the 1920s, but they reflected many of the same priorities. Most denominational fundamentalist leaders disapproved of dispensationalism on theological grounds. This was especially true for Northern Presbyterian fundamentalists, who by 1930 had suffered major defeats not just at the denomination's General Assembly but in a reorganization of Princeton Seminary that effectively removed their last bastion of institutional influence. Rather than continue at Princeton, the fundamentalist organizer and New Testament professor J. Gresham Machen declared the seminary apostate in 1929 and began an independent school, Westminster Theological Seminary, forty miles southwest in Glenside, Pennsylvania. Machen attracted other Princeton faculty, including systematic theologian John Murray and Old Testament theologian Oswald T. Allis. Both would lead the charge against dispensationalism just a few years later. In the meantime, Westminster became the theological center of the new Orthodox Presbyterian Church, founded in 1936 under the guidance of Machen to parallel the Northern Presbyterian denominational structure.

The Orthodox Presbyterian Church tolerated premillennialists in their midst as long as Machen was alive. But after his sudden death in 1937, the atmosphere shifted almost immediately. A minority faction of premillennialists led by onetime Machen student and emerging leader of separatist fundamentalism Carl McIntire broke away to form the competing Bible Presbyterian Church. McIntire also christened his own seminary, Faith Theological Seminary, drawing the few Westminster faculty who identified as premillennial and situating themselves in an increasingly fragmented Presbyterian landscape. Along with Westminster professor Allan Macrae and Wheaton College president J. Oliver Buswell, McIntire claimed his unique combination of Reformed covenantal theology and new premillennial eschatology as the true successor to Northern Presbyterian fundamentalism. Never a doctrinaire dispensationalist, McIntire taught a modified view of an approaching antichrist (usually identified with ecumenical Protestants, Catholics, and communists) and a near-though-not-imminent rapture. He ditched most other doctrines that dispensationalists like Chafer held dear, including dispensational time, free grace, and a strict church-Israel distinction. Even so, McIntire's habitual creation of new separatist institutions (including his popular magazine *Christian Beacon*, the American Council of Christian Churches, and the International Council of Christian Churches) dispersed premillennial eschatology into the less organized ranks of independent fundamentalism.

While Presbyterian fundamentalists were splitting, dispensationalists were facing new scrutiny from other representatives of the Reformed tradition. In 1931, the first academic study of premillennialism to include an analysis of "dispensationalism" appeared, by Free University of Amsterdam PhD student William H. Rutgers. Trained at Calvin Theological Seminary (Grand Rapids, Michigan) and Princeton, Rutgers was skeptical of the entire doctrine of premillennialism, but especially dispensationalism. Citing Philip Mauro's *The Gospel of the Kingdom* (1928) as "the strongest argument yet produced against dispensationalism," Rutgers was remorseless in his estimation of the system as "novel and modernistic in the strictest sense, extra-biblical and a pure invention of man."[2] Borrowing Mauro's terminology, Rutgers insisted on a distinction between "historic" and "modern" premillennialism, with his most critical comments trained on the latter, which he equated with dispensationalism. Though not a widely read work, "Premillennialism in America" showed the growing concern by conservative Reformed theologians and the outlines of a more sophisticated framework for criticism, which would be picked up by later critics.

Dispensationalists also suffered their own high-profile defections. The onetime new premillennialist Arthur W. Pink, who published a popular eschatology book, *Redeemer's Return* (1918), had abandoned the doctrine by

---

2. William H. Rutgers, "Premillennialism in America" (PhD diss., Free University of Amsterdam, 1931), 172.

1928. Pink was an adult convert to Christianity whose only formal theological education was an incomplete summer semester at Moody Bible Institute. In 1933, a series of articles appeared in Pink's magazine, *Studies in the Scriptures*, that took direct aim at dispensationalism. Like Mauro, Pink channeled the passion of a onetime disciple. He wanted to "expose the modern and pernicious error of Dispensationalism," which was "a device of the Enemy . . . wherein the wily serpent appears as an angel of light, feigning to 'make the Bible a new book' by simplifying much in it which perplexes the spiritually unlearned."[3] Dispensationalists were "would-be super expositors" and "mutilators of the Word" who undermined the unity of the Bible with their teachings of dispensational time and free grace. Having edited his magazine since before his change of heart, Pink admitted that "it is likely that some of our readers, when perusing upon the articles upon the interpretation of the Scriptures, felt more than once that we were taking undue liberty with Holy Writ."[4] No longer the case, Pink dedicated his later years to recanting his earlier views.

Pink and Mauro were joined by other defectors. One of the most prominent was G. Campbell Morgan, whose transatlantic teaching ministry was a rival to succeed Moody's around the year 1900. As the director of the Northfield Bible Conference after Moody's death and an author in *The Fundamentals*, Morgan had a better claim to succeed Moody than most. In his early works he taught dispensational time, yet by the 1930s he had left it behind entirely. With Mauro's *Visions of Patmos* (1925), a study of the book of Revelation that rejected premillennialism, Morgan claimed to be "in full agreement," and of *The Gospel of the Kingdom* (1928), he declared it to be "unanswerable." In his twilight years, Morgan had intimated publicly what he had written privately, that "the phrase 'secret Rapture' has to me for a long time been a very objectionable one" and that "the old materialistic view of the setting up of an earthly Jewish Kingdom is utterly unwarranted."[5]

---

3. Arthur W. Pink, *A Study of Dispensationalism* (1940; reprint, n.p.: Feedbooks digitized version, 2010), 3, https://archive.org/details/AStudyOnDispensationalism/page /n1/mode/2up. The series of articles appeared in *Studies in the Scriptures* in 1933–1934 and was later published as a stand-alone book. Pink's magazine published another series of articles posthumously in 1952 titled "A Critical Assessment of Dispensationalism" that is often conflated with this earlier series (both level similar criticisms).

4. Pink, *A Study of Dispensationalism*, 3.

5. Quoted in George Eldon Ladd, *The Blessed Hope: A Biblical Study of the Second Advent and the Rapture* (Grand Rapids: Eerdmans, 1956), 55; Morgan, quoted in Philip

Four theological issues claimed the most attention by defectors and covenantal critics at Westminster. These were the clearest markers of identification that distinguished dispensational and covenantal factions. The substance, while important, was often less the sticking point than were the social implications and resultant polarization of protracted and unresolvable debate.

The first issue was the historical provenance of dispensationalism, a topic raised by Mauro in the 1910s and, indeed, by critics of new premillennialism in the nineteenth century. It was clear to everyone that the church-Israel distinction and dispensational time had modern origins significantly, if not exclusively, with the teachings of the Exclusive Brethren. But was Darby recovering an earlier tradition or inventing a new one? Dispensationalists insisted that the general tenets of dispensational time were as old as the Bible itself, and that church fathers had embraced various understandings of premillennialism and dispensational time. Covenantalists described these doctrines as modern inventions that were as destructive to orthodox belief as modernist threats such as higher criticism. To these fundamentalist critics, dispensationalism was an innovation, and innovation was not authentic to historic Christianity.

A second point of contention centered on the extent of God's "two distinct purposes," especially in relation to the doctrine of salvation. In crudest terms, did Scofield, Chafer, and other dispensationalists teach that there were two ways to be saved, one under the dispensations of "law" in the Old Testament and another under the dispensation of "grace" in the New Testament? Critics read Scofield's note to John 1:17 as especially problematic. In contrasting "law" and "grace," he wrote that with the dispensation of grace, "the point of testing is no longer legal obedience as the condition of salvation, but acceptance or rejection of Christ, with good works as fruit of salvation."[6] Critics charged that the implications of dispensational time meant that the means of salvation were in flux, which, if true, would unsettle many other aspects of systematic theology. While Chafer protested this description of his views, he struggled to maintain a consistent line, as other fundamentalists identified his teachings as, at best, inconsistent on this issue.

A third and related area was the teaching of "free grace," or the doctrine that salvation meant simply acknowledging Jesus as one's Savior. While the

Mauro, "A Letter to a Dispensationalist (1933)," in *Collected Shorter Writings*, ed. Friedel Hansen (n.p.: Philip Mauro Library, 2010), 263–64.

6. *Scofield Reference Bible*, ed. Cyrus I. Scofield, rev. ed. (Oxford: Oxford University Press, 1917), 1115n2.

196 • THE DISPENSATIONALISTS

teaching of "free grace" was popular across American fundamentalism, Reformed opponents criticized its narrow focus on mental assent and lack of emphasis on the submission of a sinner's will to God. Chafer was a leading theological proponent of free grace theology and made Dallas Seminary its primary expositor. Yet Chafer was not alone. Free grace assumptions appeared in the "sinner's prayer" of early twentieth-century revivalism that would include a series of "I believe" statements, in the language of "accepting" Jesus "into your heart" popularized by radio preachers, and in the lyrics of popular revival hymns such as this: "'What must I do?' the trembling jailor cried / when dazed by fear and wonder / 'Believe on Christ!' was all that Paul replied / 'And thou shalt be saved from sin.'"[7] Covenantalists, who tended to eschew the revivalist tradition in any case, viewed free grace as a dangerous thinning out of the doctrine of salvation that both cheapened what was demanded from the convert and lessened the scope of obligations to Christian discipleship.

A fourth area of contention centered on the kingdom of God. Here eschatology entered the picture as Chafer identified the kingdom about which Jesus taught as the future kingdom of Revelation 21. The church existed as a separate (and heaven-bound) entity, whose mandate was strictly confined by the dispensations and the separation of powers God granted to Israel (earth) and the church (heaven). Covenantalists rejected this view, understanding their own churches as the emerging kingdom itself, and indeed, as the symbolic millennial reign of Christ. This was the overwhelming view of denominational fundamentalists, the majority of whom embraced the amillennial view that there would be no earthly, physical millennium set up at Christ's return beyond the existing church. Compounding the controversy, dispensationalists were often ambiguous in the application of Jesus's ethical teachings in relation to the question of kingdom. Was the Sermon on the Mount a model for the church or for the future millennial kingdom, or both?

These criticisms converged into a full-fledged covenantal assault on dispensationalism beginning in 1936. Mauro released another attack, *The Church, the Churches, and the Kingdom* (1936), that referred to dispensationalists simply as "modern Judaizers" for their support of Zionism and expectation of a literal millennium.[8] More novel were the broadsides from Westminster Theological

7. Avis B. Christiansen, "Believe on the Lord Jesus Christ," *Crusader Hymns* (Minneapolis: Billy Graham Evangelistic Association, 1966), 60. Christiansen was a lifelong Chicagoan who attended Moody's church and was affiliated with Moody Bible Institute. The hymn was written in 1920.

8. Philip Mauro, *The Church, the Churches, and the Kingdom* (1936; reprint, n.p.: Philip Mauro Library, 2008), 29.

Seminary. At the beginning of the year, Oswald T. Allis, who had taught at Princeton and then Westminster, published a scathing attack in the journal *Evangelical Quarterly* that indicted dispensationalism for destroying the "unity of scripture."[9] This was followed in May with a series of articles by Westminster professor John Murray, in the *Presbyterian Guardian*, on "modern substitutes" for Reformed theology, including "modern dispensationalism."[10] Later in the year, Allis published a follow-up to his earlier piece that criticized the law-grace distinction in Scofield's notes, diagnosing dispensationalists with "a serious misunderstanding of the true nature and purpose of the Law of God."[11] Both Allis and Murray, as well as a host of other covenantalist theologians, including William Hendriksen (at Calvin Theological Seminary), who published an influential commentary on Revelation in 1939, did not stop with one round of attacks. They hammered on dispensationalism repeatedly for the next decade.

The charges brought against dispensationalists were not new, but they were newly understood to be evidence of systematic differences rather than isolated points of contention. The designation of "modern dispensationalism" and "the dispensationalists" attached to the problematic teachings a system of interlocking logic that, for Mauro, Allis, Murray, Hendrikson, and others, inevitably produced error. Allis wrote of the "divisive tendency inherent in Dispensationalism," and Murray pleaded with fellow Presbyterians to "withdraw from a system of interpretation the logic" that leads to "disastrous consequences."[12] What Mauro and the many critics he inspired were complaining about was not a series of errors that had popped up individually in the fundamentalist movement, but a system of theology that, at its core, they believed inevitably led to error. This was a new charge, leveled by fundamentalists against fundamentalists and made on a scale hardly imaginable a decade earlier. The implications matched the scope of the charge, namely, that dispensationalism, if allowed to grow in the fundamentalist movement, would threaten fundamentalism's entire theological integrity.

9. Oswald T. Allis, "Modern Dispensationalism and the Unity of Scripture," *Evangelical Quarterly* 8, no. 1 (January 1936): 22–35.

10. John Murray, "Modern Dispensationalism," *Presbyterian Guardian* 2, no. 4 (May 18, 1936): 77–79.

11. Oswald T. Allis, "Modern Dispensationalism and the Law of God," *Evangelical Quarterly* 8, no. 3 (July 1936): 272–89.

12. Allis, "Modern Dispensationalism and the Unity of Scripture," 24; Murray, "Modern Dispensationalism," 79.

PROPHECY AND
THE CHURCH

AN EXAMINATION OF THE CLAIM OF DISPENSATIONALISTS
THAT THE CHRISTIAN CHURCH IS A MYSTERY PARENTHESIS
WHICH INTERRUPTS THE FULFILMENT TO ISRAEL OF
THE KINGDOM PROPHECIES OF THE OLD TESTAMENT

By
OSWALD T. ALLIS

*Yea, and all the prophets from Samuel and those that
follow after, as many as have spoken, have likewise
foretold of these days*

PRESBYTERIAN AND REFORMED PUBLISHING CO.
Phillipsburg, New Jersey

Figure 17. Cover of Allis's *Prophecy and the Church*. Covenantal criticism of dispensationalism hit a new high point with the publication of Oswald T. Allis's *Prophecy and the Church* in 1945. As the title indicates, prophecy was deeply entwined with ecclesiology as points of dispute between the two fundamentalist factions. Allis's lengthy subtitle revealed that by 1945 the system differences between covenantalism and dispensationalism had been sharply defined.

Feinberg, Pentecost, Ryrie, and Walvoord: The Dispensational Response

Theological disputes would have been trivial to the history of fundamentalism had they been confined to exercises in rhetoric or debate. Instead, the conflict between dispensationalists and covenantalists spurred the most frenzied period of scholarly output and institution building among conservative Protestants since the late nineteenth century. The dispensational-covenantal rift gave shape to the entire fundamentalist movement in the 1930s and 1940s, from the founding of new seminaries and parachurch organizations, to the statements of faith of countless churches, to new journals and a small mountain of new books. Dispensationalism grew into a full-fledged theological culture in response. Alongside their intellectual center at Dallas Theological Seminary, dispensationalists expanded to meet the challenge of covenantal critics. The debate between the two factions was so pronounced that virtually every fundamentalist institution of the era was forced to pick a theological side.

By the mid-1930s, dispensationalists in Dallas were on their heels and the deluge of confessional hostility from Westminster Seminary had migrated south. In 1937, denominational leaders in the Southern Presbyterian General Assembly began to investigate the teachings of Chafer. After years of hearings and heated exchanges, a special committee to investigate Chafer's views decided unanimously that his teachings were "out of accord with the system of the doctrine set forth in the Confession of Faith, not primarily or simply in the field of eschatology, but because it attacks the very heart of the Theology of our Church."[13] This "heart" was a bundle of issues related far more to Chafer's Higher Life and free grace teachings, along with his treatment of law and dispensational time, than it was to his premillennialism. After the ruling in 1944, Chafer became a pariah in his own denomination (though he was not expelled and remained a member until his death), and Dallas Seminary began to shift its student body from Presbyterians to independents and Baptists.

The systematization of dispensationalism created new internal divisions. American followers of "Bullingerism" (inspired by the teachings of E. W. Bullinger) soon had a new name: "ultradispensationalists." The term, coined by scholastic dispensationalists and their allies in the 1930s, was intended to identify and marginalize those who shared the view that the church age did not begin until midway through Paul's ministry (Bullinger himself took an even more extreme view that the church was not founded until Paul's prison epistles, dated to after the book of Acts). The consequence of either later date meant that practices such as water baptism and communion were not to be practiced by Christians. Theological systematization gave dispensationalists the vocabulary to distinguish their views from those they deemed more extreme. Harry Ironside, an Exclusive Brethren and pastor of Moody Memorial Church in Chicago, was typical in the 1930s of separating purveyors of "dispensational truth" from those who had "swung to an ultradispensationalism which is most pernicious in its effect upon one's own soul

13. "1944 PCUS Report on Dispensationalism," in *Minutes of the Eighty-Fourth General Assembly* (1944) *of the Presbyterian Church, US*, PCA Historical Center, https://www.pcahistory.org/documents/pcus1944.html, 123–27.

and upon testimony for God generally."[14] The acrimony among dispensation-alists, with the stakes now taking on systemic levels, was one of the bitter fruits of systematization.

Nonetheless, Dallas Seminary's distancing from both Southern Presbyteri-anism and ultradispensationalism set the school up for long-term success. The seminary had always been independent, but now it brimmed with students shaped by Chafer's tireless recruiting, producing graduates who became the most prodigious generation yet of dispensational leaders and scholars. By the mid-1940s, these graduates began to contribute to theological scholarship that advanced dispensationalism as a system of biblical interpretation among the growing masses of Christians with frayed institutional and intellectual ties in the aftermath of the fundamentalist-modernist controversies.

A cohort of scholars centered at Dallas Seminary were especially vital to the propagation of dispensationalism in the wider world of fundamentalism. Charles Lee Feinberg, born in an Orthodox Jewish home and a convert to Christianity in 1930, was an Old Testament scholar who also earned a ThD from Dallas and a PhD in archaeology from Johns Hopkins University. He combined expertise in biblical languages and ancient Near East history with a defense of dispensational hermeneutics. Dwight Pentecost, who earned all of his advanced degrees at Dallas, taught there for more than sixty years and wrote the most robust expression of dispensational eschatology of his gener-ation, *Things to Come* (1956). A third scholar, Charles Ryrie, was personally recruited to Dallas by Chafer as an undergraduate. Ryrie's scholastic contribu-tions were many, including a generational go-to introduction to the system, *Dispensationalism Today* (1965).

Leading Dallas Seminary was John Walvoord, the president beginning in 1952. Walvoord arrived in Dallas twenty years earlier as a recent graduate of Wheaton College, a school with a strong premillennial pedigree that annually supplied up to a quarter of all Dallas students in its early years. Displaying exceptional academic and organizational skills, Walvoord became Chafer's secretary and soon emerged as a clear successor. He helped Chafer complete his eight-volume *Systematic Theology* (1948), the most complete expression of dispensational doctrine ever produced, and offered his own contributions in the field of eschatology, especially in *The Millennial Kingdom* (1959) and the trilogy of *The Church in Prophecy* (1960), *Israel in Prophecy* (1962), and *The*

---

14. Harry Ironside, *Wrongly Dividing the Word of Truth: Ultra-Dispensationalism Exam-ined in the Light of the Holy Scriptures*, 3rd ed. (Neptune, NJ: Loizeaux Brothers, 1938), 7.

Nations in Prophecy (1967). Walvoord's tenure at Dallas, which lasted until 1986, ushered in decades of growth for the school, making it one of the largest seminaries in the world.

This Dallas cohort also oversaw the academic journal *Bibliotheca Sacra*, the oldest theological journal in the United States (founded in 1844), which was acquired from the struggling Xenia Theological Seminary in 1934. The journal was edited for fifty years by Rollin T. Chafer (Lewis's brother and the school's registrar), Lewis Chafer, and Walvoord. Though it had long been a latitudinarian venue for Protestant theological research, the journal, upon its move to Dallas, quickly became synonymous with dispensationalism, especially in its defense of the system. Virtually every major dispensational theologian from 1930 to 1960 published in "*BibSac*'s" pages, with many scholars using the journal to serialize major monographs before their publication.

Feinberg, Pentecost, Ryrie, and Walvoord—these names became ubiquitous among seminarians, pastors, and lay readers in the 1950s who undertook any type of theological education at fundamentalist schools. For some, especially at Westminster and other Reformed schools, their names were infamous. For others, their works were formative and accessible, and they provided a level of erudition above that of religious magazines and prophecy tracts. These scholastic dispensationalists produced a dizzying amount of theological writing, the vast majority intended for educational and scholarly consumption.

The Dallas cohort led a broader effort of dispensational scholarship production that included new presses, seminaries, and Bible colleges. Scholastic dispensationalists published within a relatively small print ecosystem. Historically friendly presses included the old Brethren outlet Loizeaux Brothers, alongside theologically conservative issuers such as Zondervan, Moody, and Revell. Several smaller presses also began to publish dispensational works, including Kregel (Grand Rapids, Michigan), Van Kampen (Wheaton, Illinois), and Dunham (Findlay, Ohio). The boundaries of the ecosystem became blurrier when the dozens of seminary, college, and personal presses were counted (Chafer's *Systematic Theology* was published by Dallas Theological Seminary Press, for example), but these smaller outlets often worked at a regional level to reinforce the discourse hosted by the larger national presses.

The burst of scholarship drew on a wider emerging scholastic community. In 1937, as part of a fundamentalist split in the Brethren (German Baptist) Church, a new center of advanced dispensational study called Grace Theological Seminary was created in Winona Lake, Indiana (also the historic home of revivalist Billy Sunday). It was headed by Alva J. McClain, a well-known dispensational expositor. McClain's *The Greatness of the Kingdom* (1959), the first of a planned six-volume theology that would likely have replaced Chafer's *Systematic Theology* had he finished it, was cut short by McClain's declining health in the 1960s. But his stand-alone volume became an instant dispensational classic and a widely used expression of the doctrine of the kingdom that distinguished between the "universal kingdom" of God's reign and the "mediatorial kingdom" that was offered to Israel. The latter, "to which the Biblical writings give the great preponderance of attention," McClain argued, reflected the progression of dispensational time.[15]

McClain's writing also dulled the stark dualism between heaven and earth for the sake of a more literal interpretation of Scripture, which dispensationalists, beginning with Feinberg, Ryrie, and Walvoord, started to emphasize as a defining mark of the system. Consistently reading all Scripture literally, guided by historical and grammatical context rather than typologies or dualism, was a new, and often unnoted, shift in dispensationalism brought about by systematization and the fundamentalist movement's emphasis on biblical inerrancy. Literalism of this variety was a hallmark of Grace Seminary, where the faculty included one of the founders of young-earth creationism, John C. Whitcomb.

Dallas and Grace were joined in 1952 by Talbot Theological Seminary, Biola College's new school of advanced study named after its outgoing president, Louis Talbot, a prolific dispensational writer. First led by Charles Feinberg, who became the first dean of Talbot Seminary and served until 1975, Talbot Seminary emerged as the West Coast center of dispensational scholarship and graduate education, working closely with Dallas and, along with Grace, providing advanced dispensational theological training across three regions of the United States.

As the educational pillars of scholastic dispensationalism, Dallas, Grace, and Talbot were supported by almost seventy Bible institutes, a network that continued to expand with the explosion of higher education after World War II. More urban areas featured their own Bible institutes, many of which were founded by Dallas graduates, including Washington, DC (1930), Portland, Oregon (1936), St. Louis (1938), Milwaukee (1939), and Detroit (1945). Some older Bible institutes became four-year institutions, including Kansas City Bible College (1932), Denver College (1945), Biola College (1949), and Philadelphia College of the Bible (1958)—with many making their commit-

---

15. Alva J. McClain, *The Greatness of the Kingdom: An Inductive Study of the Kingdom of God* (Grand Rapids: Zondervan, 1959), 36, 42.

ment to dispensationalism in statements of faith and yearly examinations of the faculty.

The educational apparatus of dispensationalism remained largely United States–based, but there were some exceptions: German theologian Erich Sauer; Swiss-French theologian René Pache; and Scottish minister W. Graham Scroggie were European voices writing in favor of dispensational theology. Canadian dispensationalism had a foothold in some schools, such as Prairie Bible Institute (Alberta) and Toronto Bible College, though these institutions did not make dispensational theology a cardinal teaching.

Indeed, in most cases non-American dispensationalists anticipated the theological emphases of Alva McClain and embraced a modest revision of the sharp dualism between heaven and earth, the church and Israel, and the Scofield-era distinction between the kingdom of heaven and the kingdom of God in favor of emphasizing hermeneutical literalism. The difference in theology was slight enough that in 1965 Ryrie could claim continuity between Darby, Scofield, Chafer, Sauer, McClain, and himself, even as Ryrie thanked Sauer for his tilt toward continuity and giving "strong emphasis to the unity of the Bible and prominence to God's redemptive purpose."[16]

This mini–golden age of dispensational theological production deeply shaped the history of fundamentalism. Theological polarization within fundamentalism, between covenantalists and dispensationalists, had propelled institutional growth and a rapid expansion of scholastic output and training. For fundamentalist institutions, the intellectual and theological priorities of the period 1930–1960 inevitably involved building up or tearing down the system of dispensationalism.

Ockenga, Henry, and Ladd: Neo-Evangelical Fusionism

Scholastic skirmishes highlighted how fundamentalist identity was inextricable from labeling and debating dispensationalism. Covenantalists and dispensationalists—each with their own scholars, presses, seminaries, and churches—were locked into a theological cold war of their own making.

That war had many conceptual fronts, none more active than deciding exactly what constituted the kingdom of God. Mauro's seminal critique of dispensationalism fixed attention on its "postponement theory" of the kingdom that limited its presence to the future. In Mauro's and later covenantalist attacks, this definition of the kingdom unduly warped the theology, evangelism

16. Charles Ryrie, *Dispensationalism Today* (Chicago: Moody Press, 1965), 100.

techniques, ethical considerations, and social concern of dispensationalists. This kingdom critique became one of the predominant fundamentalist attacks on dispensationalism beyond the covenantalist scholastics. It appeared in a new form in the "neo-evangelical" movement of the 1940s.

Led by evangelist Billy Graham, the neo-evangelicals (sometimes called "new evangelicals") claimed to represent a halfway point between fundamentalists and modernists. Their stated objective was to be a big tent and, through the renovated label of "evangelical," to draw together as many Christians across the spectrum of denominations and creeds that could agree to work together on the basis of a minimal shared doctrinal commitment. In this period the term "evangelical" was basically an endeavor to broker agreement between fundamentalists, Pentecostals, and conservative mainline Protestants to return attention to a broader confrontation with modernism and liberal Protestantism. Understood in this way, neo-evangelicals aimed to achieve in the religious space something akin to the more famous "fusionism" that conservatives were forging in the political arena.

In the 1940s, neo-evangelicalism would be far more accurately described as "fusing" the eschatological vision of premillennialism with the covenantal theology of the Reformed tradition. Neo-evangelicals wanted to strike "a new note in Fundamentalism," as the coiner of the label, Harold Ockenga, proclaimed in 1947.[17] Ockenga trained at Westminster Theological Seminary and was a pastor in Boston. Like Mauro, Ockenga rejected dispensational time and blamed it for "the abandonment of social fields to the secularist."[18] Unlike Mauro, he was eager to bridge, rather than widen, the chasm between fundamentalist factions.

Like dispensationalists and covenantalists, neo-evangelicals also invested in theological education, seeing seminary training and scholastic production as the pathways to saving fundamentalism. Fuller Theological Seminary, founded in 1947 in Pasadena, California, became the intellectual center of the new movement. The name of the seminary acknowledged the father of radio preacher and major donor Charles Fuller, a committed but irenic dispensationalist who had been converted at Moody's church in Chicago. In 1937, Fuller the son began a weekly radio broadcast, the *Old Fashioned Revival Hour*, that quickly gained a national following. The money from Fuller's media ministries

17. Harold Ockenga, introduction to *The Uneasy Conscience of Modern Fundamentalism*, by Carl F. H. Henry (Grand Rapids: Eerdmans, 1947), xx.
18. Ockenga, introduction to *The Uneasy Conscience*, xxi.

seeded Fuller Seminary—a school that would, ironically, become a hotbed of antidispensational scholarship.

Even as Fuller Seminary was founded with a mix of dispensational and nondispensational faculty, the school distanced itself almost immediately from scholastic dispensationalism. There were small dustups, such as a rumored comment by Charles Fuller, made to a group of seminary students, that Dallas Seminary had become "ultradispensational," for which he later apologized.[19] More substantively, the exchanges between Dallas president John Walvoord and Harold Lindsell, Fuller's first registrar, revealed deeper differences. In 1954, for example, Walvoord asked with concern if it was true that Fuller "does not limit its student body to those who are premillennial." Lindsell responded by lamenting the inability of "orthodox Christianity" to "get along with each other when it involves matters which are not basic to the Christian faith."[20] Exchanges like these were cordial enough, but lurking under the surface was an increasing recognition on both sides of divergent visions for the future of fundamentalism. The fusionism neo-evangelicals pursued would come at the expense of dispensationalists.

While dispensationalists insisted that a consistent premillennialism re-quired dispensational categories, neo-evangelicals did not. Fuller's founding faculty differed on many eschatological details but were united in rejecting dispensationalism's exclusive claim to premillennial belief. Of Fuller's original four faculty members—Carl F. H. Henry, Wilbur Smith, Everett Harrison, and Harold Lindsell—only Harrison had a direct connection to Dallas as a onetime lecturer, and that relationship had soured in the 1940s as Harrison distanced himself from the seminary's strident defense of dispensationalism. Early addi-tions to the faculty, such as Edward J. Carnell and George Eldon Ladd, were bold critics of dispensationalism. Much of the Fuller Seminary faculty agreed with the covenantalist critique that dispensationalism advanced a heterodox view of the kingdom that limited fundamentalist effectiveness and destroyed theological consensus.

Neo-evangelical fusionism was greatly elaborated in Carl F. H. Henry's book *The Uneasy Conscience of Modern Fundamentalism* (1947), which would go on to sell more than 100,000 copies. In his discussions of eschatology and the kingdom of God, Henry avoided technical terminology, preferring phrases

19. Fuller, quoted in Timothy Gale Mink, "John F. Walvoord at Dallas Theological Seminary" (PhD diss., University of North Texas, 1987), 240.
20. Lindsell, quoted in Mink, "John F. Walvoord," 240–41.

like "kingdom then preaching" to describe dispensationalism's identification of the kingdom with future Israel. In a pivotal chapter, "The Apprehension over Kingdom Preaching," Henry introduced the distinction between "non-dispensational Fundamentalism" and "dispensational Fundamentalism" to make the point that the larger fundamentalist movement had become so embittered by debates over the millennium that everyone preferred to "stay away from the kingdom."[21] The "kingdom then" theology of dispensationalism diminished the "world-relevance for the Gospel," Henry complained (48). "The great majority of Fundamentalist clergymen, during the past generation of world disintegration, became increasingly less vocal about social evils," and much of the blame lay with dispensationalism (4). This debate about terminology focused on two central Christian concepts: the nature of the kingdom of God, and the church's role in confronting social evils. In both cases, Henry found dispensationalism wanting.

Yet Henry, too, wanted to build bridges rather than raze them. He called for a détente between "the premillennialists and amillennialists" and suggested the outlines of a kingdom theology that he hoped would appeal to a critical mass of fundamentalists (17). The kingdom of neo-evangelicalism was "now and then"—present but not wholly established; future but not wholly postponed (52). In Henry's understanding, this difference over the kingdom was the issue hampering "orthodox Christian" effectiveness. Fundamentalism had an "uneasy conscience," he explained, precisely because of the contradiction of hope and pessimism fostered by dispensational theology. "This Gospel of hope coupled with prophetic despair," he explained, "has posed, during the last two generations, a problem which Fundamentalism was unable satisfactorily to resolve" (18).

Henry offered the sketch of a solution, but it would fall to others to erect a more robust kingdom theology and place neo-evangelical fusionism in this area on more solid footing. George Eldon Ladd, Henry's colleague at Fuller Seminary, would build his distinguished career on fulfilling the task. Ladd had uncritically adopted dispensational teachings and the church-Israel distinction as a teenage convert to Christianity. He then trained at Gordon Divinity School and Harvard University and began to reform his views. By the time he

21. Henry, *The Uneasy Conscience*, 42–44. Hereafter, page references from this work will be given in parentheses in the text.

Figure 18. Denominational and educational profiles, 1950. After the 1920s, factions of fundamentalist theology divided over dispensationalism. In the next three decades, they cohered into adjacent subcultures. Covenantalists and dispensationalists shared similar insular theological projects, while neo-evangelicals committed to rallying both sides as the basis for a broad postwar evangelical movement.

	Name	Denominational Affiliation	Seminary Education	Additional Degrees	Associated Seminary
Covenantalists	Oswald T. Allis (1880–1973)	Northern Presbyterian/Orthodox Presbyterian	Princeton Theological Seminary	Princeton University (MA); University of Berlin (PhD)	Princeton Theological Seminary/ Westminster Theological Seminary
	Edmund Clowney (1917–2005)	Orthodox Presbyterian Church	Westminster Theological Seminary (BT); Wheaton College (ThD)	Yale Divinity School (STM)	Westminster Theological Seminary
	William Hendriksen (1900–1982)	Christian Reformed Church	Princeton Theological Seminary (ThD)	--	Calvin Theological Seminary
	John Murray (1898–1975)	Free Presbyterian Church of Scotland	Princeton Theological Seminary (ThD)	--	Princeton Theological Seminary/ Westminster Theological Seminary
Dispensationalists	Charles Feinberg (1909–1995)	Nondenominational	Dallas Theological Seminary (ThM, ThD)	Southern Methodist University (MA); Johns Hopkins University (PhD)	Dallas Theological Seminary
	Dwight Pentecost (1915–2014)	Northern Presbyterian/ Nondenominational	Dallas Theological Seminary (ThM, ThD)	--	Dallas Theological Seminary
	Charles Ryrie (1925–2016)	Nondenominational/Southern Baptist Convention	Dallas Theological Seminary (ThM, ThD)	University of Edinburgh (PhD)	Dallas Theological Seminary
	John Walvoord (1910–2002)	Independent Fundamentalist Churches of America	Dallas Theological Seminary (ThM, ThD)	Texas Christian University (MA)	Dallas Theological Seminary
Neo-evangelicals	Edward John Carnell (1919–1967)	Northern Baptist Convention	Westminster Theological Seminary (ThM); Harvard Divinity School (ThD)	Boston University (PhD)	Fuller Seminary
	Carl F. H. Henry (1913–2003)	Northern Baptist Convention	Northern Baptist Theological Seminary (BD, ThD)	Boston University (PhD)	Fuller Seminary; Trinity Evangelical Divinity School
	George Eldon Ladd (1911–1982)	Northern Baptist Convention	Gordon Divinity School (BD)	Boston University/Harvard University (PhD)	Fuller Seminary
	Harold Ockenga (1905–1985)	Presbyterian/Congregational	Princeton Seminary/Westminster Theological Seminary (BD)	University of Pittsburgh (MA, PhD)	Fuller Seminary; Gordon-Conwell Theological Seminary

joined Fuller, he was fully disenchanted with dispensationalism. In his first two books, *Crucial Questions about the Kingdom of God* (1952) and *The Blessed Hope* (1956), Ladd spared no criticisms. He broke with dispensationalism because of "a feeling of uncertainty as to the soundness of some of its positions" and "a feeling of dissatisfaction with the quality of much of the literature which espoused this position." He had grown up in an atmosphere where "one must not talk about any Kingdom of God as existing in our generation, for this was a theme that only liberals were preaching, and any statement pointing to the Kingdom must be placed at the end of this age."[22] Such an atmosphere, in his estimation, produced a distorted sense of Christian priorities.

Like Henry, Ladd triangulated between the covenantal "amillennialists, who deny the future earthly reign of Christ," and the "premillennialists, at least of the dispensational persuasion, who tend to minimize if not deny a present spiritual kingdom inaugurated by Christ."[23] In place of both, Ladd sketched in his next books, especially *The Gospel of the Kingdom* (1959) and *Jesus and the Kingdom* (1964), an "already/not yet" kingdom theology, also called "inaugurated eschatology."[24] He celebrated diverse theological influences, including German scholars W. G. Kummel and Oscar Cullmann and Princeton theologian Geerhardus Vos, as a signal that he was escaping the "technique of desperation" that dispensationalists resorted to when they labeled nondispensational theologians dangerous to orthodoxy.[25]

The neo-evangelical theological attack on dispensationalism had institutional implications. By 1961, when Fuller revised its doctrinal statement to remove both premillennialism and biblical inerrancy as requirements for teaching, the dispensational presence at the school had all but evaporated. For a young seminary named after one of the country's most successful dispensational radio broadcasters, this was a remarkable development. As Walvoord wrote in his popular primer, *The Rapture Question* (1957), it was "not too much to say that the rapture question is determined more by ecclesiology than eschatology"—a statement that revealed how tightly wound was the bundle of

22. George Eldon Ladd, *Crucial Questions about the Kingdom of God* (Grand Rapids: Eerdmans, 1952), 13.

23. George Eldon Ladd, *The Blessed Hope: A Biblical Study of the Second Advent and the Rapture* (Grand Rapids: Eerdmans, 1956), 59.

24. George Eldon Ladd, *The Gospel of the Kingdom: Scriptural Studies in the Kingdom of God* (Grand Rapids: Eerdmans, 1959), 22–25.

25. George Eldon Ladd, review of *The Greatness of the Kingdom*, by Alva J. McClain, *Evangelical Quarterly* 31, no. 1 (1960): 50.

issues related to church, kingdom, and the future.[26] Fuller Seminary had declared that it was headed in another direction entirely from Dallas—not simply by modifying details of the end times, but by breaking from the deepest logic of the dispensational system.

Hardening Scholastic Factions

The scholastic contest came to a head in the late 1950s, at the same time the first critical histories of dispensationalism began to appear. Daniel Fuller, son of Charles Fuller, completed his studies at Northern Baptist Theological Seminary with a dissertation titled "The Hermeneutics of Dispensationalism," a four-hundred-page summary of the scholastic debates that concluded with a takedown of "dispensationalism as a system."[27] Norman Kraus, a professor at Goshen College and interlocutor with neo-evangelical theologians, published *Dispensationalism in America* (1958), drawing attention to the sectarian nature of the Exclusive Brethren as a source for the theology. Two years later, Clarence Bass, a professor of theology at neo-evangelical-influenced Bethel Seminary in St. Paul, Minnesota, published *Backgrounds to Dispensationalism* (1960), which interpreted the theology as little more than a modern version of Darby's sectarianism.

The language got heated. The president of Fuller Seminary, Edward Carnell, sparked renewed hostility when, in his 1959 defense of "orthodox Christianity," he described dispensationalism as "straight-line cultism."[28] The next year Ladd described dispensationalism as reflecting "a woeful isolation from the world of contemporary theological thought and scholarship."[29] Others offered no less decisive critiques, including Christian and Missionary Alliance luminary and popular writer A. W. Tozer, who warned in 1957 that "a widespread revival of the kind of Christianity we know today in America might prove to be a moral tragedy from which we would not recover in a hundred years." The failure of contemporary American Christianity, in Tozer's estimation, was due in large part to "the system of extreme dispensationalism" that taught salvation as free grace, which "relieved the Christian of repentance, obedience, and cross-carrying other than the most formal sense."[30]

26. John Walvoord, *The Rapture Question* (Findlay, OH: Dunham, 1957), 127, 16.
27. Daniel Fuller, "The Hermeneutics of Dispensationalism" (PhD diss., Northern Baptist Theological Seminary, 1957), 191–94.
28. Edward John Carnell, *The Case for Orthodoxy* (Philadelphia: Westminster, 1959), 118.
29. Ladd, review of *The Greatness of the Kingdom*, 50.
30. A. W. Tozer, *Keys to the Deeper Life* (Grand Rapids: Zondervan, 1957), 24.

American evangelicals were encouraged by a crop of British evangelical voices, including theologian J. I. Packer and Anglican cleric John Stott, who saw dispensationalism as a problem on both eschatological and free grace grounds. Writing in 1958, in the pages of the neo-evangelical *Christianity Today*, Packer celebrated the "exploded, if not out of fashion" trajectory of "dispensational adventism" in Great Britain.[31] Stott, writing the following year, lamented the "extremes and extravagances" associated with fundamentalism "especially in the United States" that procured an "excessively literalist interpretation of the Bible."[32] Packer and Stott's appearance in *Christianity Today* revealed something of the orientation of the flagship American magazine, which routinely criticized dispensationalism. Its executive editor was L. Nelson Bell, one of the writers of the 1944 Southern Presbyterian report condemning dispensationalism as a "fundamental divergence" from Presbyterian theology.[33]

Dispensationalists returned the favor. In the pages of *Bibliotheca Sacra*, Ryrie touted that by 1957 "evangelicals are having to give their attention increasingly to the dispensational questions," declaring that dispensationalism, "properly defined," is "the only valid system of Biblical interpretation."[34] Two years later, Walvoord charged that all nondispensationalists—including "Roman Catholic, modern liberal, and modern conservative writers"—had fallen under the influence of hermeneutical and theological errors. By offering "no defense against modern liberalism," Christians who rejected dispensational categories in favor of covenantalism were tempting fate and already sliding down the slope to modernism.[35]

The scholastic scene could seem to outsiders as little more than ivory tower sniping, a debate so heated precisely because the stakes were so low. Yet this was far from the case. The issues raised by theologians and pastors had profound effects on fundamentalist religion and social engagement. Through what lens would fundamentalist churches and organizations view culture, society, and politics? Given the structure of fundamentalist institutions and the power in this community for theological differences to organize activity, the answer would be decided as much by scholastic debate as anything else. In the same decades of covenantal, dispensational, and neo-evangelical rivalry, the prod-

31. J. I. Packer, "Fundamentalism: The British Scene," *Christianity Today*, September 29, 1958, 5.

32. John Stott, *Fundamentalism and Evangelism* (Grand Rapids: Eerdmans, 1959), 14.

33. "1944 PCUS Report on Dispensationalism."

34. Charles Ryrie, "The Necessity of Dispensationalism," *Bibliotheca Sacra* 114 (July 1957): 243, 254.

35. John Walvoord, *The Millennial Kingdom* (Findlay, OH: Dunham, 1959), 72.

ucts of fundamentalist seminaries—and the fundamentalist movement itself—ensured that dispensationalism would not remain a minor footnote to historical theology. Controversy grew rather than shrunk dispensational influence, with its key ideas gaining currency far beyond the halls of learning.

Earth, what sorrows lie before thee
Unlike it in the shadows past
The sharpest throes that ever tore thee
Though the briefest and the last!

I see the shadows of the sunset
I see the dread avenger's form
I see the Armageddon onset
But I shall be above the storm

There comes the mourning and the sighing
There comes the heart tear's heavy fall
The thousand agonies of dying
But I shall be above them all!

Horatius Bonar, "A Stranger Here,"
Hymns of Faith and Hope (1857), as quoted in
Gerald Stanton, *Kept from the Hour* (1954)

With degrees from Wheaton College and Dallas Seminary, and teaching posts at Dallas, Talbot Seminary, and Biola College, Gerald Stanton (1918–2010) was the epitome of scholastic dispensational training in the twentieth century. In his magnum opus, going through four editions over the span of nearly fifty years, Stanton answered the burning question: "Will Christ return before the Tribulation, or must the Church pass through that dreaded hour?" This framing of the stakes between "pretribulational premillennialists" and all other Christians sharpened dispensationalism's implications in all areas of thought.

13

Dispensational Politics

In the 1970s, a second generation of neo-evangelicals repeated the charge made by Carl Henry in *Uneasy Conscience* (1947) that "modern Fundamentalism does not explicitly sketch the social implications of its message for the non-Christian world." From evangelical sociologist David O. Moberg, who wrote *The Great Reversal* (1972), to historian Donald Dayton, insiders were asking: "Whatever happened to evangelicalism?" For Dayton, the answer boiled down to a mix of dispensationalism and conservative Princeton theology—both trafficking in "the same tendency toward pessimism" that "laid the basis for modern Fundamentalism."[1] This fundamentalism, Dayton charged, was entirely wrapped up in the otherworldly visions of apocalypse and heaven. This critique shaped understandings of fundamentalism and politics for the rest of the twentieth century, and to some extent still does.

Henry and Dayton were half right.[2] Neo-evangelicals diagnosed dispensationalists as severed from the evangelical traditions that had guided American Protestant social concern for generations. Some nineteenth-century evangelicals had embraced social reforms such as abolition, temperance, and poverty relief, even as others (or sometimes the very same activists) supported slavery and Jim Crow segregation. Dispensationalism had no comparable record or body of thought, rejecting the very premise that Christians were called to such earthly tasks. A large portion of neo-evangelical writings from the 1940s to the 1970s was focused on forging a comprehensive social theology that bridged

1. Donald W. Dayton, *Discovering an Evangelical Heritage* (New York: Harper & Row, 1976), 121, 132.

2. Carl F. H. Henry, *The Uneasy Conscience of Modern Fundamentalism* (Grand Rapids: Eerdmans, 1947), 39.

the divide between the present and future kingdom that was the cornerstone of dispensational theology.

For the most part, evangelical observations about a "great reversal" in social engagement were wrong, at least on the basic measures of organized activism. Fundamentalists never resigned from social or political life. Nationalist fundamentalists continued to wage a culture war for Christian America, even after the defeats of the 1920s. They opposed the teaching of evolution, opposed international entanglements, promoted free markets, preached against urban vices including sex trafficking and prostitution, supported Zionism, and questioned, or actively resisted, racial desegregation. By the time Henry was writing against fundamentalism in 1947, many of those that he decried as world renouncing had been active in politics for decades. The same was only more true in the 1970s.

Rather than a "great reversal," fundamentalists did redirect social engagement away from reform toward a defense of the status quo. They were skeptical of progressive policies and bemoaned the creeping secularization of American life. They deepened their anticommunism throughout the mid-twentieth century to both defend global missions work and to shore up the centrality of Christianity to American society. In this tapestry of views, dispensationalists contributed to a fundamentalist political tradition of popular, and populist, public engagement based on a particular understanding of Christian America and the cultural crisis in its midst. Dispensationalism was not determinative of this wider conservative Christian critique of culture, but neither was it marginal. Its newly minted "system" of theology supplied a set of heuristic tools to understand, and decode, the politics of the day. These tools—many of them based on the same Bible Reading methods pioneered in the nineteenth century that now were grouped under the name biblical literalism—gave shape to a set of political and cultural ideas with a reach far beyond theological debates, and extending far wider than the fundamentalist movement.

William Bell Riley: Forging a Dispensational Politics

Not all dispensationalists waded into social and political activism with gusto—on this point the neo-evangelicals were correct. Scholastic dispensationalists were intensely focused on the technical aspects of their system, and many pastors preached of the imminent rapture as an escape hatch that shrunk the need for Christians to relieve existing worldly suffering. The pantheon of mid-century dispensational scholars—Feinberg, Pentecost, Ryrie, Walvoord, Mc-Clain—spent far more time on the theological nature of the kingdom than on

US foreign policy—even though, as Henry and others pointed out, kingdom theology could not help but bear on politics.

More politically engaged than the scholastics were nationalist fundamentalists, those like William Bell Riley, J. Frank Norris, and John Roach Straton who organized to oppose evolution and urban vices. Nationalists tended to focus on the momentary and the specific, reacting to the most recent act of Congress, anticipating the next election, or making sense of front-page headlines. Where scholastics specialized in biblical and theological debate, nationalists like Riley advanced a populist apocalyptic hermeneutic that was meant to interpret daily events. And where scholastics published quarterly journals of theological argumentation, nationalists published weekly magazines of commentary. Where scholastics built seminaries and trained future pastors, nationalists built grassroots networks of churches that could affect politics locally and, in a few cases, nationally.

Riley, atop his fundamentalist empire in Minneapolis, was one of the most effective and controversial nationalists until his death in 1947. His politics had become truly national in the 1920s through fundamentalist organizing that linked antievolution activism across denominations and sections of the country. He was undaunted by early political defeats and continued to organize for a variety of cultural issues, blending free-market economics, social conservatism, and racial segregation with dispensational theology. Though many differences between northern and southern dispensationalists persisted, there was increasing convergence on national issues, creating the basis for a broad-based fundamentalist politics forged by those like Riley who had a national vision for organizing. Where there was sectional difference, compromise was in order. Southerners tended to mistrust corporations more than northerners, while northerners tended to bemoan the harshness of Jim Crow segregation. For the sake of a united front both sides accommodated, dispensational distinctions between heavenly and earthly priorities helped smooth over the differences.

Antievolution activism provided the blueprint for mobilization and remained the cornerstone of public campaigning for decades, even as efforts expanded to other issues, especially anticommunism. Riley represented the nationalist leadership by, beginning in the 1930s, centering his rhetoric on a growing global conspiracy that connected a variety of social concerns as preparing the way for the end times. Conspiratorial thinking had always accompanied premillennialists to some extent, dating to Darby's suspicions of the Church of Ireland and extending to speculations about the reign of Napoleon III and trends of consolidation in the early twentieth century. Riley began to theorize in earnest in the wake of his foiled antievolution activism, though he, too, had a long history of writing about elites (modernists, leftists) he thought possessed too much power. In attacking his political opponents in the 1920s, Riley repeatedly described the conspirators as "Jewish-Bolshevik Darwinist."[3] His identification of "Darwinists" was obvious enough, as was "Bolsheviks"—this Marxist movement being the newest iteration of materialist-oriented socialism that premillennialists had been railing against since the 1860s. But what about "Jewish"?

In his antisemitism, Riley participated in a much broader American discourse of the period that included industrialist Henry Ford, radio preacher Father Coughlin, and America First Committee spokesman Charles Lindbergh. Yet Riley trafficked in dispensational antisemitism, a unique form that combined racial antisemitism with a prophetic lens on world events centered on the Jewish people. "As a Fundamentalist and a Premillennialist," Riley preached in 1936, "I accord to the Jew not only a great place in past history, but also a major place in prophecy, or history to come."[4] This line was Riley's preamble to a firehose of antisemitic slurs that ended with his conclusion that "the Jew" has "no one to blame but himself" for having "become unpopular in this country."[5] He did not expound on the role of Jews in "history to come," but his prophecy analysis was entirely indebted to his conviction that "the Jewish secret organizations of the country" were "in-line with Communism," overrepresented in the Roosevelt administration, and plotting a "Russian administration for America."[6] He promoted the fabricated *Protocols of the Elders of Zion* and defended fascists in the 1930s, including the Silver Legion of America. He kept company with Gerald K. Winrod, of Wichita, Kansas (known as the "Jayhawk Nazi"), who published *The Jewish Assault on Christianity* (1935) and propounded conspiracy theories in his popular magazine *The Defender*. Even some scholastic-oriented dispensationalists were captivated by the *Protocols*, including James M. Gray and Arno C. Gaebelein, though they both soon recanted. Riley and Winrod never changed their views.

Even within the fold, however, the overtly antisemitic strain of dispensationalism had more detractors than supporters. J. Frank Norris, the popular preacher Louis Bauman, and most scholastics dissented from this line of

3. Quoted in Edward J. Larson, *Summer for the Gods: The Scopes Trial and America's Continuing Debate over Science and Religion* (New York: Basic Books, 2008), 44.
4. William Bell Riley, "The Jew and Communism," sermon transcript, October 18, 1936, 1, https://cdm16120.contentdm.oclc.org/digital/api/collection/riley/id/4894/page/0/inline/riley_4894_0.
5. Riley, "The Jew and Communism," 4.
6. Riley, "The Jew and Communism," 5, 9.

thought and were Zionists as well as critics of European antisemitism. They agreed with Riley that Jews were exceptional and occupied "a major place in prophecy," but they fixed their negative analysis of global events on communists, fascists, progressives, and evolutionists. Rather, the place of Jews in prophecy was linked to Zionism and the "restoration" of national Israel in the Holy Land. Most dispensationalists watched with great interest the geopolitical swings in the Middle East and were attuned to rising antisemitism in Europe earlier than many Americans because of this interest.

Beyond antisemitism, conspiratorial thinking informed dispensational apocalyptic geopolitical analysis, which grew by bounds in the 1930s. Here the difference between scholastic and nationalist dispensationalists was again apparent. At a New York City prophecy conference in 1942, during World War II, the scholastic theologian John Walvoord spoke on the "seven distinct principles of deterioration" that would culminate "in a grand crescendo in the tribulation." Though discussing prophecies and generalized signs of "unbelief" and "godlessness," Walvoord refrained from prognosticating about the sequence of future events. He was rather more interested in defending the conclusions of consistent dispensational hermeneutics. Dispensationalism, he described, "is a distinct system of theology, a method of interpretation of the whole Word of God, an essential element in determining the teaching of every book." He concluded with a metaphor of the artificial lakes in his hometown of Dallas that, through a complex network of underground hydraulics, supplied water to a vast number of homes and farms. "Only when one gets close to the dams can one hear the roar of the water and can see the tug of the current that syphons the water to a lower level."[7] Dispensational truth was not about the surface-level predictions of fulfilled prophecy but was about the deeper system level that revealed what Darby had in an earlier era called the "thoughts of God."

For nationalists, on the other hand, prophetic interpretation was all about making sense of the chaotic surface waters of global events. At the same 1942 conference, Louis Bauman, perhaps the most popular nationalist interpreter of prophecy in this period, speculated as to the real-world alignment of geopolitical forces and their relation to the coalition of nations in the prophetic passage of Ezekiel 38. This near-future coalition, which would invade Israel at the end of days, was an "anti-God, anti-semitic, atheistic, communistic federation of northern nations." The "Bolshevist federation," Bauman confidently claimed, was not yet formed, but the recent turn of the war, with devastating defeats

---

7. John Walvoord, "Prophecy and the Deterioration of Nations," in *The Sure Word of Prophecy*, ed. John Bradbury (1944; reprint, Chicago: Revell, 2016), 170, 167, 175.

of German forces by Soviets on the eastern front in Europe, pointed to its ascension.[8] He expanded this analysis in his book from the same year, *Russian Events in the Light of Bible Prophecy* (1942), having no qualms about revising his prophetic timeline to reflect the most recent geopolitical developments.

Walvoord and Bauman were speakers at the same prophecy conference. Their shared theological background and overlapping networks of fundamentalism meant that the division between scholastic theology meant for seminarians and what would become more popular-oriented dispensationalism was never absolute. But the analyses advanced by Walvoord and Bauman were distinct.

While Walvoord was a part of a relatively small circle of scholastics based in Dallas and a few other schools working to erect the theological system of dispensationalism, Bauman was one of dozens of nationalists who used prophecy to decode contemporary events in real time. Doing so required no specialized language skills or training. Bauman had none in any case, being ordained into full-time ministry in the German Baptist Brethren church at age eighteen. Rather than exposit dispensational time, Bauman was a popular translator of the signs of the times with columns in the *King's Business* and the *Sunday School Times*, and volumes with titles like *Light from Bible Prophecy as Related to the Present Crisis* (1936) and *"Prepare War!" or Arming for Armageddon* (1937). An advertisement for the latter volume reinforced his strengths. This was Bauman's "latest and most timely prophetic book," its contents "timely and up-to-date . . . giving the latest statistics."[9] While ostensibly a commentary on Joel 3, the book spent as much time documenting the arms buildup in Nazi Germany as any other topic.

The mix of dispensational categories and populist critiques that Bauman so skillfully combined accomplished something no previous premillennialists had accomplished, or necessarily wanted to. In the long historical arc of premillennialism, there had been no single orientation to politics. Darby had leveled a critique of the British Empire and called for the destruction of the Anglican Church. James Brookes adopted a heavenly view of the church in order to evacuate himself from the violent "worldly" contest over slavery and racial equality, while Dwight Moody used the same insight less than a decade later to work for sectional reconciliation after the Civil War. In the early twentieth century, northerner Arthur T. Pierson identified Jim Crow segregation

8. Louis Bauman, "Is the Battle of Armageddon in John's Vision on the Isle of Patmos the Same as the Battle of Ezekiel 38 and 39," in Bradbury, *The Sure Word of Prophecy*, 163–64.

9. Advertisement for *"Prepare War!," King's Business*, May 1937, 179.

as a barrier to the gospel, while southern-born Amzi Clarence Dixon saw no contradiction. In his early days of premillennialism, Philip Mauro understood the rise of American imperialism in the Philippines as deeply troubling; other premillennialists saw it as an unprecedented missionary opportunity. While there would remain a diversity of attitudes among dispensationalists, the success of nationalist commentary by Riley, Bauman, and others meant that conspiratorial and reactionary politics would be no less integral to midcentury dispensationalism than the theological concepts its name denoted.

Theology and Politics "Hand in Hand"

By the 1940s, dispensational politics had grown to the point that its propagation did not depend on individual contributors but on a shared milieu formed by hundreds of evangelists, pastors, and writers. Like the new premillennial builders of the late nineteenth century, these mid-twentieth-century media evangelists and political commentators blended church, educational, and popular appeal. Many were or had been pastors, some had careers as itinerant preachers or radio voices, most had been trained at Bible institutes, and all shared a socially conservative, free-market, and apocalyptic set of cultural and political commitments.

The dispensational analysts of the 1930s and 1940s exploited the medium of radio, translating complicated system into accessible biblical analysis and geopolitical speculation. Many of the most popular radio programs broadcast from the Los Angeles area, including Louis Talbot's *Bible Institute Radio Hour*, Charles Fuller's *Old Fashioned Revival Hour*, and J. Vernon McGee's *Thru the Bible*. The location of the broadcasts revealed the shifting centers of gravity in dispensational culture, both geographically and culturally. With all three of these programs beaming from its hills, Southern California was becoming the newest geographical anchor of dispensational culture. One of the fastest-growing regions of the country, Los Angeles and Orange Counties were changed more than any other region by the outmigration of some 10 million southerners in the decades of the 1920s–1960s. The new Sun Belt extended from east to west across the continental United States, funneling scores of families into the Southwest. Radio programs extended this culture to reach millions of weekly listeners, forming dispensational sensibilities in mass market audio format.

Upwardly mobile white migrants to the Southwest brought their religion with them, and through the mediums of print and radio blended southern sensibilities with the culture and teachings of northern fundamentalism. The blending of sectional identities was illustrated in the free roam of the same radio waves. Talbot (a Presbyterian from Australia), Fuller (a Baptist native of Los Angeles), and McGee (a Presbyterian from Texas) each had followings across the country. The cultural and media recontextualization of dispensationalism in the Sun Belt extended the reach of dispensational influence and produced a cultural resonance that was less mired in fundamentalist factionalism. Where Lewis Sperry Chafer had been rebuffed by southern denominations with his Yankee-sourced dispensationalism, Talbot, Fuller, and McGee were embraced by millions of southern transplants with similar theological teachings.

By the mid-twentieth century, the Southwest had replicated in practice many of the racially segregated social patterns of the South. Dispensationalism appealed to white Christians in this setting not because its teachings demanded racial segregation, nor because its teachings advanced racial desegregation, but because it had very little to say on the matter of race at all. God's ordained division of humanity into Israel, the church, and the nations was a toothless framework to address American race relations. And as dispensationalism suggested, humanity was currently in the dispensation of grace. American society would, like every society in every past dispensation, grow more sinful until it ended in human failure. In any case, the church was heaven-bound with no intrinsic relationship to the "world system." Dispensationalists reinforced the divides that stretched between heaven and earth, Israel and the church, and the church and the nations, that latter category including the United States. Dispensational teachings did not lead to social quietism, but to a plea to keep the existing social order. On race in particular, dispensationalism facilitated not a "great reversal" of social concern but a great defense of the status quo.

Unsurprisingly, dispensationalism in its systematized form was unappealing to the Black church, even Black fundamentalists who agreed with other doctrines of the movement. A strand of apocalypticism was present in the teachings of Black fundamentalists, most of whom were entirely excluded from white fundamentalist institutions and conversations. Positing radical reversals of social power and the imposition of divine justice, the premillennial second coming was a frequent element of Black eschatology. Interwar figures such as Eli George Biddle and Noah W. Williams included a generalized premillennialism in their teachings. After visiting Palestine in 1935, for example, Williams briefly speculated on the details of a prophesied "war of world-wide proportions" and the battle of Armageddon: "it can be seen at once that I am a Pre-Millennialist." But he eschewed details in favor of the dictum to "just read your Bible."[10] A similar hesitancy was evinced by Biddle, who embraced

10. Williams, quoted in Daniel R. Bare, *Black Fundamentalists: Conservative Christian-*

the teaching of dispensational time in the early 1920s but ultimately dropped it for a less systematized premillennial eschatology. In large part due to a failure to address race, dispensationalism was created and systematized as a white fundamentalist project, and, with a few exceptions, would remain so for the rest of the twentieth century.

As a testament to this demographic boundary of dispensationalism, the emergent civil rights movement of the 1950s was seen by dispensationalists as part of the larger project of American liberalism that failed to appreciate God's intentions for the church and for the nations. Ernest Pickering, a Dallas alumnus and leader in the Independent Fundamentalist Churches of America, typified the wider white fundamentalist fixation on the linkage between political and theological liberalism. Writing in the pivotal civil rights year of 1964, the Florida native and longtime Texan was still complaining about the *Brown v. Board of Education* ruling by the Supreme Court, which had begun the national process of school desegregation a decade earlier. "Radical political liberals," Pickering wrote in a separatist Baptist magazine, had no respect for the Constitution in seeking to satisfy their "sense of 'social justice'" through novel legal arguments. "Is it any wonder, then," he continued, "that religious liberals rally to such a standard since they too have an unholy disregard for the revealed, fixed, and authoritative truth of God—the Bible?"[11] The social ill of racism, which Pickering did in fact see as an ill, would be reconciled eschatologically in an eventuality of the kingdom after the second coming. But in the here and now, in an American society that suffered from endemic racism, the dispensational "system" limited itself to calling for individuals to repent. The best that white Christians could do was to pursue gradual desegregation. This was also the most promising path, dispensationalists in Texas, California, and Chicago could agree, to maintain the momentum of sectional reconciliation within their movement.

Pickering's pairing of political and religious liberalism worked not only to group his secular and sacred opposition under the same banner, but also to reinforce the bond between political and religious "conservatism." The term "conservative" had been used inconsistently before 1930 and the systematization of dispensationalism. It rarely described premillennial theology or politics in nineteenth-century usage. Arthur T. Pierson, in 1903, described teachers of Higher Life holiness as possessing "a conservative spirit, a tenacious clinging

---

ity and Racial Identity in the Segregation Era (New York: New York University Press, 2021), 83.

11. Ernest Pickering, "The Relation of Theological Liberalism to Political Liberalism," *Central Bible Quarterly* 7, no. 4 (1964): 8.

222 ♦ THE DISPENSATIONALISTS

to the old truths, with a corresponding suspicion of all new and strange doc-trines."[12] Still, no identification of political conservatism appeared until "world system" analysis identified progressivism as an agent of global consolidation. By the 1910s, conservatism had finally come to reflect its more contemporary alignment. William Bell Riley, in organizing fundamentalists in the late 1910s, had called for "true and evangelical conservatives" to unite.[13] But Moody and Scofield, to take two prominent examples, did not consistently identify as politically or religiously "conservative," nor as defenders of a particular po-litical theory. By the time of Pickering's article in 1964, political realignment had done just this. "Theological liberals tend to be, and to support, political liberals, while theological conservatives tend to be, and to support, political conservatives," Pickering explained. "As systems of thought and action they go hand in hand."[14]

Pickering led the Independent Fundamentalist Churches of America, an organization that balanced separatist fundamentalism and scholastic dispensa-tionalism. On the "hand in hand" relationship between theological and polit-ical conservatism that he promoted, he was in good company in both camps. The early Cold War surge in anticommunism was especially abetted by funda-mentalists and served as a way for scholastic dispensationalists and separatist fundamentalists to work together in politics in the 1950s. Carl McIntire, from his headquarters in Collingswood, New Jersey, and John R. Rice, from Whea-ton, Illinois, espoused a vigorous anticommunism that borrowed from new premillennial motifs, though never in a systematic way. Both used anticom-munism to "mainstream fundamentalism," as one biographer of Rice has put it, through creating a touch point between separatist fundamentalists and the wider fundamentalist community of covenantalists, dispensationalists, and neo-evangelicals.[15] A shared anticommunist agenda, paired with a shared self-identification as stewards of religious and political conservatism, allowed the very fractured world of fundamentalism to influence national discourse with more concerted pressure than the ecclesiastical, sectional, or theological (not to mention temperamental) status of the movement might have indicated.

The "hand in hand" pairing of theology and politics reflected dispensational systematization, a development visible in the popular Bible radio programs.

12. Arthur T. Pierson, *The Keswick Movement* (New York: Funk & Wagnalls, 1903), 108.

13. William Bell Riley, *The Menace of Modernism* (New York: Christian Alliance Pub-lishing Co., 1917), 156.

14. Pickering, "The Relation," 2.

15. Keith Bates, *Mainstreaming Fundamentalism: John R. Rice and Fundamentalism's Public Reemergence* (Knoxville: University of Tennessee Press, 2021).

As their titles suggested—*Back to the Bible, Radio Bible Class Hour, Thru the Bible*—radio shows were organized to preach through the Bible systematically. The daily or weekly format allowed hosts to relate regularly scheduled expository preaching to the news of the day, weaving together dispensational categories and the most recent national news, creating new logic and verse chains that seamlessly connected religious and political systems, much how the keyword chains of biblical concordances had remapped the meaning of Scripture on the basis of "plain" approaches to the entire Bible following dispensational assumptions.

Once connections between political and religious conservatism (and between political and religious liberalism) were established, areas of social and political thought not directly addressed by the Bible fell into place to develop a logic that appeared consistent. The power of the system was, in part, to absorb new issues and new information in a way that harmonized with previous commitments. The fundamentalist-modernist controversy had always entailed more than theological difference, but fundamentalists—and especially dispensationalists—had not initially conceived of themselves as propagating a "system." Yet by the 1940s, they were advancing interlocking commitments that circumscribed the influence of theological ideas outside the system and extrapolated ideas inside the system.

Literalism in Action

Though most dispensationalists agreed with Pickering's metaphor that religious conservatism went "hand in hand" with political conservatism, dispensational politics was not simply a veneer for ideological conservatism. Dispensational attitudes hinged on biblical interpretations that cohered to the unique insights of the theological system. As Ryrie reminded readers, dispensationalism "is a system of Biblical truth. It is not merely an interpretation of one passage in the last book of the Bible."[16] The implication was that dispensationalism touched on all "biblical truth."

New premillennialists, from Darby to Scofield, had created an evolving set of tools, including numerical structures, typologies, and dualisms, to make sense of the Bible. These aids tended to work alongside the commonsense tradition that idealized "plain" interpretations of biblical texts. As dispensationalism systematized in the 1930s and 1940s, the related ideal of biblical

16. Charles Ryrie, *The Basis of the Premillennial Faith* (New York: Loizeaux Brothers, 1953), 6.

literalism became one of the defining marks of dispensationalism. In his 1965 book *Dispensationalism Today*, Ryrie defined "a system of hermeneutics that is usually called literal interpretation" as one of the three *sine qua nons* of dispensationalism.[17] Though relatively uncontroversial in 1965 among dispensationalists, this claim would have been a surprise to Scofield, who noted hundreds of allegories in his reference Bible and favored two of the most influential premillennial commentaries packed with typologies and dualistic assumptions, Frederick Grant's *Numerical Bible* and Darby's *Synopsis of the Books of the Bible*. The modest revision suggested by Ryrie was indicative of the systematization process writ large.

By the 1930s, literal readings of all Scripture, not just prophecy, had become a hallmark of dispensationalism. As David Cooper, a professor at Biola College, described his "Golden Rule of Interpretation" in 1942: "When the plain sense of Scripture makes common sense, seek no other sense; therefore, take every word at its primary, ordinary, usual, literal meaning unless the facts of the immediate context, studied in the light of related passages and axiomatic and fundamental truths, indicate clearly otherwise."[18] Slight variations on this definition were offered time and again—in the broadcasts of J. Vernon McGee, in the pamphlets of Louis Talbot, in the devotional advice of Charles Fuller, and in the scholastic tomes of Ryrie, Pentecost, and Walvoord.

Dispensational literalism was more than a reflexive flattening of language. It was taught through historical and grammatical analysis of a text that tried to identify the original authorial meaning of the written words. The method stood in contrast to critical source and form analysis favored by modernists, or the addition of allegorical and symbolic interpretations favored by covenantalists. Unlike their forebears, dispensationalists built their identity on a full-throated commitment to consistent literal interpretation across all of Scripture. "If literal interpretation is the only valid hermeneutical principle and if it is consistently applied it will cause one to be a dispensationalist," Ryrie wrote in 1957.[19] By equating literal hermeneutics with dispensationalism, Ryrie was flipping the direction of reasoning first employed by Darby, who read prophecy literally because of his prior commitment to a heaven-earth dualism.

---

17. Charles Ryrie, *Dispensationalism Today* (Chicago: Moody Press, 1965), 45.

18. David Cooper, *The World's Greatest Library Graphically Illustrated* (Los Angeles: Bible Research Society, 1942), 37.

19. Charles Ryrie, "The Necessity of Dispensationalism," *Bibliotheca Sacra* 114 (July 1957): 250.

While the prioritization of literalism as described by Ryrie would have destabilizing effects on dispensationalism in the long run, it shored up the relationship between dispensational biblical interpretation and social engagement in the 1940s and 1950s. Through Bible reading and social analysis that linked theological categories to contemporary issues, dispensationalists created a rationale for embracing the larger platform of American conservatism, and the creative material for cultural commitments unique to dispensationalism. As it took on the trappings of a system, dispensational thought encompassed the theological topics it directly addressed—the end times, the nature of the church, the fulfillment of prophecy—but also issues less directly in its theological sight, but which would become staples of "conservative" social engagement in the mid-twentieth century. For example, dispensational educator G. Douglas Young, from his American Institute of Holy Land Studies in Jerusalem, spearheaded evangelical Christian Zionism by calling for "Bible-believing Christians" to find a "practical outlet for their pre-millennial faith" informed by literal interpretations of prophecy.[20] In little more than two decades, Young and his allies managed to vault evangelical Christians ahead of mainline Protestants as the staunchest Christian supporters of the State of Israel in American politics.

Another, and perhaps less obvious, area where the dispensational embrace of literalism coincided with changing "conservative" cultural attitudes was young-earth creationism. Though existing in the 1920s, young-earth creationism remained a minority position among fundamentalists until the 1960s, when a book by two followers of George McCready Price accelerated its adoption. *The Genesis Flood* was published in 1961 by John C. Whitcomb and Henry M. Morris, two dispensationalists who spent the 1950s modifying Price's geological dating to align with consistent literal hermeneutics. Their theory of "flood geology" reconciled the earth's natural history with the global flood narrative in Genesis and fixed the age of the earth at between six thousand and ten thousand years. When released, *The Genesis Flood* standardized and popularized a literal interpretation of Genesis 1–11 for fundamentalists of all types.

Whitcomb and Morris first met through the American Scientific Affiliation, a neo-evangelical organization that included scientists from across the fundamentalist spectrum who worked in higher education. The association's 1953 annual meeting was held at Grace Theological Seminary, one of the three

20. G. Douglas Young, *The Bride and the Wife: Is There a Future for Israel?* (Minneapolis: Free Church Publications, 1960), 88.

centers of advanced dispensational training, where a young John C. Whitcomb was teaching Old Testament. Morris, a hydraulics engineer at the University of Louisiana, presented a paper arguing for a literal reading of the flood narrative that dated it to a few thousand years ago. Already primed in this direction by his dispensational hermeneutics, Whitcomb struck up a friendship with Morris and produced a 1957 dissertation that would be the basis for their shared work.

The resulting *Genesis Flood* claimed to establish "the historicity and character" of the flood in Genesis 6–9 as a globe-spanning catastrophic event that occurred in earth's relatively recent past.[21] This argument was controversial even in fundamentalist circles when it appeared and was rejected by most neo-evangelicals, too. Pro-evolution members of the American Scientific Affiliation had already denounced the work of Price, on which Whitcomb and Morris relied heavily. Bernard Ramm, a rising neo-evangelical theologian, used his 1954 book *The Christian View of Science and Scripture* to trash the "ignoble tradition" of flood geology in favor of a "progressive creationism" that allowed for a harmonious (rather than survival of the fittest) unfolding of creation to climax with humanity.[22] Ramm's theory failed to gain a following, but his dismissal of flood geology was well in line with the scholarly reception of *The Genesis Flood*.

The story among dispensationalists was different. Acclaim for the book mounted, peaking in 1967 when Morris was awarded the W. H. Griffith Thomas Lecture at Dallas Seminary. After Morris delivered his final talk, he reported to Whitcomb that "the entire student body and faculty responded with a lengthy and most embarrassing standing ovation." Morris gleaned that most of the four hundred students and the bulk of the faculty accepted a "recent six-day creation and the world Flood."[23] Charles Ryrie came out for young-earth creationism in an article of the same year that appeared in *Bibliotheca Sacra*. The true Christian must "accept the Bible fully and plainly with the necessary consequence of rejecting evolution," he stated, concluding, "Since the Bible itself has been shown to be true in other areas (particularly in the matter of fulfilled prophecy) . . . the choice of what to accept about creation really should not be too difficult to make."[24] Ryrie's direct comparison of prophetic and creation lit-

21. John C. Whitcomb and Henry Morris, *The Genesis Flood* (Phillipsburg, NJ: Presbyterian & Reformed, 1961), xix.

22. Bernard Ramm, *The Christian View of Science and Scripture* (Grand Rapids: Eerdmans, 1954), 9.

23. Quoted in Ronald L. Numbers, *The Creationists: From Scientific Creationism to Intelligent Design*, expanded ed. (Cambridge, MA: Harvard University Press, 2006), 235.

24. Charles Ryrie, "The Bible and Evolution," *Bibliotheca Sacra*, January 1967, 67, 77–78.

erature and his insistence that both be judged by the same standards was a typical example of what was meant by dispensationalism's biblical literalism.

The reception at Dallas was not a fluke. Dispensationalists became the vanguard of young-earth creationism, advancing its concepts through the Bible college network. In 1970, when Morris decided to finally leave his engineering post as head of the prestigious civil engineering program at Virginia Polytechnic Institute, he moved to San Diego, to cofound Christian Heritage College with a Baptist pastor, Tim LaHaye, who would become one of the most popular dispensational writers of the late twentieth century. Young-earth creationism extended far beyond dispensational circles—especially in the Wisconsin Evangelical Lutheran Synod and among independent fundamentalist networks. In 2019, 40 percent of Americans agreed with what Gallup defined as "creationism": dating the human species to not more than 10,000 years old.[25] Yet for all of its popular appeal, young-earth creationism was stamped with the concerns of midcentury dispensationalism. The framework that gave life to young-earth creationism had crystallized in the decades after 1930 and flourished in the dispensational culture built on print, radio, and weekly sermons devoted to Cooper's dictum: "When the plain sense of Scripture makes common sense, seek no other sense."

Billy Graham and the Neo-Evangelical Insurgency

In the years after World War II, the theological differences between dispensationalists and other fundamentalists, including the emerging neo-evangelicals, were obscured by an overarching political conservatism rooted in Cold War anticommunism. No figure better reflected the overlap and tensions within fundamentalism than did the evangelist Billy Graham, at once an agent of fundamentalist and later neo-evangelical theology, and also an international celebrity and constant presence in the halls of American power.

Though raised in North Carolina, away from the main currents of dispensationalism, Graham was marked by its teachings throughout his life. His mother, Marrow Graham, was a devotee of the writings of Arno Gaebelein and other new premillennialists. In 1937, Graham attended the Florida Bible Institute, founded by fundamentalist and dispensationalist William T. Watson. In 1948 Graham was picked at the age of twenty-nine to become William Bell Riley's successor as president of Northwestern Bible College in Minneapolis—a job

---

25. Megan Brenan, "40% of Americans Believe in Creationism," July 26, 2019, https://news.gallup.com/poll/261680/americans-believe-creationism.aspx.

he performed mostly in absentia until 1952. And in 1954, Graham became a member of First Baptist Church in Dallas, one of the largest congregations in the world, led by dispensationalist (and prominent Southern Baptist states-man) W. A. Criswell.

In his early ministry, Graham assumed dispensational trappings himself, es-pecially in preaching impending judgment. "In this moment I can see the judg-ment hand of God over Los Angeles," he cried in his breakout 1949 crusade, implying both God's imminent wrath and the fulfillment of biblical proph-ecy.[26] He often gestured to a near future that included God's any-moment intervention. "This is the next event on God's calendar," Graham wrote of the rapture in his 1965 best seller, *World Aflame*. In Graham's globe-spanning revivals, he, like Dwight Moody fifty years earlier, reiterated time and again that "the Church has been most effective in the world when she has lived in momentary expectancy of the return of Christ."[27]

For all his invocations of the rapture, Graham's understanding of dispen-sationalism—like Moody's—remained superficial. Key doctrines, including the church-Israel distinction and the negation of a present kingdom, were hardly taught consistently. At the same 1949 crusade in which he prophesied impending doom for Los Angeles, he also declared that humans could change the future: "If we repent, if we believe, if we turn to Christ in faith and hope, the judgment of God can be stopped."[28] This minor deviation from dispensa-tionalism revealed Graham's broader project, which included but ultimately superseded the theological system. Rather, Graham shared the neo-evangelical understanding of an "already but not yet" kingdom and was committed to liberate fundamentalism from its intellectual ghetto—a ghetto he believed had been largely erected by dispensationalists and separatists.

Graham directed his personal and institutional influence, and his significant resources, not to strengthen dispensationalism but to move beyond it in ser-vice of the nation. To that end, he pushed ahead the neo-evangelical project: he was a founding board member of Fuller Seminary in the 1940s; he was the visionary for *Christianity Today* in the 1950s; he spearheaded the Lausanne Movement in the 1970s alongside British evangelist John Stott (a strident critic of dispensationalism); and he helped to spur the spread of evangelicalism across the globe, seeding a network of organizations and schools from Latin

26. Billy Graham, ed., *Revival in Our Time: The Story of the Billy Graham Evangelistic Campaigns* (Wheaton, IL: Van Kampen, 1950), 57.

27. Quoted in Matthew Avery Sutton, *American Apocalypse: A History of Modern Evangelicalism* (Cambridge, MA: Belknap Press of Harvard University Press, 2014), 327.

28. Graham, *Revival in Our Time*, 57.

America to the Indian subcontinent that were deeply skeptical of dispensational theology.

If dispensationalists had, in neo-evangelical criticisms, shrunk the calling of the church, Graham wanted to shrink the scope of the apocalypse. Carl Henry, a close collaborator with Graham, had complained in 1948 that fundamentalists, by which he meant dispensationalists, had been "preoccupied with 'rescuing the furniture' on the mistaken assumption that 'the house of humanity was totally destroyed.'" This cosmic apocalypse was anathema to both Henry and Graham. America, in its current configuration, steeped in religious modernism and declining morality, was headed toward disaster—but this was not the end of history. There was hope if Americans turned from their evil ways. "Fundamentalism was not wrong in assuming a final consummation of history," Henry clarified, "but rather in assuming that this is it."[29]

Dispensationalists and neo-evangelicals diverged over the scope of God's impending judgment, shaping the social and political trajectory of both groups. As Henry's comments suggested, neo-evangelicals owed a debt to dispensationalism all the same. In calling for revival as America's "only hope" to avoid apocalyptic ruin, neo-evangelicals had mapped the eschatological stakes of premillennialism onto the national destiny of the United States. A full century after Exclusive Brethren tried to avoid this fate, the conflation of heavenly and earthly kingdoms had returned with force. "The Church should be taking its proper place of leadership in the nation," Graham thundered in his famous sermon, "America's Hope," finishing with nothing less than a "spiritual call to arms" for the church to embrace a neo-evangelical form of Christian nationalism: "To safeguard our democracy and preserve the true American way of life, we need, we must have, a revival of genuine old-fashioned Christianity, deep, widespread, in the power of the Holy Spirit."[30] The previous fifty years had enabled the systematization of dispensationalism and the spread of its teachings, but the theology also rested on shaky ground even within fundamentalism, as Graham's haphazard invocations made clear.

29. Carl F. H. Henry, "The Vigor of the New Evangelicalism," *Christian Life and Times*, January 1948, 32.

30. Billy Graham, "America's Hope," in *Calling Youth to Christ* (Grand Rapids: Zondervan, 1950), 23, 29.

PART III

THE POP DISPENSATIONALISTS
1960–2020

Scholastic dispensationalism breeds a more popular revival of nationalist end-times teachings, especially through the best seller by Hal Lindsey and Carole C. Carlson, *The Late Great Planet Earth* ◆ Competition between scholastic and pop dispensationalism, as well as increasing criticism by competing fundamentalist and evangelical subcultures, climaxes in the 1970s ◆ A decisive break occurs within the dispensational fold, as well as in the broader world of evangelical theology ◆ Meanwhile, pop dispensationalism reaches new heights of popularity in shaping the rhetoric of the New Christian Right and in segments of religious culture including televangelism, Christian music, and megachurches ◆ Beset by critics, scholastic dispensationalism collapses in the 1990s ◆ A dismembered and commoditized pop dispensationalism scatters across vast stretches of American culture

It is not for a sign we are watching
For wonders above and below
The pouring out of vials of judgment,
The sounding of trumpets of woe;
It is not for a day we are looking
Nor even the time yet to be
When the earth shall be filled with God's glory
As the waters cover the sea;
It is not for a king we are longing
To make the world-kingdoms His own;
It is not for a judge who shall summon
The nations of earth to his throne.

Not for these, though we know they are coming;
They are but adjuncts of Him,
Before whom all glory is clouded,
Besides whom all splendor grows dim.
We wait for the Lord, our beloved,
Our Comforter, Master and Friend,
The substance of all that we hope for,
Beginning of faith and its end;
We watch for our Savior and Bridegroom,
Who loved us and made us his own;
For Him we are looking and longing;
For Jesus and Jesus alone.

Annie Johnson Flint,
"For What We Are Watching" (n.d.)

Flint's poem was written early in the twentieth century but reappeared in the 1950s in dispensational devotionals. The two stanzas helpfully captured the motivating edges of dispensational engagement at midcentury: a mix of imminent world judgment and spiritual hope.

14

Pop Dispensationalism

Thirty years into the fundamentalist movement, theological infighting was at a stalemate. Tempers continued to run high. Writing in 1957, Carl F. H. Henry bemoaned how "many fundamentalists" from the 1920s on had "identified Christianity rigidly with premillennial dispensationalism."[1] William E. Cox, writing in his *Amillennialism Today* (1966)—a direct response to Charles Ryrie's *Dispensationalism Today* (1965)—described the belief in a "literal, earthly, materialistic millennium" as a teaching "arrived at only through a hyperliteral interpretation of obscure passages of Scripture."[2] Observing how defining "evangelicalism" hinged in part on settling these doctrinal disputes, John Walvoord complained that "an evangelical [as opposed to a fundamentalist] is free to believe all that fundamentalists believe theologically"—"or if he prefers, he can deny all the fundamentals and still claim the same name." The term "evangelical," Walvoord noted with concern, "only declares one in favor of the evangel, or the gospel, but it does not in itself define the term theologically."[3]

Though consensus seemed further away than ever, the previous generation's struggle for scholastic superiority had produced another generation of theologians eager to carry on the fight. The expansive growth of Dallas Theological Seminary (DTS) under Walvoord pointed to a vibrant future for dispensationalism. Thousands of dispensationalists worked in pulpits, colleges, seminaries, nonprofits, and mission agencies across the United States and the globe. The pipeline of training grew, with advanced schools at Talbot Seminary in Los

---

1. Carl F. H. Henry, *Evangelical Responsibility in Contemporary Theology* (Grand Rapids: Eerdmans, 1957), 36.

2. William E. Cox, *Amillennialism Today* (Philadelphia: Presbyterian & Reformed, 1966), 136.

3. John F. Walvoord, "What's Right about Fundamentalism," *Eternity*, June 1957, 34.

Angeles and Grace Seminary in Winona Lake, Indiana. And there was potential for yet more growth. "Accredited schools were taking DTS graduates as faculty, though the school at that time was unaccredited," recalled one student of the seminary's halcyon 1960s.[4] Accreditation by the Southern Association of Colleges and Schools came in 1969, when enrollment soared past four hundred and the school broke ground for its largest building expansion to date.

Yet, even as Dallas Seminary was fulfilling Chafer's vision to train men in the system of dispensational theology, seismic changes were afoot. Among the more than sixty graduates in Dallas's 1962 class was Harold Lee "Hal" Lindsey, a Houston native, an ex–tugboat captain, and now the possessor of a master's degree in Greek New Testament from Dallas Seminary. In the 1970s, Lindsey's fame would outpace his teachers' and that of Dallas Seminary itself, as he became one of the most successful authors of the decade and the most important popularizer of dispensationalism in the twentieth century. The source of his notoriety began with a book marketed to baby boomers at the height of the counterculture. In 1970, after a few years as a campus ministry worker in California, Lindsey wrote a popularized version of the dispensational eschatology he learned at Dallas titled *The Late Great Planet Earth* (1970). The unabashedly unscholastic book went on to sell ten million copies in the decade, doing more to familiarize Americans with the "rapture" and the "tribulation" than any scholastic tome. It also spurred a process that would unravel the scholastic project and, indeed, lead to the demise of the system of dispensationalism itself.

Figure 19. Hal Lindsey. Harold Lee "Hal" Lindsey became the most successful popularizer of dispensationalism in the twentieth century. He is pictured here in Dallas Theological Seminary's 1962 yearbook. Courtesy of Turpin Library, Dallas Theological Seminary.

The success of *Late Great Planet Earth* propelled Lindsey into the consumer-driven world of mass-market paperbacks, which he would exploit for decades, but also further away from the influence of his scholastic teachers. Lindsey did not invent the commercialization of dispensationalism, but he monetized its

4. Mal Couch, "History of the War over Dispensationalism: Where We Stand Today, Part II," *Conservative Theological Journal* 6, no. 18 (August 2002): 221.

theological tropes more effectively than had anyone previously. In the process, he disrupted the project of scholastic dispensationalism and injected dispensational concepts into American popular culture at a moment when baby boomers were taking greater notice of religious ideas. Commercialization inflicted on dispensationalism, like so many areas of American religion, a drastic reorganization through the metrics of popularity and virality. The market evaluated the worth of religious teachings on its own terms, creating an environment where scholastic dispensationalism struggled while its popular forms thrived.

Hal Lindsey and The Late Great Planet Earth

A popular form of dispensationalism indebted to the nationalists of the 1920s thrived in an atmosphere of religious and national crisis in the 1960s. Across North America, weekly church attendance peaked in the decade, before beginning a steady decline. The sixties also witnessed the rise of "alternative religions," a term that encapsulated smaller Christian movements but also non-Christian teachings including Eastern spirituality, New Age practices, and insular communities led by charismatic leaders like L. Ron Hubbard, Jim Jones, and Sun Myung Moon. Hal Lindsey, whose primary ministry focus before becoming an author was the campus of UCLA, was perceptive in diagnosing a devolution of institutional authority and decentralization of cultural influence once held by Protestants.

With a growing public demand for accessible religious insights into the social chaos, the erudition that scholastic dispensationalists had cultivated in their struggle for theological legitimacy was, in this new context, a liability. Spiritual seekers outside the fundamentalist fold were interested not in a systematic theology but in a presentation of religion that spoke to the contemporary moment. The era's defining work in this vein was *Late Great Planet Earth*. The book was chock-full of social observations, musings on military weaponry, and armchair diplomacy, mixed with a simplified dispensational eschatology to make sense of the times. The first edition, published by evangelical press Zondervan in 1970, featured on the back cover a still-youthful-looking forty-one-year-old Lindsey and promised "Prophecy for the Now Generation." Though born in 1929, Lindsey lumped himself with the baby boomers: "We have been described as the 'searching generation,'" he explained. "We need so many answers—answers to the larger problems of the world, answers to the conditions in our nation, and most of all, answers for ourselves."[5] Truth was

5. Hal Lindsey and Carole C. Carlson, *The Late Great Planet Earth* (Grand Rapids: Zondervan, 1970), vii.

elusive in the university classroom, he diagnosed. Only pain followed from faith in philosophy, astrology, sexual freedom, or science. These faddish sources of knowledge did not have the pedigree of ancient and timeless truth enjoyed by the Bible. "Let's give God a chance to present His views," he pleaded.[6]

Late Great Planet Earth also had an air of geopolitical urgency. The book was written in the aftermath of the Arab-Israeli War in June 1967, where six days of fighting witnessed a near-total Israeli victory. Israel extended its control over the biblical Old City and East Jerusalem, the West Bank (encompassing the biblical lands of Judea and Samaria), the Golan Heights, the Gaza Strip, and the entire Sinai Peninsula. This stunning turn of events captured world attention. It also aligned with dispensational expectations that Jews would recapture the city of Jerusalem as a coda to the "time of the Gentiles" (Luke 21:24). Lindsey would articulate this expectation in nearly everything he wrote.

Regarding the Middle East, Lindsey was willing to speculate boldly where his seminary teachers were not. Rehearsing standard dispensational teachings, *Late Great Planet Earth*'s core message was straightforward. Before the rapture and the return of Christ, three prophetic events had to be fulfilled: the return of the Jewish people to their biblical land, their capture of Jerusalem, and the rebuilding of the sacrificial temple destroyed in year 70 by Roman legions. By mid-1967, two of the three steps had improbably reached fulfillment in Lindsey's estimation. He predicted, based on a typological reading of a parable in Matthew 24, that "within forty years or so of 1948, all these things could take place."[7] The qualifications—"or so," "could"—allowed Lindsey an escape hatch when 1988 came and went without a rebuilt temple or rapture, but his confidence in the accuracy of biblical prophecy was palpable.

Lindsey's analysis repackaged the content of his scholastic teachers by updating their language and writing with contemporary cultural references about geopolitics. The rapture, with his pen, became "the ultimate trip," while the antichrist assumed the nickname of "Future Fuhrer."[8] Traditional concepts remained central—rapture and antichrist, a third temple in Jerusalem and betrayal of the Jewish people, a climactic battle at Armageddon—but the style was rebellious. "This is not a complex theological treatise," Lindsey explained on the first page, "but a direct account of the most thrilling, optimistic view of what the future could hold for any individual."[9] Lindsey brooked no omnipotent third-

6. Lindsey and Carlson, *Late Great Planet Earth*, viii.
7. Lindsey and Carlson, *Late Great Planet Earth*, 43.
8. Lindsey and Carlson, *Late Great Planet Earth*, 87, 124.
9. Lindsey and Carlson, *Late Great Planet Earth*, vii.

person voices, no detached academic tones. He banished copious footnotes and welcomed instead chic prose, exclamation points, and tabloid copy.

Lindsey's innovation in form was a key ingredient to his success. He realized better than his teachers that old-time prophecy preaching could have mass appeal to a generation dropping out of institutional religion but tuning in to spirituality. It was ultimately popular with a massive segment of American readers. *Late Great Planet Earth* became the best-selling nonfiction book of the 1970s, with ten million copies printed in the decade and twenty-eight million by the end of the century. *Late Great Planet Earth* did not invoke the term "dispensationalism" once, but when it did appear in coverage of the book or in Lindsey's teachings, it became synonymous with Lindsey's apocalyptic timeline. Like the invention of the prophecy chart more than a century before, Lindsey initiated the steady process of popularization by thinning out the theology and making it tantamount to its apocalyptic scenario.

The book entered the bloodstream of American culture, pioneering a subgenre of futurist geopolitical analysis that was expanding beyond a strictly fundamentalist market. The new entries, of which Lindsey's was the most commercially successful, were aimed at a broad readership of no particular religious background. Alvin Toffler's *Future Shock* (1970), which sold six million copies, diagnosed Americans with a collective psychological trauma brought about by "too much change in too short a time," with the forecast that information overload would destabilize economies and whole societies in the years to come.[10] A few years earlier, Stanford biologist Paul Ehrlich had published *The Population Bomb* (1968), selling two million copies, offering a Malthusian vision of humanity's future defined by mass starvation, climate change, and resource wars. The marketing genius of *Late Great Planet Earth* was its genre-bending—and genre-creating—blend of prophecy, spirituality, futurology, and entertainment that landed in readers' hands at the very moment these disparate interests were combining in the real world in new ways.

After *Late Great Planet Earth* sold 500,000 copies under Zondervan, the trade press Bantam Books picked up options for a mass-market paperback (in the same years it was publishing the first original *Star Trek* novels). The book's crossover appeal resembled another Bantam mass-market sensation of the era, Erich von Däniken's best seller, *Chariot of the Gods* (1968—picked up for paperback in 1971), a book positing that ancient aliens had visited earth and guided human development. Like Däniken, Lindsey wrote with a claim to authority far outstripping his credentials. Lindsey presented himself as a popularizer of scholarly knowledge who, like Däniken, delivered better insights

10. Alvin Toffler, *Future Shock* (New York: Random House, 1970), 2.

about the world than the scientific or religious establishments. The critical scholarly reactions to both books in light of massive commercial success were microcosms of the widening ruptures in popular and scholarly knowledge taking place in the 1970s.

Unlike other futurist geopolitical books, *Late Great Planet Earth* was co-written by a woman. Lindsey's collaborator was C. C. Carlson, credited as something less than a coauthor but more than a ghostwriter ("by Hal Lindsey with C. C. Carlson"). Tucked on the back cover was her full name—Carole C. Carlson—a freelance journalist who would go on to author with Lindsey a string of hits. After *Late Great Planet Earth*, Lindsey and Carlson released *Satan Is Alive and Well on Planet Earth* (1972), *There's a New World Coming* (1973), and *The Liberation of Planet Earth* (1974). Each sold in the millions, fueling a commercial demand for dispensational-informed commentary that was addressed not only to the faithful but to entire segments of the reading public.

Five years older than Lindsey, Carlson had even less claim to represent boomers, but the stylistic flair of *Late Great Planet Earth* was her major contribution. Carlson's name is less familiar today for obvious reasons. She succeeded in her career mostly as a ghostwriter, a line of work that encouraged a low profile. Her chosen medium was also predominantly print, while Lindsey leveraged his publications into a full-blown multimedia empire that included television, film, radio, and a bustling tourism business. But just as important, Carlson was a woman writing in a genre dominated, even in the radical sixties and subversive seventies, by men. Modern-day prophets spoke in an assumed masculine vocabulary of religious and political power, wars, military technology, and government oppression: the biblical prophets (all men) told of coming political intrigues and wars (hatched and fought by men) to be won, finally, by the "Last Adam," the "Second Man"—Jesus. Thus, it made sense to dispensationalists that men, too, would bring those biblical visions to the American public. Dispensational theologians only haphazardly embraced the prophet Joel's and the apostle Peter's vision that "sons and daughters will prophesy" in the last days (Acts 2:17 NIV). Writers like Carole C. Carlson remained an exception into the twenty-first century, the gendered division of labor withstanding even the most powerful currents of mass popularization and commercialism.

Those gatekeepers, in any case, were increasingly ineffective after the success of *Late Great Planet Earth*. From the break in the dam lodged by Lindsey and Carlson tumbled forth dozens of imitators that outsold, and reached beyond, the scholastic circle of influence. The torrent was powerful, deep, and wide, shaping the contours of the evangelical movement and popular culture far into the future. Independent church pastor Tim LaHaye, who would go on to cowrite the Left Behind series, made his first mark on the apocalypse with *The Beginning of the End* (1972). Jewish convert and evangelist Zola Levitt, along with Talbot- and Dallas-trained Thomas McCall, wrote the popular apocalyptic tracts *Satan in the Sanctuary* (1973) and *Raptured* (1975) on their way to founding one of the largest Jewish mission agencies in the world. Charismatic dispensationalist Chuck Smith, whose Calvary Chapel movement spread across the country and globe from its base in Southern California, modeled his prophecy tracts *Snatched Away!* (1976) and *End Times* (1978) on Lindsey's countercultural, Jesus People prose. Steeped in dispensational thought and populist in style, these writers looked expectantly not only for the rapture and return of Christ, but for signs that America was damned and condemned, a heap of chaff whose wheat would be harvested in the twinkling of an eye.

Pop dispensationalists captured a large market, much of it unrealized before 1970. At the same time, Lindsey's success in defining dispensational language, style, and content came at the expense of the scholastic tradition that had trained him. Lindsey broke with his teachers on numerous issues: his piecemeal embrace of charismatic practices, his fuzzy maintenance of dispensational time and the church-Israel distinction, his divorce and remarriage (Lindsey would marry three times), and his penchant for date setting, the Achilles' heel of premillennial respectability since the Great Disappointment. At every turn, Lindsey's success redounded less to Dallas Seminary than to Zondervan and Bantam Books and, indeed, to Lindsey himself. The flock of pop-dispensational creators in his wake would follow his lead.

Prophets and Profits

By the summer of 1971, with sales of *Late Great Planet Earth* rocketing into the hundreds of thousands, Hal Lindsey and Carole C. Carlson were well on their way to making the "rapture" a term of wide, if shallow, popular American usage. Dozens of pop dispensational works flooded the paperback market and solidified geopolitical prophecy commentary as a burgeoning market. That these authors wrote for profit does not necessarily mean that they did not also sincerely hold to dispensationalism. Economic opportunity could just as easily encourage niche-authentic visions of the future and appeal to slices of the dispensational pie: Zola Levitt and Arnold Fruchtenbaum wrote from and for a small but growing messianic Jewish community; Tim LaHaye and Chuck Smith reached younger audiences with their growing church and media empires; Jack Van Impe and Mal Couch took to the airwaves and adapted their geopolitical analysis to televangelism.

The fusion of creativity and entrepreneurship ensured a future for geopolitical prophecy commentary, albeit an unstable one. As a case in point, by
the end of the 1970s, *Late Great Planet Earth* was stylistically passé. Conceptualized as campus ministry speaking notes, Lindsey and Carlson's book su-
perficially maintained some of the norms of scholasticism. Lindsey's seminary
credentials were in the first sentence of his author biography, and repeated
references in the text to "scholars of biblical prophecy" gave the appearance
that Lindsey was giving voice to field-wide consensus. This appeal to theological authority, made to bolster Lindsey's credibility, harkened to a passing
midcentury era of fundamentalist culture.

On the other hand, these same notes foreshadowed the populist direction
prophecy analysis would take in the 1970s. Lindsey's references consisted
mostly of magazine and newspaper stories about recent events. The sparsely
documented intellectual and theological influences charted a lineage of thought
that largely circumvented the dispensational system as it had been formed in the
previous forty years. Lindsey included notes to nineteenth-century Lutheran
minister Joseph A. Seiss, who combined biblical prophecy with pyramidology,
and John Cumming, a virulently anti-Catholic Scottish minister of the same
century who predicted the second coming would take place between 1848 and
1867. Lindsey cited as a twentieth-century inspiration the nationalist fundamentalist Louis Bauman, who published half a dozen books in the interwar period
analyzing global events in anticipation of the return of Jesus. All were marginal
voices in the scholastic dispensational canon as it had been constructed in the
mid-twentieth century. Lindsey offered no mentions of Scofield or Chafer or
of his many teachers at Dallas. *Late Great Planet Earth* was intended as much as
an evasion of the scholastic tradition as it was indebted to it.

The torrent of pop-dispensational works that followed Lindsey exhibited
even fewer references to scholastic thought, further widening the breach in
the community. *Late Great Planet Earth*'s success instead prompted new, less
theologically grounded questions for writers: Why did prophecy commentary
need any connection to the scholastics or to formal religious thought of any
kind? Why did it need to be limited to the genre of nonfiction? Why did it
need to be confined to the medium of print? Lindsey paved the way for dispensational diffusion into all types of media and popular culture in the 1970s,
including fiction, film, and music.

Popularizers in Lindsey's wake were more or less independent of oversight—by Lindsey, the scholastics, or church hierarchies. They were only ten-
uously connected to the world of scholastic dispensationalism, with many of
them, like Lindsey, claiming little more than a degree from Dallas or Moody.

They held the professors at these institutions in high esteem, but few ran their newest prophecy analyses by Walvoord or Ryrie before publishing. The successful among them were flush with money and intent on capturing the spiritual marketplace of the 1970s. They were creatives, travelers, communicators. Above all, as their fluorescence of books, pamphlets, films, television and radio shows attested, they were entrepreneurs. The money they made was reinvested into their own creations—mostly media empires and production lines—and became the source of significant personal wealth.

The creative pressures of commercialization put immense strain on the dispensational system as constructed by the scholastics. Fiction allowed for speculation and imagination on the part of writers and more easily facilitated commercialization. Credentials, tests of theological consistency, and institutional affiliations were less important than creative and marketing skills. Book after book and film after film made clear that popular entertainment, dictated by consumer tastes, made a superior dispensational product. Some creatives continued to advance theological arguments, but others paid homage to the scholastic tradition by expanding the market and simply assuming dispensational underpinnings.

Religious creativity was a permanent state of affairs in the burgeoning genre of apocalyptic fiction. Salem Kirban, an Arab Christian journalist with a degree from Temple University, was a contemporary of Lindsey's and published *How to Survive* (1968), a guidebook for those left behind after the rapture. The book sold well and likely primed the pump for *Late Great Planet Earth* a couple of years later, quickly reaching 250,000 copies, but Kirban's big hit was his first foray into apocalyptic fiction, *666* (1970), and its sequel, *1000* (1973). Telling the story of George, a postrapture convert who must survive the antichrist's reign, *666* was structured around the titular "mark of the beast" required by the totalitarian regime in order to exercise basic freedoms of movement, worship, and commerce. In the sequel, with the millennial kingdom established, *1000* dramatized the return of Satan after one thousand years and his ultimate defeat. Kirban's novels hewed closely to the established dispensational sequence of events—too close, with numerous instances of *deus ex machinas*, arbitrary shifts in narrative perspective, and awkward fulfillments of prophecy in service of biblical accuracy.

Novelists after Kirban would feel less obligated to faithfully represent the full dispensational eschatology if it conflicted with narrative quality. Diverse theological trajectories into the end times mixed with market opportunities and creative talent to offer readers new stories. There were plenty of examples, from Frank Allnutt's *The Peacemaker* (1978) to faith healer Maurice Cerullo's *The*

Omega Project (1981). Standing out from the glut was Carol Balizet, who gained attention for her skepticism of professional medical advice and wrote *The Seven Last Years* (1979), billed as "the best selling novel that takes up where *Late Great Planet Earth* left off."[11] Combining dispensationalism with her eclectic mix of beliefs, Balizet produced a narrative that included a comet destroying the island of Cyprus to announce the rapture (making it less than an any-moment event), massive earthquakes knocking the planet off its axis (creating new weather patterns resembling those of climate change), and the pope as the antichrist (resurrecting a figure of older premillennial schemes). Balizet's success in the apocalyptic market was owed to these novelistic innovations. Other writers tweaked the formula for their own ends, but for the lucky ones like Balizet—whose novels went mass-market paperback like Lindsey's—success in publishing spurred personality-based ministries and other possibilities in visual and print media.

Undergirding apocalyptic fiction was the creative milieu of dispensationalism. It supplied world-building ingredients—to be combined creatively by each author—and produced theological and prophetic details: new worlds, new characters, new scenarios. Scholastic nuances were the first victims of popular success. A difference in apocalyptic details, previously the purview of scholastic concern, lost significance when such details were treated as plot devices. Authors varied on every aspect of the theology that could conceivably intersect a fictional narrative—the timing of the rapture, the identity of the antichrist, the ideology of the one-world government and the teachings of the one-world religion, the nature of the mark of the beast. While drawing inspiration from the scholastic tradition, apocalyptic fiction used it loosely, as source material. Many readers seemed equally unconcerned about theological fidelity. The genres inspired by Lindsey prized innovation and entertainment.

Big-screen visualizations of dispensationalism were also indebted to the wave of popularity sparked by *Late Great Planet Earth*. The most important entry was *A Thief in the Night* (1972), a low-budget rapture movie that its producers estimated was eventually shown to over one hundred million viewers. The film's director, Donald Thompson, was a recent convert to Christianity when he penned the script. He relied on his friend and film producer Russell Doughton Jr. to supply the dispensational eschatology that informed the movie's key plot devices. Patty, the main character, confronted a postrapture society and the global dictatorship UNITE (United Nations Imperium for Total Emergency). Thompson's secondhand encounter with the prophecy timeline was a perfect encapsulation of the new pop dispensationalism. Seminaries, commentaries,

11. Carol Balizet, *The Seven Last Years* (New York: Bantam Books, 1979), front cover.

and monographs were far from Thompson's or Doughton's concerns. The potential character conflicts that dispensational concepts created, the dramatic tensions they made possible, and ultimately the psychological pressures that drove Patty to place her trust in Jesus were all more appealing than theological consistency. *A Thief in the Night* was produced by Mark IV Productions, named after Mark 4:33: "With many similar parables Jesus spoke the word to them, as much as they could understand" (NIV). Dispensationalism was the perfect backdrop for a parable, a thought experiment, a fictional dramatization of faith.

Mark IV would also produce *A Thief in the Night*'s three sequels—*A Distant Thunder* (1978), *Image of the Beast* (1981), and *Prodigal Planet* (1983)—and over the course of the 1970s and 1980s, apocalyptic films burgeoned into their own cottage industry. *Late Great Planet Earth* enjoyed its own film adaptation in 1978, narrated by an elderly Orson Wells. *The Second Coming* (1984), produced by the schlock-genre filmmaking Ormond family, included a poorly rendered depiction of Jesus descending from the clouds on a white horse. Character-driven films, like *Years of the Beast* (1981), used the rapture as a point of departure for a survival horror plot. Evangelistic films, created to bring viewers to the precipice of conversion, also exploited postrapture settings, from *Six Hundred and Sixty-Six* (Youth for Christ, 1972) to *Early Warning* (Missionary Productions, 1981) to *Future Tense* (Mars Hill Productions, 1990).

Uniting these diverse projects, which included wide-ranging and experimental techniques, divergent filming styles, and assorted budgets, was a dispensational milieu that most often went unspoken. The dramatic power of the rapture—its luring implications for modern transportation, communications, and economics—and the potentiality (however remote) of a global government run by a dictatorial leader overpowered alternate apocalyptic imaginations on offer in American popular culture, at least in the 1970s.

These novels and films integrated lyrics and music into their cultural punch. Forever linked to *A Thief in the Night* is Christian rock pioneer Larry Norman's single, "I Wish We'd All Been Ready" (1969), played over the opening credits and describing the hellscape of the antichrist's dictatorship after the rapture: "Life was filled with guns and war / And everyone got trampled on the floor / I wish we'd all been ready."[12] Norman's prominence in the early Christian rock scene would be hard to underestimate, but, like Lindsey, his legacy included enabling a generation of creatives to invoke and creatively combine dispensational concepts. The Jesus movement propelled Christian rock forward in the

12. Larry Norman, "I Wish We'd All Been Ready," Genius, accessed May 19, 2022, https://genius.com/Larry-norman-i-wish-wed-all-been-ready-lyrics.

1970s, with rock bands Love Song and Agape, and solo acts Norman, Barry McGuire, Keith Green, and Evie Tornquist rising in popularity as the contemporary Christian music genre took shape.

This diffusion of the rapture and Armageddon through print, film, and music introduced millions of Americans to the imagery of dispensationalism. But mass exposure through diverse media only hastened the incoherence of dispensational theology. Popularizers failed to ask how the media through which they articulated their faith shaped the meanings they conveyed. Like scholastic dispensationalists, who disregarded critical perspectives on their own hermeneutic assumptions, the producers and consumers of popular dispensationalism were oblivious to Marshall McLuhan's diagnosis, "the medium is the message."[13] They were either ignorant of or simply ignored the internal logics of commercialization—the method through which dispensationalism achieved its popularization—that decoupled the rapture, the antichrist, and the tribulation from dispensationalism's theological system. The result was haphazard engagement with dispensationalism among a broad swath of Americans—an engagement that was as much an emotive cry of alienation from postsixties American culture as it was a grappling with the ultimate truth of dispensational teachings.

Lindsey and Smith: The Jesus People

Pop dispensationalism's achievements, though rooted in commercial success, were also intertwined with the counterculture ethos of the 1960s. Hal Lindsey was a case in point. In 1968, after six years of campus ministry work with Campus Crusade for Christ, Lindsey was asked to leave because of his emphasis on eschatology. "I didn't want us to become known as a prophetic movement," recalled Campus Crusade founder Bill Bright, who was a student at Fuller Seminary but never obtained a degree. "And I surely didn't want us to ride any particular theological hobbyhorse."[14] Lindsey soon formed his own ministry, the Jesus Christ Light and Power Company. Headquartered in a former frat house at the edge of the UCLA campus, he convened weekly Bible studies that leaned heavily on the source material that would become *Late Great Planet Earth*. The discussions were not just "hobbyhorses" of Lindsey, but reflective

---

13. Marshall McLuhan, *Understanding Media: The Inventions of Man* (New York: McGraw-Hill, 1964), 7.

14. Quoted in David W. Stowe, *No Sympathy for the Devil: Christian Pop Music and the Transformation of American Evangelicalism* (Chapel Hill: University of North Carolina Press, 2011), 69.

of a type of existential searching indicative of student interests. Chris Hall, a regular attendee in the late 1960s, remembered that young people like himself "were longing to find a point of moral and spiritual clarity and stability, a rock in the midst of the storm, truth in the midst of the falsehoods of both the Right and Left, forgiveness in the midst of an increasingly jaded culture."[15]

Lindsey's end-times evangelism connected with students "looking uncomfortably to the world we inherit," as the Port Huron Statement described the radicalizing boomer generation in 1962.[16] By 1968, their inherited world was even more chaotic and violent, with a surging antiwar movement, sexual revolution, and counterculture. Sages and gurus—ranging from cult leaders to politicians—competed with wildly different visions of change. Lindsey's pop dispensationalism found credence among a segment of young people in just this context. "As Hal interpreted apocalyptic images from Daniel and Revelation, a new world opened up—a world that God controlled, even in its worst moments, and promised both to redeem and judge," Hall recalled.[17]

Many of the pop-dispensational products of the 1970s catered to habits of consumption and entertainment, but there were also flesh-and-blood communities that embodied the implications of impending judgment and social upheaval. Lindsey himself sat at the epicenter of a wider interdenominational youth movement combining Pentecostal spirituality with fundamentalist biblicism that was animated by his vision of judgment. The Jesus People movement originated in the Bay Area and was centered in Southern California, in Lindsey's backyard. This was no accident, growing as it did in the same California soil tilled by premillennialists, dispensationalists, and Pentecostals for more than half a century. Media coverage of the "Jesus freaks" pondered the blend of youth counterculture and fundamentalist theology, but to its participants, raised in the hills marked by religious radio towers, the fusion made the simplest sense. Critiques of the "world system" had never died but were once again in vogue. Dispensationalism's skepticism of global institutions, establishment authority, and modernist thought aligned with the pessimistic assessments of the world offered by student radicals and rock musicians.

Some fifty miles south of the Light and Power Company, in the city of Costa Mesa, pastor Chuck Smith and his pupil, a hippie preacher named Lonnie

15. Chris Hall, "What Hal Lindsey Taught Me about the Second Coming," *Christianity Today*, October 25, 1999, 83.

16. "Port Huron Statement," 1962, The Sixties Project, accessed May 19, 2022, http://www2.iath.virginia.edu/sixties/HTML_docs/Resources/Primary/Manifestos/SDS_Port_Huron.html.

17. Hall, "What Hal Lindsey Taught Me," 83.

Frisbee, cultivated an even larger local community of counterculture youth at Calvary Chapel, beginning what would become the Calvary Chapel movement. Smith, a lifelong Pentecostal ordained in the denomination founded by Aimee Semple McPherson, welcomed the influx by undertaking a years-long verse-by-verse study of the book of Revelation. Like Lindsey, who eventually came to work at Calvary Chapel in the 1970s, Smith's pop dispensationalism was weighted toward eschatological concerns. In his 1978 book *End Times*, Smith set a concrete date for the rapture of 1981, using the logic, borrowed from Lindsey, that "this generation shall not pass" (Matt. 24:34 KJV). "Since a generation of judgment is forty years and the Tribulation period lasts seven years, I believe the Lord could come back for His Church any time before the Tribulation starts, which would mean anytime before 1981." He clarified the math: "1948 + 40 − 7 = 1981."[18] The date came and went, of course, and many more predictions with the hedging of "could" and "may" followed. What was clear was that Smith, like Lindsey, incorporated dispensational theology here insofar as it informed this eschatological speculation.

Pop dispensationalism and the Jesus People flourished in Southern California and beyond for much of the 1970s. The movement was soon a national phenomenon, visible in cities and college campuses from Seattle to Washington, DC. Billy Graham grew out his hair a little and capitalized on the youthful energy in his crusades. Explo '72, a massive eighty-thousand-person rally organized by Campus Crusade for Christ in Dallas, attracted Graham, Johnny Cash, and Larry Norman, among others. The movement inspired most of the first generation of Christian rock musicians and roused some of the first planned megachurches in suburban America. Once the embers of impending rapture cooled in the 1980s, the Jesus People left a complicated legacy for thousands of middle-aged boomers that informed both the smaller evangelical Left and the gathering New Christian Right.

In each of these religious venues, the commercial and religious success of pop dispensationalism exposed millions of Americans to the technical language of dispensational eschatology. "Words, phrases, and symbols such as Rapture, Great Tribulation, pretribulation, posttribulation, millennium, Antichrist, Beast, and 666 were entirely new to me," Hall reminisced.[19] Yet, here, too, exposure was not to the scholastic dispensationalism of Feinberg, Walvoord, and Ryrie, but to the eschatological motifs of Lindsey, Smith, and Norman. A fractured fundamentalism, recalling Walvoord's complaint from 1957,

18. Chuck Smith, *End Times: A Report on Future Survival* (Costa Mesa, CA: Word for Today, 1978), 35.

19. Hall, "What Hal Lindsey Taught Me," 83.

could hardly offer more: the term "evangelical" "only declares one in favor of the evangel, or the gospel, but it does not in itself define the term theologically." With little to organize it but a deeply entrenched rivalry, fundamentalist theology was heavily influenced by commercial and cultural arguments.

In one sense this was a story as old as new premillennialism, harkening to the efforts of James Brookes, Joseph Seiss, and Dwight Moody in the nineteenth century. But in another sense, the Jesus People's embrace of apocalyptic theology helped to undermine the legacy and future of dispensationalism on scholastic terms. The same cultural logic that extended pop dispensationalism's reach made it vulnerable to the whims of culture and commerce. When cultural trends shifted and consumer tastes changed, pop dispensationalism would be forced to further adapt or die.

Ultimately, Lindsey's dispensational eschatology was not concerned about a broader theological framework or scholastic expertise. Pop dispensationalism severed the Jesus People's ability to integrate their prophecy expectations with an ethics, ecclesiology, or comprehensive biblical hermeneutics. "A crippling aspect of the Jesus movement as a whole was its drastically shortened exegetical perspective, a theological and historical amnesia," reflected Hall. On the prophecies in Revelation and Daniel, he observed, "I was shockingly unaware of the Christians who had read, pondered, and interpreted these texts before me."[20] The full force of the Bible Reading methods embedded in dispensationalism came to bear on the Jesus People; interpreting the Bible in anything but a plain meaning was seen as undermining biblical authority.

With the windfall profits from his best sellers, Lindsey was described by *Publishers Weekly* in 1977 as "an Adventist-and-Apocalypse evangelist who sports a Porsche racing jacket and tools around Los Angeles in a Mercedes 450 SL."[21] Lindsey's ministry had little to say about what to do until that end arrived. "We wanted our cake (Jesus to return) and to eat it too (to live however we wanted until he came back)," Hall concluded about the Jesus People movement.[22] This spirit of separation would reach beyond the Jesus People and extend to the entirety of the dispensational world over the next decade.

20. Hall, "What Hal Lindsey Taught Me," 84.
21. Quoted in Erin A. Smith, *What Would Jesus Read? Popular Religious Books and Everyday Life in Twentieth-Century America* (Chapel Hill: University of North Carolina Press, 2015), 216.
22. Hall, "What Hal Lindsey Taught Me," 85.

O soul, are you weary and troubled?
No light in the darkness you see?
There's light for a look at the Savior,
And life more abundant and free.

His Word shall not fail you, He promised;
Believe Him and all will be well;
Then go to a world that is dying,
His perfect salvation to tell!

Turn your eyes upon Jesus,
Look full in His wonderful face,
And the things of earth will grow strangely dim,
In the light of His glory and grace.

Helen Howarth Lemmel,
"The Heavenly Vision" (1922)

Helen Howarth Lemmel, a dispensationalist, taught music at Moody Bible Institute and Biola College until her death in 1961. This hymn, which would also become known as "Turn Your Eyes upon Jesus," appeared in the United States at the height of the fundamentalist-modernist controversy and became a staple of evangelical and fundamentalist hymnody in the postwar period.

15

The Great Rupture

The atmosphere was electric in the Binyenei HaUma—the largest auditorium in Jerusalem—on the evening of June 15, 1971. More than 1,500 tourists, most of them from the United States, were gathered for the Jerusalem Conference on Biblical Prophecy, sponsored jointly by Americans and the Israeli government. An opening address by eighty-four-year-old David Ben-Gurion, the first prime minister of Israel, drew on themes of Judeo-Christian values and the wisdom of the Bible. His talk would be the last of the three-day conference to be so inclusive.

For most of the proceedings, the June 1967 war was the set dressing for theological jockeying among neo-evangelicals, covenantalists, and dispensationalists. The event had been organized by Carl F. H. Henry and G. Douglas Young, the latter a longtime dispensationalist and Christian Zionist who had founded a school for evangelicals in Jerusalem. The two had butted heads repeatedly in the lead-up to the conference, with Henry hoping the gathering would rechannel evangelical apocalyptic interest in Israel into neo-evangelical themes of social engagement and missions, while Young was more interested in mobilizing evangelical political support for Israel. Left to Young, the conference, Henry worried, would amount to "a parochial eschatological sideshow reflective of one narrow segment" of theology, by which he meant dispensationalism. In a letter to a fellow evangelical, he predicted darkly that "a parochial intramural Biola mood" would infuse the conference.[1] Though

---

1. Henry to John Winston, June 12, 1970, box 5, folder 5, Carl F. H. Henry Papers, Gleason A. Archer Archives, Trinity International University, Deerfield, IL; Henry to Wilbur Smith, May 30, 1970, box 5, folder 7, Carl F. H. Henry Papers.

Biola hardly made an appearance, the program *was* parochial in the sense that it resembled an intramural contest among the theological factions of fundamentalism.

Each faction of fundamentalist theology was well represented. Alongside Charles Feinberg of Talbot Theological Seminary, John Walvoord of Dallas Theological Seminary spoke for scholastic dispensationalism. Also on the program were covenantalists Edmund Clowney, president of Westminster Theological Seminary, and Herman Ridderbos, a Dutch Reformed scholar from the Netherlands. Accompanying Henry to put forth the neo-evangelical perspective was Harold Ockenga, now president of the newly merged Gordon-Conwell Theological Seminary in Hamilton, Massachusetts. Many more dispensationalists had speaking slots, from Young to messianic Jewish missionary Alexander Wachtel, to the recent president of the Southern Baptist Convention, W. A. Criswell. Likewise, there was no shortage of opponents of dispensationalism on the platform, including British evangelical John Stott, Black American evangelist Tom Skinner, and Scottish Open Brethren theologian James M. Houston. Taken collectively, the speaker list amounted to a broad sampling of fundamentalist and evangelical theological factions.

The Jerusalem Conference on Biblical Prophecy is typically cited by historians as an early example of Christian Zionist organizing. However, the array of voices ensured that the gathering amounted to little more than the sideshow Henry predicted. The theological divisions evident in Jerusalem exposed a broader crisis of theological authority in fundamentalism. In the 1970s, even as pop dispensationalism reached millions of Americans, the project of scholastic dispensationalism began to crumble and the leadership of dispensational theology soon slipped beyond the control of its scholastic stewards. The cultural authority accrued by Dallas Seminary and others slowly drained away to the media empires of pop dispensationalists.

Although accelerated by popularizers like Hal Lindsey, the rupture of fundamentalist theology also took place among the theologians—at sites like the Binyenei HaUma. As the Jerusalem gathering made clear, the growing success of pop dispensationalism had stimulated theological opposition to dispensationalism like never before. Critics from across the conservative spectrum found common cause in stemming the tide of pop-dispensational culture. Judged by book sales and accumulated wealth, dispensational eschatology hardly suffered in the 1970s. And yet, scholastic dispensationalism witnessed dramatic, devastating, and permanent setbacks in the same years. The complex ecosystem that made scholastic dispensationalism flourish in the 1950s—a network of interdependent seminaries, publishing houses, churches, and preachers—was remaking itself in the 1970s along the lines of a postwar consumer republic and a polarizing political culture.

Walvoord and Ryrie Oversee the Scholastic Shift

Scholastic interest in popularizing dispensational eschatology existed long before Hal Lindsey and *Late Great Planet Earth*, and there were multiple forces pushing dispensationalists toward popular culture engagement in the 1960s. The Cold War and the atom bomb had stirred prophecy analysts far and wide to reinterpret the book of Revelation. For Americans wracked with anticommunist anxiety, premillennial diagnoses of the USSR's possession of nuclear weapons made intuitive sense. And a Cold War religious revival led by the likes of Billy Graham and Charles Fuller gave voice to preachers who uttered dire warnings about the state of the world. Scholastic dispensationalists discerned the shifting concerns of Americans as well as any group and spoke effectively about the reliability of the Bible for modern times.

By the 1960s, evidence of cultural decline was mounting for fundamentalists: the youth revolt and antiwar movement, free love and LSD, women's liberation, Black power. A looming apocalypse, dispensationalists observed, was not only prophesied but was in some deep sense deserved. "Even in the so-called Christian United States of America," John Walvoord wrote in 1967 while documenting the "spiritual crisis" to precede the end times, "Biblical truth has had realistic application to only a small segment of the population and has not materially influenced our national policies whether in politics, business, or educational areas of national activity."[2] The 1960s created a particular type of dispensational geopolitical analysis steeped in critical assessments for the past and future of the United States.

Also important to the rising apocalyptic interests of scholastics was the lodestar of dispensational prophecy that now seemed to have reappeared in history as the State of Israel in 1948. Postwar scholastics leaned into this unfolding future, centered in the Middle East, careening toward cosmic (and mired in terrestrial) war. Biblical prophecy was silent on the United States, but what it told about the Jewish people filled volumes of dispensational analysis. Commentaries on minor prophets and texts on systematic theology—the

---

2. John F. Walvoord, *The Nations in Prophecy* (Grand Rapids: Zondervan, 1967), 14.

building blocks of the scholastic project—would no longer suffice, especially after the Arab-Israeli War in June 1967.

The shift in scholastic style and focus toward the apocalyptic during the 1960s created a burst of production that, on its surface, appeared like another wave of scholastic output. John F. Walvoord's trilogy *Israel in Prophecy* (1962), *The Church in Prophecy* (1964), and *The Nations in Prophecy* (1967) was a comprehensive restatement of dispensational eschatology for a new generation, while Charles Feinberg's editorship of the Congress on Prophecy volumes (1964 and 1968) brought dispensational theology directly to bear on the State of Israel.

More visible than new monographs was the completion of a decade-long project in 1967: *The New Scofield Reference Bible*. A committee of nine dispensational theologians systematized Scofield's notes to conform to the most up-to-date dispensational thinking, which inevitably meant thousands of small, and a few major, alterations. Among the larger and more controversial changes, a new note to Genesis 12:1–4 integrated the Holocaust and the creation of the State of Israel in 1948 into the Bible's prophetic foreknowledge. The new note clarified that God's promise to Abraham—"I will curse those who curse you"— was "a warning literally fulfilled in the history of Israel's persecutions. It has invariably fared ill with the people who have persecuted the Jew—well with those who have protected him. For a nation to commit the sin of antisemitism brings inevitable judgment." The updated text, while dismissed by outsiders and even a few die-hard disciples of the 1917 Scofield notes, sold briskly and established continuity for another generation of dispensational thinkers.

The most lasting contribution from the decade may have been Charles Ryrie's *Dispensationalism Today* (1965), a concise synthesis of the scholastic dispensational system that served as its most cogent summation to date. Ryrie endeavored to provide a *sine qua non* of dispensationalism to clarify its contribution to Christian theology, and to do so in a way that painted it as the embodiment of a historical Christian tradition. Philip Mauro's indictment of dispensationalism as "modern" appeared on the third page of chapter 1 and haunted Ryrie's apologia. His choice of distinctives was unsurprising: "The essence of dispensationalism," he began, "is the distinction between Israel and the Church."[3] Two more flowed from the first: the "plain hermeneutics" applied equally to every book in the Bible, and an argument that the overall point of history was to glorify God (this third point, Ryrie admitted, was "a rather technical matter" that concerned a more obscure debate with covenantal theo-

3. Charles Ryrie, *Dispensationalism Today* (Chicago: Moody Press, 1965), 47.

logians). At the same time, a later chapter was devoted to distinguishing "the mainstream of dispensationalism from ultradispensationalism," the smaller tradition rooted in the teachings of E. W. Bullinger that rejected water baptism and, in some cases, the Eucharist based on a different understanding of dispensational time. Both covenantalists and neo-evangelicals had diagnosed ultradispensationalism as simply dispensationalism taken to a logical extreme, a conclusion Ryrie disputed, insisting that the two "have very basic differences."[4] Ryrie's erudition, affability, and wide engagement with critics—all in a little over two hundred pages—ensured that *Dispensationalism Today* would sell well and be a seminary staple for decades.

The *New Scofield Reference Bible* and *Dispensationalism Today* signaled the full maturation of scholastic dispensationalism as a theological system in the late 1960s. Moreover, both cemented a modest shift in doctrinal teachings, amounting in some corners of fundamentalism to the level of a "revision" on the new premillennial dualism of Darby and Scofield, and the early efforts at systematization by Chafer. This revision entailed a shift toward literal hermeneutics, rather than an a priori dualism, as the foundation of dispensational thinking. The change was subtle and went unnoticed by many practitioners (and was discussed rarely outside of select academic venues like *Bibliotheca Sacra*), but the shifting nevertheless indicated changes that would have larger effects in later decades.

For the moment, however, the success of the scholastic project created a comprehensive and deep (if narrow) theological community centered at Dallas Seminary that seemed to be having resonance among lay Christians, too. A second wave of generational scholars—most not yet having earned their PhDs—was recruited by Walvoord to Dallas in the 1950s and 1960s to bolster their ranks: S. Lewis Johnson in systematic theology, Haddon Robinson in homiletics, Bruce Waltke in Old Testament, and Zane Hodges in New Testament, among others who would teach at Dallas for decades. As their range of fields attested, dispensational scholars held diverse but interlocking theological concerns. Dispensationalism, now producing a steady stream of trained theologians, was fostering something of a fully fledged scholarly discourse. The theological work generated new insights and addressed new challenges, and for seminarians being trained in the system, the same scholars supplied confidence in dispensationalism's academic bona fides.

But even as the scholastic conversation grew, dispensational theologians took note of the mass audiences interested in prophecy. With best sellers by

4. Ryrie, *Dispensationalism Today*, 192–93, 205.

THE NEW SCOFIELD REFERENCE BIBLE

HOLY BIBLE

AUTHORIZED KING JAMES VERSION

With introductions, annotations, subject chain references,
and such word changes in the text as will help the reader

EDITOR

C.I. SCOFIELD, D.D.

EDITORIAL COMMITTEE OF THE NEW EDITION

E. SCHUYLER ENGLISH, Litt.D.
CHAIRMAN

FRANK E. GAEBELEIN, A.M., Litt.D.
HEADMASTER EMERITUS, *The Stony Brook School*

WILLIAM CULBERTSON, D.D., LL.D.
PRESIDENT, *Moody Bible Institute*

CHARLES L. FEINBERG, Th.D., Ph.D.
DEAN, *Talbot Theological Seminary*

ALLAN A. MAC RAE, A.M., Ph.D.
PRESIDENT, *Faith Theological Seminary*

CLARENCE E. MASON, JR., Th.M., D.D.
DEAN, *Philadelphia College of Bible*

ALVA J. MC CLAIN, Th.M., D.D.
PRESIDENT EMERITUS, *Grace Theological Seminary*

WILBUR M. SMITH, D.D.
EDITOR, *Peloubet's Select Notes*

JOHN F. WALVOORD, A.M., Th.D.
PRESIDENT, *Dallas Theological Seminary*

NEW YORK · OXFORD UNIVERSITY PRESS

1967

Figure 20. New Scofield Reference Bible title page. The culmination of more than a decade of scholastic collaboration, the revised edition of the *Scofield Reference Bible* (1967) was a monument to dispensationalism's scholastic project. Scholars made thousands of changes to the 1917 edition, including revisions away from Scofield's inherited dualism and interest in typological structures, all while maintaining the basic theological structure of Scofield's work.

Salem Kirban and Hal Lindsey, financial and cultural capital was up for grabs, and what the popularizers accrued was flowing away from scholastic institutions. Not content simply to concede millions of readers, the scholastics entered the growing postwar apocalyptic market, too.

Previous to 1970, scholastics understood the popular demand for apocalyptic analysis but failed to adapt to the popular forms. Dwight Pentecost, following his large scholastic tome *Things to Come* (1958), published *Prophecy for Today* (1961), a collection of sermons with titles such as "Israel's Title Deed to Palestine" and "The Coming Great World Dictator." In the same year, a collected volume of prophecy conference addresses featuring Walvoord, Feinberg, McGee, and Herman Hoyt (of Grace Theological Seminary) bridged the gap between technical theological arguments and geopolitical analysis (*The Prophetic Word in Crisis Days*). Later in the decade, while Lindsey was penning his best seller with Carlson, Charles Ryrie published a sedate apocalyptic study guide, *The Bible and Tomorrow's News* (1969). In the same year, a thirty-year-old pastor trained at Talbot named John F. MacArthur published a short pamphlet, *Israel: God's Clock* (1969), that enumerated coming events, but in a dry academic style that eluded popular accessibility.

The shift changed more dramatically after Lindsey proved there to be a vast popular market. The most notable scholastic entry into popular prophecy commentary was John F. Walvoord's *Armageddon, Oil, and the Middle East Crisis: What the Bible Says about the Future of the Middle East and the End of Western Civilization* (1974). What the work lacked in style it made up for in cutting-edge analysis. Walvoord discussed Cold War geopolitics, the global oil market, the Arab-Israeli conflict, and European economic integration. The manuscript was only half finished at the outbreak of the fourth Arab-Israeli war in October 1973, with Zondervan once again poised to benefit from a timely entry into geopolitical prophecy analysis. The press encouraged him to finish quickly, which he did by conscripting as coauthor his son, John E. Walvoord, then a doctoral student in psychology at Columbia University. The final book was released mere months after the dust had settled in the Middle East and made the case that the region was "the center of world attention of prophecies for the last days."[5]

Stripped of its prophetic language and episodic digressions into biblical interpretation, Walvoord's tract would have been hard to distinguish from a conservative policy brief, echoing the same concerns over weak US diplomacy, high oil prices, and increased Russian meddling voiced by conservative policy wonks. Walvoord offered more details than Lindsey, and his book achieved impressive sales (600,000 copies by 1976; a reissue in 1991 on the eve of the First Gulf War sold another million). But as a decade-shaping work, the Walvoords' attempt came up short. Its sales, while large, were dwarfed by more popular works. The book was an impressive imitator of *Late Great Planet Earth*, but an imitator all the same.

Armageddon, Oil, and the Middle East was only the most successful of a rash of similar outputs by scholastic dispensationalists. In each case, writers presented a more accessible writing style, vocabulary, and fluency with contemporary affairs. The books ignored systematic doctrine, lending credence

5. John F. Walvoord and John E. Walvoord, *Armageddon, Oil, and the Middle East Crisis: What the Bible Says about the Future of the Middle East and the End of Western Civilization* (Grand Rapids: Zondervan, 1974), 12.

to the popular image of dispensationalism as little more than an end-times scenario. Other scholarly popularizations included retired Dallas Seminary archaeologist Merrill Unger's *Beyond the Crystal Ball* (1973), Western Seminary biblical scholar Stanley A. Ellison's *Biography of a Great Planet* (1975), and Charles Ryrie's *The Living End* (1976). All these contributions hinted at how the center of dispensational thinking was shifting definitively from the seminary to the sales chart, influencing not just who defined dispensational content but who shaped its future. Lindsey had shed the scholasticism of his teachers. As those same teachers worked to emulate Lindsey, they were unable to grasp just how thin was the barrier separating the old scholastic and the new pop dispensationalism.

George Eldon Ladd and Premillennialism without Dispensationalism

In the wake of pop dispensationalism's stunning commercial success, the rift between the old scholastic and new popular traditions was at first hard to detect. To the outside observer, dispensationalism never looked healthier. But writing decades later, Mal Couch, a Dallas graduate who had capitalized on the popular craze of the 1970s through films, television, and radio, reflected more critically on the costs of popularization. "After the 1970s, interest in dispensationalism began to decline within the mainstream of conservative evangelicalism," he lamented in the foreword to the scholastic collaboration *Dictionary of Premillennial Theology* (1996).[6] Couch's explanations for decline were manifold, but the main thrust could be traced back to the 1970s: hyped predictions by dispensational writers failed to materialize, and Middle East geopolitics became less newsworthy after 1973. Couch pondered if television had created a generation of Christians who could not easily grasp the complexities of dispensationalism. "The do-your-own-thing generation of unsaved people, and even born-again Christians," he complained, "simply didn't have time for the apostasy and the rapture that we taught would be upon us soon."[7] Underlying this self-serving complaint was a nugget of truth: dispensational theology as a whole, if it could still be called a whole, was awash in money but shallow in rigor. For whatever reason, younger evangelicals

6. Mal Couch, ed., *Dictionary of Premillennial Theology* (Grand Rapids: Kregel, 1996), 10.

7. Mal Couch, "History of the War over Dispensationalism: Where We Stand Today, Part II," *Conservative Theological Journal* 6, no. 18 (August 2002): 223.

and fundamentalists lacked the interest to ponder the depths of scholastic dispensationalism.

From Couch's perspective, the most galling failures were unforced errors by dispensational seminaries, Bible schools, and pastors. "[A] de-emphasis on the teaching of the rapture and Bible prophecy in general" among once-strong churches signaled an alarming "paradigm shift," he warned. "Prophecy was out, and psychology was in. The teaching of doctrine was replaced by sermons on current social issues and the emotional life of the believer"—and, it could be added, political commentary masquerading as prophecy analysis.[8] Mirroring a therapeutic turn in American society that privileged individual self-expression and psychological categories of meaning, evangelical culture after the mid-1970s also became dominated by social and psychological concerns. Self-help books and family values—two sides of the new interest in personal fulfillment—had replaced grand cosmic reflections on the return of Jesus with concerns closer to, and inside, the home.

This was the scholastics' theory of decline, at least. In fact, Couch failed to see how much the tendencies he abhorred had manifested themselves within scholastic circles. One dispensational pioneer of the move to "social" and "emotional" issues was a collaborator for the *Dictionary*, who had used the attention accrued from apocalyptic analysis in the 1970s to emerge as a key voice in the culture wars of the 1980s. Tim LaHaye, after his 1972 discourse on the approaching end, teamed up with his wife, Beverly, to produce the most popular evangelical sex manual of the decade, *The Act of Marriage* (1976). He buttressed this book with help guides on depression, dating advice, and the "male temperament." These combined to fix his attention on issues of gender and sexuality over all other considerations, marshaling fundamentalists and evangelicals to organized political action in books such as *The Battle for the Family* (1982). LaHaye's decade-long publication migration from prophecy analysis to social issues fit Couch's narrative of dispensational decline, even though LaHaye would cowrite the Left Behind novels in the 1990s.

The paradoxical legacy of a figure like LaHaye is at the heart of the rupture of dispensationalism. Many of the tradition's chief proponents in the 1970s pushed into new cultural territory but did not invest in the perpetuation of scholastic dispensationalism. Whether that territory was mass culture or mass politics (and LaHaye successfully went toward both), dispensational theol-

8. Couch, *Dictionary of Premillennial Theology*, 10.

ogy was treated as a source book or an inherited cultural language rather than an active theological tradition requiring methods of self-perpetuation. Judged on its own terms, dispensational resources of time, energy, and money were all heading away from the scholastic project into newly organized and scaled cultural and political projects, from mass-market thriller novels to political activism.

But if scholastic dispensationalism was stumbling, self-inflicted wounds were only half the story. The decline of scholastic dispensationalism was also brought about by sharp criticisms leveled by fellow fundamentalists and evangelicals—covenantalists and neo-evangelicals who were more committed than ever to cutting down dispensationalism's influence in light of its growing mass and lay appeal.

No critics were better positioned to undermine the influence of scholastics than a new generation of premillennialists who traced their influences back to the old premillennial tradition rather than through new premillennialism and dispensationalism. These theologians, keeping alive the intrapremillennial rivalry that shaped so much of prefundamentalist theological discourse, disagreed with dispensational hermeneutics and taught that the kingdom of God would be centered on the church rather than Israel (among other distinctions). A renewed version of old premillennialism going by the name "historic premillennialism" flourished in the halls of neo-evangelical seminaries in the 1970s—in classrooms at Fuller Seminary, Gordon-Conwell Theological Seminary, and Trinity Evangelical Divinity School, among other centers of evangelical training. Neo-evangelicals insisted that historic premillennialism was superior on theological and missional grounds, while the conservative wing in the Southern Baptist Convention also included historic premillennialists such as SBC president from 1982 to 1984, Jimmy Draper. The New Christian Right also brought to prominence key historic premillennial social activists, including author and pro-life activist Francis Schaeffer and family values proponent James Dobson, both of whom rejected an imminent rapture and future kingdom as antithetical to urgent political organizing.

Figure 21. "Evangelical Higher Education and Eschatology in the 1970s." In the 1970s, eschatology remained a polarizing issue in fundamentalist and evangelical circles. Three camps occupied the majority of the conservative Protestant landscape: a network of dispensational institutions, a more pluralist nondispensational evangelicalism that tended to promote old (historic) premillennialism, and an amillennial Reformed community wary of all the attention paid to eschatology. The theological direction of fundamentalism and evangelicalism remained up for grabs fifty years after the fundamentalist movement was organized.

	Name	Location	Date Founded	Denominational Allegiance	Notable Contributors to Eschatology Scholarship
Dispensational Friendly Seminaries	Dallas Theological Seminary	Dallas, TX	1925	Nondenominational	John Walvoord (D), Charles Ryrie (D), Dwight Pentecost (D)
	Grace Theological Seminary	Winona Lake, IN	1937	Brethren Churches	Herman Hoyt (D), Alva McLain (D), John Whitcomb (D)
	Talbot Theological Seminary	La Mirada, CA	1952	Nondenominational	Charles Feinberg (D), Robert Saucy (D)

Notable colleges/Bible institutes: Biola College (La Mirada, CA); Moody Bible Institute (Chicago, IL); Philadelphia Bible Institute (Philadelphia, PA); The Master's College (Santa Clarita, CA)

	Name	Location	Date Founded	Denominational Allegiance	Notable Contributors to Eschatology Scholarship
Historic Premillennial Friendly Seminaries	Trinity Evangelical Divinity School	Deerfield, IL	1897	Evangelical Free Church of America	Gleason Archer (H), Paul Feinberg (D), Norman Geisler (D), Carl F. H. Henry (H), Wilbur Smith (D)
	Fuller Theological Seminary	Pasadena, CA	1947	Nondenominational	Daniel Fuller (H), George Eldon Ladd (H)
	Gordon-Conwell Theological Seminary	Hamilton, MA	1969 (merged)	Nondenominational	Gordon Fee (H), Harold Ockenga (H)

Notable colleges: Westmont College (Monticello, CA); Wheaton College (Wheaton, IL); Trinity University International (Deerfield, IL)

	Name	Location	Date Founded	Denominational Allegiance	Notable Contributors to Eschatology Scholarship
Neo-Amillennial Friendly Seminaries	Calvin Theological Seminary	Grand Rapids, MI	1876	Christian Reformed Church	Anthony Hoekema (A), Fred Klooster (A)
	Westminster Theological Seminary	Glenside, PA	1929	Orthodox Presbyterian Church	Oswald Allis (A), Cornelius Van Til (A), O. Palmer Robertson (A)

Notable colleges: Calvin College (Grand Rapids, MI); Grove City College (Grove City, PA); Northwestern College (Orange City, IA)

Legend: Dispensationalism (D), Historic Premillennialism (H), Amillennialism (A)

Among the most successful challengers to scholastic dispensationalism was a cadre of premillennial-but-not-dispensational theologians who published in New Testament studies and systematic theology through the 1970s. Robert Gundry's *The Church and the Tribulation* (1973) was a particularly influential defense of a "posttribulational rapture" that discarded the bulk of dispensational theology in favor of a covenantal and Reformed system. The most successful of these challengers by far was George Eldon Ladd, the erstwhile dispensational seminary student of the 1930s, pioneer critic of dispensationalism in the 1940s and 1950s, and professor of New Testament studies at Fuller Theological Seminary. As the banner carrier for historic premillennialism, Ladd enjoyed unprecedented success in evangelical circles in the 1970s. The definitive presentation of his method, *A Theology of the New Testament* (1974), was ranked by evangelical seminarians twelve years later as the second-most influential work of theology, behind only Calvin's *Institutes*.[9] As the theologian Russell Moore declared years later, Ladd was the chief scholarly influence behind an "emerging evangelical consensus" on historic premillennialism in the late twentieth century.[10]

One dark irony of Ladd's theological success was that it occurred as his personal and emotional life disintegrated. In addition to suffering from alcoholism and a failing marriage, Ladd became convinced that his life's work fell far short of its promise, that he had been unable to win a "seat at the table" of academic theology, in the words of his biographer John D'Elia.[11] In light of this realization, which Ladd came to after the tepid reception of his most innovative work, *Jesus and the Kingdom* (1966), he was hardly content with his secondary, and far more successful, rebuttals of dispensationalism. By 1970, Ladd had come to regard evangelical theology as an intellectual backwater. He oriented his last decade of work to the broadest possible community of Christians but made his deepest mark on those in his own evangelical community.

The most obvious difference between dispensational and historic premillennial movements in the 1970s was that the latter stayed relatively coherent while the former popularized rapidly. The relative stability and lack of popular growth in historic premillennialism initially alarmed its supporters,

9. Mark A. Noll, *Between Faith and Criticism: Evangelicals, Scholarship, and the Bible in America* (Vancouver, BC: Regent College Publishing, 2004), 212.

10. Russell Moore, *The Kingdom of Christ: The New Evangelical Perspective* (Wheaton, IL: Crossway, 2004), 138.

11. John A. D'Elia, *A Place at the Table: George Eldon Ladd and the Rehabilitation of Evangelical Scholarship in America* (New York: Oxford University Press, 2008).

who regarded "rapture theology" and apocalyptic politics as poorly conceptualized and thought dispensationalism besmirched their own reputation for theological rigor and consistency. Yet dispensationalism seemed to have the pulse of the culture. Ladd certainly found no solace in the explosion of apocalyptic literature, writing in disappointment in 1977 that "there has been little creative dialogue between dispensationalists and other schools of prophetic interpretation."[12] Basic errors of exegesis, he insisted, were endemic to dispensationalism and were only exacerbated by the imprecision of popular writings and the willingness of theologians—supposedly fellow scholars—to wade into popular commercial writing.

The lack of academic dialogue between dispensationalists and the wider Protestant community was starker in light of how Ladd and his fellow historic premillennialists had made strides toward enlarging scholarly and theoretical engagement in their own work. Ladd himself made his debt to contemporary German theology and the biblical theology movement well known. In *Jesus and the Kingdom* (reissued again in 1974 as *The Presence of the Future: The Eschatology of Biblical Realism*), Ladd proposed a "synthesis" of Protestant eschatology, citing favorably contemporary German theologians Werner Kümmel and Günther Bornkamm, Dutch theologian Herman Ridderbos, and American Presbyterian scholar J. Arthur Baird.[13] Ladd elevated American evangelical concerns, including the inerrancy of Scripture, but these did not quash his ability to draw from new academic and textual developments. While few Protestant theologians took much note of Ladd, Ladd's attention to them reshaped the scholarly landscape of evangelicalism.

As early as 1967, Ladd observed from his admittedly motivated vantage that "the successors to the fundamentalists of the 1920s have divided in two directions" based on engagement with wider theological discussions. Some "have shown little interest, indeed, a strengthening negative attitude toward interacting with the main stream of culture, philosophy, and theology" (e.g., dispensationalists), while others who possessed the same "theological heritage" of "older fundamentalism" were "convinced of the truthfulness of the fundamentals of the Christian faith, but . . . do not reflect the basic defensive,

12. George Eldon Ladd, "A Historic Premillennial Response," in *The Meaning of the Millennium: Four Views*, ed. Robert Clouse (Downers Grove, IL: IVP Academic, 1977), 93.
13. George Eldon Ladd, *The Presence of the Future: The Eschatology of Biblical Realism* (Grand Rapids: Eerdmans, 1974), 29–42.

apologetic stance of fundamentalism."[14] A decade later, Ladd's words rang true to many observers, and the acceptance or rejection of dispensationalism was one of the main fault lines of the division.

The historic premillennial commitment to wider academic engagement bore fruit through the growth of evangelical seminaries and colleges. Fuller Theological Seminary grew rapidly in the 1970s as it added a school of global missions and a school of psychology. On the other coast, Gordon-Conwell Theological Seminary, newly merged in 1969, became a safe place for historic premillennial scholarship. Neither Gordon-Conwell nor Fuller propounded a specific eschatological alternative, even as both effectively rid themselves of dispensational faculty by 1980. The maturation of Trinity Evangelical Divinity School in Deerfield, Illinois, was one of the more surprising shifts in the evangelical landscape. As the seminary for the Evangelical Free Church of America, a staunch dispensational denomination when founded in 1950, it began to host historic premillennial scholars in the 1960s, including Carl F. H. Henry. Elsewhere, Wheaton College, the "Harvard of evangelicalism," shed its last dispensational vestiges in the 1960s under the new leadership of Hudson Armerding (raised a Plymouth Brethren but ordained in the covenantal Presbyterian Church in America). Other evangelical institutions effectively marginalized dispensationalism in their faculty ranks, including Regent College, Bethel College (St. Paul), Westmont College, and Western Seminary (Portland), while a crop of Wesleyan schools became more open to the influence of neo-evangelicals, including Azusa Pacific College, Taylor University, and Houghton College. Like scholastic dispensationalists decades earlier, historic premillennialists, through these and other schools, created a network of scholars spanning the geographical breadth of the old Moody movement.

Dispensationalists and historic premillennialists disagreed over abstract, often minor, theological points. The substance, however, was a battle over institutional power and the intellectual direction of the broader fundamentalist and evangelical movement. While once quite hospitable to scholastic dispensational influence, the same institutions in the 1970s were slipping further from its grasp.

The rapid popularization of dispensationalism also ironically sowed the seeds for its theological decline. In the consumer-oriented culture that dominated pop dispensationalism and, increasingly, evangelicalism, values like

14. Quoted in Noll, *Between Faith and Criticism*, 121.

internal coherence and scholarly discourse—important cultural markers in fundamentalism—also declined. Creativity, accessibility, and innovation produced financial and cultural capital, and capital was what propelled books about the Bible (or the Bible itself) into American stores and compelled new and renewed faith commitments in American pews. For the popularizers of dispensationalism, the discarding of scholastic oversight and the flood of commercial success were for the best: provisions by God to spread the gospel, and through commercial success, to multiply the church's efforts. For the scholastics themselves, who tried to tap academic and mass-market interests alike, their inability to perpetuate a strong intellectual defense of dispensationalism, nor to outperform the popularizers, spelled a worrying future.

Dispensationalism after Fundamentalism

The split attention of scholastic dispensationalism was a disaster for the movement, and was compounded by its shrinking credibility and slowness to extend its training to new constituencies. It was not until 1966 that Dallas Seminary accepted its first Black student. A few years later, with still only a handful of Black students on campus, one of them asked John Walvoord, the president, why there was not more concerted effort at recruiting eager Black would-be seminarians. That student was Tony Evans, who would become the seminary's first Black PhD recipient and a nationally known pastor and author. Writing years later, Evans recalled Walvoord responding, "Tony, I'm not a fighter. I kind of go with the law—the protocol." Into the 1970s, the institutional leadership of scholastic dispensationalism writ large displayed the same lack of vision and imagination, perpetuating, in Evans's words, "a culture of self-segregation without the overt rejection" that concretized the limited appeal of dispensationalism beyond white circles.[15]

Like the mass-market logic that circumvented scholastic gatekeeping, the decline of authority among the gatekeepers themselves paved the way for an entirely new relationship between dispensationalism and American culture. A rising movement of Christian political activism and a new strain of nationalism—gathering steam in the 1970s and bursting forth in the New Christian Right at the end of the decade—was, like the commercial popularizers, animated not by strict theological purity but by galvanized interests in society,

15. Tony Evans, *Oneness Embraced: A Kingdom Race Theology for Reconciliation, Unity, and Justice* (Chicago: Moody Publishers, 2022), 298.

politics, and culture. Pop dispensationalism's emphasis on eschatology gave it special cachet in both commercial and political spaces. Meanwhile, the external and internal blows to the scholastic project left dispensationalism-as-a-theological-system in tatters.

Back in the 1920s, new premillennialism had helped to fuel fundamentalist organizing before it was blamed for the movement's setbacks. Philip Mauro's coining of the term "dispensationalism" in 1927 was a response to this arc of defeat. In the 1970s, a new round of scrutiny began to focus on dispensationalism, this time in anticipation of, rather than in reaction to, fundamentalist agitation. Ernest Sandeen's pathbreaking history *The Roots of Fundamentalism* (1970) began with the disclaimer that he was not writing an "obituary" of fundamentalism but that the movement "has manifested an unexpected vitality and appeal." He placed dispensationalism at the center of fundamentalist identity, defining the entire movement "partly if not largely as one aspect of the history of millenarianism."[16] Sandeen's argument would be challenged by historians later in the decade, but *The Roots of Fundamentalism* laid the groundwork for enduring scholarly and popular interpretations of the movement that centered on dispensationalism. Sandeen prioritized theology, working against previous interpreters set on "removing theological and religious variables from the analysis of controversy."[17] The result was renewed academic and journalistic focus on keywords like "dispensationalism" that ironically reinforced the centrality of dispensationalism to fundamentalism at the very moment its influence was waning.

Sandeen's magnum opus left one more legacy. In placing "fundamentalism in the context of the millenarian tradition," he collapsed the distinctions between old and new premillennialists. In many ways, he collapsed the distinctions between all fundamentalists and evangelicals, offering that fundamentalism succeeded because of an alliance of its various factions. The lumping served Sandeen's higher purpose to depict fundamentalism as a "self-conscious, structured, long-lived dynamic entity," but in this version premillennialism was a largely static theology after being imported from the British Isles in the 1860s. Its existence served his history of fundamentalism but was hardly a "dynamic entity" itself. Most historians followed Sandeen's lead. Viewed from the vantage of the history of dispensationalism, however, the line of significance was reverse: fundamentalism became an influential

16. Ernest Robert Sandeen, *The Roots of Fundamentalism: British and American Millenarianism, 1800–1930* (Chicago: University of Chicago Press, 1970), xix.

17. Sandeen, *The Roots of Fundamentalism*, x.

subplot to the story of dispensationalism, one that both spurred its creation as a system and was leading to its demise.

Sandeen's history ended in 1930, so he could be forgiven for thinking less about the subsequent generation of fundamentalists who shaped dispensationalism into a scholastic tradition. Yet his book's influence was felt precisely when the fate of midcentury dispensationalism was coming into view. Dispensational theology was in free fall, even as pop dispensationalism was conquering American culture.

Oh Lord, my God
When I, in awesome wonder
Consider all the worlds Thy hands have made
I see the stars, I hear the rolling thunder
Thy power throughout the universe displayed

And when I think that God, His Son not sparing
Sent Him to die, I scarce can take it in
That on the cross, my burden gladly bearing
He bled and died to take away my sin

When Christ shall come, with shout of acclamation
And take me home, what joy shall fill my heart
Then I shall bow, in humble adoration
And then proclaim, my God, how great Thou art

Stuart Hine, "How Great Thou Art" (1949)

The first verses of "How Great Thou Art" were inspired by Swedish poet and parliamentarian Carl Gustav Boberg, who wrote the words "O Store Gud" in 1885 or 1886. Later, in 1934, a Russian version of Boberg's song came to the attention of British Methodist missionary Stuart K. Hine, then in western Ukraine, who wrote the first verses as they are known today. When the Second World War broke out, Hine returned to Great Britain, eventually ministering to eastern European refugees who inspired a final verse, depicting a second coming that will "take me home." At Billy Graham's 1954 crusade in London, Exclusive Brethren publisher Andrew Gray (of Pickering & Inglis) handed crusade musician George Beverly Shea the "new hymn." Introduced the following year at Graham's revivals in Canada, "How Great Thou Art" became one of the most popular hymns in North America.

16

The "Humanist Tribulation"

Hal Lindsey was no one-hit wonder. While he would never repeat the sales success of *Late Great Planet Earth*, which reached fifteen million copies by 1982, he produced a string of follow-up best sellers. *The 1980s: Countdown to Armageddon* (1980) was a direct sequel, of sorts, to his original breakout hit. Celebrating the "new prophetic phenomenon," Lindsey wrote, ten years later, "I now sense an urgent, even desperate compulsion to bring readers up to date."[1] And the readers responded. *The 1980s* sold 360,000 copies in nine weeks and charted on the New York Times Best Seller list for a total of twenty weeks.

Near the end of *Late Great Planet Earth*, Lindsey had addressed the question, "Where do we go from here?" His answer focused on personal piety: convert, live for God, trust in Christ, and evangelize. Lindsey's final directive was: "plan our lives as though we will be here our whole life expectancy, but live as though Christ may come today."[2] Rarely did Lindsey connect his readers' personal obligations to the geopolitical realm in which he spent most of the book.

The 1980s broke with Lindsey's previous advice in this crucial respect. Now he posed a different question: "What about the U.S.?"[3] The leading nation in the Western world was absent from biblical prophecy, which could mean one of a few possibilities. Communists could take over or destroy the United

1. Hal Lindsey, *The 1980s: Countdown to Armageddon* (New York: Bantam Books, 1980), 7.

2. Hal Lindsey and Carole C. Carlson, *The Late Great Planet Earth* (Grand Rapids: Zondervan, 1970), 174, 176.

3. Lindsey, *The 1980s*, 129.

States, rendering the nation prophetically obsolete. Or economic stagnation could thrust the United States into second-class-nation status, possibly as a vassal of the antichrist's ten-nation confederacy.

In the face of these grim scenarios, one other option remained. "If some critical and difficult choices are made by the American people right now, it is possible to see the U.S. remain a world power."[4] Lindsey elided exactly how the United States remaining a world power could escape prophetic mention, or how reversing American decline would affect dispensational time. These details were not his concern. Instead, he gave the same directive to his readers that he had in 1970: "We should plan our lives as though we will live them out fully. But we should live each day with the idea: 'Jesus could come today.'" Ten years later, however, these words meant something different, that "we must actively take on the responsibility of being a citizen and a member of God's family." Lindsey now urged his readers to elect a new breed of politicians who "will not only reflect the Bible's morality in government but will shape domestic and foreign policies to protect our country and our way of life." More precisely, they will "clamp down on big government, cut exploitation of the welfare system, keep our strong commitments to our allies and stand up to communist expansion"—an agenda that aligned closely to the platform advanced by the Republican Party and the live presidential campaign of Ronald Reagan.[5]

The implications of Lindsey's analysis mirrored a wider pop-dispensational synthesis with Christian nationalism that saw the United States as a decisive actor in the prophetic timeline. The centrality of the United States to God's purposes was a basic Christian nationalist conceit that was centuries old, but in the 1970s it was newly fused with dispensational eschatology that had up to this point been allergic to making prophecy fulfillment conditional on Republican partisan politics. In many ways pop dispensationalists were indistinguishable from other conservative Christians, but in this sense they were instrumental for creating nationalist cooperation across fundamentalist factions for the first time since the 1920s.

The New Christian Right, as the organized expression of fundamentalist politics was named, gained followers by interpreting liberalizing cultural trends as consequences of the familiar force of theological modernism, and a more recently identified antagonist of "secular humanism." Major Supreme Court cases and cultural controversies that fundamentalists interpreted as advancing a secularizing agenda spurred them into the public square in a mass

4. Lindsey, *The 1980s*, 132.
5. Lindsey, *The 1980s*, 157.

EXHIBIT VIII
PROPHETIC OUTLINE OF HISTORY

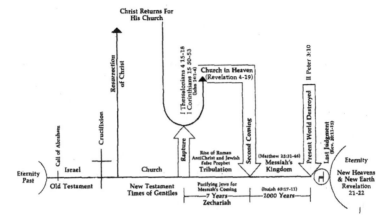

Figure 22. Hal Lindsey's "Prophetic Outline of History." Lindsey's diagram from *The 1980s: Countdown to Armageddon* bore more than a passing resemblance to the original Brethren version of the 1850s. But Lindsey also changed subtle things. He drew an unbroken line for linear time, a sign that the sharp disjuncture of dispensational time was of less interest to him than the sequence of prophesied events. He instead added numerous details, most related to the period between the rapture and the second coming, which was the center of interest in all of Lindsey's pop-dispensational writing.

organized fashion for the first time in a generation. Social changes in gender roles, race relations, and public schooling helped coalesce disparate regional and local concerns into a national cause: legal and foreign policy developments—and many in between—were seen as part of a larger anti-Christian agenda. The United States, in the New Christian Right social critique, was perilously close to becoming a nation that harmed rather than helped the church's primary purpose to spread the gospel.

But this reactive posture was only half the story. The simultaneous rise of pop dispensationalism as a consumer juggernaut, and the rupture of fundamentalist theology, restructured the relationship between fundamentalism and politics in the same years as the rise of the New Christian Right. Across the fractured theological landscape, fundamentalist and evangelical leaders spent the late 1970s and 1980s embracing "cobelligerency" that prioritized common cause in politics over theological competition. While nationalist fundamentalists led the way in promoting cobelligerency in the 1920s, it was now a much broader mix of leaders from a variety of subcultures that encouraged cobelligerency. Because of its cultural resonance among rank-and-file church members, pop dispensationalism became one of the shared theological reference points in this New Christian Right.

Tim LaHaye and the "Humanist Tribulation"

Hal Lindsey may have been the face of pop dispensationalism, but Tim LaHaye was its brain. "In Mainline Catholic and Protestant churches, you will never meet anyone who has heard of Tim LaHaye," historian Martin Marty observed in 1983. "In conservative Protestant churches, you will seldom meet anyone who has not heard of him."[6] A pastor-turned-political activist, LaHaye was a ubiquitous figure in the New Christian Right and did as much as any other single individual to channel fundamentalist Christians into organized conservative politics. LaHaye's output both in print and behind the scenes helped establish the New Christian Right in the late 1970s, shaping the direction of pop-dispensational influence from that of mass consumption toward the bedrock of a mobilized political movement.

LaHaye was well suited to the task. He was a lifelong fundamentalist and dispensationalist. Whereas Lindsey made the turn to politics in the 1970s, LaHaye, who was just three years older and born in 1926, was a veteran member of the John Birch Society, a nationwide anticommunist advocacy group that trafficked in conspiracy theories, racism, and antisemitism. Funded in part by fundamentalist J. Frank Norris, the organization was named after John Birch, a young American missionary who was killed by Chinese communists in 1945. The society took special hold in LaHaye's home region of Southern California, among its growing population of white conservatives. In the 1970s, LaHaye helped create several conservative political action groups influenced by Bircher ideas, including the Moral Majority and Religious Roundtable, both founded in 1979 to organize conservative Christians as a political force within the Republican Party.

His religious trajectory mirrored his political trajectory, embodying the "hand in hand" philosophy in dispensational thinking. Born in Detroit, LaHaye embraced the teaching of the rapture at age nine, when his father died. The funeral preacher promised, "This is not the end of Frank LaHaye; because he accepted Jesus, the day will come when the Lord will shout from heaven and descend, and the dead in Christ will rise first and then we'll be caught up together to meet him in the air."[7] LaHaye attended Bob Jones University, where,

---

6. Martin Marty, "The Humanist Conspiracy," *Christian Century*, January 26, 1983, 79.

7. Quoted in Jane Lampman, "The End of the World," *Christian Science Monitor*, February 18, 2004, https://www.csmonitor.com/2004/0218/p11s01-lire.html.

after serving in World War II, he graduated in 1950. He then attended Western Seminary in Portland, Oregon, and studied dispensational theology. He landed in the outskirts of San Diego, at a small Southern Baptist congregation that grew under his care into a multisite megachurch. From this base he created an array of organizations and media ventures advancing dispensational eschatology, biblical literalism, and political conservatism. In 1971, he founded his own school, Christian Heritage College, and in 1972 he invited young-earth creationist Henry M. Morris to establish the Institute for Creation Research.

LaHaye's earliest writings on prophecy copied unabashedly from Hal Lindsey's style. In *The Beginning of the End* (1972), LaHaye hewed to pop-dispensational themes and analysis of current events. So impressed was La-Haye with *Late Great Planet Earth* that he obtained permission from Lindsey to copy the chapter on "Russia and the Mideast" into his own book verbatim.[8] To the extent that LaHaye diverged from the pop-dispensational formula in this early work, it was introducing readers to a taste of scholastic style, such as Biola College professor David L. Cooper's "Golden Rule of Interpretation" that emphasized the "plain sense" and "common sense" interpretation of Scripture.[9] Lindsey's writings eschewed even this brief exposure of hermeneutics, but LaHaye was eager to share at least some of the fruits of the scholastic tradition.

LaHaye would eventually publish more than a dozen nonfiction books on dispensational eschatology. Collectively they displayed his ability to bridge pop- and scholastic-dispensational discourses and attach them to a robust conservative politics that emphasized anticommunism and a family values agenda. Others with LaHaye's pastor-theologian-organizer profile began to bridge the dispensational scholastic-popular divide in the 1970s, including Ed Hindson, coorganizer of the Moral Majority and longtime professor at Liberty University; Gary G. Cohen, a close collaborator with pop dispensationalist Salem Kirban; and Rick Yohn, a Dallas- and Talbot-trained pastor and frequent tour guide to Israel, among others. The split taking place in fundamentalist theology created room for mixing new cultural and political arguments that remained part of conservative evangelicalism for decades.

With a deepening concern for the fate of American society, LaHaye introduced a major conceptual innovation that would shape the thinking of the New Christian Right: the humanist tribulation. The concept appeared in LaHaye's *The Battle for the Mind* (1980), a book that situated two diametrically opposed

8. Tim LaHaye, *The Beginning of the End* (Wheaton, IL: Tyndale House, 1972), 63.
9. LaHaye, *Beginning of the End*, dedication page.

worldviews to "determine morals, values, life-style, and activities of mankind." One worldview was "secular humanism," a pervasive philosophy in LaHaye's judgment that, at its most basic level, "attempts to solve the problems of man and the world independently of God." LaHaye argued that in recent decades a conspiracy of humanists, though numbering but "a few thousand," had systematically taken over America and its key institutions of education, media, and government.[10] The same theme of consolidation that animated new premillennial writings in the early twentieth century reappeared in new form. The alternative worldview was "biblical truth," which also had a long pedigree through the Hebrew Bible, Christian church, and fundamentalist movement.[11]

The "humanist tribulation" was LaHaye's term to describe an approaching tribulation *before* the rapture that would pit humanism and Christianity in an existential struggle. Alternately, he called this prerapture period the "pretribulation tribulation." By employing traditional eschatological language, he suggested a significant alteration in traditional dispensational theology that hinged on an "any-moment" rapture. LaHaye's own warning was that "the pre-Tribulation tribulation—that is, the tribulation that will engulf this country if liberal humanists are permitted to take total control of the government—is neither predestined nor necessary."[12] LaHaye taught that it was up to the faithful to stave off this outcome. "It will deluge the entire land for the next few years, unless Christians are willing to become much more assertive in defense of morality and decency than they have been during the last three decades."[13] LaHaye's antihumanist manifesto called for rapid mobilization and a purging of all elite political and cultural institutions.

Other leaders in the New Christian Right voiced the same conceptual shift. While they professed the imminence of the rapture, in practice, and as the reason for mobilizing politically, they anticipated the humanist tribulation. Jerry Falwell, who was familiar with both Lindsey and LaHaye and was an Independent Baptist, founded and led the most important New Christian Right advocacy organization, the Moral Majority. He also admonished Christians to embrace their role in the in-between times: "Between now and the rapture of the Church, America can have a reprieve. God can bless the country and before the rapture I believe we can stay a free nation."[14] For virtually every

10. Tim LaHaye, *The Battle for the Mind* (Old Tappan, NJ: Revell, 1980), 147.

11. LaHaye, *Battle for the Mind*, 9.

12. LaHaye, *Battle for the Mind*, 217–18.

13. Quoted in Susan Harding, *The Book of Jerry Falwell: Fundamentalist Language and Politics* (Princeton: Princeton University Press, 2001), 242.

14. Harding, *Book of Jerry Falwell*, 244.

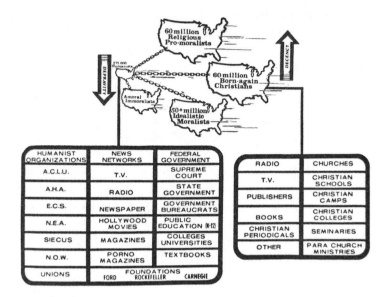

Figure 23. Tim LaHaye, diagram from *The Battle for the Mind*. LaHaye's depiction of the warring forces of "depravity" and "decency" informed the conservative culture-war framework, which he usually presented in his books in the context of dispensational time, and especially his innovation of the humanist tribulation that called on Christians to rally to the cause of global missions, via securing the political rights of churches and religious organizations, in anticipation of the rapture.

dispensationalist who embraced political mobilization in the 1970s—and especially for those like Falwell with a previous record of denouncing politics as a worldly distraction—the innovation of the humanist tribulation became a frequently invoked theological context for action.

LaHaye and Falwell stated that their goal for encouraging political mobilization was to "evangelize the world in our generation," in Falwell's words, or what LaHaye called the "great soul harvest."[15] The aims of global missions harkened back to new premillennialism a century earlier. But this was not just nostalgia. The centrality of global evangelization to New Christian Right rhetoric disclosed the basic logic of the movement. The humanist tribulation helped to clarify why in this historical moment a robust political program was required. By interpreting cultural trends not merely as signs of the end times but as obstructions to the fulfillment of the church's evangelistic mission, pop dispensationalists pioneered a version of Christian nationalism that evaluated

15. LaHaye, *Battle for the Mind*, 219.

the exceptional status of the United States in relation to the extent the country empowered the dispensational purposes of the church.

This argument, embedded in a Christian nationalism that also advanced a particular set of family values issues, was visible in Lindsey's *The 1980s*, where he listed "four reasons" why "the U.S. has been preserved as a free country."[16] They included (1) the large number of Christians among its citizenry, (2) their constant prayers for the nation, (3) American philanthropy for global missions, and (4) US support for Jews and Israel. Falwell simplified the reasons to two: "God has raised up America in these last days for the cause of world evangelization and the protection of his people, the Jews. I don't think America has any other right or reason for existence other than those two purposes."[17] For Lindsey and Falwell, the purpose of the United States was intimately bound to dispensational categories. These priorities shaped many New Christian Right efforts to obtain legal protections for Christians in the United States, religious freedom abroad, and support for Israel.

LaHaye outlined the same priorities in *The Battle for the Mind*. Late in the book he admitted that his fixation on the "religion of humanism" might prompt readers to question his "real motivation." LaHaye was "patriotic," he clarified; but he went on, "that is not my primary concern. You must understand; I am first and foremost a committed Christian." He was called to preach the gospel to every person. "That is my number-one priority," he said. In his travels La-Haye became convinced that most resources for global evangelization were sourced by the United States. He put the number at "80 to 85 percent" and listed "missionaries, technology for preaching the Gospel, and money for world missions" as the United States' key contributions. Without a free America, the entire church's mission was in peril. "If atheistic, amoral, one-world humanists succeed in enslaving our country, that missionary outlet will eventually be terminated."[18] The conditional "if" in this sentence revealed how the humanist tribulation had redramatized dispensational eschatology: from a mix of cosmic fate and individual hope to one of national fate and collective agency.

Schaeffer, Falwell, and Robertson at the "Integration Point"

The humanist tribulation was a pop-dispensational construct, but it offered a pattern for political mobilization that was intended to appeal to more people

---

16. Lindsey, *The 1980s*, 157–58.

17. "An Interview with the Lone Ranger of American Fundamentalism," *Christianity Today*, September 4, 1981, 25.

18. LaHaye, *Battle for the Mind*, 222–23.

than just dispensationalists. The wider adoption of the humanist tribulation among New Christian Right activists—ranging across the fundamentalist spectrum, from Francis Schaeffer to Pat Robertson—showed how pop dispensationalism had yet again spread beyond the dispensational faithful to inform a broader cultural and political milieu, in this case the New Christian Right.

LaHaye dedicated *Battle for the Mind* (1980) to fellow fundamentalist Francis Schaeffer, who, before gaining political notoriety in the United States, was famous for using a Reformed theological approach to engage with modern art, film, and literature as a method to understand the humanist worldview.[19] Schaeffer was perhaps the most widely cited New Christian Right thinker up to his death in 1984, especially in connecting "secular humanism" to a "culture of death" that promoted abortion, infanticide, and, he predicted, eventually euthanasia.[20] LaHaye had enlisted scholastic authority into his pop-dispensational political activism, and Schaeffer had accomplished a similar task among his own Reformed circles. The two were performing mirror works in different fundamentalist factions.

While LaHaye and Schaeffer agreed on the threat of humanism, Schaeffer rejected the teaching of dispensational time and regarded eschatological speculation of any kind as a distraction. Schaeffer studied at Faith Theological Seminary, the Reformed premillennial offshoot of Westminster Theological Seminary. Like his onetime mentor, Carl McIntire, he held to a covenantalist "unity of Scripture" that regarded the church as the vehicle for the kingdom of God, a sharp distinction from dispensationalism's insistence that the kingdom awaited the second coming.

Never especially interested in end-times doctrines, Schaeffer spoke infrequently about eschatology. Instead, he warned others against doing so. In 1972, at the same moment of *Late Great Planet Earth*'s sales explosion, he raised the alarm that "for many of the youth, prophecy, rather than being part of the larger whole of theology, has become the integration point of whatever theology they have."[21] This was an insightful (and dismissive) description of the pop-dispensational moment, which had so narrowly concentrated on near-future end-times speculation that it had become the "integration point" of the system of dispensational theology.

When it came to his rhetoric, though, Schaeffer would traffic in the humanist tribulation concept under a different guise. His pessimistic assessments of

19. LaHaye, *Battle for the Mind*, dedication page.
20. Francis A. Schaeffer and C. Everett Koop, *Whatever Happened to the Human Race? Exposing Our Rapid Yet Subtle Loss of Human Rights* (Old Tappan, NJ: Revell, 1979).
21. Francis Schaeffer, *The New Super Spirituality* (London: Hodder & Stoughton, 1973), 36.

American culture became a major source of urgency for the New Christian Right. In *A Christian Manifesto* (1981), Schaeffer's most strident call for Christians to employ every means at their disposal to turn back the tide of secular humanism, he wrote of a "unique window" of opportunity that was opened by the election of Ronald Reagan in 1980. "It is our task to use the open window to try to change that direction [toward humanism] at this very late hour," he warned.[22] The "unique window" bore more than a passing resemblance to LaHaye's "next few years" and Falwell's resolution to mobilize Christians "between now and the rapture of the Church." The thinking that animated all three was imprinted with the pop-dispensational pattern of the humanist tribulation: growing anti-Christian forces and an awakening that would strengthen America before the onslaught of the tribulation.

Schaeffer on the one hand, and LaHaye and Falwell on the other hand, represented two theologically distinct wings of the New Christian Right, two fundamentalist factions that had defined themselves in opposition to each other on theological terms and now wanted to bridge the gap by being "cobelligerents" (Schaeffer's term) in political activism.[23] The promise of victory compelled the competing factions to get along. The language and framing they settled on ensured that pop dispensationalism would be a permanent organizing principle of the New Christian Right. It would help gloss over, rather than deepen, the fault lines that had riven fundamentalism for the last half century.[24]

The centrality of pop dispensationalism to the New Christian Right was secured at a momentous 1982 meeting of fundamentalist and evangelical leaders. Representatives from across the spectrum of fundamentalism and evangelicalism were present, including Schaeffer and Falwell. The luncheon at Carl F. H. Henry's house in Washington, DC, also included a handful of other power players: fundamentalists in the Moral Majority, neo-evangelicals from the National Association of Evangelicals and *Christianity Today*, and theologians including John F. Walvoord of Dallas Seminary and Hudson Armerding of Wheaton College. The guest list, in other words, reflected the spectrum of scholastic rivalry dating to the 1930s.

At the luncheon, both Falwell and Schaeffer articulated the need to look past theological divisions and the history of infighting. Each invoked familial

22. Francis Schaeffer, *A Christian Manifesto*, rev. ed. (Westchester, IL: Crossway, 1982), 75.

23. Francis Schaeffer, *The Church at the End of the Twentieth Century* (Downers Grove, IL: InterVarsity Press, 1970), 36.

24. Quoted in Mel White, *Religion Gone Bad: The Hidden Dangers of the Christian Right* (New York: Penguin, 2006), 11.

language, with Falwell calling evangelicals his "brothers" and expecting that as they worked together politically, "healing" would occur and "the differences between them would disappear." Schaeffer, delivering a thinly veiled threat to the other attendees, explained, "If someone attacks my brother, he attacks me." Schaeffer urged a cease-fire to intrafundamentalist fighting, and his approach worked. All in attendance agreed to "be responsible to defend each other." The evangelicals in the room promised "to present Falwell fairly and favorably."[25] In effect, the summit solidified Falwell's pop-dispensational-infused politics at the top of the New Christian Right.

Of course, many factions were absent at Henry's summit, most conspicuous of which were Pentecostals or charismatics who practiced the gifts of the Spirit. Numerically, these Christians swamped the neo-evangelicals and fundamentalists, who were improbably claiming to speak for a majority of Americans. From Aimee Semple McPherson in the 1920s to the revivalist Pentecostals of the postwar period, premillennialism was one shared theological commitment between Pentecostals and fundamentalists. The doctrinal statements of the International Church of the Foursquare Gospel and the Assemblies of God, the two largest white Pentecostal denominations in the United States, taught of the "blessed hope" of the rapture and regathering (and conversion to Christianity) of "national Israel," but otherwise remained uncommitted to dispensational distinctives.[26] For their part, dispensationalists followed the lead of Lewis Sperry Chafer and distanced themselves from Pentecostals, insisting that speaking in tongues, among other spiritual gifts, had ceased in the early church and would only be revived in the millennial kingdom.

The border between fundamentalists and Pentecostals began to blur, however, with the rise of pop dispensationalism. Marion Gordon "Pat" Robertson was an unlikely example of this trend. A Southern-Baptist-turned-independent charismatic and, beginning in 1966, host of the television show *The 700 Club*, Robertson's religious influences were many, inscrutably so. He synthesized Southern Baptist, Pentecostal, and fundamentalist religious backgrounds with his upbringing as the son of a longtime US senator from Virginia. His father's prominence afforded Robertson an elite education at Washington and Lee University and Yale University. After passing the New York bar in 1955, Robertson had a conversion experience and attended the Biblical Seminary in New

25. Quoted in Neil J. Young, *We Gather Together: The Religious Right and the Problem of Interfaith Politics* (New York: Oxford University Press, 2015), 181–82.

26. "Assemblies of God 16 Fundamental Truths," Assemblies of God, accessed May 19, 2022, https://ag.org/beliefs/statement-of-fundamental-truths.

York, a small school founded in 1900 by Moody movement premillennialist Wilbur Webster White. This all formed a highly individualized faith for Robertson. His eschatological teachings and frequent predictions for the future, which were expressed through his expanding media empire, were equally difficult to define. He would at various times be labeled a premillennialist or a postmillennialist, a dispensationalist or a "Dominionist" arguing for the political reconstruction of the United States on the basis of biblical laws and values. Moreover, Robertson's penchant for conspiracy theories drew to him labels ranging from anti-Mason to antisemite.

By the mid-1970s, Robertson had come to the same conclusions as so many other future New Christian Right activists: not only was the world on the precipice of the second coming, but American society was in steep decline. Robertson rejected the imminent rapture, in large part because he rejected the idea of fixed prophetic events. He, too, integrated the pattern of the humanist tribulation, hinging future outcomes on a combination of human and divine agency. "Not everything in the future is fixed," he wrote in 1981. More precisely, he anticipated a near future of struggle and an awakening, a last chance for the world before God's final judgment was unleashed. "The World is going to see heartache," he predicted in 1983, "but God's people are going to see tremendous blessing, tremendous anointing, tremendous outpouring of the Spirit, tremendous evangelism."[27]

Robertson pinpointed Christian political agency as the bulwark to this impending tribulation. "The principles of the Kingdom of God can change the world. These principles are so revolutionary that they can change government, education, and social life."[28] Like LaHaye and Falwell, Robertson, too, looked for a revival before the end began—a "brief period of grace" that would usher in "the greatest worldwide spiritual revival ever seen in history."[29] In these statements, Robertson could sound almost like someone calling on Christians to usher in God's kingdom through political reform. Observers called this Robertson's "pragmatism and innate optimism" that made him a "somewhat unorthodox dispensationalist."[30] But his views did not diverge far from other New Christian Right leaders. He could just as easily be defined as a pop dispensationalist, prioritizing human and divine agency to reverse, for a time, the inroads of secular humanism. Robertson dismissed the any-moment rapture, but, in

---

27. Quoted in David Edwin Harrell Jr., *Pat Robertson: A Personal, Religious, and Political Portrait* (New York: Harper & Row, 1987), 147–48.

28. Harrell, *Pat Robertson*, 149.

29. Harrell, *Pat Robertson*, 147.

30. Harrell, *Pat Robertson*, 149, 148.

practice, so too had the pop dispensationalists who were mobilizing in the short term to resist the humanist tribulation. In the case of Robertson, like that of Falwell, Lindsey, LaHaye, and Schaeffer, the same message, the same "integration point," was conveyed by the leadership of the New Christian Right: Christian political mobilization needed to preserve the special role of the United States in empowering the church to fulfill its mission, so long as God tarried.

What political positions did the "integration point" of pop dispensationalism influence in the New Christian Right? In many ways, the movement was subsumed under the Republican Party and advocated views on taxes, economics, and foreign policy not much different than other conservatives. In some cases, including those of Tim LaHaye and Jerry Falwell, New Christian Right leaders actively resisted the civil rights movement and later measures of desegregation.

There were other political issues uniquely appealing to the pop-dispensationalist faction within the New Christian Right. Domestically, pop dispensationalism fueled a robust expansion of the homeschool movement, of the "textbook wars" in public schools, and a new wave of pro-life advocacy centered on overturning *Roe v. Wade*. In foreign policy, support for the State of Israel—coupled with hopes for Israeli annexation of occupied territories after the June 1967 War—was fueled in part by, and often expressed through the rhetoric of, the language of pop dispensationalism. Christian Zionist organizing and cooperation with the Israeli government confounded the diplomatic establishment of both major political parties. Interweaving the mix of moral and policy appeals on each of these issues was the context of tribulation—prophesied but also contingent on the actions of the church.

More importantly than any particular policy position, pop dispensationalism made sense of the opposition through a conspiratorial framing that connected them all. In *The Battle for Public Schools* (1983), LaHaye presented the mature details of the big conspiracy he had first introduced in *The Battle for the Mind*. An elite network of conspirators were advancing secular humanism and included "the Illuminati, Bilderbergers, Council on Foreign Relations, and more recently, the Trilateral Commission. These are only some of the suggested groups." Their goal: "to reduce the standard of living in our country so that someday the citizens of America will voluntarily merge with the Soviet Union."[31] Everything from Cold War diplomacy to public education to entertainment media was implicated in the conspiracy, either as agent or victim of corruption.

LaHaye introduced the players, the issues, and the stakes of the conspiracy, but he did not confirm its veracity. "Personally, I do not know if the conspiracy theory has any validity," he wrote. "I am not saying that all educrats are part of

31. Tim LaHaye, *The Battle for Public Schools* (Old Tappan, NJ: Revell, 1983), 46–48.

a gigantic conspiracy. I don't even know if there is one. But if a few humanist educrats . . . were part of a conspiracy, it would certainly explain a number of things."[32] The urgency of the humanist tribulation made LaHaye predisposed to see the conspiracy as more likely than not, supplying more cosmic meaning to the mobilization of Christian voters. All told, pop dispensationalism was integral to instantiating the New Christian Right and framing its politics in line with apocalyptic thinking.

Whose Apocalypse?

In the spring of 1984, in the heat of the presidential campaign between Ronald Reagan and Walter Mondale, a burst of media attention focused on the question of Reagan's end-times beliefs. "On at least five occasions in the last four years," a reporter for the *Washington Post* summarized, "Ronald Reagan has referred to his belief that Armageddon may well occur during the present generation and could come in the Middle East."[33] A documentary released weeks before the election, titled "Ronald Reagan and the Prophecy of Armageddon," raised the count to eleven.[34] The not-so-subtle intimation of this reporting spun another portentous scenario: Reagan's own apocalyptic fervor just might trigger a real nuclear apocalypse. The specter of "nuclear dispensationalism" became a widespread media concern in the mid-1980s, with its chief purveyors including LaHaye, Falwell, and Robertson.[35]

One entry into this genre of apocalyptic reporting meticulously reconstructed Reagan's religious background to document his dispensational influences. The writer, Grace Halsell, evaluated which of Reagan's family and friends might have been predisposed to the theology: his mother was a devout member of the Disciples of Christ and listened to religious radio; the evangelist George Otis and the singer Pat Boone both prayed with Reagan in 1970; Billy Graham and Reagan discussed *Late Great Planet Earth* at a dinner the following year. "There was evidence in 1971," Halsell concluded, "to indicate that Reagan, at least in that year, was a dispensationalist or a believer in the

32. LaHaye, *Battle for Public Schools*, 48.

33. Ronnie Dugger, "Does Reagan Expect a Nuclear Armageddon?" *Washington Post*, April 8, 1984, C4.

34. See John Herbers, "Religious Leaders Tell of Worry on Armageddon View Ascribed to Reagan," *New York Times*, October 21, 1984, 32.

35. Larry Jones, "Apocalyptic Eschatology in the Nuclear Arms Race," *Transformation* 5, no. 1 (1988): 25.

cult of Israel and the ideology of Armageddon."[36] Representing "Christian extremists," Reagan and his followers, she warned, "are obsessed with their own belief system, their own ideology, their own certitude that they have both the right and the power to help orchestrate not only their own End of Times, but doomsday for the rest of the species."[37] Though using different vocabulary, Halsell had identified how pop dispensationalism, in her estimation, had become lodged in the mind of the most important political officeholder in the country.

The accuracy of this portrayal of Reagan is less important than how Halsell's exposé of "Armageddon theology" copied the structure of pop-dispensational discourse, revealing how it had seeped into other parts of culture and politics. While LaHaye and Falwell spoke frequently about nuclear war as the consequence of failing to resist the Democratic-led humanist tribulation, Halsell had constructed her own scenario of world destruction that centered on the unique role of American partisan politics. She offered her own dark prophecies of a fundamentalist tribulation, and her own solution that amounted to political mobilization against the New Christian Right.[38] She exposed her readers, many of whom had likely never heard a sermon by Jerry Falwell, to the terms and style of pop-dispensational politics.

And she bestowed immense explanatory power to the style, citing it to explain the thinking of the president of the United States and the nation's nuclear policy. The scenario, true or false, validated her underlying assumptions. The same pop-dispensational logic also leaked into vast wells of American religious and popular culture in the 1980s.

36. Grace Halsell, *Prophecy and Politics: Militant Evangelists on the Road to Nuclear War* (Westport, CT: Lawrence Hill, 1986), 44.
37. Halsell, *Prophecy and Politics*, 200.
38. Jonathan Schell, *The Fate of the Earth* (New York: Knopf, 1982), 5.

Amazing grace, how sweet the sound
That saved a wretch like me
I once was lost, but now am found
Was blind, but now I see.

The earth shall soon dissolve like snow
The sun forbear to shine
But God, who called me here below
Will be forever mine.

When we've been there ten thousand years,
Bright shining as the sun
We've no less days to sing God's praise
Than when we'd first begun.

John Newton, "Amazing Grace" (1779)

Probably the most famous hymn in the English language, "Amazing Grace" originally began and ended with the first two verses above, respectively. The second verse was soon replaced with the more familiar "ten thousand years" verse, but versions varied, and still do. The imagery of the earth dissolving and the implicit dualism of calling believers from below into God's presence are themes resonant with dispensationalism, and reveal one set of issues that divided dispensationalists from other evangelicals, including other premillennialists, in the second half of the twentieth century: namely, was the "blessed hope" one of escape from a dying world, or was heaven coming to earth? (This analysis is indebted to J. Richard Middleton, *A New Heaven and a New Earth: Reclaiming Biblical Eschatology* [Grand Rapids: Baker Academic, 2014], 27–30.)

17

Saturation and Its Limits

The summer of 1988 was abuzz with talk of the rapture. An unknown writer, Edgar C. Whisenant, of Little Rock, Arkansas, had gone viral with a pamphlet titled *88 Reasons Why the Rapture Will Happen in 1988*. Over the first half of the year, more than 300,000 copies were mailed to pastors and more than four million copies were sold across the country. The upshot of Whisenant's argument was clear enough: the rapture would occur on the Jewish holiday of Rosh Hashanah, between September 11 and September 13, 1988. "Matt. 24:36 states that 'No one knows about that day or hour, not even the angels in heaven, nor the Son, but only the Father,'" Whisenant admitted, before adding, "this does not preclude or prevent the faithful from knowing the year, the month, and the week of the Lord's return."[1]

A NASA engineer-turned-prophecy expert, Whisenant diverged from any textbook definition of dispensationalism, even as he was unmistakably part of its legacy. His pamphlets included references to the early century prophecy chart designer Clarence Larkin and the *Scofield Reference Bible*, but Whisenant cited no living dispensational scholars and had no affiliations with dispensational institutions. The eighty-eight reasons he gave ranged from the familiar to the incredible. The bulk of Whisenant's arguments were based on intricate numerology. Reason 78, for example, explained that "From 28 A.D., when Jesus revealed Himself to the Apostles as the Son of God (John 5:10–38), we have 28 A.D. + (7 × 280) = 1988, the Rapture of the Church year." The math was straightforward in Whisenant's telling: "Seven means complete, and 280

---

1. Edgar Whisenant, *88 Reasons Why the Rapture Will Be in 1988* (Nashville: World Bible Society, 1988), 1.

means the gestation period (of a human child); therefore, the numbers would say that the complete gestation period of the Church has been accomplished, and the Church is now ready to be born into eternity in the House of God in heaven."[2]

Whisenant's homespun methods won him few credentialed defenders, but in the world of pop-dispensational culture he was a hit. The Associated Press reported on September 12 that pastors across the country observed increases in baptisms and last-minute evangelization drives.[3] Trinity Broadcast Network, the media center of pop-dispensational televangelism, ran special programming anticipating that millions of its viewers would no longer be on Earth.[4]

Whisenant's viral pamphlet was revealing. The New Christian Right had adapted pop dispensationalism into its political program, but this was only one part of its legacy. In the 1980s and 1990s, pop dispensationalism spread into virtually every sector of American culture: on screens and in bookstores, over airwaves and in pews. Pop-dispensational productions continued to sell in the millions to the faithful and seekers alike. Through many mutations and shifting religious cultures, pop dispensationalism itself was evolving in unexpected ways: in the "electric church" of televangelism, in Christian contemporary music, in megachurches helmed by dispensational pastors, and in other institutional contexts. All told, the saturation of pop dispensationalism was a multivalent and complex process, testifying to the resilience of pop-dispensational concepts even in the face of a rapidly disintegrating dispensational theological community.

Televangelists and Electric Dispensationalism

The heyday of televangelism in the 1970s and 1980s picked up where the initial explosion of pop-dispensational cultural production had left off. On television, as Neil Postman wrote in *Amusing Ourselves to Death* (1985), "religion, like everything else, is presented, quite simply and without apology, as entertainment." After watching hours of televangelist programming, Postman

2. Whisenant, *88 Reasons*, 55.

3. Meg Reynolds, "Thousands Prepare for Prelude to Christ's Second Coming," Associated Press, September 12, 1988, https://apnews.com/article/ede13977f4795f9d6afd69854d55b5f0.

4. Richard Abanes, *End-Time Visions: The Doomsday Obsession*, rev. ed. (Nashville: B&H, 1999), 93.

concluded that there was "no theology, and above all, no sense of spiritual transcendence" on display. In televangelism, "the preacher is tops. God comes out as second banana."[5] Pop dispensationalism's fate was implicated in the basic potential and limitations of the medium of television.

In the 1970s, Lindsey and other pop dispensationalists had used print, music, and film to market a greatly expanded subgenre of apocalypticism. While they appropriated forms and motifs from a variety of sources—scholastic dispensationalism, scientific doomsday scenarios, military technology, the counterculture—the mediums of print and film allowed for sustained argumentation (in nonfiction) and narrative (in fiction). Even the most successful pop-dispensational books included complex, multistage scenarios of the end times and the second coming. In some cases, like the humanist tribulation, pop dispensationalists added to, rather than stripped down, the classic dispensational timeline. But as pop dispensationalism gained a foothold in religious television, the key anchors were no longer the broader dispensational system but competing symbols in television culture. Pop dispensationalism was not a rival religious explanation for the state of the world, but a rival narrative context for entertainment.

The "electric church" of televangelism represented a growth edge in religious media that dated to the early postwar period.[6] Over the 1970s and early 1980s, it ballooned to include more than seventy nationally televised religious programs. The National Religious Broadcasters, an umbrella trade association that advocated for expanded Christian access to all media platforms, gave the growth some shared evangelical priorities amid rapid expansion. By 1980, weekly viewer numbers were pegged by the Nielsen ratings board at around 15 million, with more than 80 percent of programming dedicated to "independent evangelical groups."[7] Annual donations to television ministries reached the hundreds of millions of dollars by the 1980s.

Media scrutiny of televangelism was as important as viewing numbers for introducing Americans to the prominent televangelists and their pop-dispensational messages. By 1981, sociologists Jeffrey K. Hadden and Charles E. Swann were attributing at least part of the success of the New Christian Right

5. Neil Postman, *Amusing Ourselves to Death: Public Discourse in the Age of Show Business* (New York: Viking Penguin, 1985), 116–17.

6. Ben Armstrong, *The Electric Church* (Nashville: Nelson, 1979).

7. Don Cusic, *The Sound of Light: A History of Gospel and Christian Music* (Milwaukee: Hal Leonard, 2002), 314.

to televangelism.[8] Social commentators like Neil Postman were hailing tel-evangelism as the apex (or nadir) of the medium of television. Norman Lear, longtime TV show runner and founder of the liberal advocacy group People for the American Way, was producing a "televangelist survey" that routinely aggregated controversial clips to circulate among its hundreds of thousands of members.[9] The constant, often alarmist coverage of televangelists did bring attention to their excesses, but the more lasting contribution was to introduce millions of Americans, by way of sound bites and quotes, to the terminology of pop dispensationalism.

A few of the New Christian Right's leading figures, including Jerry Falwell (*Old-Time Gospel Hour*), Pat Robertson (*The 700 Club*), and the Southern Baptist firebrand James Robison (*James Robison Presents*), had built their platforms on the back of televangelism. The format, aided by new digital databases that could generate vast mailing lists, allowed for expanded fund-raising, brand awareness, and growth. The medium was gilded and glossy, depicting an idealized setting (usually touched with some southern charm, reflecting the demographics of televangelists themselves), famous guests and musical talent, and a telegenic pastor. The same qualities that produced television stars and celebrities were at work in televangelism, giving New Christian Right leaders a unique platform to spread their ideas and accrue influence.

But the televangelists with the largest audiences were less interested in directly mobilizing Christian voters. Aging stars Oral Roberts (*Oral Roberts and You*) and Rex Humbard (*Inspiration*) continued to pull some of the largest audiences. A younger generation made the most cultural impact: Jim and Tammy Faye Bakker (*The PTL Club*), Jimmy Swaggart (*The Jimmy Swaggart Telecast*), and Paul and Jan Crouch (Trinity Broadcasting Network) were all far more popular in the 1970s and 1980s, and less directly politically active, than New Christian Right televangelists. They were watched by millions of Americans, and indeed millions more global viewers, fueling media and real-world infrastructure, from satellite networks to new Bible colleges. Like Lindsey in the 1970s, their aims were independent of existing institutional interests. Their primary goals were to build their audience and accrue a war chest for further expansion.

8. Jeffrey K. Hadden and Charles E. Swann, *Prime Time Preachers: The Rising Power of Televangelism* (Reading, MA: Addison-Wesley, 1981).

9. Howard Kurtz, "Norman Lear's Crusade Widens," *Washington Post*, February 3, 1986, https://www.washingtonpost.com/archive/politics/1986/02/03/norman-lears-cru sade-widens/72fb9dde-1d34-423c-9956-b25f3deba10c/.

Televangelists pursued these goals by exploiting the strengths of television. Radio preachers had pioneered an engagement with dispensational theology that tried to apply the whole system of dispensationalism to social and cultural life. J. Vernon McGee's *Thru the Bible* and Martin Ralph DeHaan's *Radio Bible Class of the Air* were structured, even in their titles, to be an expository exercise that, through consistent and systematic engagement with the Bible, would educate listeners to be better Christians. Televangelism took a different route. The Bakkers' *PTL Club* had a variety-show format, while *Oral Roberts and You* resembled a late-night talk show. Televangelists were often ignorant of the way the medium of television shaped their theology, but they intuited well enough that certain formats entertained better than others.

On the screen, televangelists stimulated interest in charismatic renewal, but as they gained audiences, their rhetoric tended toward the common denominator that could appeal across the spectrum of fundamentalists, evangelicals, Pentecostals, charismatics, and potential converts. For virtually every televangelist, that baseline entailed a pop dispensationalism that supplied a grab bag of near-future concepts that could mix easily with Pentecostal teachings and cast a wide net for potential viewers. Engagement with pop dispensationalism rarely ranged beyond the standard scenario: cultural decline blamed on humanism, geopolitical chaos, rapture, tribulation, antichrist, Armageddon, and finally the second coming.

While there are many ways to summarize televangelism in the 1980s, encapsulating the role of dispensationalism is more difficult, in part because none of the televangelists took much interest in the inner workings of any particular theology. For the majority of televangelists, dispensationalism was mediated through their shared denominational background in the Assemblies of God and the dissemination of pop dispensationalism in the 1970s.

Largely sidelined in the fundamentalist-modernist controversies, the Assemblies of God had incorporated premillennial eschatology from its founding but otherwise developed outside the boundaries of fundamentalism. Its positions on glossolalia (speaking in tongues), divine healing, and the "latter rain" of signs and wonders ran against the fundamentalist grain. In 1943, the Assemblies of God was the largest body to join the new National Association of Evangelicals, signaling its desire to work with neo-evangelicals who wanted to pitch a wide Protestant tent in the service of a united Christian front against secularism and communism. One of the points of agreement between Pentecostals and neo-evangelicals was a shared alienation from scholastic dispensationalism. This alienation manifested conspicuously in the televangelist craze of the 1970s, where pop dispensationalism was pervasive but on-screen engagement with dispensational theology was scarce.

To paraphrase Neil Postman one more time, what happened in the 1980s was not that pop dispensationalism became the dominant content of television, but that television shows became one of the dominant purveyors of a reduced version of dispensationalism. Televangelists were indispensable in disseminating pop-dispensational understandings of end-times concepts (rapture, antichrist, tribulation, Armageddon) and the pattern of crisis thinking defined by the humanist tribulation. They, too, had become (in many cases, unwitting) representatives of the dispensational tradition and carried forth a heightened eschatological vision of the near future not just for faithful dispensationalists but for a wide swath of Americans.

CCM and the Pop-Dispensational Complex

To some observers in the 1980s it appeared as if televangelism was the wave of the future. But a string of high-profile scandals in 1987 and 1988 ensured that televangelism would not become the preeminent driver of religious culture into the 1990s. Jim and Tammy Faye Bakker, Jimmy Swaggart, and another Assemblies of God televangelist, Marvin Gorman, all fell to a mix of financial and sexual intrigue in the span of eighteen months, while Jerry Falwell and Pat Robertson saw their viewership decline dramatically because of their own assortment of scandals and public missteps. By the end of 1990, the total televangelist audience had plummeted to below 8 million weekly viewers.

This collapse was clarifying in one respect, revealing that televangelism was just one cog in a larger wheel churning pop dispensationalism into diffuse forms of religious culture. In the late nineteenth century, an institutional complex was erected by global missions-oriented new premillennialists. That older complex of institutions included Bible institutes, revival circuits, missions organizations, and religious publishers. The newer, late twentieth-century complex was comprised of televangelists, megachurches, political advocacy groups, and cultural industries, both print and electronic. The differences between the two illustrated how the underlying infrastructure of fundamentalism and evangelicalism had changed in a century. The older complex remained active—Bible institutes and seminaries continued to enroll students, prophecy conferences continued to be held, premillennial authors had no shortage of publishing options. But the locus of authority had shifted toward the new.

The change was decades in the making. Since the 1970s, the fracture in fundamentalist theology had continued to deepen, limiting the influence of older scholastic networks and confining them, year after year, to perpetuating their teachings to ever smaller circles of followers. Cobelligerency in the New Christian Right also blurred old boundaries, revealing in its barest form a widespread restructuring of American religion. Religious communities, and especially Christians, were increasingly arrayed along a newer cultural axis of traditional to progressive rather than the older fundamentalist-modernist axis that had organized so much of twentieth-century Protestantism. The term "evangelicalism," popularized in the 1970s, came to prominence in just this setting, offering not simply a theological or ecclesial identity but also a label rooted in religious, cultural, and economic interests of the postwar period.

By the 1990s, the locus of commercial power had shifted to the new pop-dispensational complex, now firmly situated in the broader evangelical consumption ecosystem. The outburst of prophecy speculation early in the decade was a stark piece of evidence illustrating how much more commercial sway pop dispensationalists held over their scholastic colleagues. On the occasion of the Gulf War in 1990, Charles Dyer, a professor at Dallas Seminary, published *The Rise of Babylon: Sign of the Times* (1991), which argued that Saddam Hussein, as dictator of Iraq and the historical land of the Babylonian Empire, was a potential prophetic figure. The book quickly sold about 300,000 copies. John Walvoord rushed to market an updated version of his 1974 primer, *Armageddon, Oil, and the Middle East*, and sold a million more copies.

These scholastic efforts were impressive relative to other religious offerings, but paled in comparison to pop-dispensational sales in the same period. Even though Lindsey's *The Magog Factor* (1992) became embroiled in a plagiarism scandal, it sold well. Lindsey's next offering, *Planet Earth: 2000 A.D., Will Humankind Survive?* (1994), also sold briskly. The following year, Tim LaHaye and fiction writer Jerry Jenkins released their first Left Behind novel; the series would go on to sell more than 80 million copies. Judged on book sales alone (and the scholastics were less well represented in every other popular medium), the 1990s were decided in favor of pop-dispensational publishing.

The pop-dispensational complex of the 1990s depended on these types of blockbuster sales. Across the religious landscape, there was no more commodifiable vocabulary than pop dispensationalism. The growth of Christian contemporary music, or CCM, was a powerful case in point. The two musical traditions that fed into CCM, southern gospel and Jesus rock music, were dominated by pop-dispensational motifs. The first annual Dove Awards in 1969, hosted by the Gospel Music Association, awarded its first Song of the Year posthumously to gospel singer Robert Emmett Winsett and his song "Jesus Is Coming Soon," then covered by the Oak Ridge Boys on their album *It's Happening!* (1967). Later on, the increasingly mainstream gospel acts continued the tradition, including Blue Ridge Quartet ("That Day Is Almost Here," 1971), Andraé Crouch ("Soon and Very Soon," 1971), Gordon Jensen ("Redemption Draweth Nigh," 1972), The Telestials ("One Way Flight," 1975), and Rusty Goodman ("I Believe He's Coming Back," 1978).

The same pop-dispensational strain was visible in Jesus music, the rock-infused songs mostly created by Jesus People in the 1970s. In the wake of Larry Norman ("I Wish We'd All Been Ready," 1969) came bands like Love Song ("Maranatha," 1970) and Petra ("Gonna Fly Away," 1974) and artists like Randy Stonehill ("Good News," 1976). The much-discussed conversion to evangelical Christianity of Bob Dylan in 1978 paved the way for his own contribution, "Are You Ready?" (1980). Both gospel and Jesus music reflected the influence not just of local churches and regional theology but also of the transcendent cultural appeal of dispensational motifs across a wide spectrum of American Christianity.

By the late 1970s, the emerging CCM genre, which soon vied for attention in larger music circles, catered to the widest possible audience while retaining the marks of pop dispensationalism. Sandi Patty, who was the Dove Awards' Female Vocalist of the Year for eleven consecutive years (1982–1992), performed as one of her iconic songs the classic meditation on the rapture, "We Shall Behold Him" (1982). Another major artist of the 1980s, Larnelle Harris, who won Male Vocalist of the Year three times in the decade, regularly performed "Don't Let the Rapture Pass You By" (1982).

As CCM progressed from a fusion of gospel and rock into its own genre, pop-dispensational themes continued to appear. DC Talk, merging CCM with R&B (rhythm and blues) influences, sang the apocalyptic "Final Days" (1989) on its self-titled debut album and later made a popular cover of "I Wish We'd All Been Ready" (2000). Pop singer Crystal Lewis released "People Get Ready . . . Jesus Is Comin'" (1996) on her breakout record, while gospel singer Ivan Parker recorded the most popular version of "Midnight Cry" (1997), a staple of his concerts based on a mash-up of the parable of the ten virgins that concluded: "Therefore keep watch, because you do not know the day or the hour" (Matt. 25:13 NIV). When the first film version of the fictional

Left Behind series was released in 2000, the official soundtrack featured more than a dozen dispensational-friendly songs from the industry's leading voices, ranging from Rebecca St. James ("Come Lord, Quickly") to Third Day ("Sky Falls Down").

It bears repeating that the thematic range of this pop-dispensational music tradition was limited to end-times themes. The doctrines of dispensational time and of the church-Israel distinction were not music-ready material, nor was an appeal to biblical literalism. Unlike worship hymns or confessional songs, CCM did not prize theological precision. Creators preferred a mix of emotive, narrative, and therapeutic lyrics that drew on the urgency and spectacle of pop-dispensational scenarios.

This limited engagement with dispensationalism also revealed the limits of pop-dispensational appeal in the genre as a whole. Other CCM visions of the future, rooted in other theological commitments, also caught fire. The popular worship song "For Future Generations" (1994) by the band 4Him, formed in 1990 in Alabama, blended southern gospel themes with pop music production values. The tune, which won *CCM Magazine*'s Song of the Year in 1994 (the same year 4Him won the Dove Award for Group of the Year), began with an assessment of the world familiar to pop-dispensational songs, warning that "the signs are obvious, they are everywhere." And yet, in 4Him's hands, this familiar refrain subverted pop-dispensational expectations. Instead of an imminent second coming, the chorus made a commitment to "tomorrow and today / I must be a light for future generations." The implicit eschatology in "For Future Generations" was nondescript, but it was certainly not dispensationalist. Rather, the song aimed to de-imminentize the eschaton and to encourage Christians to "preserve our faith." By rejecting "would-be prophets," Christians could internalize the main message: "I won't compromise in a world of desperation."[10]

Like pop-dispensational songs, this alternative eschatological vision had its own lines of influence in CCM, some advancing a more Reformed tradition and some a Pentecostalism that emphasized the kingdom's power in the here and now. By the twenty-first century, in fact, pop dispensationalism was crowded out by "already/not yet" lyrics describing a present kingdom. The dominant CCM acts in the new century—including those that made their way into thousands of church worship sets: Chris Tomlin, the David

10. 4Him, "For Future Generations," Song Lyrics, accessed May 20, 2022, http://www.songlyrics.com/4him/for-future-generations-lyrics/.

Crowder Band, and Hillsong United—had shed pop-dispensational influence. This was, in part, a natural response to the individualistic, therapeutic, and pop-oriented nature of pop music in general. CCM had traveled far from its gospel and rock roots to look much more like a Christian variation of the pop genre. But the change was also due to a more pervasive dilution and shift in the broadly evangelical religious culture reacting against the wild success of pop-dispensational saturation.

Mega-Dispensationalism and Its Limits

The success of the pop-dispensational complex could be measured in paperback and album sales. But its influence reached a wider breadth of religious culture beyond store shelves and television screens. In the 1980s, pop dispensationalism became embedded in some of the formative institutions of religious culture, none more so than the suburban megachurch. Defined as congregations with more than two thousand regular attendees (often with many more), megachurches were relatively new platforms for dispensational pastors in the late twentieth century. While they would exploit this new institutional form, they would also confront the limits of dispensationalism's appeal, as the same theological factionalism that reared its head in other areas of evangelical and fundamentalist culture manifested in megachurches, too.

The modern megachurch was preceded by the nineteenth-century institutional church. Pastors of these earlier churches often made up the elite leadership of new premillennialism—Arthur T. Pierson, Amzi Dixon, and William Bell Riley all based their personal ministries on large urban congregations. The decline of urban institutional churches and the rise of suburban megachurches in the late twentieth century were part of a larger population shift to the suburbs taking place among (largely white) middle-class Americans. Beginning in the 1950s, middle-class families migrated on a large scale to the suburbs and exurbs of major metropolitan areas. Modern megachurches emerged in these communities, and by the end of the century there were hundreds of megachurches across the United States, and especially in the Sun Belt, in suburban and exurban communities.

With the intertwined histories of premillennialism and institutional churches as a backdrop, it was no surprise that dispensationalism was part of the theological mix of the megachurch boom, too. Pastors trained at Dallas Theological Seminary helped to pioneer the modern megachurch movement. Charles R. Swindoll assumed the pastorate of the First Evangelical Free Church of Fullerton, California, in 1971, which quickly grew to more than three thousand weekly attendees and launched Swindoll on a career in national radio (*Insight for Living*) and, eventually, back to Dallas Seminary as its chancellor in the 1990s. In 2009, a poll of eight hundred evangelical pastors placed Swindoll second behind only Billy Graham as the most influential living preacher to their ministry.[11]

Other Dallas-trained pastors of the same generation followed Swindoll, including Erwin Lutzer, David Jeremiah, Robert Jeffress, Tony Evans, and Andy Stanley—all leading megachurches in major urban or suburban areas in the late twentieth century. They were joined by those trained at other centers of dispensational education. Talbot Seminary alumni included John MacArthur and Kenton Beshore. One famous graduate from Grace Theological Seminary, David Hocking, gained a large following at Calvary Church in Santa Ana, California, before he was forced to resign due to a sex scandal in 1992. Only a few months later he joined the staff of the nearby Calvary Church in Costa Mesa, the megachurch of Chuck Smith and epicenter of the Jesus People movement. These churches shared similar ministry models and an identifiable (if sometimes selective) embrace of dispensational teachings. They were located in strategic growth areas, including the greater areas of Chicago, Atlanta, and Dallas, and the sprawling terrain of Southern California.

In total, the story of modern megachurch growth could not be told without the contribution of dispensational-trained pastors. But despite this story of success, the wider megachurch growth of the 1970s revealed the demographic and theological limits of dispensationalism. The two most influential megachurch leaders in the late twentieth century—Bill Hybels and Rick Warren—made a point to dissociate from the theology and indeed from the theological factionalism that continued to roil fundamentalism and evangelicalism.

More to the point, the loose but expansive network of late-century megachurches professing New Calvinism or neo-Reformed covenantal theology posed a stark theological contrast to dispensationalism. This megachurch revival of Reformed theology beginning in the 1980s stoked the factional infighting between dispensationalists and covenantalists that had defined fundamentalism since the 1930s.[12] The leaders of New Calvinism were pre-

11. "Protestant Pastors Name Graham Most Influential Living Preacher," LifeWay Research, February 2, 2010, https://lifewayresearch.com/2010/02/02/protestant-pastors-name-graham-most-influential-living-preacher/.

12. Collin Hansen, *Young, Restless, Reformed: A Journalist's Journey with the New Calvinists* (Wheaton, IL: Crossway, 2008).

dominantly megachurch pastors, including John Piper, Tim Keller, and Kevin DeYoung, all members of the Presbyterian Church in America, as well as nondenominational Reformed teachers Charles Joseph (C. J.) Mahaney and Mark Driscoll. There also emerged a powerful Southern Baptist contingent that included Matt Chandler, R. Albert Mohler, and Mark Dever. Collaborative venues for this disparate group of New Calvinist leaders and churches included the "network of networks" umbrella of the Gospel Coalition, the pastors conference Together for the Gospel (T4G), and book publishers Crossway and LifeWay.[13]

The New Calvinism's allergy to dispensationalism was evident from the beginning. Take John Piper, a longtime pastor of Bethlehem Baptist Church in Minneapolis, Minnesota. Though born to a traveling dispensational evangelist, Piper was trained in the neo-evangelical institutions of Wheaton College and Fuller Seminary. At the latter school, Daniel P. Fuller, son of Charles Fuller and one of the leading neo-evangelical critics of dispensationalism, mentored Piper. After a stint as a New Testament professor at the neo-evangelical Bethel College and Seminary, Piper assumed the pastorate of Bethlehem Baptist Church, both in the Twin Cities. He increasingly became known for teaching a Baptist Reformed theology that rejected most key dispensational teachings (while retaining a premillennial eschatology), which paved the way for his church's rapid growth and his own leadership in the New Calvinist movement. Piper consistently objected to dispensationalism as insufficiently Reformed in its teachings of salvation and the church.

In the elite levels of New Calvinist megachurch leaders, Piper worked with another antidispensationalist, C. J. Mahaney, founder of Sovereign Grace Church in the suburbs of Washington, DC. Mahaney planted his church in 1977 as part of the Jesus People movement and was initially influenced by little more than the Bible and *Late Great Planet Earth*. "It's not a pattern I'd recommend," he reflected years later.[14] In the 1980s, with a fast-growing congregation, Mahaney was introduced to the works of the Reformed tradition—John Calvin, the Puritans, Charles Spurgeon—which largely rid him of his dispensational convictions and connected him instead to Piper and other New Calvinists. Their cooperation would become more formalized in the de-

13. "Global Resourcing," The Gospel Coalition, accessed May 20, 2022, https://www.thegospelcoalition.org/global-resourcing/.

14. Quoted in "Keeping Their Eyes on the Cross," *Washington Times*, December 23, 2002, https://www.washingtontimes.com/news/2002/dec/23/20021223-111002-4857r/.

cade 2000–2009 in networks like T4G, but would fracture again in the 2010s as allegations of mismanagement and sexual abuse in his ministries isolated Mahaney from other New Calvinists (many of whom were suffering public scandals of their own).

Outside the dispensational-covenantal megachurch face-off, still other Christians incorporated dispensational theology in ways that served their unique interests—both spreading dispensational concepts and fraying its coherence as a system. Proponents of the prosperity gospel, rooted in Pentecostalism and teaching that financial and physical health are God's will, constituted another growth vector for megachurches. To take but one example, John Hagee, founder of Cornerstone Church in San Antonio, Texas, fused prosperity teachings, dispensationalism, and New Christian Right activism to become one of the most influential pastors in the country. Hagee's father, a Pentecostal dispensational preacher, taught him that the day Israel declared its independence was "the most important day of the twentieth century."[15] The younger Hagee followed his father's footsteps. After a trip to Israel in 1978, Hagee became convinced that Christian support for Israel was not only biblically sound, based on his dispensational interpretation of Scripture, but also ethically required by Christians to atone for the church's history of anti-Judaism rooted in faulty (nondispensational) Christian interpretations of the relationship between Israel and the church. He hosted his first annual "Night to Honor Israel" in 1981, and by the 1990s had emerged as a national leader of Christian Zionism. In 2006 he founded Christians United for Israel, the largest Christian Zionist advocacy group in the United States, with more than 11 million members in 2022.

Hagee's Christian Zionism included a wide range of political and theological arguments, from geopolitical prophecy analysis to a nation-based prosperity gospel that blamed American decline on insufficient support for Israel. He based his expectations of divine blessings and curses on his reading of Genesis 12:3, where God tells Abraham:

> "I will bless those who bless you,
>   and whoever curses you I will curse." (NIV)

Hagee followed other Christian Zionists in rejecting the need for Christians to pursue the conversion of Jews on the theological basis, informed by dispen-

---

15. John Hagee, *In Defense of Israel*, rev. ed. (Lake Mary, FL: Front Line, 2007), 11.

sational categories, that God had an unwavering special relationship with the Jewish people. While maintaining high-profile friendships with a handful of Orthodox rabbis and Israeli leaders, Hagee drew accusations of antisemitism for his expositions of prophecy timelines that included lurid descriptions of destruction for the Jewish people.

Ultimately, Hagee's career illustrates another powerful manifestation of mega-dispensationalism in the twenty-first century, one deeply tied to Pentecostal networks otherwise distinct from fundamentalist, evangelical, and New Calvinist circles. The founding leadership board for Christian United for Israel included six Pentecostal megachurch pastors and an executive from the Christian Broadcasting Network. The one non-Pentecostal on the board was Jerry Falwell (who died the year after the organization's founding in 2007). As a group, this leadership team revealed how a particular political manifestation of mega-dispensationalism had found footing in the stratum of Pentecostal megachurches and had organized at a national level to influence US politics and diplomacy.

Southern Baptists and Sectional Rapprochment, Continued

Examples like Hagee point to the ways dispensationalism had made a home in the South in the middle and late twentieth century. Given dispensationalism's roots in the Great Lakes basin, this development was not inevitable, even as generations of northern new premillennialists and dispensationalists pursued sectional reconciliation. Over the decades they made consistent inroads into the region, linking the theology to real and imagined understandings of southern religion. At the same time, dispensationalism's adoption in the South was not wholesale. The role of dispensationalists in the "conservative resurgence" (or "fundamentalist takeover") of the Southern Baptist Convention in the late 1970s is a more recent case in point.

As far back as the nineteenth century, Southern Baptist leaders rarely subscribed to the tenets that would become dispensational theology. The Civil War–era publisher James Robinson Graves and the twentieth-century fundamentalist J. Frank Norris were rare new premillennialists in the denomination, and both had complicated relationships to the Southern Baptist Convention, with Graves a key founder in the separatist Landmark movement and Norris leaving the convention in the 1920s. There remained a consistent presence of lower-profile Southern Baptist ministers who adopted dispensational ideas, and certainly many in the pews who did the same. The doctrines spread piecemeal through revivalists who picked up the theology, including well-known names like Lee Roberson (of Tennessee) and Vance Havner (of South Carolina), who embarked on national revival tours beginning in the 1940s. The positioning of Dallas Theological Seminary in Texas further built a sectional bridge, even as denominational resistance by Southern Presbyterians and others blunted its influence. None of the Southern Baptist denomination's seminaries (which counted six by 1970) taught dispensationalism, and in most cases isolated its doctrines as northern imports.

As Southern Baptists began to develop into distinct moderate and conservative camps over the 1960s and 1970s, dispensationalism's profile rose in the convention. Its bona fides as a system that prized biblical inerrancy made it a resource, and its proponents ready allies, for conservatives. At the same time, the rise of Southern Baptist megachurches helped to elevate key champions of the theology. In a previous era, these megachurch pastors could have easily toiled away separately in obscurity. Instead, they helped form the network of the "conservative resurgence" and weave dispensational themes into the emerging conservative culture of the convention.

The godfather of the resurgence was a dispensationalist: past convention president and longtime pastor at First Baptist Church in Dallas, W. A. Criswell. An anomaly in Baptist circles, he had taught dispensationalism since the 1940s. "Well, people coming to hear me preach said, 'Why, that man is a premillennialist. Why, that man is a dispensationalist,'" Criswell recalled in a 1985 sermon. "I never had a premillennial teacher in my life. I never had a dispensational teacher in my life, nor had I ever read any premillennial literature."[16] This might have been true in Criswell's formal education at Baylor University and Southern Seminary, where the theology had little purchase, but his first pastorship at First Baptist Church in Muskogee, Oklahoma, had exposed him to small-town dispensationalism. By the time Criswell replaced the famous George W. Truett, a committed postmillennialist, in the Dallas pulpit in 1941, he insisted that he was merely following an expository preaching style and employing a literal hermeneutic, not trafficking in a Yankee "ism."

Criswell and his close ally, fellow dispensationalist and president of the new Criswell College in Dallas, Paige Patterson, campaigned for another dispensationalist, Adrian Rogers, to win the convention's presidency as the

16. W. A. Criswell, "The Rising of Israel," W. A. Criswell Sermon Library, sermon transcript, July 21, 1985, https://wacriswell.com/sermons/1985/the-rising-of-israel/.

first committed conservative in 1979. They were joined by other conservatives who were not interested in dispensationalism, including Bailey Smith and James Draper—both also megachurch pastors. For these leaders, the plan for a decade of unbroken conservative convention presidents would usher in conservative appointments at every level of the denomination, from seminary presidents to officials in mission agencies and trustees. The goal was not just advancing theological conservatism, but entrenching a social conservatism, as well, that protected Southern Baptists' privileged place in southern culture and limited the impingement of the federal government on regulating discrimination in churches and seminaries. Rogers won the 1979 election and began an unbroken chain of conservative presidents through the end of the century that included some professing dispensationalists such as Charles Stanley and Jerry Vines (presidents from 1985 to 1990).

Dispensationalists would continue to have influence at the highest levels of the convention, but the second generation of conservative leadership in the 1990s was overwhelmingly covenantalist in orientation. This included R. Albert Mohler, president of Southern Baptist Theological Seminary and cofounder of Together for the Gospel, as well as Mohler's mentee, Russell Moore, whose first book, *The Kingdom of Christ: The New Evangelical Perspective* (2004), sided decisively with covenantalist neo-evangelical theology. Other Southern Baptist conservatives, including Wayne Grudem, David Dockery, and Owen Strachan, all were New Calvinists, as well. A 2009 poll showed that across the six Southern Baptist seminaries, covenantal premillennialism was the majority view. The flagship, Southern Baptist Theological Seminary, reported no dispensational faculty, reflecting the strong currents of New Calvinism at the school.[17]

The legacy of dispensationalism in the Southern Baptist Convention is a window into how both scholastic dispensational production and pop dispensationalism enabled dispensational ideas to spread in areas, especially in the South, that had a history of reticence. Over generations of sectional reconciliation, dispensationalism eventually found a wide hearing in the South, both at the level of theological education and in popular religious culture.

At the same time, dispensationalism's uneven fate in Southern Baptist circles mirrored its struggles in northern fundamentalism. In neither set-

17. David Roach, "END TIMES: Scholars Differ on What Bible Says about Subject," *Baptist Press*, December 30, 2009, https://web.archive.org/web/20120105064313/http://www.bpnews.net:80/BPnews.asp?ID=31963.

ting did scholastic dispensationalism continue its momentum, or even take permanent root, after the 1960s. Among Southern Baptists, too, scholastic dispensationalism was the purview of a shrinking community of pastors and seminary professors, even as pop dispensationalism flourished on television and in Christian bookstores. In many cases, where pop dispensationalism continued to make inroads, it did so at the cost of decaying theological coherence and scholastic authority.

"You have to admit, when people disappear, some rules go out the window."

Rayford Steele, in Tim LaHaye and
Jerry B. Jenkins, *Left Behind* (1995)

These days of toil—what matters it
  So short this life of tears and pain
Lift up thy face! What dost thou fear?
  Thou hast not given thine all in vain.
Soon thou shalt walk with Him in white.
  Who knoweth? It may be to-night.

Adelaide Allison, "October Sixth" (1894)

The sentiment of *Left Behind*'s main protagonist, airliner pilot Rayford Steele, in light of the rapture, had deep resonances in the history of premillennialism. Allison's poem, quoted favorably by later dispensationalists, evoked the mix of fatalism, expediency, and anticipation that could often define dispensational culture. These sentiments manifested not just in fiction and poetry, but in the lives of pop dispensationalism into the twenty-first century.

18

Collapse

As pop dispensationalism advanced into American politics and popular culture, scholastic efforts to manage its reception had vacillated between mimicking pop-dispensational outputs and critiquing pop dispensationalism as insufficiently rigorous. The former could be seen in John Walvoord's *Armageddon, Oil, and the Middle East* (1974) and Charles Ryrie's *The Final Countdown* (1982), to name a few books in the same popular style as Lindsey. With each attempt, though, the multimedia commercial reach and cultural influence of pop dispensationalism easily prevailed.

The scholastics' other approach, to criticize pop dispensationalism's sensationalism and accommodation to popular culture, was harder to detect for outsiders to the tradition. In 1984 John Walvoord, then in the twilight years of his leadership of Dallas Seminary, distanced his school from Lindsey by telling *Christianity Today* that the popularizer "goes beyond our teaching." Walvoord further explained that pop dispensationalists like Lindsey were inconsistent literalists, preferring to interpret biblical prophecy in ways that accommodated modern military technology rather than maintaining a strictly literal approach.[1]

Scholastics consistently leveled this line of critique at the popularizers of their theology. A few years later, Walvoord published a beefy reference work, *The Prophecy Knowledge Handbook* (1990), in which he contrasted scholastic interpretation on all types of issues to that of the pop dispensationalists. Once again, he was concerned that popularizers had traded literalism for hype. The prophesied "great star" of Wormwood foretold to fall "from heaven, blazing like a torch" during the tribulation was not, as Lindsey maintained, a symbol for nuclear war but "a large object naturally blazing as it entered the at-

---

1. "Critics Fear That Reagan Is Swayed by Those Who Believe in a 'Nuclear Armageddon,'" *Christianity Today*, December 14, 1984, 48.

mosphere and apparently having chemicals that made the water bitter." The prophecy was, in other words, to be taken as literally as possible. Likewise, Charles Ryrie, in a similar barb at popularizers, insisted that the plague of "locusts" of Revelation 9:9 was not a symbol of Apache helicopters or futuristic soldiers, as pop-writer Salem Kirban speculated, but in fact was a plague of locusts.[2] In example after example, scholastics resisted siding with the pop interpretations of prophecy that, admittedly, stimulated more popular interest.

In the 1990s, outside observers rarely remarked on these tensions. They preferred to emphasize the similarities among dispensationalists rather than understand their differences. Yet, in doing so they missed the significance of these internal squabbles. Scholastic attempts to correct pop-dispensational sensationalism signaled a theological tradition in the midst of a crisis of authority. While pop dispensationalism barreled into the 1990s on the momentum of commercial success, the scholastic credibility of dispensationalism was rapidly diminishing. By the end of the century, the tradition had more or less hollowed out its own institutions and ceased to train a younger generation of theologians and pastors in the teachings of Scofield and Chafer.

The collapse happened along multiple fronts. A resurgent faction of post-millennial fundamentalists going under the name "Christian reconstructionists" waged a vicious print war with dispensationalists in the 1980s that left both sides battered and the targets of wider opprobrium. At the same time, John F. MacArthur, a popular Talbot Seminary–trained author and megachurch pastor, publicly broke with scholastic dispensationalists over what it meant to be "born again." His attack launched a decades-long "Lordship salvation controversy" that signaled a broader defection of scholastic dispensationalists to covenantal theology. Third, a scholastic revision to the tradition that became known as "progressive dispensationalism" coalesced at Dallas Seminary in the 1990s and created a split between "progressive" and "traditional" dispensationalists. By the year 2010, a stunning state of affairs had come to pass: dispensationalism looked to be on its last legs as a theological tradition. It continued to be taught in some sectors of fundamentalism, and pop dispensationalism continued to churn out content and shape religious culture, but the enduring theological legacy of dispensationalism was clouded in uncertainty.

2. Quoted in Lisa Vox, *Existential Threats: American Apocalyptic Beliefs in the Technological Era* (Philadelphia: University of Pennsylvania Press, 2017), 134–35.

The Reconstructionists: Eschaton Redux

Every fundamentalist needs a conversion story, and the band of arch-Calvinist fundamentalists known as Christian reconstructionists were no exception. Many of their leaders had grown up dispensationalists. "From 1966 until 1975 I was a dispensationalist," wrote theologian Kenneth Gentry in his polemical *House Divided: The Break-up of Dispensational Theology* (1989). In a preface titled "Why I Could Not Remain a Dispensationalist," the onetime student at Grace Theological Seminary recounted how he had transferred to Reformed Theological Seminary (Jackson, Mississippi) after encountering Oswald Allis's classic covenantalist critiques of dispensationalism. Already questioning his received theology, Gentry recalled that Allis's book *Prophecy and the Church* (1945) "bulldozed the residue of [his] collapsed dispensationalism."[3]

When he arrived in Mississippi, Gentry had yet more theological road to travel. He began to be discipled by one of his new professors, Greg Bahnsen, whose brief tenure on the faculty was defined by controversy. Under Bahnsen's tutelage, Gentry began "as an anti-theonomic amillennialist," but later he "came out as a theonomic postmillennialist." The technical language and syllabic drudgery were part of the charm in this corner of fundamentalism. Gentry had embraced his teacher's positions of "theonomy," a Christian political agenda seeking to rule society through divine law, and postmillennialism, an eschatological vision that sees such a divinely ruled society as preparation for the second coming.

Bahnsen was dismissed from Reformed Seminary for teaching these views in 1979, but by then both professor and student were part of the burgeoning "theonomic postmillennialist" movement known as Christian reconstructionism. The leading lights of the movement were staunch Calvinists who embraced a robust conservative theo-political agenda also known as Dominionism. They included theologian Rousas John Rushdoony and his son-in-law, free-market economist and ethicist Gary North. Rushdoony's think tank, the Chalcedon Foundation (Vallecito, California), and North's educational organization, the Institute for Christian Economics (Tyler, Texas), anchored the movement, which found a small, incendiary following especially among fundamentalist Presbyterian churches.

Gentry's conversion story from dispensationalism was shared by other leaders of the movement. North gladly admitted: "I was an ultradispensationalist in the early spring of 1964" while Ray Sutton, pastor of the reconstructionist hot spot

---

3. Greg L. Bahnsen and Kenneth Gentry Jr., *House Divided: The Break-up of Dispensational Theology* (Tyler, TX: Institute for Christian Economics, 1989), xlvii.

of Westminster Presbyterian Church in Tyler, Texas, had trained at Dallas Seminary.[4] The shared fundamentalist heritage intensified the rivalry that followed.

At the heart of their criticism of fellow fundamentalists, reconstructionists blamed the failure of the church to assert its God-ordained authority over society on dispensationalist teachings that encouraged social quietism until the rapture. Their movement's name was inspired by the project to "reconstruct" the American church to carry out this agenda, and especially to rescue rank-and-file fundamentalists from their captivity to dispensationalism. As North wrote in 1989, reconstructionists had worked for nearly a decade "to flush into the open some dispensational scholar—not just a Hal Lindsey . . . but a true academic spokesman of the movement"—in order to provoke a confrontation.[5]

The reconstructionist provocations did prompt dispensational responses, but never from a "true academic spokesman." The strongest rebuttal came from Hal Lindsey himself. In the most scholarly toned book of his career, Lindsey took on Christian reconstructionism in *The Road to Holocaust* (1989). The title, which implicated "the Dominion Theology movement" in the potential destruction of the United States, the church, and Israel, was fittingly overblown for a debate among two small circles of fundamentalist theologians. Using the ill-advised metaphor of holocaust, Lindsey described Christian reconstructionism as the most recent villain in the long history of Christian anti-semitism. The "trail from [third-century church father] Origen to Auschwitz" traveled through generations of "supersessionists" who perpetuated the "false prophetic premise of the Church" that "it was the sole possessor of Israel's covenant promises."[6] As dissenters from the historic "replacement theology" that saw the church as the heir to Israel's covenant with God, dispensationalists were largely exonerated on this count.

Looking at reconstructionism, which called the church to seize its God-given power over worldly institutions, Lindsey concluded that he was witnessing "history repeating itself."[7] "Let the true Christian never again give a theological framework from which unscrupulous men can promote another holocaust for the children of Israel," he petitioned. He also took a victory lap, pointing to the "nineteen years since the *Late Great Planet Earth* was written" as a time when "virtually all the things that were anticipated in the book have emerged and fit into the prophetic scenario." In light of his accuracy, Lind-

4. Bahnsen and Gentry, *House Divided*, xlv.
5. Bahnsen and Gentry, *House Divided*, xxxii.
6. Hal Lindsey, *The Road to Holocaust* (New York: Bantam Books, 1989), 11–13.
7. Lindsey, *The Road to Holocaust*, 27.

sey complained, it was "amazing" that a movement like reconstructionism "should arise and deny it all." Then again, he concluded, "I really shouldn't be surprised, because such false teaching was predicted."[8]

Lindsey set the tone of an acrimonious debate that both sides joined together. Pop-dispensational writer Dave Hunt's *Whatever Happened to Heaven?* (1988) and Tim LaHaye's *No Fear of the Storm* (1992) were defenses of the rapture that promised that the church's destiny was to avoid, rather than overcome, current politics or looming tribulations. Another pro-dispensationalist response was *Dominion Theology: Blessing or Curse?* (1988), written by two younger writers in the more scholarly mode, H. Wayne House and Thomas Ice. They concluded that reconstructionism posed "undeniable dangers" to Christians and to American society.[9] Elsewhere Ice proclaimed reconstructionists to be "the most dangerous trend within Evangelical Christianity" because "the call for Believers to exercise a premature dominion is at the heart of Satan's promise to Eve in the Garden."[10]

The dispensationalist defense spurred renewed institution building, as well. Ice worked with Tim LaHaye to found in 1994 the Pre-Trib Research Center, modeled on the Powerscourt Conferences of the early 1830s. The center hosted a yearly gathering and produced a flood of publications combating reconstructionists and postmodernists (Pre-Trib members saw deep connections between the spiritualized biblical hermeneutics of the former and the epistemological relativism of the latter). At its height, the center counted more than two hundred members, with many leading their own ministries and media platforms, or holding faculty positions. In 2005 the center moved to Liberty University, the burgeoning and loosely dispensational school founded and led by Jerry Falwell.

For their part, reconstructionists advanced familiar lines of critique. Gary North wrote close to fifty books, managed his own Dominion Press, and edited a variety of newsletters and journals, including *Christian Reconstruction* (1977–1996) and *Bible Economics Today* (1978–1996), with much of his attention after 1985 dedicated to denouncing dispensationalism. He popularized the research of David MacPherson, a journalist and ex-dispensationalist who had spent decades attempting to discredit the origins of the rapture by tracing them to a mentally unstable teenage girl, Margaret MacDonald, who saw vi-

8. Lindsey, *The Road to Holocaust*, 283, 282.

9. Wayne House and Thomas Ice, *Dominion Theology: Blessing or Curse?* (Portland, OR: Multnomah, 1988).

10. Thomas Ice, "What Is Dominion Theology?" Scholars Crossing, May 2009, https://digitalcommons.liberty.edu/pretrib_arch/74.

sions in 1830, and from whom John Nelson Darby purportedly stole the idea of an imminent rapture. In books ranging from *The Incredible Cover Up* (1975) to *The Rapture Plot* (1995), MacPherson hammered the same conspiracy theory even as nonpartial experts found the scenario unlikely. The critique stuck in reconstructionist circles, however, and was frequently repeated.

Historical origins played a role in another key area of debate. Both sides charged the other with lacking premodern precedents for their theology, and so the long debate over the provenance of millennial doctrines was rehashed once more. Dispensationalists like Ice charged that postmillennialism did not develop until the writings of English theologian Daniel Whitby in the seventeenth century, while reconstructionists pointed to the even later introduction of key dispensational concepts in the nineteenth century. Just as dispensationalists had mined the church fathers for precedents to their doctrines, so too did reconstructionists. Especially in his commentary on the book of Revelation, *Days of Vengeance* (1987), reconstructionist theologian David Chilton insisted that the earliest Christians were "preterists" who understood much of the prophetic material in the New Testament to have been fulfilled in the first century, a scenario that accommodated the particular strand of postmillennial eschatology advanced by reconstructionists.

More than marshaling new arguments, both sides traded in overblown declarations of decisive victory. "I will say it again: Dispensationalism is dying . . . Sayonara Scofield!" North declared in his book *Rapture Fever: Why Dispensationalism Is Paralyzed* (1993), concluding, "We are witnessing dispensationalism's terminal generation."[11] His colleague Kenneth Gentry edited a magazine encouraging the decline, *Dispensationalism in Transition* (1988–1995), the final issue of which began, "In January 1988, I launched this newsletter. This month, I am ending it. The target—dispensationalism—is now catatonic."[12] The dispensationalist Thomas Ice wrote around the same time of his undaunted confidence that his was the superior theology, "since the Bible teaches only a single viewpoint on any issue, amillennialism and postmillennialism are nowhere to be found, but premillennialism is found on every page of the Bible, from Genesis to Revelation."[13] Fundamentalists directed their militant and pugilistic rhetoric with equal verve to their fellow fundamentalists as they did to the more distant liberal Protestants or secular humanists.

11. Gary North, *Rapture Fever: Why Dispensationalism Is Paralyzed* (Tyler, TX: Institute for Christian Economics, 1993), 201, 221.

12. Gary North, "What Ever Happened to Scofield's Dispensationalism?" *Dispensationalism in Transition* 9, no. 12 (December 1995): 1.

13. Thomas D. Ice, "The Unscriptural Theologies of Amillennialism and Postmillennialism," Scholars Crossing, May 2009, https://digitalcommons.liberty.edu/pretrib_arch/54.

The heat subsided after the mid-1990s, but the damage had been done. The Christian reconstructionists brought to light troubling trends in scholastic dispensationalism: its aging theological leadership, its shrinking Christian college footprint, its lingering weaknesses on historical and hermeneutical debates. Reconstructionism itself would never gain a broad popular following, though its influence on some leaders in the New Christian Right fascinated journalists. Its legacy advanced half of what North had hoped: a scholarly struggle that cornered dispensationalists and removed some of the sheen from the theology's popular appeal.

The "Lordship Salvation Controversy": Deeper Cracks in Scholastic Dispensationalism

As vitriolic as the Christian reconstructionist critique could get, it had ultimately failed to "flush into the open" a "true academic spokesman" of dispensationalism to engage in debate. In 1993, North complained bitterly of the "continuing silence" of Dallas Seminary faculty in response to repeated broadsides by reconstructionist theologians. Those faculty "have become theological deaf-mutes" and poor defenders of their theology, he concluded.[14]

Engaging with the likes of Gary North was hardly an appealing proposition to the deans of dispensationalism, but their avoidance of this particular debate was more likely due to the many other fires burning on the theological front. While reconstructionists were lobbing their attacks, a growing number of Dallas-trained scholars were defecting into broadly Reformed covenantalist seminaries and churches. The trend was visible at the lay level, with thousands of rank-and-file examples, but just as alarming were the scholastic defections.

To take but two examples, Gregory K. Beale and Bruce Waltke, both generation-defining biblical scholars in their fields, moved into covenantalist circles after their training at Dallas Seminary. Beale, who graduated from Dallas in 1976, soon ditched his dispensational commitments while teaching at Gordon-Conwell Seminary and Westminster Seminary. Ordained in the Orthodox Presbyterian Church, he promoted biblical inerrancy on Presbyterian terms while rejecting dispensational categories. Bruce Waltke began his career teaching at Dallas Seminary before leaving for positions at a string of Reformed seminaries that included Westminster and the more recent Knox Theological Seminary in Fort Lauderdale, Florida. He eventually became an Anglican and published numerous influential works on the Old Testament from a broadly Reformed (and Reformational) perspective.

14. North, *Rapture Fever*, 198.

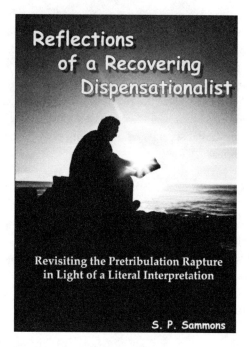

Figure 24. *Reflections of a Recovering Dispensationalist* book cover. Works like this, self-published in 2012, grew in number in the twenty-first century. The author, a pastor in California, rejected dispensational theology but insisted he remained a biblical literalist. This book was notable for gaining the endorsements of numerous evangelical (covenantal) scholars, including Gordon Fee and Ben Witherington III.

Beale's and Waltke's breaks with dispensationalism were confined to scholastic and intrachurch chatter. More public was the departure of Sam Storms, a pastor and theologian who graduated from Dallas Seminary in 1977 and made his way into Reformed and charismatic leadership, including John Piper's Desiring God Ministries and the Reformed church-planting network, Acts 29. As an illustration of the diverse communities he represented, Storms also worked for a time in the charismatic Apostolic-Prophetic movement. A sprawling collection of pastors and churches headquartered in Kansas City, the Apostolic-Prophetic movement embraced charismatic theology and rejected dispensational eschatology. In fact, the movement became known for its dominionist "Seven Mountains Mandate" teachings that pushed Christians to overtake the institutions and spheres in society as a preparatory work for the second coming. As a charismatic leader with New Calvinist credentials, Storms moved out of premillennial circles, which was the subject of his popular 2013 book, *Kingdom Come: The Amillennial Alternative.*

The most significant break from scholastic dispensationalism was only a partial defection, which made the episode even messier. John F. MacArthur, son of a Canadian dispensationalist preacher, became the pastor of Grace Community Church in 1969 and also founded The Master's Seminary, both of which were in the northern suburbs of Los Angeles. He was trained at Bob Jones University and then Talbot Theological Seminary, and his first publications in the 1960s reflected his indebtedness to scholastic dispensationalism. By the mid-1980s, however, he had begun to question parts of the tradition. And by 2005, MacArthur was a headliner at New Calvinist conferences, representing something of a token dispensationalist in the movement and lending the resurgent Reformed some broader credibility. MacArthur acknowledged as much, calling himself (tongue in cheek) a "leaky dispensationalist" who told his new Reformed colleagues, as early as the 1980s, "I was much more one of you than one of them."[15]

MacArthur's grievances with dispensationalism were not with the church-Israel distinction or the imminent rapture, which he continued to teach. Rather, he complained about a longtime dispensational difference with the Reformed tradition on the definition of salvation, or being "born again." The free grace salvation taught by Scofield, Chafer, and other dispensationalists featured a low barrier of entry into the saving grace of Jesus. Sometimes called "mental assent salvation," the threshold was for an individual to make a simple intellectual or mental acknowledgment of the proposition that Jesus is Savior. A prime popular example of this "free grace" teaching could be found in Hal Lindsey's *Liberation of Planet Earth* (1974), which ended with an unadulterated free grace appeal: "Let me tell you right now, if while you've been reading this book, you've said to yourself, 'This is true and I believe it. I don't understand it all, but I believe what I do understand,' then I guarantee you that you've become a child of God."[16]

MacArthur took aim at this popular view, starting with its predominance in televangelism, before developing a larger critique of how dispensational theology enabled its spread. In *The Gospel according to Jesus* (1988), which broke the debate into the open, MacArthur began by sketching the sorry state of affairs. "It now appears that the church of our generation will be remembered chiefly for a series of hideous scandals that uncovered the rankest exhibitions of depravity in the lives of some highly visible televangelists." As worrying as the sins of Jim Bakker and Jimmy Swaggart were, MacArthur was more

---

15. MacArthur, quoted in *Stand: A Call for the Endurance of the Saints*, ed. Justin Taylor and John Piper (Wheaton, IL: Crossway, 2008), 129.

16. Hal Lindsey, *Liberation of Planet Earth* (Grand Rapids: Zondervan, 1974), 137–38.

perturbed by the way "conservative, fundamentalist, evangelical" leaders had taught rank-and-file Christians to respond, or rather, fail to respond. "Most troubling of all is the painful reality that most Christians continue to view these [disgraced] people as insiders, not as wolves and false shepherds who have crept in among the flock."[17]

The problem plaguing Christians was not tribalism or theological ignorance, according to MacArthur, but an insufficient understanding of what was required to be "born again." Christians, he warned, "have been told that the only criterion for salvation is knowing and believing some basic facts about Christ" (17). He called this "easy-believism" (196). If knowing was the only necessary condition of salvation, then someone could seemingly live a sinful life but claim to "follow Jesus" and still be considered "born again" (16–17). In the era of pop dispensationalism, this free grace doctrine had come home to roost: "The character of the visible church reveals the detestable consequence of this theology." Polling by Gallup revealed that close to one-third of all Americans considered themselves "born again," which put this matter at the forefront of public life. "Those figures surely represent millions who are tragically deceived," MacArthur warned. "Theirs is a damning false assurance" (16).

By the time he had investigated the matter thoroughly, MacArthur identified the source of the free grace error as none other than the leading lights of scholastic dispensationalism, beginning with Lewis Sperry Chafer. The founder of Dallas Seminary was "a brilliant man," MacArthur acknowledged, but he was also deeply flawed. Chafer pioneered a "tendency" among dispensationalists "to get carried away with compartmentalizing truth to the point that they can make unbiblical distinctions." The dichotomy of law and grace that underpinned dispensational time was the excess that led to the free grace heresy. By defining the current dispensation as one of "pure grace," Chafer deposited free grace into the very core of the scholastic tradition (25–27).

The position was not just Chafer's. Ryrie defended it in *So Great Salvation* (1977), which was republished in 1989. But none did more to promote "free grace" than Zane Hodges, a professor of New Testament at Dallas Seminary from 1959 to 1986, who attacked the traditional Reformed view that to be saved required not just belief but active repentance from sins and acknowledgment of Jesus as Lord. In his response to MacArthur, titled *Absolutely Free! A Biblical Reply to Lordship Salvation* (1989), he charged that what MacArthur was teach-

17. John F. MacArthur, *The Gospel according to Jesus* (Grand Rapids: Zondervan, 1988), 16–17. Hereafter, page references from this work will be given in parentheses in the text.

ing led to "a kind of faith/works synthesis which differs only insignificantly from official Roman Catholic dogma."[18]

The "Lordship salvation controversy," so-called for the two sides' disagreement on whether salvation required acknowledging Jesus as Savior or as both Savior and Lord, spurred dozens of pamphlets, books, conference panels, and sermons. The controversy also attracted outsiders to the dispensationalist-covenantalist conflict, like philosopher Dallas Willard. In his popular *The Divine Conspiracy* (1998), Willard dedicated an early chapter to dismissing the "free grace" position as little more than a "gospel of sin management" that reduced the idea of salvation to one of individual guilt and absolution. Willard rejected Ryrie's and MacArthur's narrow basis for debate, that "being saved is a forensic or legal condition rather than a vital reality or character." And yet, Willard admitted, this view thoroughly dominated the "interpretation of salvation in the evangelical and conservative churches of North America."[19] Willard's outside perspective highlighted the contraction of fundamentalist theological concerns in the wake of its ongoing factionalism, and also hinted at the ways "free grace" teachings were in steep decline among a wider circle of evangelical theologians by the end of the century.

In any case, the rhetoric remained charged, with accusations of "false doctrine" coming from all sides. MacArthur invoked a long list of historic and contemporary theologians on his side, including many of the most famous fundamentalist opponents of dispensationalism: J. Gresham Machen, Oswald T. Allis, and Arthur Pink. Yet, on the free grace side was the large network of Dallas alumni and the revivalist-theological tradition that extended from Moody to Sunday to Lindsey and LaHaye. As Arthur Pink, the staunch opponent of dispensationalism, admitted in 1937, "The terms of Christ's salvation are erroneously stated by the present-day evangelist. With very rare exception he tells his hearers that salvation is by grace and is a free gift."[20] MacArthur's critique was a newly potent, if familiar, grievance against the traditions that fed into dispensationalism, and which dispensationalism itself had bolstered.

Like Beale, Waltke, and Storms, MacArthur's change in thinking began to be reflected in his affiliations. He became increasingly at home among the New Calvinist circles that shared his views on salvation. One of the first endorsers

---

18. Zane Hodges, *Absolutely Free! A Biblical Reply to Lordship Salvation* (Grand Rapids: Zondervan, 1989), 20.

19. Dallas Willard, *The Divine Conspiracy: Rediscovering Our Hidden Life in God* (New York: Harper, 1998), 52–56.

20. Arthur Pink, "Signs of the Times," *Studies in the Scriptures* 16 (1937): 373.

of *The Gospel according to Jesus* had been John Piper, and it was through that vote of confidence that MacArthur and Piper struck up a lasting friendship. In a later conversation, in 2008, he told Piper, "I was really not moving in Reformed circles at the time."[21] That all changed in the wake of the controversy. By the end of the 1990s, he had appeared at numerous conferences with Reformed apologist R. C. Sproul and Anglican theologian J. I. Packer, and in the decade 2000–2009 he was a regular speaker at T4G and Gospel Coalition events.

MacArthur's continuing allegiance to teachings like the church-Israel distinction made him a lightning rod in the ongoing scholastic defections from dispensationalism, suggesting that some dispensational teachings continued even as he leveled severe critiques on others. But in the broader view, he was not that unique. Faced with a resurgent postmillennialism and consistent attacks by ex-dispensationalists, the scholastic dispensational tradition entered the 1990s more weakened than it had been for decades. But the rolling collapse had yet another turn—the most devastating one yet that tore at the very roots of the tradition.

Progressive Dispensationalism: Baseline Fracture

In the same years of reconstructionist harangues and Reformed defections, scholastic dispensationalists faced an even more existential crisis when a revisionist school of thought emerged at Dallas Seminary, the institutional and geographical center of the tradition. In the 1990s, a younger generation of dispensational scholars openly broke with the older generation and joined a broader neo-evangelical consensus on issues of covenants, eschatology, and salvation. They called themselves "progressive dispensationalists." This development started the final chapter to one of the key contests of fundamentalist theology that had begun half a century earlier. Besieged on the outside and now in its own institutions, scholastic dispensationalism was on its last legs.

By 1994, when Moody Press published a volume on the deepening fault lines within scholastic dispensationalism, the rise of a new progressive dispensationalism had all but incapacitated the tradition. The volume, *Issues in Dispensationalism*, was needed, its editors wrote, "to stimulate positive interaction and discussion within current dispensational dialogue."[22] The contributors included "the patriarchs of dispensationalism" as well as "younger, less published individuals." Of the twenty-four advanced degrees awarded to

---

21. Quoted in Taylor and Piper, *Stand*, 129.

22. Wesley R. Wills, John R. Master, and Charles Ryrie, eds., *Issues in Dispensationalism* (Chicago: Moody Press, 1994), 11.

the twelve contributors, twenty were earned at Dallas Theological Seminary, revealing how small the scholastic community remained. They were all defenders of a "traditional dispensationalism" that traced itself through the legacy of Scofield and Chafer, and the now-emeritus dean of Dallas Seminary, Ryrie, presided over the volume.

The concentration of scholastic firepower revealed the significant threats to "traditional dispensationalism" that the volume was intended to address. In *Dispensationalism Today* (1965), Ryrie had argued for a united dispensationalist front. He had proposed an ahistorical and clear-cut, three-point *sine qua non* of dispensationalism that took hold, at least for a short time, among the wider scholastic community. In that book he had cast the theology's chief opponents as being outside of the tradition—covenantalists, ultradispensationalists, and, of course, modernists. Thirty years later, these opponents were the least of Ryrie's worries. Bowing to deepening internal debate, he now employed a new nomenclature. In his opening chapter he contrasted "normative" dispensationalists like Scofield and Chafer with a new insurgency of "progressive dispensationalists"—a younger generation, many of them trained at Dallas. These younger "progressives" could hardly be counted as dispensationalists at all, he mused. He described their work as an "aberration" and a worrying "rapprochement" with covenantal theology.[23]

By the 1990s, progressive dispensationalism had become a full-fledged school of thought, threatening to snuff out the "normative" tradition established by Scofield, Chafer, Walvoord, and Ryrie. The chief architects of progressive dispensationalism were three Dallas Seminary professors—theologian Craig A. Blaising, New Testament scholar Darrell Bock, and Old Testament scholar Kenneth Barker—and a Talbot Seminary theologian, Robert L. Saucy. Barker and Saucy were older, having been trained at Dallas Seminary in the early 1960s, while Blaising and Bock were graduates from the 1970s. They all came of age during or immediately in the wake of the rupture in fundamentalist theology. They responded to the unsettled theological territory by revising, modifying, and altering the system of dispensationalism as it had been handed down to them. The rupture of authority in dispensationalism had finally reached the inner sanctum.

The term "progressive" was a clue to how this younger generation of dispensationalists positioned themselves. The term was not necessarily polemical (nor political) but was intended to define the newly understood relationship between dispensations, especially regarding the current dispensation. Instead

23. Wills, Master, and Ryrie, *Issues in Dispensationalism*, 20–21.

of the traditional view that the current dispensation represented a "parenthesis" in God's redemptive history that postponed the kingdom, progressives asserted a fundamental continuity, or progression, from one dispensation to the next. In effect, this seemingly minor shift forced a reevaluation of a vast scope of once-settled dispensational theology, from the tradition's vaunted consistent literal biblical hermeneutics to the nature of the kingdom, the church-Israel distinction, and the purpose of God's covenants. On these core issues, progressives first marked their differences with fellow dispensationalists cautiously in the 1980s, and by the 1990s sparked a widespread and, as it developed, unbridgeable split in the already-beleaguered scholastic community.

While progressive dispensationalists produced new scholarship, they were hitting on points of disagreement decades old. One issue was the distinction by Chafer, following Scofield and the Brethren, between the "kingdom of God" and "kingdom of heaven." Chafer had taught that these two kingdoms were separate—the kingdom of God was the spiritual rule emanating from heaven, and the kingdom of heaven was the material Davidic kingdom promised to Israel. The kingdom of God was the destiny of the church, while the kingdom of heaven was the destiny of Israel. As separate kingdoms, their covenantal relationships with God were further points of discussion—were both kingdoms covered under one covenant, two covenants, or one covenant with two parts? Dispensationalists had debated these points in their academic journals and seminar classrooms for decades, with Chafer's view dominant but with minority views always in dialogue.

The stark dichotomy in the kingdom issue was replicated in other areas of scholarship through the 1990s, from the church-Israel distinction to the law-grace dichotomy. In each case, the commitment of progressive dispensationalists to find continuity where "traditionalists" had emphasized discontinuity shaped the debate. On a variety of fronts, progressives nuanced, softened, or erased category distinctions that had animated dispensational thought for more than half a century. Barker began a reevaluation of hermeneutical and doctrinal themes in the early 1980s—declaring in his presidential address to the Evangelical Theological Society in 1981 that on the church-Israel distinction, "we [dispensationalists] have compartmentalized too much."[24] Blaising and Bock teamed up in the mid-1980s for a slew of articles in *Bibliotheca Sacra* that historicized dispensationalism and explored new areas of biblical interpretation. They introduced a "complementary hermeneutics," which affirmed the literal (earthly) fulfillment of Old Testament prophecies but also allowed for multiple fulfill-

24. Kenneth L. Barker, "False Dichotomies between the Testaments," *Journal of the Evangelical Theological Society* 25, no. 1 (March 1982): 12.

ments, some of which may not have been intended in the original utterance of the prophecy. "There also is such a thing as complementary aspects of meaning," they later wrote, "where an additional angle on the text reveals an additional element of its message or a fresh way of relating the parts of a text's message."[25] With such a hermeneutical principle in place, the fulfillment of prophecy did not need to be confined to a single future or strictly literal fulfillment.

In 1985, theologian Robert L. Saucy's home institution of Talbot Seminary hosted the annual meeting of the Evangelical Theological Society, the largest gathering of evangelical theologians in the country. Here Saucy wanted to expand the discourse around progressive issues and assembled a wide range of evangelical theological voices. The following year he launched the Dispensational Study Group, which presented papers and met yearly alongside the society's meetings, providing a venue for a regular and intensive exchange of ideas. By the early 1990s, book projects begun in the study group helped to formally coin the term "progressive dispensationalism." The most decisive contributions included the collected volume edited by Blaising and Bock, *Dispensationalism, Israel, and the Church: The Search for a Definition* (1992), followed by their coauthored *Progressive Dispensationalism* (1993) and Saucy's *The Case for Progressive Dispensationalism* (1993). As one nondispensationalist reviewer of Saucy's book noted with surprise, in one chapter with "96 exhaustive footnotes," not a single reference to Chafer or Walvoord appeared, while covenantal scholars abounded: "Ridderbos, Ladd, Perrin, Cranfield, Barrett, and even O. T. Allis are extensively—and favorably—quoted."[26]

The flurry of scholarship meant the broader evangelical theological community was being drawn into the progressive dispensationalism conversation. Vern Poythress, a covenantalist professor at Westminster Seminary, wrote one of the first of a new wave of critiques of dispensationalism with *Understanding Dispensationalists* (1987). This was followed by a run of covenantal broadsides, including a volume by two Dallas Seminary graduates, Curtis Crenshaw and Grover E. Gunn, and covenantal theologian Keith A. Mathison's *Dispensationalism: Rightly Dividing the People of God?* (1995). Though representing divergent perspectives, these books uniformly hailed progressive dispensationalism as a positive development and encouraged the decline of dispensational theology.

The Dispensational Study Group developed alongside this literature, inviting Poythress to its 1987 meeting. It continued to host Reformed and Pen-

25. Darrell L. Bock and Craig A. Blaising, *Progressive Dispensationalism* (Wheaton, IL: Victor, 1993), 68.
26. Walter Elwell, "Dispensationalisms of the Third Kind," *Christianity Today*, September 12, 1994, 28.

tecostal scholars, among others, who were eager to further diminish scholastic dispensational influence. Meetings in the early 1990s included papers presented by Old Testament scholar Tremper Longman III, trained at Westminster Seminary and a professor at the neo-evangelical Westmont College (Santa Barbara, California), and Doug Oss, a Westminster-trained Assemblies of God theologian who attacked the traditional dispensational commitment to the cessation of spiritual gifts, including speaking in tongues. The communities that these voices represented illustrated the extent of theological isolation that scholastic dispensationalism was already experiencing in the 1990s.

Hovering over the wider discourse was the "inaugurated eschatology" of neo-evangelical scholar George Eldon Ladd and his influence on progressive dispensationalism. Ryrie was alarmed by the sellout of "traditional" dispensationalism and wrote in his update to *Dispensationalism Today*, now just titled *Dispensationalism* (1995), that "critics of progressive dispensationalism see it as having already changed to covenant premillennialism"—a term that signified Ladd's position.[27] One of those critics, Walter Elwell, a covenantal theologian at Wheaton College, observed approvingly that "the newer [progressive] dispensationalism looks so much like the nondispensationalist premillennialism, that one struggles to see any real difference."[28]

Traditional dispensationalist Robert Lightner, who taught systematic theology at Dallas Seminary from 1968 to 2015, represented the old guard when he complained that progressive dispensationalism had sprung up in the "seedbed for dispensational thinking"—his own seminary.[29] "The founders and the heavy promoters of progressive dispensationalism are Dallas graduates," he lamented.[30] The situation was a disaster not just in seminary classrooms but also in the wider religious landscape. "There are already progressive dispensationalists on mission fields, heading up mission boards, and in Bible Colleges and Seminaries all across the country, with some schools completely overtaken by it."[31] The advance would only accelerate.

By the first decade of the new century, progressive dispensationalism had become an unavoidable, and in many places predominant, perspective at Dallas, Talbot, and Grace seminaries, as well as at Bible colleges including Moody Bible Institute and Philadelphia School of the Bible (renamed Cairn University). Many

27. Charles Ryrie, *Dispensationalism* (Chicago: Moody Press, 1995), 178.
28. Elwell, "Dispensationalisms of the Third Kind," 28.
29. Robert A. Lightner, "Progressive Dispensationalism," *Conservative Theological Journal* 4, no. 11 (April 2000): 55.
30. Lightner, "Progressive Dispensationalism," 55–56.
31. Lightner, "Progressive Dispensationalism," 62.

of the leading colleges and universities founded by dispensationalists—Biola University, Gordon College, Multnomah College, Trinity International University—continued to grow and even thrive as schools, but they joined each other in ditching distinctly dispensational curricula. Most faculty at these schools claimed little influence and found little inspiration from scholastic dispensationalism, and most students left having little or no knowledge of the system, either.

Traditional dispensationalism continued to be taught in small pockets—at Tyndale Seminary (Hurst, Texas), Virginia Beach Theological Seminary (Virginia Beach, Virginia), Southern California Seminary (El Cajon, California), and Faith Baptist Theological Seminary (Ankeny, Iowa), among others. It retained a foothold in other schools through the early twenty-first century—at Colorado Christian University (Lakewood, Colorado), Western Seminary (Portland, Oregon), Moody Bible Institute, and The Master's Seminary (Sun Valley, California), among others. The Conservative Theological Society, which published the *Conservative Theological Journal* (later renamed *Journal of Dispensational Theology*), was set up to maintain traditionalist scholarship. But this reach paled in the light of the tradition's status just a few decades earlier. Across the sweep of evangelicalism, the scholastic tradition was now traveling under the progressive banner or banished to the margins altogether.

A Lonely Wake for Dispensationalism

Almost no one outside the circles of fundamentalist and evangelical scholastic conversation attended to the collapse of scholastic dispensationalism. The Left Behind series, with the first volume published in 1995, would push pop dispensationalism to new heights of commercial success in the early twenty-first century, but as an organizing principle for religious belonging, dispensational theology started the new millennium at a great disadvantage.

Historians and journalists were looking elsewhere: at the growth of fundamentalist political and cultural power. Paul Boyer's magisterial study of prophecy belief in post–World War II American culture, *When Time Shall Be No More* (1992), represented both the potential and the weakness of this gaze. Boyer blurred the distinction between scholarly and popular dispensationalism (and between old and new premillennialism) to declare that the "belief system" of end-times prophecy—which included everyone from Seventh-day Adventists to Christian rock bands—was "far more pervasive than many realize."[32] He

---

32. Paul Boyer, *When Time Shall Be No More: Prophecy Belief in Modern American Culture* (Cambridge, MA: Belknap Press of Harvard University Press, 1992), 17.

documented its commercial power and its ascent to national politics in the New Christian Right and other sectors, including the "Israeli-premillennialist nexus" that influenced US–Israel diplomacy.[33] The book left readers with a strong sense of the extent of popular end-times belief, but with less of a grasp of the religious and theological landscape into which it fit.

Boyer had built his study on a research tradition dating to the late 1970s that interrogated how dispensationalism helped the political rise of the New Christian Right. This research asked how dispensationalism influenced politicized Christian fundamentalism—rather than the reverse. For all their merits, these works narrowed outside interest in dispensationalism to its influence on fundamentalism, rather than the networks of dispensational people, institutions, and practices that were already shrinking.

By the 2010s, academic interest in dispensational theology had reached its nadir. There had not been a historical survey since the early 1960s, while at the same time there was a boom of pathbreaking scholarship on premillennialism and pop dispensationalism as consumer and cultural phenomena, much of it grappling with the success of the Left Behind series and the New Christian Right. Historians elevated the centrality of apocalypticism in evangelical identity, but none of this work gave sustained attention to the ways fundamentalism had reshaped and ultimately helped to destroy dispensationalism. Nor could it readily explain the precipitating decline of premillennialism in evangelicalism in the 2010s: its abandonment by seminaries and Christian colleges, denominational shifts like the decision by the Evangelical Free Church of America to declare premillennialism "nonessential" and remove it from its statement of faith, or the rapid growth of "network Christianity" teaching Pentecostal and charismatic postmillennialism.[34]

Of course, elite and institutional influence was only one measure of success. In the pulpits and pews, dispensational themes continued to resonate. To take one example, a 2015 volume resembling the 1994 *Issues in Dispensationalism* took a victory lap, claiming that "dispensationalism is an enduring and essential facet of the evangelical landscape." The volume exhibited some of the same insularities as twenty years earlier (seven of the ten 2015 contributors held appointments at Dallas Seminary, and all but one had earned a

33. Boyer, *When Time*, 205.

34. Daniel Silliman, "EFCA Now Considers Premillennialism a Non-Essential," *Christianity Today*, August 23, 2019, https://www.christianitytoday.com/news/2019/august /efca-drops-premillennialism-evangelical-free-church-teds.html; Brad Christerson and Richard Flory, *The Rise of Network Christianity: How Independent Leaders Are Changing the Religious Landscape* (New York: Oxford University Press, 2017).

degree there), yet the volume had a point. The question was where the "facet" was located. "Dispensationalism is a popular, and populist, movement," one of the editors wrote. "Dispensational teaching is so widespread that a lot of people read the Bible this way, even if they are unaware that their position is dispensational. For many of them, it is all they know."[35] Indeed, a general premillennial orientation toward world events and church apostasy could be found across evangelicalism, as could more specific teachings on the rapture and the special eschatological role of the State of Israel. In many cases, pastors trained at dispensational schools continued to teach the theology long after the schools themselves had moved on. In other cases, the confluence of media, culture, and pastoral influence reinforced pop-dispensational eschatology. Pastors often drew from the deep historical wells of dispensational-influenced hymnody and visual culture, which kept at least some expressions of the tradition afloat.

Yet, all this popular interest drew on rapidly depleting stores of historical resources. With little institutional support, the prospects for their replenishment were bleak. Pop-dispensational culture, which is what overwhelmingly shaped evangelical churches and media, was poor sustenance for anything but populist and commercial folk religion. With the crack-up of fundamentalist theology after the 1970s, dispensationalism was the clear loser. Forged in a moment of heightened introspection about the failures of fundamentalist activism in the 1920s, dispensationalism would never escape its fractious origins, which culminated in its marginalization later in the century. As fundamentalist theology ruptured, dispensationalism's theological fate declined. The vacuum that accompanied scholastic dispensationalism's collapse extended across the wider fundamentalist and evangelical worlds, and this, too, is where the story of dispensationalism's rise and fall finds its most salient legacy today.

35. D. Jeffrey Bingham and Glenn R. Kreider, eds., *Dispensationalism and the History of Redemption: A Developing and Diverse Tradition* (Chicago: Moody Publishers, 2015), 13, 16–17.

My hope is built on nothing less
Than Scofield's notes and Moody Press
I dare not trust this Thompson's chain
But wholly lean on Scofield's fame

Anonymous

This doggerel of the first verse of the classic hymn "My Hope Is Built on Nothing Less" makes fun of dispensational productions (including the *Scofield Reference Bible* and *Thompson's Chain-Reference Bible*) as providing a narrow basis for theological reasoning. While the provenance of the satire is unknown, it has enjoyed popularity on Reformed message boards (such as The Puritan Board) and communities like Reddit's Reformed-Humor: Humor in the Reformed Tradition. Dispensationalists have tried their own hand, to middling success, in spaces such as the Facebook page "Semi-serious memes for dispensational postmillenialist teens," which has close to ten thousand likes.

19

Surveying the Aftermath

In 2004—the same year the twelfth Left Behind novel appeared on store shelves—the religion scholar Amy Johnson Frykholm published a study titled *Rapture Culture*. Like so many scholars of dispensationalism, Frykholm had a personal connection to the tradition. "In my mind's eye," she wrote, "I see my grandmother's *Scofield Reference Bible*, a text from which she read every day of her life, a text that told her of the coming of the rapture."[1] *Rapture Culture* offered insights into the appeal of rapture fiction and the way, as Frykholm described it on the first page, the Left Behind series brought "dispensationalist premillennialism" from the margins of culture "into the mainstream."[2] Speaking to a reporter years later, Frykholm sharpened her sense of the theology's ascendancy: "I don't think this is a subculture. This may be the dominant American culture, and the rest of us are subcultures."[3]

In light of the history of dispensationalism recounted so far, Frykholm's observations were both true and incomplete. Undoubtedly, the popular cultural reach of dispensationalism had achieved an apotheosis in the early twenty-first century. The Left Behind series was the most visible sign of this success, and in many other forms of media—nonfiction books, films, music—the American appetite for "rapture culture" seemed insatiable.

At the same time, the fate of dispensationalism as a living theological tradition had never been more under threat. The sales success of Left Behind—and

1. Amy Frykholm, *Rapture Culture: Left Behind in Evangelical America* (New York: Oxford University Press, 2004), 4.

2. Frykholm, *Rapture Culture*, 3.

3. Frykholm, quoted in Alex Morris, "Donald Trump: The End-Times President," *Rolling Stone*, October 30, 2020, https://www.rollingstone.com/politics/politics-features/donald-trump-christians-fundamentalists-end-times-rapture-1083131.

the broader success of pop dispensationalism—was a minor consolation. In 2004, dispensationalism was a movement with no vested national leaders, a scholastic tradition with no young scholars, a commercial behemoth with no internal cohesion. Frykholm's study had made this abundantly clear. She concluded that the Left Behind series, far from a "monolithic force" that taught its readers dispensational theology, was a "multiple, dynamic, contradictory system" with "cracks and fissures" that illustrated "just how broad and diffuse evangelicalism is in American culture."[4] The series had most likely introduced more readers to the concept of the rapture than had any writing since *Late Great Planet Earth*, but to what end? The authors LaHaye and Jenkins had done little more than toss a fictional account of dispensational eschatology into the ocean of American popular culture.

Dispensationalism's scholastic collapse in the 1990s did not mean it immediately disappeared. Vast amounts of cultural and institutional influence remained. Whether cognizant of the reality or not, twenty-first-century American evangelicals lived in a religious culture deeply imprinted by the dispensational system, whose ideas did not vanish, as Frykholm perceptively documented, but whose theological integrity was laid low. The parts of dispensationalism had been scattered, no longer organized in the service of a seemingly broken "system" but pulled into powerful currents of popular culture and politics where they continued to shape and form Christians in powerful ways.

Religious Culture: Pop-Dispensational Fumes

The most identifiable signs of dispensationalism in the early twenty-first century were the unbroken streaks of pop-dispensational cultural productions, running on tried-and-true concepts such as the rapture and the antichrist. Most of the Left Behind series' 80 million sales occurred in the new century, and the additions of briskly-selling pop-dispensational fiction continued: political thrillers and apocalyptic novels by Joel Rosenberg, Jamie Lee Gray, and Jonathan Cahn; films, including *Final: The Rapture* (2013) and *The Remaining* (2014); a *Left Behind: Eternal Forces* (2006) video game and then a film reboot starring Nicholas Cage in 2014, and still another on-screen adaptation featuring Kevin Sorbo nearing completion in 2022. In each of these productions, the theology of dispensationalism hovered in the background, informing plot points and an overall Christian didacticism that encouraged consumers toward the values that aligned with fundamentalism, even as they freely borrowed, modified, or discarded dispensational theology.

4. Frykholm, *Rapture Culture*, 183.

The same pop-dispensational lack of interest in theology was visible in prophecy analysis, which entered the twenty-first century deeply tied to New Christian Right arguments about society and culture. The Y2K bug illustrated the point. Concerns about Y2K were shared widely across American society, with fears of the ability of computers to respond to the year code changing from 99 to 00, making the year 2000 potentially indistinguishable from 1900. Pop dispensationalists were constant promoters of the worry. Jerry Falwell sold survival food by hotline and produced a film, *A Christian's Guide to the Millennium Bug*, that he promoted through his *Old-Time Gospel Hour*. Like the humanist tribulation, which was adopted by all types of New Christian Right leaders in the 1980s, Y2K alarmism also appealed to nondispensational fundamentalists. For the Reformed covenantalist pastor D. James Kennedy, the threat of Y2K posed a "very dark cloud" that will catch many "unprepared and drench them like they've never been drenched."[5] For Christian reconstructionist Gary North, Y2K was nothing less than the "biggest problem the modern world has ever faced" and a potential breakthrough for theonomic politics.[6] In each case, Y2K speculation was detached from theological discourse and embedded in the political agenda of the New Christian Right, where pop dispensationalism had also made a home.

The same context made space for pop-dispensational geopolitical analysis in the wake of the terrorist attacks of September 11, 2001. Hal Lindsey was one of the first to capitalize with *The Everlasting Hatred: The Roots of Jihad* (2002), which foregrounded radical Islam over the defunct Soviet Union as the most malignant force in the world, prophetically speaking. Lindsey was frank about his evolving views in 2002, explaining, "when I wrote *The Late Great Planet Earth* in 1969, the Muslim nations were nothing like the threat they are now. Because of Bible prophecy, I recognized that with Russian help, Muslims had to be one of the power blocs of the Last Days."[7] This spirit of adaptability had been anticipated by pop-dispensational writers in the 1990s, for example, in John Hagee's *Final Dawn over Jerusalem* (1999), which foregrounded a clash with Islam as the major new horizon in prophecy analysis. But the shift was even more pronounced after 2001. Joining Lindsey's book were Mark Hitchcock's *The Coming Invasion of Israel* (2002) and Mike Evans's *Beyond Iraq: The Next Move* (2003). With few references to the scholastic tradition and

---

5. Quoted in Hank Hanegraaff, *The Millennium Bug Debugged* (Minneapolis: Bethany House, 1999), 24.

6. Quoted in Joanna Glasner, "Y2K Alarmist: Wha' Happened?" *Wired*, January 5, 2000, https://www.wired.com/2000/01/y2k-alarmist-wha-happened/.

7. Hal Lindsey, *The Everlasting Hatred: The Roots of Jihad* (Washington, DC: WND Books, 2002), 231.

each featuring an idiosyncratic timeline for the unfolding of prophecy, these takes on the post-9/11 situation deepened the already strong suspicion of Islam among New Christian Right readers and tacitly or explicitly endorsed the War on Terror as a prophetically significant struggle.

A raft of best sellers combined post-9/11 geopolitical guessing with pop-dispensational-inspired scenarios beyond the War on Terror, including John Hagee's *The Four Blood Moons* (2013) and a book by Tim LaHaye's pastoral successor in El Cajon, California, David Jeremiah, titled *The Book of Signs* (2020). Many more authors joined the conversation, including the filmmaker and author Joel Richardson and the Israeli Christian author Amir Tsarfati, each publishing multiple prophecy books in the early 2020s. What united these authors was not shared seminary training or broader denominational heritage. Nor was it regional or social proximity. Rather, it was decades of engagement in conservative political organizations and causes on the part of the authors. There were no theological gatekeepers for pop dispensationalism, but there remained a uniformity of political and cultural prescriptions curated by a New Christian Right that continued to exhibit a pop-dispensational sensibility.

Counter to critics' expectations, pop dispensationalists had seamlessly adapted their analysis to a post–Cold War geopolitical order—just as previous generations of premillennialists had done after other conflicts. The difference this time was the extensive commercial and political reach of pop dispensationalism. Like sports commentators picking winners for the upcoming season, or movie buffs predicting next year's Oscar awards, the appeal of pop-dispensational prophecy analysis did not hinge on accuracy. Neither did its appeal wane as predictions shifted. As Lindsey's ceaseless sales proved, what mattered was that the exploration of relevant data was entertaining, that the predictions reinforced existing political and cultural commitments, and that the host was authentic in the conviction of the rightness of his predictions.

Repeating the fascination with Reagan's end-times beliefs in 1984, journalists twenty years later were drawn to a reported conversation between US president George W. Bush and French president Jacques René Chirac in the lead-up to the Iraq War in early 2003. The "born again" Bush speculated that "Gog and Magog are at work in the Middle East. Biblical prophecies are being fulfilled." In reference to the War on Terror, Bush explained, "This confrontation is willed by God, who wants to use this conflict to erase His people's enemies before a new age begins."[8] The exchange was first reported years later

---

8. Bush, quoted in Stephen Spector, "Gog and Magog in the White House: Did Biblical Prophecy Inspire the Invasion of Iraq?" *Journal of Church and State* 56, no. 3 (September 2014): 545.

by a University of Lausanne theology professor who was contacted by the French government for advice on the references. The entire conversation's provenance has been hotly debated, with senior officials of the Bush administration claiming it to be "utterly and completely false."[9] Accuracy aside, few critics or observers wondered where this heterodox dispensational scenario came from. By the year 2000, pop dispensationalism had so thoroughly permeated American political culture that genealogical analyses, such as those undertaken on Reagan's views in 1984, would have been pointless. The beliefs had become part of popular discourse all the same.

The humanist tribulation, already detached from the theology that shaped it, moved even further into the political and culture currents of the New Christian Right with the election of Donald Trump in 2016. A prime example was the best-selling *The Trump Prophecies* (2017). The subtitle read "The Astonishing True Story of the Man Who Saw Tomorrow . . . and What He Says Is Coming Next." The "man" was author Mark Taylor, an ex-firefighter who claimed as early as 2011 to have experienced visions of a Trump presidency that essentially would reverse the humanist tribulation and re-Christianize America. Taylor had no seminary training and was largely discredited outside certain New Christian Right circles. But his book was listed routinely as a best seller on Amazon, and a film version, *The Trump Prophecy* (2018), was produced in collaboration with Liberty University's Cinematic Arts program.

In the nineteenth century, new premillennialism had erected an entire institutional complex to create its distinctive religious subculture. New premillennialists were never apolitical, but they were oriented toward a different end goal than political power. The overarching aim of the new premillennial complex was global missions—a project embedded in American power—but it was also otherworldly in the most literal sense of the term. The kingdom for which new premillennialists evangelized lay across a metaphysical chasm that they, almost uniquely in the history of Christianity, placed entirely outside the present world. Pursuing such a mission, generation after generation, required a particular set of institutions and commitments dedicated to its success.

This premillennial complex of the early twentieth century was deeply compromised by the end of the century. Theological tensions at the heart of fundamentalist factionalism had led to the decisive crack-up in the 1970s that paved the way for a rival complex based on the goals of cultural and political power.

9. Will Inboden, "It's Impossible to Count the Things Wrong with the Negligent, Spurious, Distorted New Biography of George W. Bush," *Foreign Policy*, August 15, 2016, https://foreignpolicy.com/2016/08/15/its-impossible-to-count-the-things-wrong-with -the-negligent-spurious-distorted-new-biography-of-george-w-bush/.

The materials for this structure were not new; they were evident in the nationalist faction of the fundamentalist movement, in the fundamentalist embrace of anticommunism, in the dispensational insistence that theology and political commitments walk "hand in hand." But unlike the premillennial complex of the early twentieth century, the new complex assumed very little of an otherworldly agenda. Its chief patrons were just as easily (and eagerly) classified as consumers as they were Christians, as voters as they were missionaries.

Every twist on twenty-first-century pop dispensationalism had some precedent in the twentieth century. But not until the collapse of scholastic dispensationalism in the 1990s did the center of gravity shift decisively to the new political and cultural project, centered in the institutions of the New Christian Right and religious media. By the twenty-first century, this political-cultural pop-dispensational complex had become entirely autonomous from scholastic discourse and, in many ways, from established religious institutions of any type.

Popular Culture: Entertaining a Premillennal Nation

American culture in the twenty-first century was awash in pop-dispensational motifs with no explicit link to the theology of dispensationalism—and yet were indebted all the same. By dispensing with the theological system, producers of pop dispensationalism managed to reach virtually every medium of entertainment in the twenty-first century. In concert with other trends of the era, pop dispensationalism supplied Americans with an essentially premillennial vision of the future, though rarely was the term or its theological context overt. Rather, Americans of many backgrounds assumed a secularized premillennial expectation of declining social cohesion and rising existential threats that would end in era-defining catastrophe.

In the twenty-first century, countless films, television shows, and video games borrowed from pop-dispensational end-times imagery and vocabulary without acknowledgment. Explicit examples included films such as *This Is the End* (2013) and *Rapture-Palooza* (2013), both big-budget Hollywood comedies drawing on specific dispensational concepts: the rapture, the antichrist, and literal prophecy fulfillment. More generalized scenarios of a sudden cataclysmic disruption heralding the end of the world were popularized through zombie, dystopian, and disaster films. Each of these subgenres existed independent of pop dispensationalism, but their rising popularity coincided with pop dispensationalism's cultural success. Most creators were uninterested in sourcing their inspirations and made no reference to dispensationalism as such.

Dispensational concepts were used for more dramatic effect in the HBO series *The Leftovers* (2014–2017), based on a 2011 novel of the same name by Tom

Perrotta. The central plot device in the series was the sudden disappearance of 2 percent of the world's population. Neither of the two creative minds behind the show was an adherent of dispensationalism. But, reflecting on his inspirations for the plot, Perrotta cited the Millerites of the 1840s and the apocalyptic motif of a decimated humanity that focuses on survivors. The pop-dispensational rapture "flipped" this script, he explained to a journalist, and he pondered a story in which only a small number of random humans disappeared with no explanation. In *The Leftovers*, "it looked like the rapture, but it wasn't the rapture; it didn't choose Christians over anybody else."[10] The assumption behind the premise was that Americans of all types grasped the basic outlines of the dispensational teaching of the rapture. But more creatively interesting than a rules-based rapture, in Perrotta's mind, was an arbitrary one. The book and series won awards and critical acclaim, and introduced millions of viewers to an idea indebted to dispensationalism but strategically severed from its theological origins.

A similar influence was evident on an even larger scale in the Marvel superhero movies by Disney. In "Phase III" of the franchise, which encompassed eleven films from 2016 to 2019 that grossed more than $13 billion, the threat to the heroes centered on a galactic villain named Thanos, whose plan involved assembling a magical glove, the Infinity Gauntlet, that could disappear half of all humanity in an instant with a snap of the finger. The culminating movie of Phase III, *Avengers: End Game* (2019—the highest-grossing film in history at the time), began with the aftermath of the "Snapture." The first minutes of the movie were essentially a classic rapture scene, while a follow-up television series pondered the classic rapture quandary of where the select went when they disappeared.

The Infinity Gauntlet plot dated to a run of early 1990s comics, but the success of the Marvel movies made the rapture motif one of the most identifiable in all of cinema.[11] Just as with other examples of pop-dispensational diffusion, the Marvel universe had no traceable connection to religious institutions, and its use of the "Snapture" could be discussed entirely without reference to dispensationalism. When the two were compared, critics asked how the Bible stacked up against Marvel rather than the reverse. One popular blog examined

10. Kate Tuttle, "Tom Perrotta on 'The Leftovers' and How We Behave in Times of Fear and Loss," *Boston Globe*, March 31, 2020, https://www.bostonglobe.com/2020/03/31/arts/tom-perrotta-leftovers-how-we-behave-times-fear-loss/.

11. See Glen Weldon, "OK, Let's Talk about the Ending of 'Avengers: Infinity War,'" NPR, April 30, 2018, https://www.npr.org/2018/04/30/607093337/ok-lets-talk-about-the-ending-of-avengers-infinity-war and Leah Schnelbach, "Snapture vs. Rapture: Where *Avengers: Infinity War* Sticks with Biblical Lore, and Where It Departs," *Tor.com*, April 23, 2019, https://www.tor.com/2019/04/23/snapture-vs-rapture-avengers-infinity-war/.

"where *Avengers: Infinity War* [the previous film that introduced the 'Snapture'] sticks with biblical lore, and where it departs"—making dispensationalism (and the Bible) yet one more interesting source to mine for background lore in the far more culturally relevant Marvel Cinematic Universe.

Other mediums proved just as eager to incorporate pop-dispensational motifs into their imagined worlds. *Everybody's Gone to the Rapture* (2015) was a popular video game released for the Playstation 4 that allowed the player to investigate a slow-moving disappearance of inhabitants of an English village. The departures were eventually discovered to be the work of "The Pattern," a godlike force that, like the dispensational rapture, united people in an otherworldly dimension. Another example was the pop-punk band Ludo, in its concept album *Broken Bride* (2005), which told the story of a brokenhearted time traveler seeking to reverse the death of his wife. In one time jump, he accidently lands in a postapocalyptic zombie future and takes to manning the barricades of the last human city. The chorus of the song blares "Save our city / Keep our souls, Lord / Through the rapture of this world." Awash in biblical apocalyptic imagery, the song imagines a theologically unmoored, yet dispensationally resonant, scenario of the battle of Armageddon.

From the comedy of Bo Burnham, to television shows ranging from *Arrested Development* to *The Righteous Gemstones*, to the music of Kelly Clarkson, pop-dispensational resonances pulsed through American culture in the twenty-first century. The looming "secular" apocalypses of climate change and global pandemics, which culture creators addressed with more frequency beginning in the COVID-19 pandemic of 2020, affirmed a general resignation that the future looked bleak and, whatever the immediate outcome, the outlines of what was next were hazy and ominous. Screeds against environmental degradation, big data, and systemic injustice permeated the 2010s like utopian visions and optimistic speculations of space exploration soaked the popular culture of the 1950s. Commentators like Ross Douthat called the current culture "decadent," while others, such as writer Ta-Nehisi Coates, disabused readers of "the comforting narrative of divine law, toward fairy tales that imply some irrepressible justice."[12] The various sectors of American culture seemed to agree that the old ideological foe of premillennial time, the idea of inevitable historical progress, was down for the count.

All told, the dispersion of dispensational ideas, especially the shape of its premillennial telos and its unique eschatological concepts, reached dizzying cultural

---

12. Ross Douthat, *The Decadent Society: How We Became the Victims of Our Own Success* (New York: Simon & Schuster, 2020); Ta-Nehisi Coates, *Between the World and Me* (New York: One World, 2015), 70.

heights in the twenty-first century. The success shaped Americans' religious beliefs, too, at least when judged by polling data. A 2004 *Newsweek* poll indicated that 55 percent of Americans agreed that "faithful believers will be taken up to heaven in the rapture."[13] There was evidence everywhere that the rapture was more popular in the first decades of the twenty-first century than ever before, and yet the scholastic health of dispensationalism had already flatlined.

Political Culture: To the Ends of the Internet

Alongside its religious and popular reach, pop dispensationalism also advanced a complicated legacy on the Internet: in the message boards that perpetuated fundamentalist theological conflict, in the apocalyptic conspiracy theories that pulsed through online communities and real-world politics, and in the social-media-fueled polarization that came to define American society in the twenty-first century. In each arena, imprints of New Christian Right politics and pop-dispensational culture worked in tandem and interlaced in both predictable and novel ways.

Dispensational Bible Reading methods were enhanced by the radical advances in digital tools that allowed hypertext linking, keyword searches, and interpretive collaboration on a scale never before imagined. Popular study platforms like Logos Bible Software were built on digital Bible databases including the CDWordLibrary project at Dallas Theological Seminary. Logos built a massive library of ebooks that eventually counted more than 200,000 titles, including hundreds of study Bibles and translations, and most of the entire corpus of new premillennial and scholastic dispensational theology. From the collected works of John Nelson Darby and Lewis Sperry Chafer, to Chuck Swindoll's entire New Testament commentary, to back issues of obscure midcentury theological journals, Logos empowered pastors and lay researchers in ways that the first promoters of biblical concordances could only have dreamed of.

In other corners of the Internet, where fundamentalists debated theology, Christian reconstructionists, New Calvinists, and ex-dispensationalists continued to hammer on dispensationalism's weaknesses. Many of the most active conversations took place on message boards and blogs, from the harshly covenantal threads to more moderate forums. A 2011 Puritan Board thread titled "Am I a Dispensationalist?" allowed for members to diagnose the theology as if it was a sickness, and to prescribe Reformed doctrine for the cure.[14] Another

---

13. David Gates, "The Pop Prophets," *Newsweek*, May 24, 2004, 48.
14. "Am I a Dispensationalist?" *Puritan Board*, September 27, 2011, https://www.puritanboard.com/threads/am-i-a-dispensationalist.70127/.

thread, "What Was Your Last Straw for Dispensationalism?," attracted stories of disillusionment. One user recalled in 2019, "The last straw that broke my resolve in being able to coexist and endure [in a dispensationalist church] was when the pastor decided to preach expositionally through the Book of Revelation. Those crazy Clarence Larkin charts still haunt me."[15]

Antidispensationalism was present in numerous blogs and resource libraries, from the Reformed Forum, an educational organization linked to the International Council of Reformed Churches, to the theological database and blog Monergism, which compiled dozens of critical writings and videos. Separatist fundamentalists targeted dispensationalism, too, such as the YouTube controversialist and independent Baptist pastor Stephen Anderson, who produced multiple documentaries, including *After the Tribulation* (2016) and *Marching to Zion* (2017) that rehashed criticisms as old as fundamentalism itself. The vitriol of intrafundamentalist squabbling did not subside in the twenty-first century, even if the factions had changed in size and influence.

New Calvinism, whether in the Bible-nerd style of John Piper or the militant masculinity of megachurch pastor Mark Driscoll, ballooned in online presence at the same time that dispensational theology shrank. Driscoll's pioneering online preaching was one example, as was the fast expansion of the Gospel Coalition website, becoming one of the largest Web publishing platforms in all of American religion. By the beginning of the twenty-first century, New Calvinism had positioned itself as the heir to evangelical social thought for the rank-and-file laity that was once occupied by New Christian Right leaders such as Falwell and LaHaye, and long ago by "world system" critics and the heads of the Moody movement. New Calvinists advanced models of "biblical manhood and womanhood" that defaulted to twentieth-century cultural norms of family values. This was undoubtedly a continuation of similar efforts under pop-dispensational and New Christian Right leadership, albeit in much more theologically sophisticated formulations. The continuity between pop-dispensational and New Calvinist leadership circles revealed deep contours that spanned the breadth of white evangelicalism in the twenty-first century. Even so, this homogeneity existed alongside, and amid, seismic shifts that continued to shape the evangelical community.

As a declining theological tradition, scholastic dispensationalism had few online hubs that could rival the energy and content production of Reformed cov-

15. "What Was Your Last Straw for Dispensationalism?" *Puritan Board*, September 24, 2019, https://www.puritanboard.com/threads/what-was-your-last-straw-for-dispensationalism.99413/.

Figure 25. RaptureReady.com home page, 2022. Rapture Ready (raptureready.com) was an aggregator of pop-dispensational content in an era when most dispensational sites had gone defunct. The visual style of the site was a mix of the Left Behind film reboot of 2014 and cable news. As a sign of the political commitments of Rapture Ready, by 2020 the site also hosted raptureready.tv, which streamed the right-wing NewsMax when not offering original content.

enantal critics. One exception was Rapture Ready (raptureready.com), which aggregated news on "end-times events" and maintained up-to-date reading lists on pop-dispensational-related culture. A few sites acted as repositories of dispensational writing, including the Pre-Trib Research Center and the digital commons of Liberty University, but these were unmistakably "Web 1.0" technologies with little user-generated interactions or growing audiences. Aging televangelists could still make waves, especially through memified clips, such as in February 2022 when ninety-one-year-old Pat Robertson came out of retirement to declare that Russian president Vladimir Putin's invasion of Ukraine was a "staging ground" for the battle of Armageddon.[16] The political rather than theological core of these sites indicated what united pop dispensationalists after 2010: a shared loathing of liberalism, progressivism, and modernism.

The legacy of pop dispensationalism was more visible at the convergence of the New Christian Right and the Internet, which had merged to aid Donald Trump's

16. Timothy Bella, "Pat Robertson Says Putin Was 'Compelled by God' to Invade Ukraine to Fulfill Armageddon Prophecy," *Washington Post*, February 28, 2022, https://www.washingtonpost.com/world/2022/03/01/pat-robertson-putin-god-russia-ukraine/.

presidential election in 2015–2016 and provided his most loyal base of support even after his defeat in 2020. By the 2010s, pop dispensationalism was feeding into a resurgent Christian nationalist movement that continued to see itself as the rightful stewards of American culture. Christian nationalists rallied around a series of causes—the antibailout Tea Party after the 2008 banking crisis, the 2013 Birtherism controversy questioning the legitimacy of the presidency of Barack Obama, and the QAnon conspiracy, which began in 2017. Each episode had trace elements of pop-dispensational influence. Increasing media and political attention focused on police brutality after the death of Michael Brown in Ferguson, Missouri, in 2014 fueled a renewed narrative of world-system consolidation among many pop-dispensational observers. The polarization over racial justice and other issues served as confirmation of anti-Christian consolidation, just as secular humanism had served a previous generation of pop dispensationalists.

Combining many of these substrata of white evangelical culture was the QAnon conspiracy theory, which began on the edges of (avowedly nonreligious) 4Chan Internet culture, but soon gained a following that was disproportionally represented by those most likely to be influenced by pop dispensationalism, namely, white evangelicals. In the nearly five thousand posts by the mysterious Q from 2017 to 2020 were dozens of biblical passages and predictions ("Qdrops") related to the political fortunes of Donald Trump. There was no dominant apocalyptic motif in these posts, but the general outlines of the humanist tribulation were simply assumed. The revelations of Q heralded a "Great Awakening," led by Donald Trump, that would beat back a vast conspiracy of liberals, progressives, secularists, and other enemies of the American people. A vague deliverance, possibly supernatural, lay at the other end of "The Storm," Q's term for the coming tribulation.

Much of the coverage of QAnon fixated on the wild details of the conspiracy—deep-state child sex trafficking rings and satanic rituals—but more cogent to its appeal was the pattern of history that Q endorsed: tribulation, awakening, and deliverance. By the 2010s, this was a pattern structuring the political identity of the New Christian Right for more than a generation via politicized and commercialized pop dispensationalism and mediated through media and political messaging. Ed Stetzer, an evangelical pastor, declared in 2021 that "QAnon is a train that runs on the tracks that religion has already put in place."[17] A more precise metaphor in light of the fall of dispensationalism was that QAnon jumped the tracks at the spot where pop dispensationalists

---

17. Quoted in Kaleigh Rogers, "Why QAnon Has Attracted So Many White Evangelicals," FiveThirtyEight, March 4, 2021, https://fivethirtyeight.com/features/why-qanon-has-attracted-so-many-white-evangelicals/.

had departed scholastic dispensationalism a generation earlier, with both ca-reening into a folk-religious landscape defined by the anarchism of the Internet and the illogic of the culture wars.

By 2021, polling indicated that white evangelicals were overrepresented among QAnon followers, though the extent varied from a few percentage points to an October 2020 survey that showed close to 50 percent of all white evangelicals "agreed" or "strongly agreed" with some specific QAnon beliefs.[18] Whatever the number, it was clear that for a mix of religious, political, and cultural reasons both immediate and long term that were impossible to dis-entangle, a swath of white evangelicals were uniquely receptive to QAnon.

The similarities between Q and pop-dispensational rhetoric were a common feature of journalistic reporting on QAnon. As one reporter (and self-described ex-dispensationalist) assessed the situation in 2020, the Bible reading method followers applied to QAnon posts "is startlingly similar to a news-obsessed strain of Christian theology called premillennial dispensationalism."[19] Another reporter for *Rolling Stone* (also a self-described ex-dispensationalist) centered "rapture theology" at the heart of Trump's appeal and the polarization in Amer-ican society: "we can expect that rapture theology will not go away, will not cede the privileged position Trump has granted it. And from that privileged position, we can expect that it will continue to tear Americans apart."[20]

From the rise of electronic Bible software to the dark corners of Internet message boards, the legacy of dispensationalism was scattered across the digital landscape. With the system compromised, the constituent parts mixed into other movements and contexts. Political pop dispensationalism was one mani-festation (of many) in a long theological tradition that extended back nearly two hundred years. But more immediately, the proliferation of pop dispensation-alism kept the theology relevant in the new landscape of American media.

Tony Campolo: Deconstructing Dispensationalism

A telltale sign of dispensationalism's fate was its exclusion from the vital move-ments in evangelicalism in the early twenty-first century: the New Calvinists, the emergent church, the prosperity gospel, the evangelical Left, the "exvan-

18. Paul A. Djupe and Ryan P. Burge, "A Conspiracy at the Heart of It: Religion and Q," *Religion in Public,* November 6, 2020, https://religioninpublic.blog/2020/11/06/a-con spiracy-at-the-heart-of-it-religion-and-q/.

19. Sam Thielman, "When the News Becomes Religion," *Columbia Journalism Re-view,* August 11, 2020, https://www.cjr.org/first_person/qanon-conspiracy-religion -journalism.php.

20. Morris, "Donald Trump."

gelical" community—and many other pockets besides—all derided, ignored, or excluded dispensationalists.

Even so, the specter of dispensationalism was never far from early twenty-first-century evangelical discussions. It was invoked early and often—usually as outdated, harmful, and wrong. Brian McLaren, a key voice in the emergent church and born into a Plymouth Brethren family, wrote dismissively, in his popular *A Generous Orthodoxy* (2004), of "this pop-Evangelical eschatology" that amounted to "a skyhook Second Coming, wrapping up the whole of creation like an empty candy wrapper and throwing it in the cosmic dumpster so God can finally bring our souls to heaven."[21] At the same time, other evangelical outlets posted blog entries with titles like "Dispensationalism: A Doctrine More Dangerous Than Hell Itself," while the Twitter hashtag #RaptureAnxiety emerged in 2017 alongside #ChurchToo and other social media causes.[22] Evangelical theologians writing against Christian Zionism continued to blame pro-Israel politics on dispensationalism, and evangelical Bible scholars writing against literalist hermeneutics continued to dismiss dispensational interpretations of Scripture.

Prominent critics of conservative evangelicalism such as Tony Campolo, a sociologist, pastor, and leader of the evangelical Left, typified the way dispensationalism was represented in twenty-first-century evangelical discourse. In a 2003 speech to moderate Baptists who had left the Southern Baptist Convention, he blamed much of the denomination's dysfunction on "dispensationalism . . . a weird little form of fundamentalism that started like a hundred fifty years ago." Directing his anger at the New Calvinist stronghold of Southern Baptist Theological Seminary, Campolo scoffed that the school "has now enshrined Calvin. Well, if you're going to enshrine Calvin at least accept his eschatology, which would put 'Left Behind' out of business tomorrow."[23]

The comment was confusing. In fact, there were very few, if any, faculty at Southern Seminary who would be counted as dispensationalists in 2003. But it was revealing that Campolo made the charge anyway. By the year 2000, dispensationalism was nothing if not shorthand for sectarian fundamentalism—an ironic legacy given its leaders' longing to avoid this very fate. As white

21. Brian D. McLaren, *A Generous Orthodoxy* (Grand Rapids: Zondervan, 2004), 237.

22. Matthew Distefano, "Dispensationalism: A Doctrine More Dangerous Than Hell Itself," *Unfundamentalist Christians* (*Patheos* blog), October 6, 2016, https://www.patheos.com/blogs/unfundamentalistchristians/2016/10/dispensationalism-a-doctrine-more-dangerous-than-hell-itself/.

23. Gregory Tomlin, "Campolo: Opposition to Women Preachers Evidence of Demonic Influence," *Baptist Press*, June 27, 2003, https://www.baptistpress.com/resource-library/news/campolo-opposition-to-women-preachers-evidence-of-demonic-influence/.

evangelicalism continued to debate and separate itself over issues of justice, race, politics, and culture, the significance of dispensationalism had changed with it. Rather than a set of theological doctrines, dispensationalism had come to mean a certain perspective on politics. As Campolo described it, "That whole sense of the rapture, which may occur at any moment, is used as a device to oppose engagement with the principalities, the powers, the political and economic structures of our age"—a vivid, though unwitting, channeling of Philip Mauro's original critiques close to a century earlier.[24]

In the examples of Campolo and #RaptureAnxiety, opprobrium was directed foremost at pop dispensationalism, and especially Left Behind. Few critics found the energy to trash the works of Walvoord, Ryrie, or Pentecost, even as theological luminaries in other pockets of conservative evangelicalism—the Christian reconstructionist R. J. Rushdoony or the Reformed theologian Wayne Grudem—were widely discussed. The dire straits of scholastic dispensationalism were evident in the prominence of Hal Lindsey and Tim LaHaye as the tradition's foremost representatives. They had ushered dispensationalism into the center of American popular culture, pioneered its restructuring around culture and politics, and acted as agents of its dispersion into virtually every form of media and the center of the New Christian Right. By the twenty-first century, they had as strong a claim to the legacy of dispensationalism as anyone else.

One significant change over the century that bridged Dwight Moody and Tony Campolo was the extension of premillennial categories from overtly religious contexts such as revivals and missions agencies to the popular forms that deposited bits of dispensationalism into mainstream cultural and political discourse. The success of pop dispensationalism, as Campolo inadvertently revealed in his catalogue of recent New Christian Right political victories, was that its motifs and messages had been severed from the theological system to which it had once been attached. Campolo's charge against Southern Seminary was both misdirected—few dispensationalists worked at the institution—and insufficient—pop dispensationalism had very little to do with contemporary theological discourse. The end-times scenarios that authors used in their novels, and the prophetic timelines that many pastors still referenced in their sermons, advanced a humanist tribulation threat and a New Christian Right kingdom fashioned not by theologians but by the theologically uninterested or illiterate.

24. Tomlin, "Campolo."

And I heard a loud voice from the throne saying, "Look! God's dwelling place is now among the people, and he will dwell with them. They will be his people, and God himself will be with them and be their God. 'He will wipe every tear from their eyes. There will be no more death' or mourning or crying or pain, for the old order of things has passed away." He who was seated on the throne said, "I am making everything new!"

Revelation 21:3–5a NIV

Epilogue: Maranatha

Christianity is not just a system of beliefs or a set of ethical teachings. It is also a story that begins with the creation of the world and ends with the eschaton. The theologian Lesslie Newbigin described the Bible as a "universal, cosmic history" that "interprets the entire story of all things from creation to consummation."[1] Understood in this way, Christianity is inescapably eschatological. The last verses in the book of Revelation speak to the promise of Christ's return: "'Yes, I am coming soon.' Amen. Come, Lord Jesus" (Rev. 22:20 NIV). From the earliest creedal statements of the church to the last verses of many hymns, the Christian way of thinking and being is one with a telos toward ultimate completion, or the Hebrew word *shalom*.

This eschatological thrust has undoubtedly been one of dispensationalism's most significant contributions to American Christianity. It has supplied dispensationalists with vast amounts of energy and purpose, and deeply shaped the spiritual lives of millions of Christians both within and outside its direct influence. If nothing else, dispensationalism has prompted those who have encountered its teachings to take stock of the eschatological dimensions of the historic Christian tradition. Even in arguing against dispensationalism, other Christians have sharpened their own understandings of the kingdom of God and the consummation of history. The unwillingness of many dispensationalists to understand their own commitments in historical terms makes their story all the more tragic but their contributions no less substantial.

In the wake of dispensationalism's collapse, the eschatological sight of the American church has blurred. "Good!" skeptical readers might exclaim—

---

1. Lesslie Newbigin, *The Gospel in a Pluralist Society* (Grand Rapids: Eerdmans, 1989), 89.

better a vague vision than a false one. And yet the story of dispensationalism does not allow for such an easy judgment. The theological void left by dispensationalism—one of only a few sustained attempts to create a fundamentalist theological system in the twentieth century—has not remained empty. Evangelicals, and Americans more broadly, have only multiplied doomsday speculation since the collapse of dispensational theology in the 1990s. Its remnants in pop dispensationalism have been thrust into an ocean of raging American apocalypticisms that includes doomsayers of the Anthropocene, Replacement Theory extremists, QAnon trolls, techno pessimists, and neo-Malthusians. For all the problems that theological apocalypticism posed in the twentieth century, it is likely that irreligious apocalypticism in the twenty-first century will prove to be even more disruptive. To paraphrase political scientist Samuel Goldman's law of the conservation of religion: there is a relatively constant supply of apocalyptic energy in American society. What varies—and what makes all the difference—is how and where it is expressed.[2]

There are signs that Newbigin's frame of "cosmic history," taken up by evangelical theologians working within Anglican and Reformed traditions to transcend fundamentalist factionalism, will replace the void left by dispensationalism, but it is still too early to tell. At minimum, the influence of biblical studies, from that of Old Testament scholar J. Richard Middleton to that of New Testament scholar N. T. Wright, points to a cohering evangelical "holistic eschatology" that bridges the old covenantal-dispensational rift with a shared language of new creation, consummation, kingdom, and final cosmic renewal.

In books like Middleton's *A New Heaven and a New Earth* (2014), a type of "biblical eschatology" embraces the full sweep of the biblical narrative, "from creation to eschaton," and places the church at the center of God's eschatological realization of the kingdom.[3] Middleton and others in this vein continue to confront the legacy of dispensationalism—often through critical dialogue but no less framed by foregrounding the eschatological sweep of the Bible's story. This is a theme that remains largely dormant in much of the Christian church outside of American evangelicalism.

2. Goldman quoted in Shadi Hamid, "America without God," *The Atlantic*, April 2021, https://www.theatlantic.com/magazine/archive/2021/04/america-politics-religion/618072/.

3. J. Richard Middleton, *A New Heaven and a New Earth: Reclaiming Biblical Eschatology* (Grand Rapids: Baker Academic, 2014), 37.

The dialogue often centers, fittingly, on long-standing hermeneutical issues that frame much more significant theological claims. To take one example, British theologian N. T. Wright's popular *Surprised by Hope* (2008) reopened a more than century-old debate (originally hatched between old and new pre-millennialists in the late nineteenth century) about the precise direction of the rapture. Wright wanted to reclaim the term from its dispensational usage by arguing that the key passage describing "meeting" the Lord "in the air" was a vision of believers escorting Jesus victoriously to earth rather than escaping to heaven. The direction mattered, Wright contended, because in his reading, being a "citizen of heaven" (Phil. 3:20) did not imply that raptured Christians would find their true home "away from earth." Rather, "raptured" Christians would be those who escorted their victorious king to the earth to "put everything to rights."[4] Wright's goal in this interpretation was not to diminish the eschatological fervor of Christians but to rechannel that energy into working for the kingdom of God in anticipation of (though not, as postmillennialism would have it, in preparation for) Christ's return.

The signs of a living and integrated eschatological vision after dispensationalism are even more hopeful outside of the United States. In writings that predate those of Wright and Middleton, Latin American evangelical theologians such as René Padilla and Samuel Escobar offered a "holistic eschatology" in contrast to the "dualistic spiritualization that had come to be prevalent in the practice of [American] Evangelical missionaries."[5] These Latin American theologians, who were exposed to dispensationalism through the global missions movement, readily agreed that "Jesus's historical mission can only be understood in connection with the Kingdom of God," as Padilla wrote. But they dissented from the "dualism" that sat at the heart of dispensationalism, which consigned the kingdom of God to a future dispensation and called the church to a task focused only on saving souls. As Padilla concluded, Jesus's "mission here and now is a manifestation of the Kingdom as a reality present among men and women in his own person and action, in his preaching of the gospel and in his works of justice and mercy."[6] Such a critique of dispensation-

4. N. T. Wright, *Surprised by Hope: Rethinking Heaven, the Resurrection, and the Mission of the Church* (New York: HarperOne, 2008), 133.

5. Escobar, quoted in Miguel G. Echevarria Jr., "Middleton and Wright Have We Loved, but Padilla and Escobar? North American Eschatologies and Neglected Latino Voices," *Southeastern Theological Review* 11, no. 2 (Fall 2020): 54.

6. Quoted in Echevarria, "Middleton and Wright," 56.

alism also did not seek, as so many others had, to simply weaken eschatological fervency but to orient it in another direction.

Holistic eschatology is also gaining momentum beyond the field of theology. This is a development for which dispensationalists can rightfully take some measure of historical credit, albeit not straightforwardly. An eschatologically fueled vision of redemptive "kingdom work" that looks expectantly to the new creation animates some of the brightest spots in contemporary evangelical integrative thought, from the vocational writings of the Faith and Work movement to the redemptive entrepreneurial initiatives of organizations like Praxis; from the science and faith advocacy work of Biologos to the projects of "thinking Christianly" on university campuses hosted by Christian study centers and ministries such as InterVarsity Christian Fellowship.

New signs of holistic eschatology are also visible in evangelical media and culture, a sector once dominated by pop dispensationalism. Examples include BibleProject, a digital animation studio producing short videos on biblical themes, which has garnered millions of viewers in dozens of languages since it was launched in 2014. The project's tagline that "the Bible is a unified story that leads to Jesus" contains a strong eschatological thrust (and its cofounder and chief theological influence, Tim Mackie, trained with dispensational scholar John Sailhamer at Western Seminary in Portland, Oregon). The videos themselves often point to the fulfillment of history.[7]

Similar themes are weaved into Christian art by musicians such as Andrew Peterson, Fernando Ortega, and Sara Groves. While their songs have tended not to make the worship sets of megachurch bands, they have garnered sizable followings all the same. Broader artist collectives founded in recent decades, like the Rabbit Room and Art House America, emphasize "new creation" and express similar themes. Though hardly a self-conscious tradition like scholastic or pop dispensationalism, Christian artists exploring holistic eschatology and new creation have found dedicated followings across the evangelical world. Magazines, from *Comment* to *Image Journal*, travel in the same theological direction.

The biblical eschatology of Wright and Middleton, the holistic eschatology of Padilla and Escobar, and the creative explorations of both are in part responses to the once-dominant theology of dispensationalism that have found new vibrancy in the wake of its collapse. The rise and fall of dispensationalism

---

7. "Who We Are," Bible Project, accessed May 23, 2022, https://Bibleproject.com/about/.

remains an incomplete story. The story is incomplete because dispensation-alism's legacy is inseparable from what comes next. As a popular religious culture, a folk religion, and a scholastic endeavor, the project of dispensation-alism was too big, too sustained, and too consequential to have a clean ending. It remains another chapter, one not yet complete, in the "thrilling romance of orthodoxy" that has labored for a hundred generations over the meaning of that Aramaic cry by the apostle Paul: Maranatha! "Our Lord, Come!"[8]

8. G. K. Chesterton, *Orthodoxy* (London: John Lane, 1909), 185.

Acknowledgments

I began to write this book in earnest while in the doldrums of my fourth, and as it turned out final, year on the academic job market. In hindsight, the project's scope and my desire to publish with a Christian press were not-so-subtle signals that my heart, and ultimately my future, lay outside the tenure track. In the summer of 2019 I joined Upper House, a Christian study center located on the campus of my alma mater, the University of Wisconsin–Madison. I soon embraced its mission to maintain a faithful Christian presence within the intellectual and institutional life of the university. In ways big and small, this book is indelibly marked by my recent formation at Upper House and by the thoughtful conversations and perspectives of my colleagues, led by Upper House's executive director, John Terrill. The stability and support of Upper House's community, as well as the support of the Stephen and Laurel Brown Foundation, are models for how the growing movement of study centers across North America should continue to step into the gap and support Christian scholarship in the twenty-first century.

Though my job is university-adjacent, I am deeply indebted to those inside the academy who are scholars of American religious history. Their thoughtful critiques and encouragement helped this book become what it is. Special thanks go to Mark Edwards and Chuck Cohen, both of whom read the manuscript multiple times. Thanks to Kevin Walters, Skye Doney, Matt Sutton, and Timothy Padgett for reading the manuscript in its entirety. The larger community of scholars (historians and many otherwise) who discussed with me key themes of the book in various settings include: Cam Anderson, Yaakov Ariel, Vincent Bacote, Jon Beltz, Eric Carlsson, Heath Carter, Vaneesa Cook, Jon Dahl, Darren Dochuk, Ian Van Dyke, David Fields, Maggie Flamingo, Bob Frykenberg, Jeff Hardin, Rick Lindroth, George Marsden, J. Richard Middleton, Adam Nelson, Stanley Payne, Jennifer Ratner-Rosenhagen, Ulrich Rosenhagen, Daniel Silliman, David Swartz, Lauren Turck, Daniel K. Williams, John Wigger, and John Wilsey. The communities of the Midwest Intellectual History Group, UW–Madison's Intellectual History Group, and the Interdisciplinary Religion Group hosted by UW's Center for Religion and Global Citizenry were great sounding boards and sources of feedback for parts of this manuscript. The team at Eerdmans has been a delight to work with. David Bratt saw promise in the project from the start. James Ernest, Jenny Hoffman, Andrew Knapp, Tom Raabe, and Caroline Jansen have all improved the book immensely.

Blackhawk Church has been a valuable community for thinking through the multidimensional legacies of dispensationalism. Emeritus pastor Chris Dolson was generous with his time, with his recollections of Dallas Theological Seminary, and in his donation to me of a major haul of classic dispensational publications. Thanks to the friends in our community group and various reading groups (including Blackhawk Book Club) for patience when listening to me clarify exactly how dispensationalism connected with everything, everywhere, in modern Christianity.

Dispensationalism is deeply intertwined on both sides of my family. It is with some trepidation that I undertook an examination of the tradition, and with even more tentativeness when I discerned a "rise and fall" arc to the history. I thank Mom and Dad for their patience and curiosity through the process of writing this book, and for Dad's feedback on the final manuscript. To both: thank you for the deep reverence and authority you instilled in me for the Bible; thank you for walking the Lyon Street neighborhood with a seven-year-old boy to pray the Sinner's Prayer; thank you for indulging a thirteen-year-old's quest to get Jerry Jenkins to autograph Book 6 of the Left Behind series; thank you for exposing me to the breadth of the evangelical tradition and modeling the balance of conviction and irenicism.

Finally, my greatest debt is to my wife, Veronica, who partnered with me to make this book a reality. Near the beginning, her obligations entailed occasional nights and weekends on her own while I wrote (not counting all the dinner chatter about obscure theologians). Near the end, it meant balancing both of our hybrid work commitments and coparenting the three little boys we welcomed into the world in the meantime. The joy of raising David, Jack, and Benjamin knows no bounds, but our reserves of energy do! I wouldn't want to be forever tired with anyone else.

Glossary

Covenantal theology   An approach to biblical interpretation and system of theology that emphasizes the continuity of God's covenants with humanity, formulated in the sixteenth century during the Calvinistic Reformation. By and large, adherents, here called covenantalists, reject the key teachings of dispensationalism, including its eschatological schemes, the divisions of dispensational time, and the church-Israel distinction. In the twentieth century, fundamentalist covenantalists, especially those associated with Westminster Theological Seminary, were theological rivals with dispensationalists; the groups made up two of the primary factions of fundamentalism and later evangelicalism. In the late twentieth century, New Calvinists articulated a renewed fundamentalistic covenantalism.

Fundamentalism   A coalition of institutional networks and theological factions that joined efforts beginning in the 1920s in opposition to Protestant modernism and progressivism. The term "fundamentalism" appeared in 1920 to designate factions of Northern Baptists and Presbyterians organizing to reverse modernist trends in their denominations. It soon delineated all types of antimodernist Protestants. I identify and follow three factions in particular—denominational, nationalist, and interdenominational fundamentalists—who held overlapping convictions but divergent priorities and strategies. New premillennialism was most influential among interdenominational fundamentalists and least important among denominationalists, setting up a culture of competition in the 1930s between covenantalists (with denominational roots in denominational fundamentalism) and dispensationalists (with roots in interdenominational fundamentalism). Nationalist fundamentalists denote a wide spectrum who privileged cultural over religious and theological engagement.

Great Lakes basin The region of origin of new premillennialism from the Midwest to New England (Minnesota and Missouri to Maine). I use the term especially in tracing the reception of Exclusive Brethren teachings and the locus of power in the Moody movement. I also trace how premillennialism moves from a theology embraced by this region to one that, over the course of the twentieth century and the systematization of dispensationalism, develops major centers of production and influence in the South and on the West Coast.

Modernism The movement, located especially in denominational Protestantism, to adapt Christianity to address the ills of industrialization and advances in historical and scientific knowledge. Modernists tended to accept biblical higher criticism, Darwinian evolution, and a progressive view of history. They helped to advance the Social Gospel movement, applying Christian ethics to social problems. Though they rejected premillennialism, their roots are intertwined with those of the Moody movement and the wider issues of religion and culture that gave rise to new premillennialism and, eventually, dispensationalism.

Moody movement A historically influential network of white evangelicalism traced through connections with Dwight Moody and his revivalism that emerged in the 1870s and advanced traditions of revivalism, global missions, and premillennialism through the 1920s, when it became a victim of the fracture in Protestantism broadly, and fundamentalism specifically.[1]

New premillennialism The eschatological innovations of the Exclusive Brethren and other radical dissenter groups in Great Britain beginning in the 1820s that find an American reception (and alterations) beginning in the 1850s. Three key teachings of new premillennialism, which build on the broader school of premillennialism, are the church-Israel distinction, dispensational

---

1. This term is borrowed from Michael S. Hamilton, "The Interdenominational Evangelicalism of Dwight Moody and the Problem of Fundamentalism," in *American Evangelicalism: George Marsden and the State of American Religious History*, ed. Darren Dochuk, Thomas S. Kidd, and Kurt W. Peterson (Notre Dame, IN: University of Notre Dame Press, 2014), 230–80.

time, and the imminent rapture. All three reinforce the teaching that the kingdom of God awaits earthly inauguration until the end times. New premillennialism is a major tradition that informs dispensationalism in the twentieth century and, while not a response to it, stands in contrast to covenantalism.

Old premillennialism   A theological tradition since the sixteenth century that sees biblical prophecy as referring mostly to past historical and predicted future events. Unlike new premillennialism, old premillennialism has no concept of imminent rapture or church-Israel distinction (though sometimes reserving a special role for Jews in the end times). New premillennialism and old premillennialism have much overlap, of course, but also decisive differences. The neo-evangelical movement of the mid-twentieth century (see chap. 15) can be interpreted as a revival of old premillennialism in reaction to new premillennialism and dispensationalism, which was itself a modified form that usually went under the name historic premillennialism.

Pop dispensationalism   A branch of dispensationalism that emerges after the 1960s as a popularized version of dispensational eschatology that includes the rapture, the figure of the antichrist, and the mark of the beast. Pop dispensationalists, led by Hal Lindsey, maintained increasingly strained ties to religious institutions and were more notable for their media and political expansion, especially through television, film, novels, and the New Christian Right. In my telling, pop dispensationalism consistently distilled dispensational teachings and amputated the eschatological scenario from the larger body of dispensational thought, giving it ever greater potential for cultural diffusion.

Scholastic dispensationalism   A branch of dispensationalism that forms in the 1930s in the wake of the early fundamentalist movement's failures to achieve their stated objectives. Led by Lewis Sperry Chafer and Dallas Theological Seminary, scholastics worked to construct a theological system out of the constituent parts of new premillennialism, biblical literalism, revivalism, and fundamentalism. While expanding through the 1960s, scholastic dispensationalism met increasing resistance from other fundamentalist factions, as well as competition from pop dispensationalism. By the twenty-first century, scholastic dispensationalism had collapsed, with most onetime dispensational institutions abandoning the theology, adopting the modified view of progressive dispensationalism, or embracing a pop-dispensational-infused Christian nationalism.

Sectional reconciliation   The post–Civil War project by white northern evangelicals to overcome the divisions of North-South sectionalism by uniting around shared white Christian identity to the exclusion of racial justice efforts and Black Christians. Dwight Moody was a major proponent of sectional reconciliation, which he promoted in order to strengthen global missions support. The project became widely embraced by dispensationalists in the twentieth century and paved the way for the theology to gain ground in the South and the Sun Belt.

World system   In premillennial and dispensational social analysis, the deleterious forces that govern modern society. The term was originally embedded in a populist critique of industrialization and modernist Protestantism that interpreted the predominant trend of the age as one toward "consolidation" in all areas of life. The world system had deep theological and eschatological significance as being run by Satan and the object that Christ will crush in the end of days.

Bibliographic Essay

Introduction

The following bibliographic essay will make clear my indebtedness to a broad range of scholarship. Here I want to highlight the seven books that have most deeply shaped my understanding of the history of dispensationalism. These are the works with which I am in most constant dialogue. The particular points of engagement will become evident below.

These key books include the following: Donald Harman Akenson's two volumes on early Brethren thought: *Exporting the Rapture: John Nelson Darby and the Victorian Conquest of North-American Evangelicalism* (Oxford University Press, 2018) and *Discovering the End of Time: Irish Evangelicals in the Age of Daniel O'Connell* (McGill-Queen's University Press, 2016); Paul Boyer, *When Time Shall Be No More: Prophecy Belief in Modern American Culture* (Belknap Press of Harvard University Press, 1992); Brendan Pietsch, *Dispensational Modernism* (Oxford University Press, 2015); Ernest Sandeen, *The Roots of Fundamentalism: British and American Millenarianism, 1800–1930* (University of Chicago Press, 1970); R. Todd Mangum, *The Dispensational-Covenantal Rift: The Fissuring of American Evangelical Theology from 1936 to 1944* (Wipf & Stock, 2007); and Matthew Avery Sutton, *American Apocalypse: A History of Modern Evangelicalism* (Belknap Press of Harvard University Press, 2014).

Chapter 1

The history of the Exclusive Brethren and Darby's original ideas has benefited from some excellent scholarship in recent years. I was most influenced by Akenson, *Exporting the Rapture*; Akenson, *Discovering the End of Time*;

Timothy C. F. Stunt, *Elusive Quest of the Spiritual Malcontent* (Wipf & Stock, 2015); Mark S. Sweetnam and Crawford Gribben, "J. N. Darby and the Irish Origins of Dispensationalism," *Journal of the Evangelical Theological Society* 52, no. 3 (2009): 569–77; Timothy Stunt, *From Awakening to Secession: Radical Evangelicals in Switzerland and Britain, 1815–35* (T&T Clark, 2000); and Sandeen, *The Roots of Fundamentalism.*

Historians have recently downplayed the direct influence of the Brethren on American premillennialism. Pietsch, *Dispensational Modernism,* 214n10, argues for the Brethren's "hermeneutic or aesthetic influence, rather than direct doctrinal impact" and especially diminishes the role of Darby. Pietsch is undoubtedly correct that most accounts of dispensationalism, especially those focused on the twentieth-century fundamentalist movement, "simply assume his influence through direct transmission of ideas" (215n10). A notable exception to this is Alan Terlep, "Inventing the Rapture: The Formation of American Dispensationalism, 1850–1875" (PhD diss., University of Chicago, 2010). Turlep emphasizes the role of James Inglis as an American intermediary. Other works cite Darby as an important influence but do not elucidate how his ideas spread, including Timothy Weber, *Living in the Shadow of the Second Coming: American Premillennialism, 1875–1925* (Oxford University Press, 1983), and Boyer, *When Time Shall Be No More.*

In highlighting the importance of Brethren besides Darby, I leaned into themes of print culture and popular religion, and a wider sense of Brethren encounters with Americans. On these themes, I was especially indebted to Candy Gunther Brown, *The Word in the World: Evangelical Writing, Publishing, and Reading in America, 1789–1880* (University of North Carolina Press, 2004); Kathryn Long, *The Revival of 1857–58: Interpreting an American Religious Awakening* (Oxford University Press, 1998); David Paul Nord, *Faith in Reading: Religious Publishing and the Birth of Mass Media in America* (Oxford University Press, 2004); and Timothy L. Smith, *Revivalism and Social Reform: American Protestantism on the Eve of the Civil War,* rev. ed. (Wipf & Stock, 2004).

Chapter 2

Darby's North American travels have been a key point of interest for understanding his legacy. Those who find Darby's travels significant to the growth and spread of dispensationalism include Sandeen, *The Roots of Fundamentalism,* which contains the standard account of Darby's journeys. Daniel P. Fuller, "The Hermeneutics of Dispensationalism" (PhD diss., Fuller Theological Seminary, 1957), and Clarence Bass, *Backgrounds to Dispensationalism: Its Historical Genesis and Ecclesiastical Implications* (Eerdmans, 1960), do not detail Darby's travels but emphasize his personal contribution to dispensationalism. Larry V. Crutchfield, *The Origins of Dispensationalism: The Darby Factor* (University Press of America, 1992), offers one of the most forceful acknowledgments by a dispensationalist of Darby's direct influence.

In telling the American reception of Brethren ideas, Scottish commonsense philosophy and the Baconian scientific method are front and center. Both were prevalent in nineteenth-century evangelicalism, as discussed in Theodore Dwight Bozeman, *Protestants in an Age of Science: The Baconian Ideal and Antebellum American Religious Thought*, 2nd ed. (University of North Carolina Press, 2009); George Marsden, *Fundamentalism and American Culture*, 2nd ed. (Oxford University Press, 2006); and Mark A. Noll, "Common Sense Traditions and American Evangelical Thought," *American Quarterly* 37, no. 2 (July 1985): 216–38. The relationship of Baconianism to dispensationalism is explored in Pietsch, *Dispensational Modernism*, esp. 101–6, and William S. Sailer, "Francis Bacon among the Theologians: Aspects of Dispensational Hermeneutics," *Evangelical Journal* 6 (1988): 71–82. David Anthony Schmidt, "Scripture beyond Common Sense: Sentimental Bible Study and the Evangelical Practice of 'the Bible Reading,'" *Journal of Religious History* 41, no. 1 (2017): 60–80, helpfully moves the commonsense framework into religious devotional territory.

Brethren typology, and especially the distinctive typologizing of biblical historical (as opposed to prophetic) literature, is explored in Akenson, *Discovering the End of Time*; Ronald M. Henzel, *Darby, Dualism, and the Decline of Dispensationalism* (Fenestra Books, 2003); and Floyd Saunders Elmore, "A Critical Examination of the Doctrine of the Two Peoples of God in John Nelson Darby" (ThD diss., Dallas Theological Seminary, 1990). A helpful discussion of typology and gender is in Margaret Bendroth, *Fundamentalism and Gender, 1875 to the Present* (Yale University Press, 1996).

Chapter 3

I emphasize the importance of the Civil War and Reconstruction to the appeal of Brethren ideas in America. On the Civil War's religious significance, I found particularly helpful George C. Rable, *God's Almost Chosen Peoples: A Religious History of the American Civil War* (University of North Carolina Press, 2010); Mark Noll, *The Civil War as a Theological Crisis* (University of North Carolina Press, 2006); and George Fredrickson, *The Inner Civil War: Northern Intellectuals and the Crisis of the Union* (Harper, 1968).

The fate of border-state evangelicals during the Civil War and Reconstruction is illuminated in April E. Holm, *A Kingdom Divided: Evangelicals, Loyalty, and Sectionalism in the Civil War Era* (Louisiana State University Press, 2017), and Luke E. Harlow, *Religion, Race, and the Making of Confederate Kentucky, 1830–1880* (Cambridge University Press, 2016). There is no critical biography of James Hall Brookes. The most important record of his life was written by his son-in-law, David Riddle Williams, *James H. Brookes: A Memoir* (Presbyterian Board of Publication, 1897), but it is eulogistic. The theological analysis of Carl E. Sanders, *The Premillennial Faith of James Brookes: Reexamining the Roots of American Dispensationalism* (University Press of America, 2001), makes the case that Brookes should be understood as an Old School Presbyterian premillennialist rather than a disciple of Darby. Sanders's analysis helps to correct loose connections made by Sandeen and others to paint Brookes as merely a proto-dispensationalist. Both Brethren influences and Brookes's Presbyterianism are important to understanding his development, an argument made stronger by the treatment of Brookes in Terlep, "Inventing the Rapture."

There is also no critical biography of Joseph A. Seiss, though two dissertations have focused on his dual legacies as a Lutheran and a premillennialist: Lawrence R. Rast, "Joseph A. Seiss and the Lutheran Church in America" (PhD diss., Vanderbilt University, 2003), and Samuel R. Zeiser, "Joseph Augustus Seiss: Popular Nineteenth-Century Lutheran Pastor and Premillennialist" (PhD diss., Drew University, 2001). Zeiser helpfully uses unpublished autobiographical writings of Seiss. Situating Seiss in a longer history of (old) premillennialism is owed to Robert Kieran Whalen, "Millenarianism and Millennialism in America, 1790–1880" (PhD diss., State University of New York at Stony Brook, 1972). The connection between Seiss and James Robinson Graves is made in Danny Eugene Howe, "An Analysis of Dispensationalism and Its Implications for the Theologies of James Robinson Graves, John Franklyn Norris, and Wallie Amos Criswell" (PhD diss., Southwestern Baptist Theological Seminary, 1988).

Chapter 4

Twentieth-century dispensationalists have tended to emphasize the long provenance of their ideas. Charles Ryrie, *Dispensationalism Today* (Moody Press, 1965), and Arnold Ehlert, *A Bibliographic History of Dispensationalism* (Baker, 1965), both claim a deep history for dispensational ideas, if not the system, stretching to the early church. Theological critics of dispensationalism have in turn emphasized the novelty of Darby's teachings and his direct influence. This is especially true of Oswald T. Allis, *Prophecy and the Church* (Presbyterian & Reformed, 1945), and C. Norman Kraus, *Dispensationalism in America: Its Rise and Development* (John Knox, 1958).

Both sides have tended to obscure the diversity of views within nineteenth-century premillennialism. The distinctive elements of historicist and futurist schools (what I have called old and new premillennialism), as well as the cultural context of nineteenth-century premillennialism, have received needed clarity in Martin Spence, *Heaven on Earth: Reimagining Time and Eternity in Nineteenth-Century British Evangelicalism* (Wipf & Stock, 2015). The distinction between the two schools has received more attention in contemporary theological discourse, especially among conservative Protestants. See Alan Hultberg, ed., *Three Views on the Rapture: Pretribulation, Prewrath, or Posttribulation* (Zondervan, 2018); Darrell L. Bock, ed., *Three Views on the Millennium and Beyond* (Zondervan, 1999); and Robert G. Clouse, ed., *The Meaning of the Millennium: Four Views* (InterVarsity Press, 1977).

Numerology and pyramidology have been treated as fringe aspects of premillennialism, in part because of their association with figures such as Charles Taze Russell. Yet in the late nineteenth century, these areas of inquiry were popular, if still suspect to most theologians. On the general allure of numbers in prophecy culture, see Boyer, *When Time Shall Be No More*.

Chapter 5

Moody's centrality to interdenominational evangelicalism is established in Sandeen, *The Roots of Fundamentalism*, and Marsden, *Fundamentalism and American Culture*. It is given renewed focus and helpfully framed as the "Moody movement" in Michael S. Hamilton, "The Interdenominational Evangelicalism of Dwight Moody and the Problem of Fundamentalism," in *American Evangelicalism: George Marsden and the State of American Religious History*, ed. Darren Dochuk, Thomas S. Kidd, and Kurt W. Peterson (University of Notre Dame Press, 2014), 230–80.

The best biography of Moody remains James Findlay, *Dwight L. Moody: American Evangelist, 1837–1899* (Wipf & Stock, 2007), originally published in 1969 by the University of Chicago Press. I found helpful the insights into Moody's theology, including links to Brethren, in Stanley N. Gundry, *Love Them In: The Life and Theology of D. L. Moody* (Moody Press, 1999). Edward J. Blum, *Reforging the White Republic: Race, Religion, and American Nationalism, 1865–1898* (Louisiana State University Press, 2005), helps immensely to situate

Moody at the forefront of white sectional reconciliation during Reconstruction. Moody's religious formation and work in Chicago are explored in Barbara Dobschuetz, "Fundamentalism and American Urban Culture: Community and Religious Identity in Dwight L. Moody's Chicago, 1864–1914" (PhD diss., University of Illinois at Chicago, 1996). The Spafford saga is told in Jane Fletcher Geniesse, *American Priestess: The Extraordinary Story of Anna Spafford and the American Colony in Jerusalem* (Doubleday, 2009).

Chapter 6

The importance of the Niagara Bible Conference is gleaned from Sandeen, *The Roots of Fundamentalism*; Mark Sidwell, "'Come Apart and Rest a While': The Origin of the Bible Conference Movement in America," *Detroit Baptist Seminary Journal* 15 (2010): 75–98; Walter Unger, "Earnestly Contending for the Faith: The Role of the Niagara Bible Conference in the Emergence of American Fundamentalism, 1875–1900" (PhD diss., Simon Fraser University, 1981); and Larry Dean Pettegrew, "The Historical and Theological Contributions of the Niagara Bible Conference to American Fundamentalism" (ThD diss., Dallas Theological Seminary, 1976). Placing Niagara in a broader context of religious networks in the late nineteenth century is helped by T. R. Noddings, "Main Street Jesus: Small-City Revivalism, Chautauqua, and the Birth of Religious Conservatism, 1880–1930" (PhD diss., Northwestern University, 2019).

Recent scholarship has emphasized the importance of nineteenth-century business practices to the growth of evangelical Christianity, both theologically and institutionally. Timothy Gloege does this for the Moody Bible Institute: *Guaranteed Pure: The Moody Bible Institute, Business, and the Making of Modern Evangelicalism* (University of North Carolina Press, 2015). Other recent studies on business and religion with a nineteenth-century starting point include Daniel Vaca, *Evangelicals Incorporated: Books and the Business of Religion in America* (Harvard University Press, 2019), and Nicole C. Kirk, *Wanamaker's Temple: The Business of Religion in an Iconic Department Store* (NYU Press, 2018).

Biographies of new premillennial builders are invaluable resources. Arthur T. Pierson's life is explored in Dana L. Robert, *Occupy until I Come: A. T. Pierson and the Evangelization of the World* (Eerdmans, 2003). The best biography of William E. Blackstone is Jonathan David Moorhead, "Jesus Is Coming: The Life and Work of William E. Blackstone (1841–1935)" (PhD diss., Dallas Theological Seminary, 2008). On A. J. Gordon, founder of Boston Missionary Training Institute, see Scott M. Gibson, *A. J. Gordon: American Premillen-*

nialist (University Press of America, 2001). And on Albert B. Simpson, see Daryn Henry, *A. B. Simpson and the Making of Modern Evangelicalism* (McGill-Queen's University Press, 2019).

The rise of the Bible institutes is captured in Virginia Brereton, *Training God's Army: The American Bible School, 1880–1940* (Indiana University Press, 1990), and Glenn Miller, *Piety and Profession: American Protestant Theological Education, 1870–1970* (Eerdmans, 2007). The explosion of "faith missions" in the 1880s is documented in Klaus Fiedler, *Interdenominational Faith Missions in Africa: History and Ecclesiology* (Mzuni Press, 2018). The foremost expert on Jewish missions is Yaakov Ariel, especially his *Evangelizing the Chosen People: Missions to the Jews in America, 1880–2000* (University of North Carolina Press, 2000).

Alongside Sandeen's recounting of the decline of the Niagara conference in *The Roots of Fundamentalism*, 209–11, see Larry D. Pettegrew, "The Rapture Debate at the Niagara Falls Conference," *Bibliotheca Sacra* 157 (2000): 331–47.

Chapter 7

The importance of Lyman Stewart and the Bible Institute of Los Angeles is established in Darren Dochuk, *Anointed with Oil: How Christianity and Crude Made Modern America* (Basic Books, 2019); Christina A. Copland, "Faith, Finances and the Remaking of Southern California Fundamentalism, 1910–1968" (PhD diss., University of Southern California, 2018); and Brendan Pietsch, "Lyman Stewart and Early Fundamentalism," *Church History* 82, no. 3 (2013): 617–46. On Biola University, see also James O. Henry, "History of Biola University since 1908" (unpublished manuscript, 1996).

The theological contours of early Pentecostalism are explored in Edith L. Blumhofer, *Restoring the Faith: The Assemblies of God, Pentecostalism, and American Culture* (University of Illinois Press, 1993); Donald W. Dayton, *Theological Roots of Pentecostalism* (Baker Academic, 1987), and Grant Wacker, *Heaven Below: Early Pentecostals and American Culture* (Harvard University Press, 2003). Gerald Wayne King, "Disfellowshiped: Pentecostal Responses to Fundamentalism in the United States, 1906–1943" (PhD diss., University of Birmingham, 2009), documents the fracturing and borrowing between early Pentecostals and fundamentalists.

On sectional reconciliation and racial attitudes of early twentieth-century interdenominational evangelicals, see Nathaniel Grimes, "The Racial Ideology of Rapture," *Perspectives in Religious Studies* 43, no. 3 (2016): 211–21; Michael Phillips, *White Metropolis: Race, Ethnicity, and Religion in Dallas, 1841–2001*

(University of Texas Press, 2010); and Blum, *Reforging the White Republic*. Sutton, *American Apocalypse*, demonstrates how prophecy interpretation broke along racial lines in this era.

Chapter 8

The production and reception of the *Scofield Reference Bible* are best documented in Pietsch, *Dispensational Modernism*, and R. Todd Mangum and Mark S. Sweetnam, *The Scofield Bible: Its History and Impact on the Evangelical Church* (Paternoster, 2012). Arno C. Gaebelein's firsthand account is a crucial primary source: *The History of the "Scofield Reference Bible"* (1943; reprint, CrossReach Publications, 2017)—as are the biographies of him: Michael D. Stallard, *The Early Twentieth-Century Dispensationalism of Arno C. Gaebelein* (Mellen, 2002), and David A. Rausch, *Arno C. Gaebelein, 1861–1945: Irenic Fundamentalist and Scholar* (Mellen, 1983). Scofield's direct links to the Brethren are explored in David J. MacLeo, "Walter Scott, a Link in Dispensationalism between Darby and Scofield?" *Bibliotheca Sacra* 153, no. 610 (April 1996): 155–78.

Chapter 9

Mauro's role in premillennial social criticism has not received much attention, but he does appear in Sutton, *American Apocalypse*, and in T. Andrew Coates, "The Senses of Fundamentalism: A Material History of Sensing Bodies in Early Twentieth-Century American Fundamentalism" (PhD diss., Duke University, 2016).

The "world system" was deeply implicated in evangelical attitudes toward capitalism. See Dochuk, *Anointed with Oil*; Gloege, *Guaranteed Pure*; and Kirk, *Wanamaker's Temple*. On premillennial attitudes toward Progressive Era social reform and the Social Gospel, see Sutton, *American Apocalypse*; Weber, *Living in the Shadow of the Second Coming*; Douglas Frank, *Less Than Conquerors: How Evangelicals Entered the Twentieth Century* (1986; reprint, Wipf & Stock, 2009); and Betty A. DeBerg, *Ungodly Women: Gender and the First Wave of American Fundamentalism* (Fortress, 1990).

The most valuable account of *The Fundamentals* is in Gloege, *Guaranteed Pure*. For the importance of *The Fundamentals* to fundamentalism, see Marsden, *Fundamentalism and American Culture*, and, for a sympathetic account, Gerald Priest, "A. C. Dixon, Chicago, and *The Fundamentals*," *Detroit Baptist Seminary Journal* 1 (1996): 113–34. Coates, "The Senses of Fundamentalism," helpfully situates *The Fundamentals* within a broader understanding of emerging fundamentalist religion.

On premillennialism and World War I, see Sutton, *American Apocalypse*; Marsden, *Fundamentalism and American Culture*; Weber, *Living in the Shadow of the Second Coming*; Richard Kent Evans, "'A New Protestantism Has Come': World War I, Premillennial Dispensationalism, and the Rise of Fundamentalism in Philadelphia," *Pennsylvania History: A Journal of Mid-Atlantic Studies* 84, no. 3 (Summer 2017): 292–312; and Adam Petersen, "'The Premillennial Menace': Shailer Mathews' Theological-Political Battle against Premillennialism during the First World War," *Journal of Church and State* 60, no. 2 (May 2018): 271–98. For the wider theological stakes of World War I between premillennialists and postmillennialists, see J. Michael Utzinger, *Yet Saints Their Watch Are Keeping: Fundamentalists, Modernists, and the Development of Evangelical Ecclesiology, 1887–1937* (Mercer University Press, 2006).

Chapter 10

Early and critical accounts of fundamentalism include Stewart G. Cole, *The History of Fundamentalism* (R. R. Smith, 1931), and Norman Furniss, *The Fundamentalist Controversy, 1918–1931* (Yale University Press, 1954). Cole's study spearheaded the social psychological analysis of the movement. Sandeen's *The Roots of Fundamentalism* subsumed fundamentalism as an outgrowth of millenarianism, while George Marsden introduced a more comprehensive definition of fundamentalism as "organized opposition to 'modernism,'" in *Fundamentalism and American Culture* (1st ed. 1980), that included cultural as well as theological attitudes. Recent histories of fundamentalism have been especially interested in fundamentalist political and cultural engagement, and so have modified Marsden's emphasis on antimodernism (to the extent the term denotes sectarian and social isolation) and interpreted fundamentalism as a manifestation of various aspects of modern culture, religion, and economics. Such works include those previously cited by Sutton, Gloege, and Coates, as well as Darren Dochuk, *From Bible Belt to Sunbelt: Plain-Folk Religion, Grassroots Politics, and the Rise of Evangelical Conservatism* (Norton, 2009) and *Anointed with Oil*; Daniel K. Williams, *God's Own Party: The Making of the Christian Right* (Oxford University Press, 2010); and Mary Beth Swetnam Mathews, *Doctrine and Race: African American Evangelicals and Fundamentalism between the Wars* (University of Alabama Press, 2018).

The most recent scholarship has moved away from theological definitions toward cultural, communication, and consumption definitions of fundamentalism, focusing especially on racism and sexism as dominant motifs, often to establish continuity with later evangelical attitudes. See, for example, Kristin Kobes Du Mez, *Jesus and John Wayne: How White Evangelicals Corrupted a Faith and Fractured a Nation* (Norton, 2021), and Anthea D. Butler, *White Evangelical Racism: The Politics of Morality in America* (University of North Carolina Press, 2021). For a recent historiographical intervention on the related definition of evangelicalism, see Daniel Silliman, "An Evangelical Is Anyone Who Likes Billy Graham: Defining Evangelicalism with Carl Henry and Networks of Trust," *Church History* 90, no. 3 (September 2021): 621–43.

On the history of denominational fundamentalist activity, see Marsden, *Fundamentalism and American Culture*; Bradley Longfield, *Presbyterian Controversy: Fundamentalists, Modernists, and Moderates* (Oxford University Press, 1994); and Thomas S. Kidd and Barry Hankins, *Baptists in America: A History* (Oxford University Press, 2015). On the social-economic resemblances between denominational modernists and fundamentalists, see Paul Austin Hunt, "Closer Than They Appear: The Surprising Similarities between Clarence Macartney and Harry Emerson Fosdick," *Journal of Presbyterian History* 96, no. 2 (2018): 62–74.

On nationalist fundamentalists, especially their antievolution activism, see Adam Laats, *Fundamentalism and Education in the Scopes Era: God, Darwin, and the Roots of America's Culture Wars* (Palgrave Macmillan, 2014); Ronald L. Numbers, *The Creationists: From Scientific Creationism to Intelligent Design*, expanded ed. (Harvard University Press, 2006); and Leo Ribuffo, *The Old Christian Right: The Protestant Far Right from the Great Depression to the Cold War* (Temple University Press, 1983). On the importance of Prohibition to fundamentalism, see Barry Hankins, *Jesus and Gin: Evangelicalism, the Roaring Twenties, and Today's Culture Wars* (St. Martin's, 2014).

Chapter 11

In carving out a separate fundamentalist lane for interdenominationalists, I am drawing on a distinction made by historian LeRoy Moore, made in dialogue with Ernest Sandeen, between "doctrinaire fundamentalists" and fundamentalism as a "party movement." The latter, according to Moore, was an interdenominational coalition that saw itself as combating modernism and cultural liberalism. See LeRoy Moore, "Another Look at Fundamentalism: A Response to Ernest R. Sandeen," *Church History* 37 (June 1968): 196. A similar taxonomy dividing denominational and interdenominational fundamentalism, though this time for the South, is offered in William R. Glass, *Strangers in Zion: Fun-*

damentalists in the South, 1900–1950 (Mercer University Press, 2001). The locus of this interdenominational fundamentalism in the World Conference on Fundamentals Association is offered by Nathan Lentfer, "A History of the World's Christian Fundamentals Association (1919–1952)" (PhD diss., Bob Jones University, 2011).

In comparing William Bell Riley to Lewis Sperry Chafer, I am drawing on William Vance Trollinger, *God's Empire: William Bell Riley and Midwestern Fundamentalism* (University of Wisconsin Press, 1990), and John D. Hannah, *An Uncommon Union: Dallas Theological Seminary and American Evangelicalism* (Zondervan, 2009). The tensions between what I identify as competing nationalist and scholastic commitments in the WCFA are documented in Daniel W. Draney, *When Streams Diverge: John Murdoch MacInnis and the Origins of Protestant Fundamentalism in Los Angeles* (Paternoster, 2008). This tension is also expressed by fundamentalist historians themselves. See George W. Dollar, *A History of Fundamentalism in America* (Bob Jones University Press, 1973), and Jim Owen, *The Hidden History of the Historic Fundamentalists, 1933–1948: Reconsidering the Historic Fundamentalists' Response to the Upheavals, Hardship, and Horrors of the 1930s and 1940s* (University Press of America, 2004). Dollar and Owen are cited here as illustrative of the internal tensions among fundamentalists that distinguish different networks of individuals and institutions oriented toward, roughly, scholastic/theological and nationalist/cultural-political agendas.

On separatist fundamentalists, and especially their uneven relationship to dispensationalism, see Barry Hankins, *God's Rascal: J. Frank Norris and the Beginnings of Southern Fundamentalism* (University Press of Kentucky, 1996); Mark Taylor Dalhouse, *An Island in the Lake of Fire: Bob Jones University, Fundamentalism, and the Separatist Movement* (University of Georgia Press, 1996); and Matthew Lee Lyon, "John R. Rice and Evangelism: An Essential Mark of Independent Baptist Fundamentalism" (PhD diss., Southern Baptist Theological Seminary, 2019).

Chapter 12

The formative struggles between Westminster Seminary covenantalists and Dallas Seminary dispensationalists in the 1930s and 1940s are explored in Mangum, *The Dispensational-Covenantal Rift*.

On covenantal theology after the 1930s, see Mangum, *The Dispensational-Covenantal Rift*; Darryl Hart, *Between the Times: The Orthodox Presbyterian Church in Transition, 1945–1990* (OPC Committee for the Historian, 2011); and the reflections of theologian John Frame in "Machen's Warrior Children," in *Alister E. McGrath and Evangelical Theology: A Dynamic Engagement*, ed. Sung Wook Chung (Baker, 2003), 113–57.

On the scholastic dispensational tradition, see Hannah, *An Uncommon Union*; Timothy Gale Mink, "John F. Walvoord at Dallas Theological Seminary" (PhD diss., University of North Texas, 1987); Darrell L. Bock and Craig A. Blaising, *Progressive Dispensationalism* (BridgePoint Academic, 1993); R. Todd Mangum, "The Modernist-Fundamentalist Controversy, the Inerrancy of Scripture, and the Development of American Dispensationalism," in *Interdisciplinary Perspectives on the Authority of Scripture: Historical, Biblical, and Theoretical Perspectives*, ed. Carlos R. Bovell (Wipf & Stock, 2015), 46–70; and Jared Burkholder and Mark Marston Norris, *Becoming Grace: Seventy-Five Years on the Landscape of Christian Higher Education in America* (BMH Books, 2015). On the contrast between German theologian Erich Sauer and American scholastic dispensationalism, see Christopher Lee Thompson, "The Life and Writings of Erich Sauer (1898–1959): His Relationship to and Influence upon American Dispensationalism" (PhD diss., Southeastern Baptist Theological Seminary, 2011). Chafer's travails with the Southern Presbyterian denomination are covered in B. Dwain Waldrep, "Lewis Sperry Chafer and the Roots of Nondenominational Fundamentalism in the South," *Journal of Southern History* 73, no. 4 (November 2007): 807–36.

In 1993, Donald Dayton, in a review of George Marsden's institutional history of Fuller Seminary, made a case for paying more attention to anti-dispensationalism as a defining feature of neo-evangelicalism. See Donald Dayton, "The Search for Historical Evangelicalism: George Marsden's History of Fuller Seminary as a Case Study," *Christian Scholars Review* 23, no. 1 (September 1993): 12–31. On the specific points of departure by neo-evangelicals from dispensational theology, see Russell Moore, "The Kingdom of God in the Social Ethics of Carl F. H. Henry: A Twenty-First Century Evangelical Reappraisal," *Journal of the Evangelical Theological Society* 55, no. 2 (June 2012): 377–97; John A. D'Elia, *A Place at the Table: George Eldon Ladd and the Rehabilitation of Evangelical Scholarship in America* (Oxford University Press, 2008); and Troy Neal Rust, "The Preaching of Harold John Ockenga as a Response to the Perceived Excesses of Fundamentalism" (PhD diss., Southern Baptist Theological Seminary, 2009). For the ways Canadian evangelicals distinguished themselves from US dynamics of fundamentalist factionalism, see John G. Stackhouse Jr., *Canadian Evangelicalism in the Twentieth Century: An Introduction to Its Character* (Regent College Publishing, 1998).

I was inspired by the model of tracing social polarization within fundamentalism through theological terminology from a study of a later era of evangelical social polarization over biblical inerrancy: Gerald T. Sheppard, "Biblical Hermeneutics: The Academic Language of Evangelical Identity," *Union Seminary Quarterly Review* 32, no. 2 (Winter 1977): 81–94.

Chapter 13

Fundamentalist politics in the interwar years—including strains of antisemitism, anticommunism, and Christian nationalism—are explored in Sutton, *American Apocalypse*. Historians of conservatism have converged on the same developments, especially Williams, *God's Own Party*; Dochuk, *From Bible Belt to Sunbelt*; and Lisa McGirr, *Suburban Warriors: The Origins of the New American Right* (Princeton University Press, 2001). Historians of business have documented the connection between fundamentalism and free-market conservatism in Sarah Ruth Hammond, *God's Businessmen: Entrepreneurial Evangelicals in Depression and War*, ed. Darren Dochuk (University of Chicago Press, 2017); Darren E. Grem, *The Blessings of Business: How Corporations Shaped Conservative Christianity* (Oxford University Press, 2016); Kevin M. Kruse, *One Nation under God: How Corporate America Invented Christian America* (Basic Books, 2016); and Bethany Moreton, *To Serve God and Wal-Mart: The Making of Christian Free Enterprise* (Harvard University Press, 2009).

For the rise of young-earth creationism, see Numbers, *The Creationists*, and Adam Laats, *Creationism USA: Bridging the Impasse on Teaching Evolution* (Oxford University Press, 2020). For a survey of Christian Zionism, see Donald M. Lewis, *A Short History of Christian Zionism: From the Reformation to the Twenty-First Century* (IVP Academic, 2021), and Yaakov Ariel, *On Behalf of Israel: American Fundamentalist Attitudes toward Jews, Judaism, and Zionism, 1865–1945* (Carlson Publishing, 1991). For a broader analysis of biblical literalism and American conservatism, see Vincent Crapanzano, *Serving the Word: Literalism in America from the Pulpit to the Bench* (New Press, 2000).

The politics of the early Cold War is explored in Axel R. Schäfer, *Countercultural Conservatives: American Evangelicalism from the Postwar Revival to the New Christian Right* (University of Wisconsin Press, 2011). On the important role of separatist fundamentalists, see Keith Bates, *Mainstreaming Fundamentalism: John R. Rice and Fundamentalism's Public Reemergence* (University of Tennessee Press, 2021), and Markku Ruotsila, *Fighting Fundamentalist: Carl McIntire and the Politicization of American Fundamentalism* (Oxford University Press, 2015).

The centrality of Billy Graham to neo-evangelical politics is explored in Kruse, *One Nation under God*; Steven P. Miller, *Billy Graham and the Rise of the Republican South* (University of Pennsylvania Press, 2009); and Aaron Griffith, *God's Law and Order: The Politics of Punishment in Evangelical America* (Harvard University Press, 2020).

Chapter 14

Apocalypticism in postwar American culture is helpfully contextualized by Lisa Vox, *Existential Threats: American Apocalyptic Beliefs in the Technological Era* (University of Pennsylvania Press, 2017), and Angela M. Lahr, *Millennial Dreams and Apocalyptic Nightmares: The Cold War Origins of Political Evangelicalism* (Oxford University Press, 2007). The rise of "futurism" in the 1970s is explored in Matthew Connelly, "Future Shock: The End of the World as They Knew It," in *The Shock of the Global: The 1970s in Perspective*, ed. Niall Ferguson et al. (Belknap Press of Harvard University Press, 2010), 337–50. Though usually ignored in studies of the divergence of expert and populist authorities of knowledge in the postwar period, dispensationalism is a helpful example. For a broader assessment of this phenomenon in evangelicalism, see Randall J. Stephens and Karl W. Giberson, *The Anointed: Evangelical Truth in a Secular Age* (Belknap Press of Harvard University Press, 2011).

While no comprehensive biography of Hal Lindsey exists, there is excellent work on his influence. On the writing and reception of *Late Great Planet Earth*, I was most helped by Erin A. Smith, *What Would Jesus Read? Popular Religious Books and Everyday Life in Twentieth-Century America* (University of North Carolina Press, 2015). Lindsey's role as a pioneer of pop dispensationalism is captured in Mark S. Sweetnam, "Hal Lindsey and the Great Dispensational Mutation," *Journal of Religion and Popular Culture* 23, no. 2 (July 2011): 217–35. In this article Sweetnam also coins the term "pop dispensationalism."

The pop-dispensational consumer market is explored by Boyer, *When Time Shall Be No More*, and in wider surveys of the era such as Steven P. Miller, *The Age of Evangelicalism: America's Born-Again Years* (Oxford University Press, 2014). A helpful mapping of evangelical finances (especially on popular culture [television, books, and music] in relation to other industries) is found in Michael S. Hamilton, "More Money, More Ministry: The Financing of American Evangelicalism Since 1945," in *More Money, More Ministry: Money and Evangelicals in Recent North American History*, ed. Larry Eskridge and Mark A. Noll (Eerdmans, 2000), 102–41.

The standard account of the Jesus People movement is Larry Eskridge, *God's Forever Family: The Jesus People Movement in America* (Oxford University Press, 2013), and the critical importance of music is further explored by Shawn Young, *Gray Sabbath: Jesus People USA, the Evangelical Left, and the Evolution of Christian Rock* (Columbia University Press, 2015), and David W. Stowe, *No Sympathy for the Devil: Christian Pop Music and the Transformation of American Evangelicalism* (University of North Carolina Press, 2011).

Chapter 15

A longer narrative of the Jerusalem Conference on Biblical Prophecy in June 1971 is in Daniel G. Hummel, "A 'Practical Outlet' to Premillennial Faith: G. Douglas Young and the Evolution of Christian Zionist Activism in Israel," *Religion and American Culture* 25, no. 1 (2015): 37–81.

My account of the 1970s rupture in fundamentalist and evangelical theology, written from the perspective of dispensationalism, is informed by a few works: Hannah, *An Uncommon Union*; Mark A. Noll, *Between Faith and Criticism: Evangelicals, Scholarship, and the Bible in America* (Regent College Publishing, 2004); and Gary Dorrien, *The Remaking of Evangelical Theology* (Westminster John Knox, 1998).

On the revival of historic premillennialism, see Craig L. Blomberg and Sung Wook Chung, eds., *A Case for Historic Premillennialism: An Alternative to "Left Behind" Eschatology* (Baker Academic, 2009); D'Elia, *A Place at the Table*; and Stanley J. Grenz, *The Millennial Maze: Sorting Out Evangelical Options* (IVP Academic, 1992).

The importance of Sandeen's *The Roots of Fundamentalism* to the academic understanding of fundamentalism in the 1970s is made clear in Matthew Avery Sutton, "New Trends in the Historiography of American Fundamentalism," *Journal of American Studies* 51, no. 1 (February 2017): 235–41. Marsden first responded to Sandeen's book in George Marsden, "Defining Fundamentalism," *Christian Scholars Review* 1, no. 2 (Winter 1971): 141–51, with Sandeen replying in "Defining Fundamentalism: A Reply to Professor Marsden," *Christian Scholars Review* 1, no. 3 (Spring 1971): 227–33. David Rausch had a narrower focus but employed a theological definition of fundamentalism that attended to more detail (such as the division between new and old premillennialists). See especially *Zionism within Early American Fundamentalism, 1878–1918: A Convergence of Two Traditions* (Mellen, 1978).

Chapter 16

The literature on the New Christian Right is vast, while the standard text is Williams, *God's Own Party*. Also helpful are Frances FitzGerald, *The Evangelicals:*

The Struggle to Shape America (Simon & Schuster, 2017), and J. Flippen, *Jimmy Carter, the Politics of Family, and the Rise of the Religious Right* (University of Georgia Press, 2011).

The most important scholar of the "humanist tribulation" in the New Christian Right is Susan Harding in *The Book of Jerry Falwell: Fundamentalist Language and Politics* (Princeton University Press, 2000). Other scholarship explores innovations in broadly dispensational end-times scenarios that supported New Christian Right politics, including Stephen O'Leary, *Arguing the Apocalypse: A Theory of Millennial Rhetoric* (Oxford University Press, 1994), and the polemical but useful Dwight Wilson, *Armageddon Now! The Premillenarian Response to Russia and Israel Since 1917* (Institute for Christian Economics, 1991).

The importance of intrafundamentalist cobelligerency is the subject of Neil J. Young, *We Gather Together: The Religious Right and the Problem of Interfaith Politics* (Oxford University Press, 2015). Robert Wuthnow's classic, *The Restructuring of American Religion: Society and Faith Since World War II* (Princeton University Press, 1988), provides a broader sociological lens on the same phenomenon.

Grace Halsell represents the numerous journalists and social scientists (many of them with some personal familiarity to fundamentalism) who helped to create the body of knowledge on evangelicals in the 1980s that amplified the importance of the New Christian Right. This development is covered in L. Benjamin Rolsky, "Producing the Christian Right: Conservative Evangelicalism, Representation, and the Recent Religious Past," *Religions* 12, no. 3 (March 2021): 171, and D. G. Hart, *Deconstructing Evangelicalism: Conservative Protestantism in the Age of Billy Graham* (Baker Academic, 2005).

Chapter 17

Some early attempts at grappling with the significance of televangelism are Quentin J. Schultze, *Televangelism and American Culture: The Business of Popular Religion* (Baker, 1991), and Razell Frankl, *Televangelism: The Marketing of Popular Religion* (Southern Illinois University Press, 1987). More recent studies have helped to contextualize televangelism in the broader religious landscape, including Richard G. Kyle, *Popular Evangelicalism in American Culture* (Routledge, 2017). The best single volume on televangelism that I consulted was John Wigger, *PTL: The Rise and Fall of Jim and Tammy Faye Bakker's Evangelical Empire* (Oxford University Press, 2017).

I am indebted to the idea of a pop-dispensational complex from the related concept by Skye Jethani: "The Evangelical Industrial Complex and Rise of Ce-

lebrity Pastors, Part 1," *Christianity Today*, February 20, 2012, www.christianity
today.com/le/2012/february-online-only/evangelical-industrial-complex-rise
-of-celebrity-pastors.html. On the economy of religious consumption that pop
dispensationalism adapted to, see Vincent J. Miller, *Consuming Religion: Christian Faith and Practice in a Consumer Culture* (Continuum, 2003); Wade Clark
Roof, *Spiritual Marketplace: Baby Boomers and the Remaking of American
Religion* (Princeton University Press, 1999); and R. Laurence Moore, *Selling
God: American Religion in the Marketplace of Culture* (Oxford University Press,
1994). To grasp the industry history of Christian Contemporary Music, I relied
on Don Cusic, *The Sound of Light: A History of Gospel and Christian Music*
(Hal Leonard, 2002), and for an insightful intellectual history of the same
music, Lester Ruth and Lim Swee Hong, *A History of Contemporary Praise and
Worship: Understanding the Ideas That Reshaped the Protestant Church* (Baker
Academic, 2021).

On the rise of suburban megachurches, see David A. Snow et al., "A Team
Field Study of the Appeal of Megachurches: Identifying, Framing, and Solv-
ing Personal Issues," *Ethnography* 11, no. 1 (2010): 165–88; Kimon Howard
Sargeant, *Seeker Churches: Promoting Traditional Religion in a Nontraditional
Way* (Rutgers University Press, 2000); and Jessica Johnson, "Megachurches,
Celebrity Pastors, and the Evangelical Industrial Complex," in *Religion and
Popular Culture in America* (University of California Press, 2017), 159–76. The
contemporary "white evangelicals" of Kristin Du Mez's *Jesus and John Wayne*'s
subtitle are, with a few exceptions, megachurch leaders in New Calvinist net-
works or affiliated with that faction. For more on the New Calvinists, see Brad
Vermurlen, *Reformed Resurgence: The New Calvinist Movement and the Battle
over American Evangelicalism* (Oxford University Press, 2020).

Chapter 18

Christian reconstructionism is explored in Julie J. Ingersoll, *Building God's
Kingdom: Inside the World of Christian Reconstruction* (Oxford University
Press, 2015), and its origins and coverage by the media are also addressed in
Molly Worthen, "The Chalcedon Problem: Rousas John Rushdoony and the
Origins of Christian Reconstructionism," *Church History* 77, no. 2 (June 2008):
399–437.

Little has been written from a historical perspective on the Lordship salvation controversy. While the controversy dates to the mid-1980s and especially
the publication of John F. MacArthur's *The Gospel according to Jesus* (1988),
the specific issues of concern regarding salvation are much older. A sum-

mary of the debate that focused on MacArthur and Hodges may be found in Richard P. Belcher, *A Layman's Guide to the Lordship Controversy* (Crowne Publications, 1990).

Progressive dispensationalism has also received minimal attention from historians of American religion. Insiders have narrated its emergence, including the traditionalist account: Ron J. Bigalke Jr. and Thomas D. Ice, "History of Dispensationalism," in *Progressive Dispensationalism: An Analysis of the Movement and Defense of Traditional Dispensationalism*, ed. Ron J. Bigalke Jr. (University Press of America, 2006), xvii–xlii; and the progressive account: Craig A. Blaising, "The Extent and Varieties of Dispensationalism," in *Progressive Dispensationalism*, ed. Darrell L. Bock and Craig A. Blaising (BridgePoint Academic, 1993), 9–56. The institutional account from the perspective of Dallas Theological Seminary is found in Hannah, *An Uncommon Union*. For a brief account of Grace Theological Seminary, which suffered a broader denominational split in the early 1990s that involved traditional and progressive dispensational divides, see Burkholder and Norris, *Becoming Grace*, 199–203.

Another way to track the influence of progressive dispensationalism and the decline of traditional dispensationalism is in disciplinary surveys of scholarship related to eschatology, such as Michael C. Thompson, "Book of Revelation," in *The State of New Testament Studies: A Survey of Recent Research*, ed. Scot McKnight and Nijay K. Gupta (Baker Academic, 2019), 459–75, and J. Richard Middleton, *A New Heaven and a New Earth: Reclaiming Biblical Eschatology* (Baker Academic, 2014), 283–311.

Dispensationalism's demise as a theological tradition, while mostly ignored, has been noted in a few spots. Liberal Protestant theologian Gary Dorrien, in *The Remaking of Evangelical Theology* (Westminster John Knox, 1998), observed that 1990s shifts in evangelical theology were seen as a "disaster" (11) by dispensational scholars. Mark Noll noted the same trend in *The Scandal of the Evangelical Mind* (Eerdmans, 1994). Though it was the "most self-conscious theological system supporting" fundamentalism, it had encouraged "several kinds of simple anti-intellectualism" (122–23). While noting the tradition's decline, Noll was also more interested in understanding dispensationalism as an anti-intellectual foil to evangelicalism than as its own dynamic tradition.

Taking the cue from Marsden, Noll, and others, many recent works of evangelical history barely mention dispensationalism, including Molly Worthen, *Apostles of Reason: The Crisis of Authority in American Evangelicalism* (Oxford University Press, 2013); Du Mez, *Jesus and John Wayne*; Randall Balmer, *Bad Faith: Race and the Rise of the Religious Right* (Eerdmans, 2021); and Butler,

White Evangelical Racism. One prominent exception is Sutton's *American Apocalypse*, though Sutton's interest is in the popular political, rather than theological, career of dispensationalism.

Chapter 19

"Rapture culture," explored in Amy Frykholm's book by the same name, has received increased attention by scholars and journalists as its intersections with right-wing politics have multiplied in the twenty-first century. Examples include Robin Globus Veldman, *The Gospel of Climate Skepticism: Why Evangelical Christians Oppose Action on Climate Change* (University of California Press, 2019); Timothy Weber, *On the Road to Armageddon: How Evangelicals Became Israel's Best Friend* (Baker Academic, 2004); Crawford Gribben, "After Left Behind: The Paradox of Evangelical Pessimism," in *Expecting the End: Millennialism in Social and Historical Context*, ed. Kenneth G. C. Newport and Crawford Gribben (Baylor University Press, 2006), 113–30; and Melani McAlister, "Prophecy, Politics, and the Popular: The 'Left Behind' Series and Christian Fundamentalism's New World Order," *South Atlantic Quarterly* 102, no. 4 (Fall 2003): 773–98. Relatedly, dispensationalism has been used to explain evangelical anti-Muslim sentiments in Grayson R. Robertson, "The Influence of Dispensationalist Theology on Evangelical Perceptions of Muslims Post-9/11" (MA thesis, Georgetown University, 2011).

The influence of dispensationalism on popular American perceptions of the end times is explored in Vox, *Existential Threats*; Anthony Aveni, *Apocalyptic Anxiety: Religion, Science, and America's Obsession with the End of the World* (University Press of Colorado, 2016); and Richard G. Kyle, *Apocalyptic Fever: End-Time Prophecies in Modern America* (Wipf & Stock, 2012). For some analysis of how covenantalists have succeeded in establishing themselves online, see Vermurlen, *Reformed Resurgence*.

Studies of pop-dispensational apocalypticism in nonreligious media include Jesse Kavadlo, *American Popular Culture in the Era of Terror: Falling Skies, Dark Knights Rising, and Collapsing Cultures* (Praeger, 2015); and Andrew Crome, "Left Behind or Left Below? Parodies of Christian End-Times Fiction in American Popular Culture," *Journal of American Culture* 38, no. 4 (December 2015): 386–400.

Index